Western Civilization

A Brief Survey

Western Civilization

A Brief Survey

Volume I: To 1789

Marvin Perry

Baruch College,
City University of New York

George W. Bock, Editorial Associate

Houghton Mifflin Company **Boston**

Dallas   Geneva, Illinois   Palo Alto   Princeton, New Jersey

Copyright © 1990 by Houghton Mifflin Company.

Printed in the U.S.A.

Library of Congress Catalog Card Number: 89-80955

ISBN: 0-395-52989-1

BCDEFGHIJ-A-9543210

Contents

List of Maps

Preface

Western civilization is a grand but tragic drama. The West has forged the instruments of reason that make possible a rational comprehension of physical nature and human culture, conceived the idea of political liberty, and recognized the intrinsic worth of the individual. But the modern West, though it has unravelled nature's mysteries, has been less successful at finding rational solutions to social ills and conflicts between nations. Science, the great achievement of the Western intellect, while improving conditions of life, has also produced weapons of mass destruction. Though the West has pioneered in the protection of human rights, it has also produced totalitarian regimes that have trampled on individual freedom and human dignity. And although the West has demonstrated a commitment to human equality, it has also practiced brutal racism.

Despite the value that Westerners have given to reason and freedom, they have shown a frightening capacity for irrational behavior and a fascination for violence and irrational ideologies, and they have willingly sacrificed liberty for security or national grandeur. The world wars and totalitarian movements of the twentieth century have demonstrated that Western civilization, despite its extraordinary achievements, is fragile and perishable.

Western Civilization: A Brief Survey is an abridged version of *Western Civilization: Ideas, Politics, and Society.* Like the longer text, this volume examines the Western tradition—those unique patterns of thought and systems of values that constitute the Western heritage. While focusing on key ideas and broad themes, the text also provides economic, political, and social history for students in Western civilization courses.

The text is written with the conviction that history is not a meaningless tale. Without a knowledge of history, men and women cannot fully know themselves, for all human beings have been shaped by institutions and values inherited from the past. Without an awareness of the historical evolution of reason and freedom, the dominant ideals of Western civilization, commitment to these ideals will diminish. Without a knowledge of history, the West cannot fully comprehend or adequately cope with the problems that burden its civilization and the world.

In attempting to make sense out of the past, the author has been careful to avoid superficial generalizations that oversimplify historical events and forces and arrange history into too neat a structure. But the text does strive to interpret and synthesize in order to provide students with a frame of reference with which to comprehend the principal events and eras in Western history.

Distinctive Features

This brief edition was prepared for Western Civilization courses that run for one term only, for instructors who like to supplement the main text with primary-source readers, novels, or monographs, and for humanities courses in which additional works on literature and art will be assigned. In abbreviating the longer text by about a third, the number of chapters has been reduced from 37 to 22. The emphasis on the history of ideas and culture has been retained, but the amount of detail has of necessity been reduced.

The text contains several pedagogical features. Chapter introductions provide comprehensive overviews of key themes and give a sense of direction and coherence to the flow of history. Many chapters contain concluding essays that treat the larger meaning of the material. Facts have been carefully selected to illustrate key relationships and concepts and to avoid overwhelming students with unrelated and disconnected data. Each chapter concludes with an annotated bibliography and review questions. The questions refer students to principal points and aim at eliciting thoughtful answers. In addition to the many illustrations and 32 maps, there is a color art insert. The art captions include questions that call on students to draw historical inferences from what they see.

This text is published in both single-volume and two-volume editions. Volume I treats the period from the first civilizations in the Near East through the Age of Enlightenment in the eighteenth century (Chapters 1–10). Volume II covers the period from the Renaissance and the Reformation to the contemporary age (Chapters 8–22), and incorporates the last three chapters in Volume I: "Transition to the Modern Age: Renaissance and Reformation," "Political and Economic Transformation: National States, Overseas Expansion, Commercial Revolution," and "Intellectual Transformation: The Scientific Revolution and the Age of Enlightenment." Volume II also contains a comprehensive introduction that surveys the ancient world and the Middle Ages; the introduction is designed particularly for students who have not taken the first half of the course.

Ancillaries

Learning and teaching ancillaries, including a *Study Guide, Instructor's Manual with Test Items,* and *Map Transparencies* also contribute to the text's usefulness. The *Study Guide* has been prepared by Professor Lyle E. Linville of Prince George's Community College. For each text chapter, the *Study Guide* contains an introduction, learning objectives, words to know, identifications, a map study exercise, chronological/relational exercises, multiple-choice and essay questions, and a "transition," which reflects back on the chapter and looks forward to the next chapter's topic. The map study has outline maps, and students are asked to locate geographical features on them. A duplicate set of maps appears at the back of the book and may be removed for use in class quizzes. In the chronological/relational exercises, students are asked to put a list of items in their chronological order; then in an exercise that develops critical thinking skills, students are asked to write a paragraph indicating the relationship of the items to one another, along with their historical significance.

The *Instructor's Manual with Test Items* was also prepared for the brief edition by Professor Linville. The *Manual* contains chapter outlines, learning objectives, lecture topics, a film/video bibliography, essay and discussion questions, multiple-choice questions, and identifications. In addition, a set of 30 map transparencies is available on adoption.

Acknowledgments

In preparing this abridgement, I have made extensive use of the chapters written by my colleagues for *Western Civilization: Ideas, Politics, and Society*. Chapter 8, "Transition to the Modern Age: Renaissance and Reformation," and Chapter 9, "Political and Economic Transformation: National States, Overseas Expansion, Commercial Revolution," are based largely on James R. Jacob's and Margaret C. Jacob's chapters in the longer volume. Chapter 10, "Intellectual Transformation: The Scientific Revolution and the Age of Enlightenment," is drawn largely from Margaret C. Jacob's material. Much of Chapter 14, "The Industrial Revolution: The Transformation of Society," and Chapter 15, "Europe in the Industrial Age: Modernization and Imperialism," is drawn from Myrna Chase's chapters. Chapter 18, "The Soviet Union: Modernization and Totalitarianism," and the two concluding chapters—"Europe After 1945: Recovery, Realignment, Division" and "The New Globalism: Problems and Prospects"—are an abridgement of Theodore H. Von Laue's chapters. To a lesser or greater extent, my colleagues' material has been abridged, restructured, and rewritten to meet the needs of this volume. Therefore, I alone am responsible for all interpretations and any errors. I wish to thank my colleagues for their gracious permission to use their words and thoughts.

Also, I would like to thank the following instructors for their critical reading of sections of the manuscript:

John W. Arnot, *West Los Angeles College*

Achilles Avraamides, *Iowa State University*

Stuart T. Cooke, *College of San Mateo*

Roger P. Davis, *Kearney State College*

Donald S. Gochberg, *Michigan State University*

William E. Gohlman, *State University College of New York at Geneseo*

Robert W. Roetger, *Emerson College*

Many of their suggestions were incorporated into the final version. I am also grateful to the staff at Houghton Mifflin Company who lent their considerable talents to the project. I would like to express my gratitude to George Bock who assisted in the planning of the text from its inception and who read the manuscript with an eye for major concepts and essential relationships. As ever, I am grateful to my wife, Phyllis G. Perry, for her encouragement.

M.P.

Western Civilization
A Brief Survey

Roman Relief: Praetorian Soldiers. (*Giraudon/Art Resource*)

I · The Ancient World: Foundation of the West

To A.D. 500

Chapter • I

The Ancient Near East:
The First Civilizations

Civilization was not inevitable; it was an act of human creativity. The first civilizations emerged about 5,000 years ago, in the Near Eastern river valleys of Sumer and Egypt. Before that time stretched the vast ages of prehistory, when our ancestors did not dwell in cities and knew nothing of writing. Today, when civilization is threatened by a nuclear holocaust, we might reflect on humanity's long and painful climb to a civilized state. ✪

The Rise to Civilization

The Paleolithic Age

The period called the Paleolithic Age, or Old Stone Age, began with the earliest primitive tool-making human beings who inhabited East Africa nearly 3 million years ago. It ended about 10,000 years ago in parts of the Near East when people discovered how to farm. Our Paleolithic ancestors lived as hunters and food gatherers. Because they had not learned how to farm, they never established permanent villages. When their food supplies ran short, they abandoned their caves or tentlike structures of branches and searched for new dwelling places.

Human social development was shaped by this 3-million-year experience of hunting and food gathering. For survival, groups of families formed bands consisting of around thirty people; members learned how to plan, organize, cooperate, trust, and share. Hunters assisted each other in tracking and killing game, finding cooperative efforts more successful than individual forays. By sharing their kill and bringing some back to their camp for the rest of the group, they reinforced the social bond. Bands that did not cooperate in the hunt or distribute meat to everyone were unlikely to survive.

Although human progress was very slow during the long centuries of the Paleolithic Age, developments occurred that influenced the future enormously. Paleolithic people developed spoken language and learned how to make and use tools of bone, wood, and stone. With these simple but useful tools, Paleolithic human beings dug up roots, peeled the bark off trees, trapped, killed, and skinned animals, made clothing, and fashioned fishnets. They also discovered how to control fire, which allowed them to cook their meat, and provided warmth and protection.

Like toolmaking and the control of fire, language was a great human achievement. Language enabled individuals to acquire and share knowledge, experiences, and feelings with one another. Thus language was the decisive factor in the development of culture and its transmission from one generation to the next.

Most likely, our Paleolithic ancestors developed mythic-religious beliefs to explain the mysteries of nature, birth, sickness, and death. They felt that living powers operated within and beyond the world they experienced, and they sought to establish friendly relations with these powers. To primitive peoples, the elements—sun, rain, wind, thunder, and lightning—were alive. The natural elements were spirits; they could feel and act with a purpose. To appease these forces of nature, hunters and gatherers made offerings. Gradually shamans, medicine men, and witch doctors emerged who, through rituals, trances, and chants, seemed able to communicate with these spirits. Also, Paleolithic people began the practice of burying their dead, sometimes with offerings, which suggests belief in life after death.

Between 30,000 and 12,000 years ago, Paleolithic people sought out the dark and silent interior of caves, which they probably viewed as sanctuaries, and, with only torches for light, they painted remarkably skillful and perceptive pictures of animals on the cave walls. When these prehistoric artists drew an animal with a spear in its side, they probably believed that this act would make them successful in hunting; when they drew a herd of animals, they probably hoped that this would cause game to be plentiful.

The Neolithic Revolution

Some 10,000 years ago, the New Stone Age or Neolithic Age began in the Near East. During the Neolithic Age, human beings discovered farming, domesticated animals, established villages, polished stone tools, made pottery, and wove cloth. So important were these achievements that they are referred to as the Neolithic Revolution.

Agriculture and the domestication of animals revolutionized life. Whereas Paleolithic hunters and food gatherers had been forced to use whatever nature made available to them, Neolithic farmers altered their environment to satisfy human needs. Instead of spending their time searching for grains, roots, and berries, women and children grew crops near their homes; instead of tracking animals over great distances, men could slaughter domesticated goats or sheep nearby. Farming made possible a new kind of community. Since farmers had to

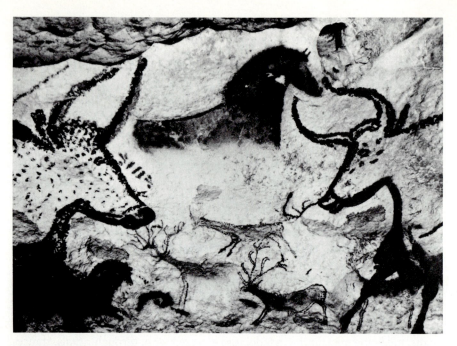

Cave Painting from Lascaux, France, Paleolithic Period.   Produced as a part of the mythic-religious rites of hunting, cave paintings display considerable artistic merit. (*French Government Tourist Office*)

live near their fields and could store food for the future, farming led to the rise of permanent settlements.

Villages changed the patterns of life. A food surplus freed some people to devote part of their time to sharpening their skills as basket weavers or tool-makers. The demand for raw materials and the creations of skilled artisans fostered trade, sometimes across long distances, and the formation of trading settlements. An awareness of private property emerged. Hunters had accu-mulated few possessions, since belongings only presented a burden when mov-ing from place to place. Villagers, however, acquired property that they were determined to protect from one another and from outsiders who might raid the village. Hunting bands were egalitarian; generally, no one member had more possessions or more power than another. In farming villages, a ruling elite emerged that possessed wealth and wielded power.

Neolithic people made great strides in technology. By shaping and baking clay, they made pottery containers for cooking and for storing food and water. The invention of the potter's wheel enabled them to form bowls and plates more quickly and precisely. Stone tools were sharpened by grinding them on rock. The discoveries of the wheel and the sail improved transportation and promoted trade, and the development of the plow and the ox yoke made tilling the soil easier for farmers.

The Neolithic period also marks the beginning of the use of metals. First used was copper, which was easily fashioned into tools and weapons. Implements made from copper lasted longer than those made of stone and flint, and they could be recast and reshaped if broken. In time, artisans discovered how to make bronze by combining copper and tin in the proper ratio. Bronze was harder than copper, which made a sharper cutting edge possible.

During the Neolithic Age, the food supply became more reliable, village life expanded, and the population increased. Families that acquired wealth gained a higher social status and became village leaders. Religion grew more formal and structured; nature spirits evolved into deities, each with specific powers over nature or human life. Altars were erected in their honor, and ceremonies were conducted by priests, whose power and wealth increased as people gave offerings to the gods. Neolithic society was growing more organized and complex; it was on the threshold of civilization.

The First Civilizations

What we call *civilization* arose some 5,000 years ago in the Near East (in Mesopotamia and Egypt) and then later in the Far East (in India and China). The first civilizations began in cities that were larger, more populated, and more complex in their political, economic, and social structure than Neolithic villages. Because the cities depended on the inhabitants of adjacent villages for their food, farming techniques must have been developed sufficiently to produce food surpluses. Increased production provided food for urban inhabitants who engaged in nonagricultural occupations—merchants, craftsmen, bureaucrats, and priests.

The invention of writing enabled the first civilizations to preserve, organize, and expand knowledge; it allowed government officials and priests to conduct their affairs more efficiently. Civilized societies also possessed organized governments that issued laws and defined the boundary lines of their states. On a scale much larger than Neolithic communities, the inhabitants erected buildings and monuments, engaged in trade, and used specialized labor for different projects. Religious life grew more organized and complex, and a powerful and wealthy priesthood emerged. These developments—cities, specialization of labor, writing, organized government, monumental architecture, and a complex religious structure—differentiate the first civilizations from prehistoric cultures.

Religion was the central force in these primary civilizations. It provided satisfying explanations for the operations of nature, helped to ease the fear of death, and justified traditional rules of morality. Law was considered sacred, a commandment of the gods. Religion united people in the common enterprises needed for survival—for example, the construction and maintenance of irrigation works and the storage of food. Religion also promoted creative achievements in art, literature, and science. In addition, the power of rulers, who were regarded either as gods or as agents of the gods, derived from religion.

The emergence of civilization was a great creative act and not merely the inevitable development of agricultural societies. Many communities had learned how to farm, but only a handful made the leap into civilization. How was it possible for Sumerians and Egyptians, the creators of the earliest civilizations, to make this breakthrough? Most scholars stress the relationship between civilizations and river valleys. Rivers deposited fertile silt on adjoining fields, provided water for crops, and served as avenues for trade. But environmental factors alone do not adequately explain the emergence of civilization. What cannot be omitted is the human contribution—capacity for thought and cooperative activity. Before these rivers could be of any value in producing crops, swamps around them had to be drained, jungles had to be cleared, and dikes, reservoirs, and canals had to be built. To construct and maintain irrigation works required the cooperation of large numbers of people, a necessary condition for civilization.

In the process of constructing and maintaining irrigation networks, people learned to formulate and obey rules and developed administrative, engineering, and mathematical skills. The need to keep records stimulated the invention of writing. These creative responses to the challenges posed by nature spurred the early inhabitants of Sumer and Egypt to make the breakthrough to civilization, thereby altering the course of human destiny.

Mesopotamian Civilization

Mesopotamia is the Greek word for "land between the rivers." It was here, in the valleys of the Tigris and Euphrates rivers, that the first civilization began. The first people to develop an urban civilization in Mesopotamia were the Sumerians, who colonized the marshlands of the lower Euphrates, which, joined by the Tigris, flows into the Persian Gulf.

Through constant toil and imagination, the Sumerians transformed the swamps into fields of barley and groves of date palms. Around 3000 B.C. their hut settlements gradually evolved into twelve independent city-states, each consisting of a city and its surrounding countryside. Among the impressive achievements of the Sumerians were a system of symbol writing on clay tablets (cuneiform) to represent ideas; elaborate brick houses, palaces, and temples; bronze tools and weapons; irrigation works; trade with other peoples; an early form of money; religious and political institutions; schools; religious and secular literature; varied art forms; codes of law; medicinal drugs; and a lunar calendar.

The history of Mesopotamia is marked by a succession of conquests. To the north of Sumer was a Semitic* city called Akkad. About 2350 B.C., the people of Akkad, led by Sargon the Great, the warrior king, conquered the Sumerian cities. He built the world's first empire, which extended from the Persian Gulf

---

*Semites included Akkadians, Hebrews, Babylonians, Phoenicians, Canaanites, Assyrians, and Aramaeans. Hebrew and Arabic are Semitic languages.

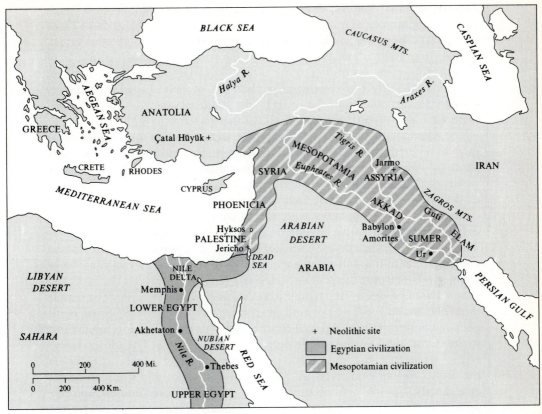

Map 1.1   Mesopotamian and Egyptian Civilizations

to the Mediterranean Sea. The Akkadians adopted Sumerian cultural forms and spread them beyond the boundaries of Mesopotamia with their conquests. Mesopotamian religion became a blend of Sumerian and Akkadian elements.

In succeeding centuries, the Sumerian cities were incorporated into various kingdoms and empires. The Sumerian language, replaced by a Semitic tongue, became an obscure language known only to priests, and the Sumerians gradually disappeared as a distinct people. But their cultural achievements endured. Akkadians, Babylonians, Elamites, and others adopted Sumerian religious, art, legal, and literary forms. The Sumerian legacy served as the basis for a Mesopotamian civilization that maintained a distinct style for 3,000 years.

Religion: The Basis of Mesopotamian Civilization

Religion lay at the center of Mesopotamian life. Every human activity—political, military, social, legal, literary, artistic—was generally subordinated to an overriding religious purpose. Religion was the Mesopotamians' frame of reference for understanding nature, society, and themselves; it dominated and inspired all other cultural expressions and human activities. Wars between cities, for instance, were interpreted as conflicts between the gods of those cities, and victory ultimately depended on divine favor, not on human effort. Myths—narratives about the activities of the gods—explained the origins of the human species. According to the earliest Sumerian myths, the first human beings issued forth from the earth like plant life, or were shaped from clay by divine craftsmen and granted a heart by the goddess Nammu, or were formed from the blood of two gods sacrificed for that purpose.

The Mesopotamians believed that people were given life so that they could execute on earth the will of the gods in heaven. No important decisions were made by kings or priests without first consulting the gods. To discover the wishes of the gods, priests sacrificed animals and then examined their entrails; or the priests might find their answers in the stars or in dreams.

The cities of Mesopotamia were sacred communities dedicated to serving divine masters, and people hoped that appeasing the gods would bring security and prosperity to their cities. Each city belonged to a particular god, who was the real owner of the land and the real ruler of the city; often a vast complex of temples was built for the god and the god's family.

Supervised by priests, the temple was the heart of the city's life. The temple probably owned most of the land in its city; temple priests collected rents, operated businesses, and received contributions for festivals. Most inhabitants of the city worked for the temple priests as tenant farmers, agricultural laborers, or servants. Priests coordinated the city's economic activity: supervising the distribution of land, overseeing the irrigation works, and storing food for emergencies. Temple scribes kept records of expenditures and receipts. By serving as stewards of the city's gods and managing their earthly estates, the priests sustained civilized life.

Mesopotamians believed that the gods controlled the entire universe and everything in it. The moon, the sun, and the storm; the city, the irrigation works, and the fields—each was directed by a god. Mesopotamians saw gods and demons everywhere in nature. There was a god in the fire and another in the river; evil demons stirred up sandstorms, caused disease, endangered women in childbirth. To protect themselves from hostile forces, Mesopotamians wore charms and begged their gods for help. When misfortune befell them, they attributed it to the gods. Even success was not due to their own efforts, but to the intervention of a god who had taken a special interest in them. Compared to the gods, an individual was an insignificant and lowly creature.

Life in Mesopotamia was filled with uncertainty and danger. Sometimes the unpredictable waters of the rivers broke through the dikes, flooding fields, ruining crops, and damaging cities. At other times an insufficient overflow deprived the land of water, causing crops to fail. Mesopotamia had no natural barriers to invasion. Feeling themselves surrounded by incomprehensible and often hostile forces, Mesopotamians lived in an atmosphere of anxiety that permeated their civilization.

Contributing to this sense of insecurity was the belief that the gods behaved capriciously, malevolently, vindictively. What do the gods demand of me? Is it ever possible to please them? To these questions Mesopotamians had no reassuring answers, for the gods' behavior was a mystery to mere human beings.

A mood of uncertainty and anxiety, an awareness of the cosmos as unfathomable and mysterious, a feeling of dread about the fragility of human existence and the impermanence of human achievement—these attitudes are as old as the first civilization. The *Epic of Gilgamesh,* the finest work of Mesopotamian literature, masterfully depicts this mood of pessimism and despair. The *Gilgamesh* deals with a profound theme: the human protest against death. Confronted with the reality of his own death, Gilgamesh yearns for eternal life. But this, he learns, was denied human beings when the gods created them, allotting death as their portion at life's end. "Where is the man who can clamber to heaven? Only the gods live forever . . . but as for us men, our days are numbered, our occupations are a breath of wind."[1]

Government, Law, and Economy

Bestowed on a man by the gods, kingship was the central institution in Mesopotamian society. Unlike Egyptian pharaohs, Mesopotamian kings did not consider themselves to be gods, but great men selected by the gods to represent them on earth. Gods governed through the kings, who reported to the gods about conditions in their land (which was the gods' property) and petitioned the gods for advice.

The king administered the laws, which came from the gods. The principal collection of laws in ancient Mesopotamia was the famous code of Hammurabi (1792–1750 B.C.), the Babylonian ruler. Unearthed by French archaeologists in 1901–1902, the code has provided invaluable insights into Mesopotamian society. In typical Mesopotamian fashion, Hammurabi claimed that his code rested on the authority of the gods; to violate it was to contravene the divine order.

The code reveals social status and mores in that area and time. Women were subservient to men, although efforts were made to protect women and children from abuse. By making death the penalty for adultery, the code probably sought to preserve family life. Punishments were generally severe—"an eye for an eye and a tooth for a tooth." The code prescribed death for housebreaking, kidnapping, aiding the escape of slaves, receiving stolen goods, and bearing false witness, but it also allowed consideration of extenuating circumstances. Class distinctions were expressed in the code. For example, a person received more severe punishment if he had harmed a noble than he would if he had harmed a commoner. Government officials who engaged in extortion or bribery were harshly punished. The code's many provisions relating to business transactions show the importance of trade to Mesopotamian life.

The economy of Mesopotamian cities depended heavily on foreign and domestic trade. Because of trade's importance to the life of the city, governments instituted regulations to prevent fraud. Business transactions had to be re-

Couple from Nippur, 2500 B.C.
Large eyes and geometrical beard
and hair characterize Sumerian
figures. The intimacy and informal-
ity of the pose contrast with the
rigidity of the Egyptian couple (opposite). (*Courtesy of the Oriental Institute, University of Chicago*)

corded in writing. Enterprising businessmen set up trading outposts in distant
lands, making the Mesopotamians pioneers in international trade.

Mathematics, Astronomy, and Medicine

The Mesopotamians made some impressive achievements in mathematics.
They devised multiplication and division tables, including even cubes and cube
roots. They determined the area of right-angle triangles and rectangles, divided
a circle into 360 degrees, and had some understanding of principles that centuries later would be developed into the Pythagorean theorem and quadratic
equations. But the Babylonians, who made the chief contribution in mathematics, barely advanced to the level of devising theories; they did not formulate
general principles or furnish proofs for their mathematical operations.

By carefully observing and accurately recording the positions of planets and
constellations of stars, Babylonian sky watchers took the first steps in developing the science of astronomy, and they devised a calendar based on the
cycles of the moon. As in mathematics, however, they did not form theories to
coordinate and illuminate their data. They believed that the position of the
stars and planets revealed the will of the gods. Astronomers did not examine
the heavens to find what we call cause and effect connections between the
phenomena. Rather, they aspired to discover what the gods wanted. With this

Mycerinus and Queen, c. 2525 B.C.
Swelling chests and hips idealize the
royal couple's humanity, but the
cubic feeling of the sculpture and the
rigid confidence of the pose proclaim
their unquestioned divinity. (*Courtesy Museum of Fine Arts, Boston*)

knowledge, people could organize their political, social, and moral lives in accordance with divine commands, and they could escape the terrible consequences that they believed resulted from ignoring the gods' wishes.

Consistent with their religious world-view, the Mesopotamians believed that disease was caused by gods or demons. To cure a patient, priest-physicians resorted to magic; through prayers and sacrifices they attempted to appease the gods and eject the demons from the sick body. Nevertheless, in identifying illnesses and prescribing appropriate remedies, Mesopotamians demonstrated some accurate knowledge of medicine and pharmacology.

Egyptian Civilization

During the early period of Mesopotamian civilization, the Egyptians developed their civilization in the fertile valley of the Nile. Without this mighty river, which flows more than 4,000 miles from central Africa northward to the Mediterranean Sea, virtually all Egypt would be a desert. When the Nile overflowed its banks, the floodwaters deposited a layer of fertile black earth that, when cultivated, provided abundant food to support Egyptian civilization. The Egyptians learned how to control the river—a feat that required cooperative effort and ingenuity, as well as engineering and administrative skills. In addition to water and fertile land, the Nile provided an excellent transportation link between Upper (southern) and Lower (northern) Egypt. Natural barriers—mountains, deserts, cataracts in the Nile, and the Mediterranean Sea—protected Egypt from attack, allowing the inhabitants to enjoy long periods of peace and prosperity. Thus, unlike Mesopotamians, Egyptians derived a sense of security from their environment.

From the Old Kingdom to the Middle Kingdom

About 2900 B.C., a ruler of Upper Egypt, known as Narmer, or Menes, conquered the Nile Delta and Lower Egypt. By 2686 B.C., centralized rule had been firmly established, and great pyramids, which were tombs for the pharaohs, were being constructed. During this Pyramid Age, or Old Kingdom (2686–2181 B.C.), the essential forms of Egyptian civilization crystallized.

The Egyptians believed the pharaoh to be both a man and a god, the earthly embodiment of the deity Horus. He was an absolute ruler of the land and kept the irrigation works in order, maintained justice in the land, and expressed the will of heaven.

In time, the nobles who served as district governors gained in status and wealth and gradually came to undermine the divine king's authority. The nobles' growing power and the enormous expenditure of Egypt's human and material resources on building pyramids led to the decline of the Old Kingdom. From 2181 to 2040 B.C., called the First Intermediate Period, rival families competed for the throne, thus destroying the unity of the kingdom. The civil wars and the collapse of central authority required to maintain the irrigation system cast a pall of gloom over the land.

During what is called the Middle Kingdom (2040–1786 B.C.), strong kings reasserted pharaonic rule and reunited the state. With political stability restored, cultural life was reinvigorated and economic activity revived. Pharaohs extended Egyptian control south over the land of Nubia (modern Sudan), which became a principal source of gold. A profitable trade was carried on with Palestine, Syria, and Crete.

About 1800 B.C., central authority again weakened. In the era known as the Second Intermediate Period (1786–1570 B.C.), the nobles regained some of their power, the Nubians broke away from Egyptian control, and the Hyksos (a mixture of Semites and Indo-Europeans) invaded Egypt. The Hyksos succeeded in dominating Egypt for about a hundred years, until they were driven out in 1570 B.C. The period of empire building known as the New Kingdom (1570–1085 B.C.) then began.

The basic features of Egyptian civilization had been forged during the Old and Middle Kingdoms. Egyptians looked to the past, believing that the ways of their ancestors were best. For almost 3,000 years, Egyptian civilization sought to retain a harmony with that order of nature instituted at creation. Believing that the universe was changeless, the Egyptians did not value change or development—what we call progress—but venerated the institutions, traditions, and authority that embodied permanence.

Religion: The Basis of Egyptian Civilization

Religion was omnipresent in Egyptian life and accounted for the outstanding achievements of Egyptian civilization. Religious beliefs were the basis of Egyptian art, medicine, astronomy, literature, and government. The great pyramids were tombs for the pharaohs, man-gods. Magical utterances pervaded medical practices, for disease was attributed to the gods. Astronomy evolved to determine the correct time to perform religious rites and sacrifices. The earliest examples of literature dealt wholly with religious themes. Pharaoh was a sacrosanct monarch who served as an intermediary between the gods and human beings. The Egyptians developed an ethical code, which they believed had been approved by the gods.

Egyptian polytheism took many forms, including the worship of animals, for the people believed that gods manifested themselves in both human and animal shapes. The Egyptians also believed great powers in nature—sky, sun, earth, the Nile—to be gods. Thus, the universe was alive with divinities, and human lives were tied to the movements of the sun and the moon and to the rhythm of the seasons. In the heavens alive with gods, Egyptians found answers to the great problems of human existence.

A crucial feature of Egyptian religion was the afterlife. Through pyramid-tombs, mummification to preserve the dead, and funerary art, Egyptians showed their yearning for eternity and their desire to overcome death. Mortuary priests recited incantations to ensure the preservation of the dead body and the continuity of existence. Inscribed on the pyramids' interior walls were "pyramid texts" written in *hieroglyphics*—a form of picture writing in which figures, such as crocodiles, sails, eyes, and so forth, represented words, or sounds that would be combined to form words. The texts contained fragments from myths, historical annals, and magical lore and provided spells to assist the king in ascending to heaven. To Egyptians, the other world contained the same pleasures enjoyed on earth—friends, servants, fishing, hunting, paddling a canoe, picnicking with family members, entertainment by musicians and dancers, and good food. Because earthly existence was not fundamentally unhappy, however, Egyptians did not yearn for death.

Divine Kingship

Divine kingship was the basic institution of Egyptian civilization. Egyptians believed that rule by a god-king was the only acceptable political arrangement, that it was in harmony with the order of the universe, and that it brought justice and security to the nation.

The power of the pharaoh extended to all sectors of society. Peasants were drafted to serve in labor corps as miners or construction workers. Foreign trade was a state monopoly conducted according to the kingdom's needs. As the supreme overlord, the pharaoh oversaw an army of government officials who collected taxes, supervised construction projects, checked the irrigation works, surveyed the land, kept records, conducted foreign trade, and supervised government warehouses where grain was stored as insurance against a bad harvest. All Egyptians were subservient to the pharaoh, whose word was regarded as a divine ordinance. Most pharaohs took their responsibilities seriously and tried to govern as benevolent protectors of the people.

The pharaoh was seen as ruling in accordance with Ma'at, which means justice, law, right, and truth. To oppose the pharaoh was to violate the order of Ma'at and to bring disorder to society. Because Egyptians regarded Ma'at as the right order of nature, they believed that its preservation must be the object of human activity—the guiding norm of the state and the standard by which individuals conducted their lives. Those who did Ma'at and spoke Ma'at would be justly rewarded. Could anything be more reassuring than this belief that divine truth was represented in the person of the pharaoh?

Science and Mathematics

Like the Mesopotamians, the Egyptians made practical advances in the sciences. They demonstrated superb engineering skills in building pyramids and fashioned an effective system of mathematics that enabled them to solve relatively simple problems based more on experience than on reasoning. The Egyptians' solar calendar, which enabled them to know when the Nile would overflow, was more accurate than the Babylonians' lunar calendar.

In the area of medicine, Egyptian doctors were more capable than their Mesopotamian counterparts. They were able to identify illnesses; they recognized that uncleanliness encouraged contagion; they had some knowledge of anatomy and performed operations—circumcision and perhaps the draining of abscessed teeth. But their knowledge of medicine, like that of the Mesopotamians, was handicapped by their belief that gods caused illnesses.

The New Kingdom and the Decline of Egyptian Civilization

The New Kingdom began in 1570 B.C. with the war of liberation against the Hyksos, which gave rise to an intense militancy that found expression in empire building. Military-minded pharaohs conquered territory that extended as far east as the Euphrates River. From its subject states, Egypt acquired tribute and slaves. Conquests led to the expansion of the bureaucracy, the rise of a professional army, and the increased power of priests, whose temples shared in the spoils. The formation of the empire ended Egyptian isolation and accelerated commercial and cultural intercourse with other peoples. Egyptian art, for example, showed the influence of foreign forms during this period.

A growing cosmopolitanism was paralleled by a movement toward monotheism during the reign of Pharaoh Amenhotep IV (c. 1369–1353 B.C.). Amenhotep sought to replace traditional polytheism with the worship of Aton, a single god of all men who was represented as the sun disk. Amenhotep took the name Akhenaton ("It is well with Aton"), and moved the capital from Thebes to a newly constructed holy city called Akhataten (near modern Tell el-Amarna). The city had palaces, administrative centers, and a temple complex honoring Aton. Akhenaton and his wife, Nefertiti, dedicated themselves to Aton—the creator of the world, the maintainer of life, and the god of love, justice, and peace. Akhenaton (or Ikhneton) also ordered his officials to chisel out the names of other gods from inscriptions on temples and monuments. With awe Akhenaton glorified Aton:

> How manifold are thy works!
> They are hidden from man's sight.
> O sole god, like whom there is no other.
> Thou hast made the earth according to thy desire.[2]

Akhenaton's "monotheism" had little impact on the masses of Egyptians, who retained their ancient beliefs, and was resisted by priests, who resented his changes. After Akhenaton's death, a new pharaoh had the monuments to Aton destroyed, along with records and inscriptions bearing Akhenaton's name.

The most significant historical questions concerning Akhenaton are: Was his religion genuine monotheism, which pushed religious thought in a new direction? And if so, did it influence Moses, who led the Israelites out of Egypt about a century later? These last questions have aroused controversy among historians. The principal limitation on the monotheistic character of Atonism is that there were really two gods in Akhenaton's religion—Aton and the pharaoh himself, who was still worshiped as a deity. Nor is there any evidence that Akhenaton influenced the monotheism of Moses.

Late in the thirteenth century, Libyans, probably seeking to settle in the more fertile land of Egypt, attacked from the west, and the Peoples of the Sea, as unsettled raiders from the Aegean Sea area and Asia Minor were called, launched a series of strikes at Egypt. A weakened Egypt abandoned its empire. In the succeeding centuries Egypt came under the rule of Libyans, Nubians, Assyrians, Persians, and finally Greeks, to whom Egypt lost its independence in the fourth century B.C.

Egyptian civilization had flourished for almost 2,000 years before it experienced an almost 1,000-year descent into stagnation, decline, and collapse. During its long history the Egyptians tried to preserve the ancient forms of their civilization, revealed to them by their ancestors and representing for all time those unchanging values that are the way of happiness.

Empire Builders

The rise of an Egyptian empire during the New Kingdom was part of a wider development in Near Eastern history after 1500 B.C.—the emergence of international empires. Empire building led to the intermingling of peoples and cultural traditions and to the extension of civilization well beyond the river valleys.

One reason for the growth of empires was the migration of peoples known as Indo-Europeans. Originally from a wide area ranging from southeastern Europe to the region beyond the Caspian Sea, Indo-Europeans embarked on a series of migrations around 2000 B.C. that eventually brought them into Italy, Greece, Asia Minor, Mesopotamia, Persia, and India. From a core Indo-European tongue there emerged the Greek, Latin, Germanic, Slavic, Persian, and Sanskrit languages.

Hittites

Several peoples established strong states in the Near East around 1500 B.C.—the Hurrians in northern Mesopotamia, the Kassites in southern Mesopotamia, and the Hittites in Asia Minor.

The Hittites wanted to control the trade routes that ran along the Euphrates River into Syria. In the 1300s, the Hittite empire reached its peak. Its leaders ruled Asia Minor and northern Syria, raided Babylon, and challenged Egypt for control of Syria and Palestine.

The Hittites borrowed several features of Mesopotamian civilization, including cuneiform, legal principles, and literary and art forms. Hittite religion blended the beliefs and practices of Indo-Europeans, native inhabitants of Asia Minor, and Mesopotamians. The Hittites were probably the first people to develop a substantial iron industry. At first, they apparently used iron only for ceremonial and ritual objects, and not for tools and weapons. However, because iron ore was more readily available than copper or tin (needed for bronze), after 1200 B.C. iron weapons and tools spread throughout the Near East, although bronze implements were still used. Around 1200 B.C., the Hittite empire fell, most likely to Indo-European invaders from the north.

Small Nations

During the twelfth century B.C. there was a temporary lull in empire build-ing, which permitted a number of small nations in Syria and Palestine to assert their sovereignty. Three of these peoples—Phoenicians, Aramaeans, and He-brews*—were originally Semitic desert nomads. The Phoenicians were descen-dants of the Canaanites, a Semitic people who had settled Palestine about 3000 B.C. Those Canaanites who migrated northwest into what is now Lebanon were called Phoenicians.

Settling in the coastal Mediterranean cities of Tyre, Byblos, Berytus (Beirut), and Sidon, the Phoenicians were naturally drawn to the sea. These daring explorers established towns along the coast of North Africa, on the islands of the western Mediterranean, and in Spain, and they became the greatest sea traders of the ancient world. The Phoenicians (or their Canaanite forebears) devised the first alphabet, which was a monumental contribution to writing. Since all words could be represented by combinations of letters, it saved memorizing thousands of diagrams and aided the Phoenicians in transmitting the civilizations of the Near East to the western Mediterranean.

The Aramaeans, who settled in Syria, Palestine, and northern Mesopotamia, performed a role similar to the Phoenicians'. As great caravan traders they carried both goods and cultural patterns to various parts of the Near East. The Hebrews and the Persians, for example, acquired the Phoenician alphabet from the Aramaeans.

Assyria

In the ninth century B.C., empire building resumed with the Assyrians, a Semitic people from the region around the upper Tigris River. Although they had made forays of expansion in 1200 and 1100 B.C., the Assyrians began their march to "world" empire three centuries later. In the eighth and seventh centuries the Assyrians became a ruthless fighting machine that steamrolled through Mesopotamia—including Armenia and Babylonia—as well as Syria, Palestine, and Egypt.

The Assyrian king, who was the representative and high priest of the god Ashur, governed absolutely. Nobles appointed by the king kept order in the provinces and collected tribute. The Assyrians improved roads, established messenger services, and engaged in large-scale irrigation projects to facilitate effective administration of their conquered lands and to promote prosperity. To keep their subjects obedient, the Assyrians resorted to terror and to depor-tation of troublesome subjects from their home territories.

---

* The Hebrews are discussed in Chapter 2.

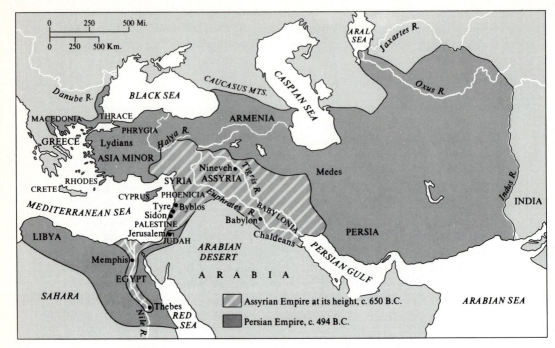

Map 1.2   The Assyrian and Persian Empires

Despite their harsh characteristics, the Assyrians maintained and spread the culture of the past. They copied and edited the literary works of Babylonia, adopted the old Sumerian gods, and used Mesopotamian art forms. The Assyrian king Ashurbanipal (669–626 B.C.) maintained a great library that contained thousands of clay tablets. After a period of wars and revolts by oppressed subjects weakened Assyria, a coalition of Medes from Iran and Chaldeans, or Neo-Babylonians, sacked the Assyrian capital of Nineveh in 612 B.C., destroying Assyrian power.

Persia: Unifier of the Near East

The destruction of the Assyrian empire made possible the rise of a Chaldean empire that included Babylonia, Assyria, Syria, and Palestine. Under Nebuchadnezzar, who ruled from 604 to 562 B.C., the Chaldean or Neo-Babylonian empire reached its height. After Nebuchadnezzar's death, the Chaldean empire was torn by civil war and threatened by a new power—the Persians, an Indo-European people who had settled in southern Iran. Under Cyrus the Great and his son and successor, Cambyses, the Persians conquered all lands between the Nile in Egypt and the Indus River in India. This conquest took twenty-five years, from 550 to 525 B.C.

The Near Eastern conception of absolute monarchy justified by religion reached its culminating expression in the person of the Persian king, who, with

Persepolis: Great Ceremonial Staircase and Audience Hall.   Persepolis was the ceremonial center of the Persian Empire. The repetitive geometric tribute bearers in bas relief along the staircase continue artistic traditions from distant Sumerian times. (*Courtesy of the Oriental Institute, University of Chicago*)

divine approval, ruled a vast empire, "the four quarters of the earth." Persian kings developed an effective system of administration—based in part on an Assyrian model—that gave stability and a degree of unity to their extensive territories. The Persian empire was divided into twenty provinces (*satrapies*), each one administered by a governor (*satrap*) responsible to the emperor. To guard against subversion, the king employed special agents—"the eyes and ears of the Emperor"—who supervised the activities of the governors. Persian kings allowed the provincials a large measure of self-rule. They also respected local traditions, particularly in matters of religion, as long as subjects paid their taxes, served in the royal army, and refrained from rebellion.

The empire was bound together by a uniform language, Aramaic (the language of the Aramaeans of Syria), used by government officials and merchants. Aramaic was written in letters based on the Phoenician alphabet. By making Aramaic a universal language, the Persians facilitated written and oral communication within the empire. The empire was further unified by an elaborate network of roads, an efficient postal system, a common system of weights and measures, and an empire-wide coinage based on an invention of the Lydians from western Asia Minor.

In addition to providing impressive political and administrative unity, the Persians fused and perpetuated the various cultural traditions of the Near East. Persian palaces, for example, boasted the terraces of Babylon, the colonnades of Eygpt, the winged bulls that decorated Assyrian palace gates, and the craftsmanship of Median goldsmiths.

The political and cultural universalism of the Persian empire had its counterpart in the emergence of a higher religion, Zoroastrianism, which contained both monotheistic and dualistic elements. Named for its founder, the Persian prophet Zoroaster, this religion taught belief in Ahura Mazda—the Wise Lord—god of light, of justice, wisdom, goodness, and immortality. But in addition to the Wise Lord, there existed Ahriman, the spirit of darkness, who was evil and destructive; Ahriman was in conflict with the ultimately triumphant Ahura Mazda. People were free to choose whom they would follow. To serve Ahura Mazda, one had to speak the truth and be good to others; the reward for such behavior was life eternal in paradise, the realm of light and goodness. Followers of the evil spirit were cast into hell, a realm of darkness and torment. In contrast to the traditional religions of the Near East, Zoroastrianism rejected magic, polytheism, sacrifices, and temples, and instead stressed ethics.

Persia unified the nations of the Near East into a world-state, headed by a divinely appointed king, and synthesized the region's cultural traditions. Soon it would confront the city-states of Greece, whose political system and cultural orientation differed from that of the Near East.

The Religious Orientation of the Near East

All features of Near Eastern society—law, kingship, art, and science—were generally interpenetrated with and dominated by religion. Religion was the source of the vitality and creativity of Mesopotamian and Egyptian civilizations. Near Eastern art was inspired by religion; literature and history dealt with the ways of the gods; science was permeated with religion. And priest-kings or god-kings, their power sanctioned by divine forces, furnished the necessary authority to organize large numbers of people in cooperative ventures.

A Myth-making World-View

A religious or mythopoeic (myth-making) view of the world gives Near Eastern civilization its distinctive form and allows us to see it as an organic whole. Myth-making was humanity's first way of thinking. Appealing primarily to the imagination and emotions, not to reason, myth-making was the earliest attempt to make nature and life comprehensible.

Originating in sacred rites, ritual dances, feasts, and ceremonies, myths depicted the deeds of gods who, in some remote past, had brought forth the world and human beings. Holding that human destiny was determined by the gods, Near Eastern people interpreted their experiences through myths. Myths also enabled Mesopotamians and Egyptians to make sense out of nature, to explain the world of phenomena. Through myths the Near Eastern mind sought to give coherence to the universe, to make it intelligible. These myths gave Near Eastern peoples a framework with which to pattern their experiences into a meaningful order, justify their rules of conduct, and try to overcome the uncertainty of existence.

Religion determined the Near Eastern view of nature. Gods and demons resided within nature: the sun and stars, the rivers and mountains, the wind and lightning were either gods or the dwelling places of gods. To an Egyptian or a Mesopotamian, natural phenomena—a falling rock, a thunderclap, a rampaging river—were experienced as life facing life. If a river flooded the region, destroying crops, it was because it wanted to; the river or the gods desired to punish the people. Near Eastern peoples did not view nature as a physical entity, as an *it,* inanimate, impersonal, and governed by universal law; rather, they saw every object in nature mythically, as a *thou,* suffused with life.

> In other words, the ancients told myths instead of presenting an analysis or conclusions. We would explain, for instance, that certain atmospheric changes broke a drought and brought about rain. The Babylonians observed the same facts but experienced them as the intervention of the gigantic bird Imdugud which came to their rescue. It covered the sky with the black storm clouds of its wings and devoured the Bull of Heaven, whose hot breath had scorched the crops.[3]

The myth-making mind of the ancient Near East was not troubled by contradictions; it did not seek logical consistency; it did not analyze nature systematically and rationally; it did not structure and explain reality by means of hypothesis, logical analysis, and general rules. It had no awareness of repetitive laws inherent in nature, but attributed physical occurrences to divine powers.

Of course, Near Eastern people did engage in rational forms of thought and behavior. They certainly employed reason in building irrigation works, in preparing a calendar, and in performing mathematical operations. But, because rational or logical thought remained subordinate to a mythic-religious world-view, Near Eastern people did not arrive at a *consistently* and *self-consciously* rational method of inquiring into physical nature and human culture. They did not fashion a body of philosophic and scientific ideas that were logically structured, discussed, and debated.

Near Eastern civilization reached the first level in the development of science—observing nature, recording data, and improving technology in mining, metallurgy, and architecture. But it did not advance to the level of self-conscious philosophic and scientific thought—that is, logically deduced abstractions, hypotheses, and generalizations. These later developments were the singular achievement of Greek philosophy, which gave a "rational interpretation to natural occurrences which had previously been explained by ancient mythologies. . . . With the study of nature set free from the control of

Chronology 1.1 ⊕ The Near East	
3200 B.C.*	Rise of civilization in Sumeria
2900	Union of Upper and Lower Egypt
2686–2181	Old Kingdom; essential forms of Egyptian civilization take shape
2180	Downfall of Akkadian empire
1792–1750	Hammurabi of Babylon brings Akkad and Sumer under his control and fashions a code of laws
1570	Egyptians drive out Hyksos and begin building an empire
1369–1353	Amenhotep IV; a movement toward monotheism
1200	Fall of Hittite empire
612	Fall of Assyrian empire
604–562	Reign of Nebuchadnezzar; height of Chaldean empire
550–525 B.C.	Persian conquests form a world empire
	* Most dates are approximations.

mythological fancy, the way was opened for the development of science as an intellectual system."[4]

Near Eastern Achievements

Sumerians and Egyptians demonstrated enormous creativity and intelligence. They built irrigation works and cities, organized governments, charted the course of heavenly bodies, performed mathematical operations, constructed large-scale monuments, engaged in international trade, established bureaucracies and schools, and advanced the level of technology considerably. And without the Sumerian invention of writing—one of the great creative acts in history—what we mean by *civilization* could not have emerged.

Many elements of ancient Near Eastern civilization were passed on to the West. The wheeled vehicle, the plow, and the phonetic alphabet—all important to the development of civilization—derive from the Near East. In the realm of medicine, the Egyptians knew the value of certain drugs, such as castor oil; they also knew how to use splints and bandages. The innovative divisions that gave 360 degrees to a circle and 60 minutes to an hour originated in Mesopotamia. Egyptian geometry and Babylonian astronomy were utilized by the Greeks and became a part of Western knowledge. In Christian art, too, one finds connections to the Mesopotamian art forms—for example, the Assyrians depicted winged angel-like beings.

The belief that a king's power comes from a heavenly source also derives from the Near East. Both the Hebrews and the Greeks borrowed Mesopotamian literary themes. For example, some biblical stories—the Flood, the quarrel between Cain and Abel, and the Tower of Babel—stem from Mesopotamian antecedents. A similar link exists between the Greek and the earlier Mesopotamian mythologies.

Thus, many achievements of Egyptians and Mesopotamians were inherited and assimilated by both Greeks and Hebrews. Even more important for an understanding of the essential meaning of Western civilization are the ways in which Greeks and Hebrews rejected or transformed elements of the older Near Eastern traditions to create new points of departure for the human mind.

Notes

1. *The Epic of Gilgamesh*, with an introduction by N. K. Sandars (Baltimore: Penguin Books, 1965), pp. 69, 104.
2. From *The Culture of Ancient Egypt* by John A. Wilson (1951): 227. © 1951 The University of Chicago.
3. Henri Frankfort, et al., *Before Philosophy* (Baltimore: Penguin Books, 1949), p. 15.
4. Samuel Sambursky, *The Physical World of the Greeks* (New York: Collier Books, 1962), pp. 18–19.

Suggested Reading

Campbell, Bernard G., *Humankind Emerging* (1982). The world of prehistory.

David, Rosalie A., *The Ancient Egyptians* (1982). Focuses on religious beliefs and practices.

Frankfort, Henri, et al., *The Intellectual Adventure of Ancient Man* (1946); paperback edition is entitled *Before Philosophy*. Brilliant discussions of the role of myth in the ancient Near East by distinguished scholars.

Gowlett, John, *Ascent to Civilization* (1984). An up-to-date study with excellent graphics.

Hallo, W. W., and Simpson, W. K., *The Ancient Near East* (1971). An authoritative survey of the political history of the Near East.

Moscati, Sabatino, *The Face of the Ancient Orient* (1962). An illuminating survey of the various peoples of the ancient Near East.

Oppenheim, A. L., *Ancient Mesopotamia* (1964). Stresses social and economic history.

Wilson, John A., *The Culture of Ancient Egypt* (1951). An interpretation by a distinguished Egyptologist.

Review Questions

1. Why is the development of the Neolithic Age referred to as the Neolithic Revolution?
2. What is meant by civilization? Under what conditions did it emerge?
3. How did religion influence Mesopotamian civilization?
4. What achievements did the Mesopotamians make in trade, mathematics, and science?
5. How did the Egyptians' religious beliefs affect their civilization?
6. What is the significance of Akhenaton?
7. How did the Persians give unity to the Near East?
8. What advances in science were made by Near Eastern civilization? How was science limited by a myth-making view of nature?
9. What were the accomplishments of the civilizations of the Near East? What elements of Near Eastern civilization were passed on to Western civilization?

Chapter ⍟ 2

The Hebrews: A New View of God and the Individual

Ancient Mesopotamia and Egypt, the birthplace of the first civilizations, are not the spiritual ancestors of the West; for the origins of the Western tradition, we must turn to the Hebrews (Jews) and the Greeks. As Egyptologist John A. Wilson says:

The Children of Israel built a nation and a religion on the rejection of things Egyptian. Not only did they see God as one, but they ascribed to him consistency of concern for man and consistency of justice to man. . . . Like the Greeks, the Hebrews took forms from their great neighbors; like the Greeks, they used those forms for very different purposes.[1]

In this chapter we examine one source of the Western tradition, the Hebrews, whose conception of God broke with the outlook of the Near East and whose ethical teachings helped to fashion the Western idea of the dignity of the individual. ⍟

Early Hebrew History

The Hebrews originated in Mesopotamia and migrated to Canaan, a portion of which was later called Palestine. The Hebrew patriarchs—Abraham, Isaac, and Jacob, so prominently depicted in the Old Testament—were chieftains of seminomadic clans that roamed Palestine and occasionally journeyed to Mesopotamia and Egypt. The early Hebrews absorbed some features of Mesopotamian civilization. For example, there are parallels between biblical law and the Mesopotamian legal tradition. Several biblical stories—the Creation, the Flood, the Garden of Eden—derive from Mesopotamian sources.

Some Hebrews journeyed from Canaan to Egypt to be herdsmen and farmers, but they eventually became forced laborers for the Egyptians. Fearful of becoming permanent slaves of pharaoh, the Hebrews yearned for an opportunity to escape. In the late thirteenth century B.C. an extraordinary leader rose among them called Moses, who was accepted by his people as a messenger of God. Leading the Hebrews in their exodus from Egypt, Moses transformed them during their wanderings in the wilderness of Sinai into a nation, welded together and uplifted by a belief in Yahweh, the one God.

The wandering Hebrews returned to Canaan to rejoin other Hebrew tribes that had not migrated to Egypt. The conquest of the Canaanites, who possessed a material culture superior to the Hebrews', took many generations. Threatened by the Philistines (originally from the islands of the Aegean Sea and the coast of Asia Minor), the twelve Hebrew tribes united under the leadership of Saul, a charismatic hero whom they acclaimed as their first king. Under Saul's successor, David, a gifted warrior and poet, the Hebrews (or Israelites) broke the back of Philistine power and subdued neighboring peoples.

David's son Solomon built a royal palace in Jerusalem and beside it a magnificent temple honoring God. Under Solomon, ancient Israel was at the height of its political power and prosperity, but opposition to Solomon's tax policies and his favored treatment of the region of Judah in the south led to the division of the kingdom after his death in 922 B.C. The tribes loyal to Solomon's son belonged to the Kingdom of Judah, while the other tribes organized the northern Kingdom of Israel.

In 722 B.C., Israel fell to the Assyrians, who deported many Hebrews to other parts of the Assyrian empire. These transported Hebrews merged with neighboring peoples and lost their identity as the people of the one God. In 586 B.C., the Chaldeans conquered Judah, destroyed the temple, devastated the land, and deported several thousand Hebrews to Babylon. This time was the darkest moment in the history of the Hebrews. Their state was gone, and neighboring peoples had overrun their land; their holy temple, built during the reign of King Solomon, was in ruins; thousands had died in battle or had been executed; others had fled to Egypt and other lands, and thousands more were in exile in Babylon. This exile is known as the Babylonian Captivity.

Still the Hebrews, in what is a marvel of history, survived as a people. Although many of the exiles in Babylon assimilated Babylonian ways, some remained faithful to their God, Yahweh, and the Law of Moses and longed to return to their homeland. Thus, their faith enabled them to endure conquest and exile. When the Persians conquered Babylon, King Cyrus, in 538 B.C., permitted the exiles to return to Judah, now a Persian province, and to rebuild the temple.

The Jews eventually lost their independence to Rome and became a dispersed people. But they never relinquished their commitment to God and his Law as recorded in the Hebrew Scriptures. Called *Tanak* by Jews (and Old Testament by Christians), these Scriptures consist of thirty-nine books* by

---

* In ancient times, the number of books was usually given as twenty-four. Certain books are now divided into two parts and the twelve works by the minor prophets are now counted as individual books.

Dura-Europos Synagogue Mural, Third Century A.D.   This scene depicts Aaron, the original high priest of the Hebrews and brother of Moses. The mural of biblical scenes consisted originally of about sixty panels, of which only thirty remain intact. (*Dura-Europos Collection, Yale University Art Gallery*)

several authors who lived in different centuries. Jews call the first five books—Genesis, Exodus, Leviticus, Numbers, and Deuteronomy—the Torah. Often the Torah is referred to as the Pentateuch, a Greek word meaning "five books."

The Old Testament represents Hebrew literary and oral tradition dating from about 1250 to 150 B.C. Compiled by religious devotees, not research historians, it understandably contains factual errors, imprecisions, and discrepancies. However, there are also passages that contain reliable history, and historians find the Hebrew Scriptures an indispensable source for studying the ancient Near East. Students of literature study it for its poetry, legends, and themes, all of which are an integral part of the Western literary tradition. But it is as a work of religious inspiration that the Old Testament attains its profoundest importance.

These Scriptures are the record of more than 1,000 years of ancient Jewish history; containing Jewish laws, wisdom, hopes, legends, and literary expressions, they describe an ancient people's efforts to comprehend the ways of God. They emphasize and value the human experience; their heroes are not demigods but human beings. They depict human strength as well as weakness. Some passages exhibit cruelty and unseemly revenge, while others express the highest ethical values. As set forth in the Hebrew Scriptures, the Hebrew idea of God and his relationship to human beings is one of the foundations of the Western tradition.

God: One, Sovereign, Transcendent, Good

The Hebrew view of the one God marked a profound break with Near Eastern religious thought. Pagan gods were not truly free; their power was not without limits. Unlike Yahweh, Near Eastern gods were not eternal, but were born or created; they issued from some prior realm. They were also subject to biological conditions, requiring food, drink, sleep, and sexual gratification. Sometimes they became ill, or grew old, or died. When they behaved wickedly, they had to answer to fate, which demanded punishment as retribution; even the gods were subject to fate's power.

The Hebrews regarded God as *fully* sovereign. He ruled all and was subject to nothing. Yahweh's existence and power did not derive from a preexisting realm as pagan gods' did. The Hebrews believed that no realm of being preceded God in time or surpassed him in power. They saw God as eternal, the source of all in the universe, and having a supreme will.

Whereas Near Eastern divinities dwelt within nature, the Hebrew God was *transcendent,* above nature and not a part of it. Yahweh was not identified with any natural force and did not dwell in a particular place in heaven or on earth. Since God was the creator and ruler of nature, there was no place for a sun-god, a moon-god, a god in the river, or a demon in the storm. Nature was God's creation but was not itself divine. Therefore, when the Hebrews confronted natural phenomena, they experienced God's magnificent handiwork, not objects with wills of their own. All natural phenomena—rivers, mountains, storms, stars—were divested of any supernatural quality. The stars and planets were creations of Yahweh, not divinities or the abodes of divinities. The Hebrews neither regarded them with awe nor worshiped them. This removal of the gods from nature is a necessary prerequisite for scientific thought.

The Hebrews demythicized nature, but, concerned with religion and morality, they did not create theoretical science. As testimony to God's greatness, nature inspired people to sing the praises of the Lord; it invoked worship of God, not scientific curiosity. When Hebrews gazed at the heavens, they did not seek to discover mathematical relationships, but admired God's handiwork. The Hebrews did not view nature as a system governed by natural law. Rather, they saw the rising sun, spring rain, summer heat, and winter cold as God intervening in an orderly manner in his creation. The Hebrews, unlike the Greeks, were not philosophers. They were concerned with God's will, not the human intellect; with the feelings of the heart, not the power of the mind; with righteous behavior, not abstract thought.

Unlike the Greeks, the Hebrews did not speculate about the origins of all things and the operations of nature; they knew that God had created everything. For the Hebrews, God's existence was based on religious conviction, not on rational inquiry; on revelation, not reason. It was the Greeks, not the Hebrews, who originated rational thought. But Christianity, born of Judaism, retained the Hebrew view of a transcendent God and the orderliness of his creation—concepts that could accommodate Greek science.

The Hebrews also did not speculate about God's nature. They knew only that he was *good* and that he made ethical demands on his people. Unlike Near Eastern gods, Yahweh was not driven by lust or motivated by evil, but was "merciful and gracious, long-suffering, and abundant in goodness and truth . . . forgiving iniquity and transgression and sin" (Psalm 145:8).*[2] In contrast to pagan gods, who were indifferent to human beings, Yahweh was attentive to human needs. By asserting that God was *one, sovereign, transcendent,* and *good,* the Hebrews effected a religious revolution that separated them entirely from the world-view held by the other peoples of the ancient Near East.

The Individual and Moral Autonomy

This new conception of God made possible a new awareness of the individual. In confronting God, the Hebrews developed an awareness of *self* or *I,* of one's own person, moral autonomy, and personal worth. The Hebrews believed that God, who possessed total freedom, had bestowed on people moral freedom— the capacity to choose between good and evil.

Fundamental to Hebrew belief was the insistence that God did not create people to be his slaves. The Hebrews regarded God with awe and humility, with respect and fear, but they did not believe that God wanted people to grovel before him; rather, he wanted them to fulfill their moral potential by freely making the choice to follow or not to follow God's Law. Thus, in creating men and women in his own image, God granted them autonomy and sovereignty. In God's plan for the universe, human beings were the highest creation, subordinate only to God. Of all his creations, only they had been given the freedom to choose between righteousness and wickedness, between "life and good, and death and evil" (Deuteronomy 30:15).

God demanded that the Hebrews have no other gods and that they make no images "nor any manner of likeness, of any thing that is in heaven above, or that is in the earth beneath. . . . thou shalt not bow down unto them nor serve them" (Exodus 20:4–5). The Hebrews believed that the worship of idols deprived people of their freedom and dignity; people cannot be fully human if they surrender themselves to a lifeless idol. Hence the Hebrews had to destroy images and all other forms of idolatry. A crucial element of Near Eastern religion was the use of images—art forms that depicted divinities—but the Hebrews believed God, the Supreme Being, could not be represented by pictures or sculpture fashioned by human beings. The Hebrews rejected entirely the belief that an image possessed divine powers that could be manipulated for human advantage. Ethical considerations, not myth or magic, were central to Hebrew religious life.

By making God the center of life, Hebrews could become free moral agents; no person, no human institution, no human tradition could claim their souls.

---

*The Bible passages in this chapter are quoted from *The Holy Scriptures.*

Because God alone was the supreme value in the universe, only he was worthy of worship. Thus, to give *ultimate* loyalty to a king or a general violated God's stern warning against the worship of false gods. The first concern of the Hebrews was righteousness, not power, fame, or riches, which were only idols and would impoverish a person spiritually and morally.

There was, however, a condition to freedom. For the Hebrews, people were not free to create their own moral precepts or their own standards of right and wrong; freedom meant voluntary obedience to commands that originated with God. Evil and suffering were not caused by blind fate, malevolent demons, or arbitrary gods, but resulted from people's disregard of God's commandments. The dilemma is that in possessing freedom of choice, human beings are also free to disobey God, to commit a sin, which leads to suffering and death. Thus, in the Genesis story Adam and Eve were punished for disobeying God in the Garden of Eden.

For Hebrews, to know God was not to comprehend him intellectually, to define him, or to prove his existence; to know God was to be righteous and loving, merciful and just. When men and women loved God, the Hebrews believed, they were uplifted and improved. Gradually they learned to overcome the worst elements of human nature and to treat people with respect and compassion. The Jews came to interpret the belief that man was created in God's image to mean that each human being has a divine spark in him or her, giving every person a unique dignity that cannot be taken away.

By giving devotion to God, the Hebrews asserted the value and autonomy of human beings. Thus the Hebrews conceived the idea of moral freedom, that each individual is responsible for his or her own actions. Also inherited by Christianity, the ideas of human dignity and moral autonomy are central to the Western tradition.

The Covenant and the Law

Central to Hebrew religious thought and decisive in Hebrew history was the covenant—God's special agreement with the Hebrew people: if they obeyed his commands, they would "be unto Me a kingdom of priests and a holy nation" (Exodus 19:6). By this act the Israelites as a nation accepted God's lordship.

The Hebrews became conscious of themselves as a unique nation, as a "chosen people," for God had given them a special honor, a profound opportunity, and (as they could never forget) an awesome responsibility. The Hebrews did not claim that God had selected them because they were better than other peoples or because they had done anything special to deserve God's election. They believed that God had selected them to receive the Law so that their nation would set an example of righteous behavior and ultimately make God and the Law known to the other nations.

This responsibility to be the moral teachers of humanity weighed heavily on

Mosaic: The Sacrifice of Isaac.   In Hebrew art, images of human beings are rare because of the Second Commandment injunction against graven images. This mosaic showing Abraham about to sacrifice his son is from the pavement of the Beth Alpha Synagogue. (*Wiener Library, London*)

the Hebrews. They believed that God had revealed his Law—including the moral code known as the Ten Commandments—to the Hebrew people as a whole, and obedience to the Law became the overriding obligation of each Hebrew.

Israelite law incorporated many elements from Near Eastern legal codes and oral traditions. But by making people more important than property, by expressing mercy toward the oppressed, and by rejecting the idea that law should treat the poor and the rich differently, Israelite law demonstrated a greater ethical awareness and a more humane spirit than other legal codes of the Near East. Thus, there were laws to protect the poor, widows, orphans, resident aliens, hired laborers, and slaves:

You shall not steal nor deal falsely, nor lie to one another. . . . You shall not oppress your neighbor or rob him. . . . You shall do no injustice in judgment; you shall not be partial to the poor or defer to the great, but in righteousness shall you judge your neighbor. . . . When a stranger sojourns with you in your land, you shall not do him wrong. . . . [He] shall be to you as the native among you, and you shall love him as yourself. (Leviticus 19:11, 13, 33)

Like other Near Eastern societies, the Jews placed women in a subordinate position. The husband was considered his wife's master, and she often addressed him as a servant or subject would speak to a superior. A husband could divorce his wife, but she could not divorce him. Only when there was no male heir could a wife inherit property from her husband or a daughter inherit from her father. Outside the home, women were not regarded as competent witnesses in court and played a lesser role than men in organized worship.

On the other hand, the Jews also showed respect for women. Wise women and prophetesses like Judith and Esther were respected by the community and were consulted by its leaders. Prophets compared God's love for the Hebrews with a husband's love for his wife. Jewish law regarded the woman as a person, not as property. Even female captives taken in war were not to be abused or humiliated. The law required a husband to respect and support his wife and never to strike her. One of the Ten Commandments called for honoring both father and mother.

The Hebrew Idea of History

Their idea of God made the Hebrews aware of the crucial importance of historical time. Holidays commemorating such specific historical events as the Exodus from Egypt and the receiving of the Ten Commandments on Mount Sinai kept the past alive and vital. Egyptians and Mesopotamians did not have a similar awareness of the uniqueness of a given event; to them, today's events were repetitions of events experienced by their ancestors. To the Jews, the Exodus and the covenant were singular, nonrepetitive occurrences, decisive in shaping their national history. This historical uniqueness and importance of events derived from the idea of a universal God profoundly involved in human affairs—a God who cares, teaches, and punishes.

The Jews valued the future as well as the past. Regarding human history as a process leading to a goal, they envisioned a great day when God would establish on earth a glorious age of peace, prosperity, happiness, and human brotherhood. This utopian notion has become deeply embedded in Western thought.

The Jews saw history as a divine drama filled with sacred meaning and moral significance. Historical events revealed the clash of human will with God's commands. Through history's specific events, God's presence was disclosed and his purpose made known. When the Hebrews suffered conquest and exile, they interpreted these events as retribution for violating God's Law and as punishments for their stubbornness, sinfulness, and rebelliousness. For the Hebrews, history also revealed God's compassion and concern. Thus the Lord liberated Moses and the Israelites at the Red Sea and appointed prophets to plead for the poor and the oppressed. Because historical events revealed God's attitude toward human beings, these events possessed spiritual meaning, and therefore were worth recording, evaluating, and remembering.

The Prophets

Jewish history was marked by the emergence of spiritually inspired persons called *prophets,* who felt compelled to act as God's messengers. The prophets cared nothing for money or possessions, feared no one, and preached without invitation. Often emerging in times of social distress and moral confusion, the prophets pleaded for a return to the covenant and the Law. They exhorted the entire nation and taught that when his people forgot God and made themselves the center of all things, they would bring disaster on themselves and their community. The prophets saw national misfortune as an opportunity for penitence and reform. They were remarkably courageous people who did not quake before the powerful.

The flowering of the prophetic movement—the age of classical or literary prophecy—began in the eighth century B.C. In attacking oppression, cruelty, greed, and exploitation, the classical prophets added a new dimension to Israel's religious development. These prophets were responding to problems emanating from Israel's changed social structure. The general lack of class distinctions characterizing a tribal society had been altered by the rise of Hebrew kings, the expansion of commerce, and the growth of cities. By the eighth century, there was a significant disparity between the wealthy and the poor. Small farmers in debt to moneylenders faced the loss of their land or even bondage; the poor were often dispossessed by the greedy wealthy. To the prophets, these social evils were religious sins that would bring ruin to Israel. In the name of God, they denounced the hypocrisy and pomp of the heartless rich, and demanded justice. God is compassionate, they insisted. He cares for all, especially the poor, the unfortunate, the sufferer, and the defenseless. God's injunctions, declared Isaiah, were to

> *Put away the evil of your doings*
> *From before mine eyes,*
> *Cease to do evil;*
> *Learn to do well;*
> *Seek justice, relieve the oppressed,*
> *Judge the fatherless, plead for the widow.*
> *(Isaiah 1:17)*

Dead Sea Scroll.   The sacredness of the biblical text and the authority of the recorded word of God remain a unifying factor in ancient as well as modern Jewish history. Found in caves near Khirbet Qumran, the Dead Sea Scrolls contain a copy of a complete Hebrew text of Isaiah that differs insignificantly from the modern version, yet the scroll dates from the second century B.C. and is the earliest text extant. (© *John C. Trever, 1970*)

Prophets de-emphasized sacrifices and rituals and stressed the direct spiritual-ethical encounter between the individual and God. It was the inner person more than the outer forms of religious activity that concerned the prophets. Holding that the essence of the covenant was universal righteousness, the prophets criticized priests whose commitment to rites and rituals was not supported by a deeper spiritual insight nor matched by a zeal for morality in daily life. To the prophets, an ethical sin was far worse than a ritual omission. Above all, said the prophets, God demands righteousness. To live unjustly, to mistreat one's neighbors, to act without compassion—these actions violated God's law and endangered the entire social order.

The prophets thus created a social conscience that has become part of the Western tradition. They held out the hope that life on earth could be improved, that poverty and injustice need not be accepted as part of an unalterable natural order, and that the individual was capable of elevating himself or herself morally and could respect the dignity of others.

Chronology 2.1 ◈ The Hebrews

1250 B.C.*	Hebrew exodus from Egypt
1024–1000	The reign of Saul, Israel's first king
1000–961	The creation of a united monarchy under David
961–922	The reign of Solomon; construction of the first temple
750–430	The age of classical prophecy
722	Kingdom of Israel falls to Assyrians
586	Kingdom of Judah falls to Chaldeans; the temple is destroyed
586–539	Babylonian exile
538	Cyrus of Persia allows exiles to return to Judah
515 B.C.	Second temple is dedicated

*Most dates are approximations.

Two tendencies were present in Hebrew thought: parochialism and universalism. Parochial-mindedness stressed the special nature, destiny, and needs of the chosen people, a nation set apart from others. This outlook was offset by universalism, a concern for all humanity, which found expression in those prophets who envisioned the unity of all people under God. All people were equally precious to God.

The prophets were not pacifists, particularly if a war were being waged against the enemies of Yahweh. But some prophets denounced war as obscene and looked forward to its elimination. They maintained that when people glorify force, they dehumanize their opponents, brutalize themselves, and dishonor God. When violence rules, there can be no love of God and no regard for the individual.

The prophets' universalism was accompanied by an equally profound awareness of the individual and his or her worth to God. Before the prophets, virtually all religious tradition had been produced communally and anonymously. The prophets, however, spoke as fearless individuals who, by affixing their signatures to their thoughts, fully bore the responsibility of their religious inspiration and conviction.

Prophets emphasized the individual's responsibility for his or her own actions. In coming to regard God's law as a *command to conscience, an appeal to the inner person,* the prophets heightened the awareness of the human personality. They indicated that the individual could not know God only by following edicts and by performing rituals; the individual must experience God. Precisely this I-Thou relationship could make the individual fully conscious of self and could deepen and enrich his or her own personality. At Mount Sinai, God gave the Law to a tribal people who obeyed largely out of fear and compulsion; by the prophets' time, the Jews appeared to be autonomous individuals who heeded the Law because of a deliberate, conscious, and inner commitment.

Monotheism had initiated a process of self-discovery and self-realization unmatched by other peoples of the Near East. The prophets' ideals helped sustain the Jews throughout their long and often painful historical odyssey, and they remain a vital force for Jews today. Incorporated into the teachings of Jesus, these ideals, as part of Christianity, are embedded in the Western tradition.

Notes

1. John A. Wilson, "Egypt—the Kingdom of the 'Two Lands,' " in E. A. Speiser, *At the Dawn of Civilization* (New Brunswick, N.J.: Rutgers University Press, 1964), pp. 267–268.

Volume I in *The World History of the Jewish People.*
2. From *The Holy Scriptures,* copyright 1917. Reprinted by permission of The Jewish Publication Society of America.

Suggested Reading

Anderson, Bernhard, *Understanding the Old Testament,* 2nd ed. (1966). An excellent survey of the Old Testament in its historical setting.

Boadt, Lawrence, *Reading the Old Testament* (1984). A study of ancient Israel's religious experience by a sympathetic Catholic scholar.

Bright, John, *A History of Israel* (1972). A thoughtful, clearly written survey; the best of its kind.

Heschel, Abraham, *The Prophets,* 2 vols.

(1962). A penetrating analysis of the nature of prophetic inspiration.

Kaufmann, Yehezkel, *The Religion of Israel* (1960). An abridgment and translation of Kaufmann's classic multivolume work.

Kuntz, Kenneth J., *The People of Ancient Israel* (1974). A useful introduction to Old Testament literature, history, and thought.

Zeitlin, Irving M., *Ancient Judaism* (1984). A sociologist examines the history and thought of ancient Israel.

Review Questions

1. How did the Hebrew view of God mark a revolutionary break with Near Eastern religious thought?
2. How did Hebrew religious thought promote the idea of moral autonomy?
3. Provide examples showing that Hebrew law expressed a concern for human dignity.
4. Why did the Hebrews consider history to be important, and how did they demonstrate its importance?
5. What role did the prophets play in Hebrew history? What is the enduring significance of their achievement?
6. Why are the Hebrews regarded as one source of Western civilization?

Chapter ⍟ 3

The Greeks:
From Myth to Reason

The Hebrew conception of ethical monotheism, with its stress on human dignity, is one source of the Western tradition. The other source derives from ancient Greece. Both Hebrews and Greeks absorbed the achievements of Near Eastern civilizations, but they also developed their own distinctive viewpoints and styles of thought that set them apart from the Mesopotamians and Egyptians. The great achievements of the Hebrews lay in the sphere of religious-ethical thought; those of the Greeks lay in the development of rational thought.

The Greeks conceived of nature as following general rules, not acting according to the whims of gods or demons. They saw human beings as having a capacity for rational thought, a need for freedom, and a worth as individuals. Although the Greeks never dispensed with the gods, they increasingly stressed the importance of human reason and human decisions; they came to assert that reason is the avenue to knowledge and that people—not the gods—are responsible for their own behavior. In this shift of attention from the gods to human beings, the Greeks broke with the myth-making orientation of the Near East and created the rational humanist outlook that is a distinctive feature of Western civilization. ⍟

Early Aegean Civilizations

Until the latter part of the nineteenth century, historians placed the beginning of Greek (or Hellenic) history in the eighth century B.C. Now it is known that two civilizations preceded Hellenic Greece—the Minoan and the Mycenaean. Although the ancient Greek poet Homer spoke of an earlier Greek civilization in his works, historians believed that Homer's epics dealt with myths and legends, not with a historical past. In 1871, however, a successful German businessman, Heinrich Schliemann, began a search for earliest Greece. In excavating several sites mentioned by Homer, Schliemann discovered tombs, pottery, ornaments, and the remains of palaces of what hitherto had been a lost Greek civilization. The ancient civilization was named after Mycenae, the most important city of the time.

In 1900, Arthur Evans, a British archaeologist, excavating on the island of Crete, southeast of the Greek mainland, unearthed a civilization even older than that of the Mycenaean Greeks. The Cretans, or Minoans, were not Greeks and did not speak a Greek language, but their influence on mainland Greece was considerable and enduring. Minoan civilization lasted about 1350 years (2600 B.C. to 1250 B.C.), and reached its height during the period from 1700 to 1450 B.C.

The centers of Minoan civilization were magnificent palace complexes, whose construction was evidence of the wealth and power of Minoan kings. The palaces housed royal families, priests, and government officials, and contained workshops that produced decorated silver vessels, daggers, and pottery for local use and for export.

Judging by the archaeological evidence, the Minoans were peaceful. Minoan art did not generally depict military scenes, and Minoan palaces, unlike the Mycenaean, had no defensive walls or fortifications. Thus the Minoans were vulnerable to the warlike Mycenaean Greeks, whose invasion contributed to the decline of Minoan civilization.

Who were these Mycenaeans? About 2000 B.C., Greek-speaking tribes moved southward into the Greek peninsula where, together with the pre-Greek population, they fashioned the Mycenaean civilization. In the Peloponnesus, the Mycenaeans built palaces that were based in part on Cretan models. In these palaces, Mycenaean kings conducted affairs of state and priests and priestesses performed religious ceremonies. Potters, smiths, tailors, and chariot builders practiced their crafts in the numerous workshops, much like their Minoan counterparts. Mycenaean arts and crafts owed a considerable debt to Crete. A script that permitted record keeping also probably came from Crete.

Mycenaean civilization reached its height in the period from 1400 to 1230 B.C. Following that, constant warfare among the Mycenaean kingdoms (and perhaps foreign invasions) led to destruction of the palaces and abrupt disintegration of the Mycenaean civilization about 1100 B.C. But to the later Greek civilization, the Mycenaeans left a legacy of religious forms, pottery making, metallurgy, agriculture, language, a code of honor immortalized in the Homeric epics, and myths and legends that offered themes for Greek drama.

Evolution of the City-States

From 1100 to 800 B.C., the Greek world passed through the Dark Age, an era of transition between a dead Mycenaean civilization and a still unborn Hellenic civilization. The Dark Age saw the migration of Greek tribes from the barren mountainous regions of Greece to more fertile plains, and from the mainland to Aegean islands and the coast of Asia Minor. During this period the Greeks experienced insecurity, warfare, poverty, and isolation.

After 800 B.C., however, town life revived. Writing again became part of the Greek culture, this time with the more efficient Phoenician script. The population increased dramatically, there was a spectacular increase in the use of metals, and overseas trade expanded. Gradually Greek cities founded settlements on the islands of the Aegean, along the coast of Asia Minor and the Black Sea, and to the west in Sicily and southern Italy. These colonies, established to relieve overpopulation and land hunger, were independent, self-governing city-states, not possessions of the homeland city-states. During these two hundred years of colonization (750–550 B.C.), trade and industry expanded and the pace of urbanization quickened.

Homer, Shaper of the Greek Spirit

The poet Homer lived during the eighth century B.C., just after the Dark Age. His great epics, the *Iliad* and the *Odyssey,* helped to shape the Greek spirit and Greek religion. Homer was the earliest molder of the Greek outlook and character.

For centuries Greek youngsters grew up reciting the Homeric epics and admiring the Homeric heroes. The *Iliad* deals in poetic form with a small segment of the last year of the Trojan War, which had taken place centuries before Homer's time during the Mycenaean period.

The wrath of Achilles is Homer's theme. In depriving "the swift and excellent" Achilles of his rightful prize (the captive girl, Briseis), King Agamemnon has gravely insulted Achilles' honor and has violated the solemn rule that warrior heroes treat each other with respect. Achilles, his pride wounded by this offense to his honor, refuses to rejoin Agamemnon in battle against Troy. Achilles plans to retain his honor by demonstrating that the Greeks need his valor and military prowess. Not until many brave men have been slain, including his dearest friend Patroclus, does Achilles set aside his quarrel with Agamemnon and enter the battle.

Homer employs a *particular* event, the quarrel between an arrogant Agamemnon and a revengeful Achilles, to demonstrate a *universal* principle—that "wicked arrogance" and "ruinous wrath" will cause much suffering and death. Homer grasps that there is an internal logic to existence, a significant order to human affairs. For Homer, says British classicist H. D. F. Kitto, "actions must have their consequences; ill-judged actions must have uncomfortable results."[1] People, even the gods, operate within a certain unalterable framework; their deeds are subject to the demands of fate, or necessity. With a poet's insight, Homer sensed what would become a fundamental attitude of the Greek mind: there is a universal order to things. Later Greeks would formulate it in philosophical terms.

In Homer we also see the origin of the Greek ideal of *areté*, excellence. The

Attic Black-Figure Vase: Achilles Slaying Penthesilea, the Amazon Queen, c. 530 B.C. The making of vases, ordinarily a craft, became high art in the archaic and classical periods of Greek civilization. Exekias, one of the most exceptional painters of Athens, employed the black-silhouette technique with engraved detail in decorating this vase. Hundreds of examples of such signed works allow us to talk of individual artists for the first time in history. (*Reproduced by Courtesy of the Trustees of the British Museum*)

Homeric warrior expresses a passionate desire to assert himself, to demonstrate his worth, to gain the glory that poets would immortalize in their songs. In the warrior-aristocrat world of Homer, *excellence* was principally interpreted as bravery and skill in battle. Homer's portrayal also bears the embryo of a larger conception of human excellence, one that combines thought with action. A man of true worth, says the wise Phoenix to a stubborn Achilles, is both "a speaker of words and a doer of deeds." In this passage, we find the earliest statement of the Greek educational ideal—the molding of a man who, says classicist Werner Jaeger, "united nobility of action with nobility of mind," who realized "the whole of human potentialities."[2] Thus, in Homer we find the beginnings of Greek humanism—a concern with man and his achievements.

Homer's works are essentially an expression of the poetic imagination and mythical thought. But his view of the eternal order of nature and his conception of the individual striving for excellence form the foundations of the Greek outlook.

Homer did not intend his poetry to have any theological significance, but his

gods had important religious implications for the Greeks. In
rmed the basis of the Olympian religion accepted throughout
cipal gods were said to reside on Mount Olympus, and on its
the palace of Zeus, the chief deity. Religion pervaded daily
traditional religion was challenged and undermined by a
secular and rational spirit.

The Break with Theocratic Politics

Greek society from 750 B.C. to the death of Alexander the Great in 323 B.C. comprised many small independent city-states. The city-state based on tribal allegiances was generally the first political association during the early stages of civilization. Moreover, Greece's many mountains, bays, and islands—natural barriers to political unity—favored this type of political arrangement.

The scale of the city-state, or *polis*, was small; most city-states had fewer than 5,000 male citizens. Athens, which was a large city-state, had some 35,000 male citizens at its height in the fifth century B.C.; the rest of its population of 350,000 consisted of women, children, resident aliens, and slaves, none of whom could participate in lawmaking. The polis gave individuals a sense of belonging, for its citizens were intimately involved in the political and cultural life of the community.

In the fifth century B.C., at its maturity, the Greeks viewed their polis as the only avenue to the good life—"the only framework within which man could realize his spiritual, moral, and intellectual capacities," in the words of Kitto.[3] The mature polis was a self-governing community that expressed the will of free citizens, not the desires of gods, hereditary kings, or priests. In the Near East, religion dominated political activity, and to abide by the mandates of the gods was the ruler's first responsibility. The Greek polis also had begun as a religious institution in which the citizens sought to maintain an alliance with their deities. But gradually the citizens de-emphasized the gods' role in political life and based government not on the magic powers of divine rulers, but on human intelligence as expressed through the community. The great innovation introduced by the Greeks into politics and social theory was the principle that law did not derive from gods or divine kings but from the human community.

The emergence of rational attitudes did not, of course, spell the end of religion, particularly for the peasants, who remained devoted to their ancient cults, gods, and shrines. Worshiping the god of the city remained a required act of patriotism to which Greeks unfailingly adhered. Thus, the religious-mythical tradition never died in Greece, but existed side by side with a growing rationalism and became weaker as time passed. When Athenian democracy reached its height in the middle of the fifth century B.C., religion was no longer the dominant factor in politics. Athenians had consciously come to rely on human reason, not divine guidance, in their political and intellectual life.

What made Greek political life different from that of earlier Near Eastern civilizations, as well as of enduring significance, was the Greeks' gradual realization that community problems are caused by human beings and require human solutions. The Greeks also valued free citizenship. An absolute king who ruled arbitrarily and by decree, who was above the law, was abhorrent to them.

The ideals of political freedom are best exemplified by Athens. But before turning to Athens, let us examine another Greek city, which followed a different political course.

Sparta: A Garrison State

Situated on the Peloponnesian peninsula, Sparta conquered its neighbors, including Messenia, in the eighth century B.C. Instead of selling the Messenians abroad, the traditional Greek way of treating a defeated foe, the Spartans kept them as state serfs, or *helots*. Helots were owned by the state rather than by individual Spartans. Enraged by their enforced servitude, the Messenians, also a Greek people, desperately tried to regain their freedom. After a bloody uprising was suppressed, the fear of a helot revolt became indelibly stamped on Spartan consciousness.

To maintain their dominion over the Messenians, who outnumbered them

Map 3.1   The Aegean Basin

ten to one, the Spartans—with extraordinary single-mindedness, discipline, and loyalty—transformed their own society into an armed camp. Agricultural labor was performed by helots; trade and crafts were left to the *perioikoi,* conquered Greeks who were free but who had no political rights; and the Spartans learned only one craft, soldiering.

They were trained in the arts of war and indoctrinated to serve the state. Military training for Spartan boys began at age seven; they exercised, drilled, competed, and endured physical hardships. Other Greeks admired the Spartans for their courage, obedience to law, and achievement in molding themselves according to an ideal. Spartan soldiers were better trained and disciplined and were more physically fit than other Greeks. But the Spartans were also criticized for having a limited conception of areté.

Athens: The Rise of Democracy

The contrast between the city-states of Athens and Sparta is striking. Whereas Sparta was a land power and exclusively agricultural, Athens was located on

The Acropolis of Athens.   Crowned by the Parthenon (right) and the Temple of Athene Nike, the Acropolis dominated Athens. The impressive monuments were symbols of Athenian civic pride. (*A. F. Kersting*)

the peninsula of Attica near the coast, possessed a great navy, and was the commercial leader among the Greeks. To the Spartans, freedom meant preserving the independence of their fatherland; this overriding consideration demanded order, discipline, and regimentation. The Athenians also wanted to protect their city from enemies, but unlike the Spartans, they valued political freedom and sought the full development and enrichment of the human personality. Thus, while authoritarian and militaristic Sparta became culturally sterile, the relatively free and open society of Athens became the cultural leader of Hellenic civilization.

Greek city-states generally moved through four stages: rule by a king (monarchy), rule by landowning aristocrats (oligarchy), rule by one man who seized power (tyranny), and rule by the people (democracy). In a monarchy, the first stage, the king, who derived his power from the gods, commanded the army and judged civil cases.

The second stage, an oligarchy, was instituted in Athens during the eighth century B.C., when aristocrats usurped power from hereditary kings. In the next century, aristocratic regimes experienced a social crisis. Peasants who borrowed from the aristocracy, pledging their lands as security, lost their property and even became enslaved for nonpayment of their debts. In Athens the embittered and restless peasants demanded and were granted one concession. In 621 B.C., the aristocrats appointed Draco to draw up a code of law. Although Draco's code let the poor know what the law was and reduced the possibilities of aristocratic judges behaving arbitrarily, penalties were extremely severe, and the code provided no relief for the peasants' economic woes. Athens was moving toward civil war as the poor began to organize and press for the cancellation of their debts and the redistribution of land.

Solon, the Reformer   In 594 B.C. Solon (c. 640–559 B.C.), a traveler and poet with a reputation for being wise, was elected chief executive. He maintained that the wealthy landowners, through their greed, had disrupted community life and brought Athens to the brink of civil war. Solon initiated a rational approach to the problems of society by reducing the gods' role in human affairs: he attributed the city's ills to the specific behavior of individuals; he sought practical remedies for these ills; and he held that written law should be in harmony with *Diké,* the principle of justice that underlies the human community.

Solon aimed at restoring a sick Athenian society to health by restraining the nobles and improving the lot of the poor. To achieve this goal, he canceled debts, freed Athenians enslaved for debt, and brought back to Athens those who had been sold abroad, but he refused to confiscate and redistribute the nobles' land as the extremists demanded. He permitted all classes of free men, even the poorest, to sit in the Assembly, which elected magistrates and accepted or rejected legislation proposed by a new Council of Four Hundred, and opened the highest offices in the state to wealthy commoners, who had previously been excluded from these positions because they lacked noble birth. Thus, Solon undermined the traditional rights of the hereditary aristocracy and initiated the transformation of Athens from an aristocratic oligarchy into a democracy.

Solon also instituted ingenious economic reforms. Recognizing that the poor soil of Attica was not conducive to growing grain, he urged the cultivation of grapes for wine and the growing of olives, whose oil could be exported. To encourage industrial expansion, he ordered that all fathers teach their sons a trade and granted citizenship to foreign craftsmen willing to migrate to Athens. These measures and the fine quality of the native reddish-brown clay allowed Athens to become the leading producer and exporter of pottery. Solon's economic policies transformed Athens into a great commercial center. Solon's reforms, however, did not eliminate factional disputes among the aristocratic clans nor relieve all the discontent of the poor.

Pisistratus, the Tyrant In 546 B.C., Pisistratus (c. 605–527 B.C.), an aristocrat, took advantage of the general instability to become a one-man ruler, driving into exile those who had opposed him. Tyranny thus replaced oligarchy. Tyranny occurred frequently in the Greek city-states. Almost always aristocrats themselves, tyrants generally posed as champions of the poor in their struggle against the aristocracy. Pisistratus sought popular support by having conduits constructed to increase Athens's water supply; like tyrants in other city-states, he gave to peasants land confiscated from exiled aristocrats, and granted state loans to small farmers.

Pisistratus' great achievement was the promotion of cultural life. He initiated grand architectural projects, encouraged sculptors and painters, arranged for public recitals of the Homeric epics, and founded festivals that included dramatic performances. In all these ways he made culture, formerly the province of the aristocracy, available to commoners. Pisistratus thus launched a policy that eventually led Athens to emerge as the cultural capital of the Greeks.

Cleisthenes, the Democrat Shortly after Pisistratus' death, a faction headed by Cleisthenes, an aristocrat sympathetic to democracy, assumed leadership. By an ingenious method of redistricting the city, Cleisthenes ended the aristocratic clans' traditional jockeying for the chief state positions, which had caused so much divisiveness and bitterness in Athens. Cleisthenes replaced this practice, rooted in tradition and authority, with a new system devised by reason to ensure that historic allegiance to tribe or clan would be superseded by loyalty to the city as a whole.

Cleisthenes hoped to make democracy the permanent form of government for Athens. To safeguard the city against tyranny, he introduced the practice of *ostracism*. Once a year Athenians were given the opportunity to inscribe on a potsherd (*ostracon*) the name of anyone who they felt endangered the state. An individual against whom sufficient votes were cast was ostracized, that is, forced to leave Athens for ten years.

Cleisthenes firmly secured democratic government in Athens. The Assembly, which Solon had opened to all male citizens, was in the process of becoming the supreme authority in the state. But the period of Athenian greatness lay in the future; the Athenians first had to fight a war of survival against the Persian Empire.

The Persian Wars

In 499 B.C., the Ionian Greeks of Asia Minor rebelled against their Persian overlord. Sympathetic to the Ionian cause, Athens sent twenty ships to aid the revolt. Bent on revenge, Darius I, king of Persia, sent a small detachment to Attica. In 490 B.C. on the plains of Marathon, the citizen army of Athens defeated the Persians—for the Athenians, one of the finest moments in their history. Ten years later, Xerxes, Darius' son, organized a huge invasion force of some 250,000 men and over 500 ships with the aim of reducing Greece to a Persian province. Setting aside their separatist instincts, most of the city-states united to defend their independence and their liberty.

The Persians crossed the waters of the Hellespont (Dardanelles) and made their way into northern Greece. Herodotus describes their encounter at the mountain pass of Thermopylae with 300 Spartans, who were true to their training and ideal of areté and "resisted to the last with their swords if they had them, and if not, with their hands and teeth, until the Persians, coming on from the front over the ruins of the wall and closing in from behind, finally overwhelmed them." Northern Greece fell to the Persians, who continued south, burning a deserted Athens.

When it appeared that the Greeks' spirit had been broken, the Athenian statesman and general Themistocles (c. 527–460 B.C.), demonstrating in military affairs the same rationality that Cleisthenes had shown in political life, lured the Persian fleet into the narrows of the Bay of Salamis. Unable to deploy their more numerous ships in this cramped space, the Persian armada was destroyed by Greek ships. In 479 B.C., a year after the Athenian naval victory at Salamis, the Spartans defeated the Persians in the land battle of Plataea. The inventive intelligence with which the Greeks had planned their military operations and a fierce desire to preserve their freedom had enabled them to defeat the greatest military power the Mediterranean world had yet seen.

The Persian Wars were decisive in the history of the West. The confidence and pride that came with victory propelled Athens into a golden age, but it also roused the Athenian urge for dominance in Greece. The Persian Wars had ushered in an era of Athenian imperialism that had drastic consequences for the future. Immediately after the wars, more than 150 city-states organized a confederation, the Delian League, to protect themselves against a renewed confrontation with Persia. Because of its wealth, its powerful fleet, and the restless energy of its citizens, Athens assumed leadership of the Delian League. Athenians consciously and rapaciously manipulated the league for their own economic advantage, seeing no conflict between imperialism and democracy. Athens forbade member states to withdraw, stationed garrisons on the territory of confederate states, and used the league's treasury to finance public works in Athens. Although member states did receive protection from both pirates and Persians, were not overtaxed, and enjoyed increased trade, they resented Athenian domination.

The Mature Athenian Democracy

Athenian imperialism was one consequence of the Persian Wars; another was the flowering of Athenian democracy and culture. The Athenian state was a direct democracy, in which the citizens themselves, not elected representatives, made the laws. In the Assembly, which was open to all adult male citizens and which met some forty times a year, Athenians debated and voted on key issues of state—they declared war, signed treaties, and spent public funds. The low-liest cobbler, as well as the wealthiest aristocrat, had the opportunity to express his opinion in the Assembly, to vote, and to hold office. By the middle of the fifth century, the will of the people as expressed in the Assembly was supreme.

The Council of Five Hundred (which had been established by Cleisthenes to replace Solon's Council of Four Hundred) managed the ports, military installations, and other state properties and prepared the agenda for the Assembly. Because its members were chosen annually by lot and could not serve more than twice in a lifetime, the Council could never supersede the Assembly. Some 350 magistrates, also chosen by lot, performed administrative tasks. The ten generals, because of the special competence their posts required, were not chosen by lot, but were elected by the Assembly.

Athens has been aptly described as a government of amateurs; there were no professional civil servants, no professional soldiers and sailors, no state judges, no elected lawmakers. The duties of government were performed by ordinary citizens. Such a system rested on the assumption that the average citizen was capable of participating intelligently in the affairs of state, that he would, in a spirit of civic patriotism, carry out his responsibilities to his city. In fifth-century Athens, excellence was equated with good citizenship.

Athenian democracy achieved its height in the middle of the fifth century B.C. under the leadership of Pericles (c. 495–429 B.C.), a gifted statesman, orator, and military commander. In the opening stage of the monumental clash with Sparta, the Peloponnesian War (431–404 B.C.), Pericles delivered an oration in honor of the Athenian war casualties. The oration, as reported by Thucydides, the great Athenian historian of the fifth century B.C., contains a glowing description of the Athenian democratic ideal:

> *Our constitution is called a democracy because power is in the hands not of a minority but of the whole people. When it is a question of settling private disputes, everyone is equal before the law; when it is a question of putting one person before another in positions of public responsibility, what counts is not membership of a particular class, but the actual ability which the man possesses. No one, so long as he has it in him to be of service to the state, is kept in political obscurity because of poverty. And, just as our political life is free and open, so is our*

> *day-to-day life in our relations with each other. . . . We are free and*
> *tolerant in our private lives; but in public affairs we keep to the law.*
> *This is because it commands our deep respect.*[4]

Athenian democracy undoubtedly had its limitations and weaknesses. Modern critics point out that resident aliens were almost totally barred from citizenship and therefore from political participation. Slaves, who constituted about one-fourth of the Athenian population, enjoyed none of the freedoms that Athenians considered so precious. The Greeks regarded slavery as a necessary precondition for civilized life; for some to be free and prosperous, they believed, others had to be enslaved. Slaves were generally prisoners of war or captives of pirates. In Athens some slaves were Greeks, but most were foreigners. Slaves usually did the same work as Athenian citizens—farming, commerce, manufacturing, and domestic chores. However, those slaves who toiled in the mines suffered a grim fate.

Athenian women comprised another group denied legal and political rights. Women were barred from holding public offices in Athens and generally could not appear in court without a male representative. Since it was believed that a woman could not act independently, she was required to have a guardian—normally her father or husband—who controlled her property and supervised her behavior. A girl usually married at the age of fourteen to a man twice her age, and the marriage was arranged by a male relative. Although either spouse could obtain a divorce, the children remained with the father. In the belief that financial dealings were too difficult for women and that they needed to be protected from strangers, men did the marketing, not the women. Greek women received no formal education, although some young women learned to read and write at home.

The flaws in Athenian democracy should not cause us to undervalue its extraordinary achievement. The idea that the state represented a community of free citizens remains a crucial principle of Western civilization. Athenian democracy embodied the principle of the legal state—a government based not on force but on laws debated, devised, altered, and obeyed by free citizens.

This idea of the legal state could only have arisen in a society that had an awareness of and a respect for the rational mind. In the same way that the Greeks demythicized nature, they also removed myth from the sphere of politics. Holding that government was something that people create to satisfy human needs, the Athenians regarded their leaders neither as gods nor as priests, but as men who had demonstrated a capacity for statesmanship.

Both systematic political thought and democratic politics originated in Greece. There, people first asked questions about the nature and purpose of the state, rationally analyzed political institutions, speculated about human nature and justice, and discussed the merits of various forms of government. It is to Greece that we ultimately trace the idea of democracy and all that accompanies it—citizenship, constitutions, equality before the law, government by law, reasoned debate, respect for the individual, and confidence in human intelligence.

The Decline of the City-States

Although the Greeks shared a common language and culture, they remained divided politically. A determination to preserve city-state sovereignty prevented the Greeks from forming a larger political grouping, which might have contained the intercity warfare that ultimately cost the city-state its vitality and independence. But the creation of a Pan-Hellenic union would have required a radical transformation of the Greek character, which for hundreds of years had regarded the independent city-state as the only suitable political system.

The Peloponnesian War

Athens' control of the Delian League engendered fear in the Spartans and their allies in the Peloponnesian League. Sparta and the Peloponnesian states decided on war because they felt that their independence was threatened by a dynamic and imperialistic Athens. At stake for Athens was control over the Delian League, which gave Athens political power and contributed to its economic prosperity. Neither Athens nor Sparta anticipated the catastrophic consequences the war would have for Greek civilization.

The war began in 431 B.C. and ended in 404 B.C. When a besieged Athens, with a decimated navy and a dwindling food supply, surrendered, Sparta dissolved the Delian League, left Athens with only a handful of ships, and forced the city to pull down its long walls—ramparts designed to protect it against siege weapons.

The Peloponnesian War shattered the spiritual foundations of Hellenic society. During its course, men became brutalized, selfish individualism triumphed over civic duty, moderation gave way to extremism, and in several cities, including Athens, politics degenerated into civil war between oligarchs and democrats. Oligarchs, generally from the wealthier segments of Athenian society, wanted to concentrate power in their own hands by depriving the lower classes of political rights. Democrats, generally from the poorer segment of society, sought to preserve the political rights of all adult male citizens. Strife between oligarchs and democrats was quite common in the Greek city-states even before the Peloponnesian War.

The Fourth Century

The Peloponnesian War was the great crisis of Hellenic history. The city-states never recovered from their self-inflicted spiritual wounds. The civic loyalty and confidence that had marked the fifth century waned and the fourth century was dominated by a new mentality that the leaders of the Age of Pericles would have abhorred. A concern for private affairs superseded devotion to the general good of the polis. Increasingly, the tasks of government were administered by professionals instead of by ordinary citizens, and mercenaries began to replace citizen soldiers.

In the fourth century the quarrelsome city-states formed new systems of alliances and persisted in their ruinous conflicts. While the Greek cities battered one another in fratricidal warfare, a new power was rising in the north—Macedonia. To the Greeks, the Macedonians, a wild mountain people who had acquired a sprinkling of Hellenic culture, differed little from other non-Greeks, whom they called barbarians. In 359 B.C., twenty-three-year-old Philip (382–336 B.C.) became Philip II, king of Macedonia. Philip converted Macedonia into a first-rate military power and began a drive to become master of the Greeks.

Incorrectly assessing Philip's strength, the Greeks were slow to organize a coalition against Macedonia. In 338 B.C. at Chaeronea, Philip's forces inflicted a decisive defeat on the Greeks, and all of Greece was his. The city-states still existed, but they had lost their independence. The world of the small, independent, and self-sufficient polis was drawing to a close and Greek civilization was taking a different shape.

The Dilemma of Greek Politics

Philip's conquest of the city-states points to a fundamental weakness of Greek politics. Despite internal crisis and persistent warfare, the Greeks were unable to fashion any other political framework than the polis. The city-state was fast becoming an anachronism, but the Greeks were unable to see that in a world moving toward larger states and empires, the small city-state could not compete. An unallied city-state with its small citizen army could not withstand the powerful military machine that Philip had created. A challenge confronted the city-states—the need to shape some form of political union, a Pan-Hellenic federation, that would end the suicidal internecine warfare, promote economic well-being, and protect the Greek world from hostile states. Because they could not respond creatively to this challenge, the city-states ultimately lost their independence to foreign conquerors.

The waning of civic responsibility among the citizens was another reason for the decline of the city-states. The vitality of the city-state depended on the willingness of its citizens to put aside private concerns for the good of the community. The Periclean ideal of citizenship dissipated, as Athenians neglected the community to concentrate on private affairs or sought to derive personal profit from public office. The decline in civic responsibility could be seen in the hiring of mercenaries to replace citizen soldiers and in the indifference and hesitancy with which Athenians confronted Philip.

Greek political life demonstrated both the best and the worst features of freedom. On the one hand, as Pericles boasted, freedom encouraged active citizenship, reasoned debate, and government by law. On the other hand, as Thucydides lamented, freedom could degenerate into factionalism, demagoguery, unbridled self-interest, and civil war.

Greek politics also revealed both the capabilities and the limitations of reason. Originally the polis was conceived as a divine institution in which the citizen had a religious obligation to obey the law. As the rational and secular outlook became more pervasive, the gods lost their authority. When people no longer conceived of law as an expression of sacred traditions ordained by the gods, but as a merely human contrivance, respect for the law diminished, weakening the foundations of the society. The results were party conflicts, politicians who scrambled for personal power, and moral uncertainty. Although the Greeks originated the lofty ideal that human beings could regulate their political life according to reason, their history, marred by intercity warfare and internal violence, demonstrates the extreme difficulties involved in creating and maintaining a rational society.

Philosophy in the Hellenic Age

The Greeks broke with the mythopoeic outlook of the Near East and conceived a new way of viewing nature and human society that is the basis of the Western scientific and philosophic tradition. By the fifth century B.C., the Greeks had emancipated thought from myth and gradually applied reason to the physical world and to all human activities. This emphasis on reason marks a turning point for human civilization.

The development of rational thought in Greece is a process, a trend, not a finished achievement. The process began when some advanced intellects became skeptical of Homer's gods and went beyond mythical explanations for natural phenomena. The nonphilosophic majority did not, however, totally eliminate the language, attitudes, and beliefs of myth from their life and thought. Even in the mature philosophy of Plato and Aristotle, mythical modes of thought persisted. What is of immense historical importance is not the degree to which the Greeks successfully integrated the norm of reason, but that they originated this norm, defined it, and applied it to their intellectual development and social and political life.

The first theoretical philosophers in human history emerged in the sixth century B.C. in the Greek cities of Ionia in Asia Minor. Curious about the essential composition of nature and dissatisfied with earlier creation legends, the Ionians sought physical, rather than mythic-religious, explanations for natural occurrences. In the process, they arrived at a new concept of nature and a new method of inquiry. They maintained that nature was not manipulated by arbitrary and willful gods and that it was not governed by blind chance. The Ionians said that underlying the seeming chaos of nature were principles of order—general laws ascertainable by the human mind. This discovery marks the beginning of scientific thought.

The Cosmologists: A Rational Inquiry into Nature

Ionian philosophy began with Thales (c. 624–c. 548 B.C.) of Miletus, a city in Ionia. He was a contemporary of Solon of Athens, and concerned himself with how nature came to be the way it was. Thales said that water was the basic element, the underlying substratum of nature, and that through some natural process—similar to the formation of ice or steam—water gave rise to everything else in the world.

Thales revolutionized thought because he omitted the gods from his account of the origins of nature and searched for a natural explanation of how all things came to be. Thales also broke with the commonly held belief that earthquakes were caused by Poseidon, god of the sea, and offered instead a naturalistic explanation for these disturbances: he thought that the earth floated on water, and that when the water experienced turbulent waves, the earth was rocked by earthquakes.

Anaximander (c. 611–547 B.C.), another sixth-century Ionian, rejected Thales' theory that water was the original substance. He rejected any specific substance and suggested that an indefinite substance, which he called the Boundless, was the source of all things. From this primary mass, which contained the powers of heat and cold, he believed that there gradually emerged a nucleus, the seed of the world. He said that the cold and wet condensed to form the earth and its cloud cover, while the hot and dry formed the rings of fire that we see as the moon, the sun, and the stars. The heat from the fire in the sky dried the earth and shrank the seas. From the warm slime on earth arose life, and from the first sea creatures there evolved land animals, including human beings. Anaximander's account of the origins of the universe and nature understandably contained fantastic elements. Nevertheless, by offering a natural explanation for the origin of nature and life, it surpassed the creation myths.

Like his fellow Ionians, Anaximenes, who died about 525 B.C., made the transition from myth to reason. He also maintained that a primary substance—air—underlay reality and accounted for the orderliness of nature. Air

Wrestlers: Relief from a Statue Base, Athenian, Late Sixth Century B.C.   Physical fitness and athletics were highly prized by the Greeks. Poets sang the praise of Olympic champions, and sculptors captured the beauty of athletic physiques for an admiring public. (*National Archaeological Museum/TAPService, Athens*)

that was rarefied became fire, while wind, clouds, and water were formed from condensed air. When condensed still further, water turned to earth, and when condensed even more, water turned to stone. Anaximenes also rejected the old belief that a rainbow was the goddess Iris; instead, he said that the rainbow was caused by the sun's rays falling on dense air.

The Ionians have been called "matter philosophers" because they held that everything issued from a particular material substance. Other sixth-century B.C. thinkers tried a different approach. Pythagoras (c. 580–c. 507 B.C.) and his followers, who lived in the Greek cities in southern Italy, did not find the nature of things in a particular substance but in mathematical relationships. The Pythagoreans discovered that the intervals in the musical scale can be expressed mathematically. Extending this principle of proportion found in sound to the universe at large, they concluded that the cosmos also contained an inherent mathematical order. Thus the Pythagoreans shifted the emphasis from matter to form, from the world of sense perception to the logic of mathematics. The Pythagoreans were also religious mystics who believed in the immortality and transmigration of souls. Consequently, they refused to eat animal flesh, fearing that it contained former human souls.

Parmenides (c. 515–450 B.C.), a native of the Greek city of Elea in southern Italy, challenged the fundamental view of the Ionians that all things emerged from one original substance. In developing his position, Parmenides applied to philosophic argument the logic used by the Pythagoreans in mathematical thinking. In putting forth the proposition that an argument must be consistent and contain no contradictions, Parmenides became the founder of formal logic. Reality is one, eternal, and unchanging, asserted Parmenides; it is made known not through the senses, which are misleading, but through the mind— not through experience, but through reason. Truth is reached through abstract thought alone.

Democritus (c. 460–370 B.C.), from the Greek mainland, renewed the Ionians' concern with the world of matter and reaffirmed their confidence in knowledge derived from sense perception. But he also retained Parmenides' reverence for reason. His model of the universe consisted of two fundamental realities—empty space and an infinite number of atoms. Eternal, indivisible, and imperceptible, these atoms moved in the void. All things consisted of atoms, and combinations of atoms accounted for all change in nature. In a world of colliding atoms, everything behaved according to mechanical principles.

Concepts essential to scientific thought thus emerged in embryonic form with Greek philosophers: natural explanations for physical occurrences (Ionians); the mathematical order of nature (Pythagoras), logical proof (Parmenides), and the mechanical structure of the universe (Democritus). By giving to nature a rational, rather than a mythical, foundation and by holding that theories should be grounded in evidence and be capable of being defended logically, the early Greek philosophers pushed thought in a new direction. Their achievement made possible theoretical thought and the systematization of knowledge—as distinct from the mere observation and collection of data.

This systematization of knowledge extended into several areas. Greek mathematicians, for example, organized the Egyptians' practical experience with land measurements into the logical and coherent science of geometry. Both Babylonians and Egyptians had performed fairly complex mathematical operations, but unlike the Greeks, they made no attempt to prove underlying mathematical principles. In another area, Babylonian priests had observed the heavens for religious reasons, believing that the stars revealed the wishes of the gods. The Greeks used the data collected by the Babylonians, but not in religion; they sought to discover the geometrical laws that underlie the motions of heavenly bodies.

A parallel development occurred in medicine. No Near Eastern medical text explicitly attacked magical beliefs and practices. In contrast, Greek doctors associated with the medical school of Hippocrates (c. 460–377) asserted that diseases have a natural, not a supernatural, cause.

The Sophists: A Rational Investigation of Human Culture

In their effort to understand the external world, the cosmologists had created the tools of reason. Greek thinkers then turned away from the world of nature and attempted a rational investigation of people and society. Exemplifying this shift in focus were the Sophists, professional teachers who wandered from city to city teaching rhetoric, grammar, poetry, gymnastics, mathematics, and music. The Sophists insisted that it was futile to speculate about the first principles of the universe, for such knowledge was beyond the grasp of the human mind; they urged instead that individuals improve themselves and their cities by applying reason to the tasks of citizenship and statesmanship.

The Sophists answered a practical need in Athens, which had been transformed into a wealthy and dynamic imperial state after the Persian Wars. Because the Sophists claimed that they could teach *political* areté—the ability to formulate the right laws and policies for cities and the art of eloquence and persuasion—they were sought as tutors by politically ambitious young men, especially in Athens. The Western humanist tradition owes much to the Sophists, who examined political and ethical problems, cultivated the minds of their students, and invented formal secular education.

The Sophists were philosophical relativists; that is, they held that no truth is universally valid. Protagoras, a fifth-century Sophist, said that "man is the measure of all things." By this he meant that good and evil, truth and falsehood, are matters of individual judgment—there are no universal standards that apply to all people at all times.

In applying reason to human affairs, the Sophists attacked the traditional religious and moral values of Athenian society. Some Sophists taught that speculation about the divine was useless; others went further and asserted that religion was just a human invention to ensure obedience to traditions and laws.

The Sophists also applied reason to law, with the same effect—the undermining of traditional authority. The laws of a given city, they asserted, did not derive from the gods; nor were they based on any objective and universal standards of justice and good, for such standards did not exist. Some Sophists argued that law was merely something made by the most powerful citizens for their own benefit. This principle had dangerous implications: since law rested on no higher principle than might, it need not be obeyed.

Some Sophists combined this assault on law with an attack on the ancient Athenian idea of *sophrosyne*—moderation and self-discipline—because it denied human instincts. Instead of moderation, they urged that people should maximize pleasure and trample underfoot those traditions that restricted them from fully expressing their desires.

In subjecting traditions to the critique of reason, the radical Sophists triggered an intellectual and spiritual crisis. Their doctrines encouraged disobedience to law, neglect of civic duty, and selfish individualism. These attitudes became widespread during and after the Peloponnesian War, dangerously weakening community bonds. Conservatives sought to restore the authority of law and a respect for moral values by renewing allegiance to those sacred traditions undermined by the Sophists.

Socrates: The Rational Individual

Taking a different approach was Socrates (c. 470–399 B.C.), one of the most extraordinary figures in the history of Western civilization. Socrates attacked the Sophists' relativism, holding that people should regulate their behavior in accordance with universal values. He felt that the Sophists taught skills, but that they had no insights into questions that really mattered. What is the purpose of life? What are the values by which man should live? How does man perfect his character? Here the Sophists failed, said Socrates; they taught the ambitious to succeed in politics, but persuasive oratory and clever reasoning do not instruct a man in the art of living. He felt that the Sophists had attacked the old system of beliefs, but had not provided the individual with a constructive replacement.

Socrates' central concern was the perfection of individual human character, the achievement of moral excellence. Moral values, for Socrates, did not derive from a transcendent God as they did for the Hebrews. They were attained when the individual regulated his life according to objective standards arrived at through rational reflection, that is, when reason became the formative, guiding, and ruling agency of the soul. For Socrates, true education meant the shaping of character according to values discovered through the active and critical use of reason.

Socrates wanted to subject all human beliefs and behavior to the clear light of reason, and in this way to remove ethics from the realm of authority, tradition, dogma, superstition, and myth. Socrates believed that reason was the only proper guide to the most crucial problem of human existence—the question of good and evil.

Dialetics   In urging Athenians to think rationally about the problems of human existence, Socrates offered no systematic ethical theory, no list of ethical precepts. What he did supply was a method of inquiry called *dialectics,* or logical discussion. As Socrates used it, a dialectical exchange between individuals, a *dialogue,* was the essential source of knowledge. It forced people out of their apathy and smugness and compelled them to examine their thoughts critically, to confront illogical, inconsistent, dogmatic, and imprecise assertions, and to express their ideas in clearly defined terms.

Dialectics affirmed that the acquisition of knowledge was a creative act. The human mind could not be coerced into knowing; it was not a passive vessel into which a teacher poured knowledge. The dialogue compelled the individual to play an active role in acquiring the ideals and values by which he was to live. In a dialogue, individuals became thinking participants in a search for knowledge. Through relentless cross-examination, Socrates induced his partner to explain and justify his opinions through reason, for only thus did knowledge become a part of one's being.

Dialogue implied that reason was meant to be used in relations between human beings, and that they could learn from each other, help each other, teach each other, and improve each other. It implied further that the human mind could and should make rational choices. To deal rationally with oneself and others is the distinctive mark of being human.

The Execution of Socrates   Socrates devoted much of his life to his mission—persuading his fellow Athenians to think critically about how they lived their lives. Through probing questions, he tried to make people realize how directionless and purposeless their lives were.

For many years, Socrates challenged Athenians without suffering harm, for Athens was generally distinguished by its freedom of speech and thought. In the uncertain times during and immediately after the Peloponnesian War, though, Socrates made enemies. When he was seventy, he was accused of corrupting the youth of the city, and of not believing in the city's gods but in other new divinities. Underlying these accusations was the fear that Socrates was a troublemaker, a subversive who threatened the state by subjecting its ancient and sacred values to the critique of thought.

Socrates denied the charges and conducted himself with great dignity at his trial, refusing to grovel and beg forgiveness. Convicted by an Athenian court, he was ordered to drink poison. Had he attempted to appease the jurors, he probably would have been given a light punishment, but he would not alter his principles even under threat of death.

Socrates did not write down his philosophy and beliefs. We are able to construct a coherent account of his life and ideals largely through the works of his most important disciple, Plato.

Plato: The Rational Society

Plato (c. 429–347 B.C.) used his master's teachings to create a comprehensive system of philosophy that embraced both the world of nature and the social world. Virtually all the problems discussed by Western philosophers for the past two millennia were raised by Plato. We shall focus on two of his principal concerns, the theory of Ideas and that of the just state.

Theory of Ideas   Socrates had taught that universal standards of right and justice exist and that these are arrived at through thought. Building on the insights of his teacher, Plato insisted on the existence of a higher world of reality, independent of the world of things that we experience every day. This higher reality, he said, is the realm of Ideas or Forms—unchanging, eternal, absolute, and universal standards of beauty, goodness, justice, and truth.

Truth resides in this world of Forms and not in the world made known through the senses. For example, a person can never draw a perfect square, but the properties of a perfect square exist in the world of Forms. Similarly, the ordinary person only forms an opinion of what beauty is from observing beautiful things; the philosopher, aspiring to true knowledge, goes beyond what he sees and tries to grasp with his mind the Idea of beauty. The ordinary individual lacks a true conception of justice or goodness; such knowledge is available only to the philosopher whose mind can leap from worldly particulars to an ideal world beyond space and time. Thus, true wisdom is obtained through knowledge of the Ideas, not the imperfect reflections of the Ideas that are perceived with the senses.

Plato was a champion of reason who aspired to study and to arrange human life according to universally valid standards. In contrast to sophistic relativism, he maintained that objective and eternal standards do exist.

The Just State   In adapting the rational legacy of Greek philosophy to politics, Plato constructed a comprehensive political theory. What the Greeks had achieved in practice—the movement away from mythic and theocratic politics—Plato accomplished on the level of thought: the fashioning of a rational model of the state.

Like Socrates, Plato attempted to resolve the problem caused by the radical Sophists—the undermining of traditional values. Socrates tried to dispel this spiritual crisis through a moral transformation of the individual, whereas Plato wanted the entire community to conform to rational principles. Plato said that if human beings are to live an ethical life, they must do it as citizens of a just and rational state. In an unjust state, people cannot achieve Socratic wisdom, for their souls will mirror the state's wickedness.

Plato had experienced the ruinous Peloponnesian War and Socrates' trial and execution. Disillusioned by the corruption of Athenian morality and democratic politics, he came to believe that under the Athenian constitution, neither the morality of the individual Athenian nor the good of the state could be enhanced, and that Athens required moral and political reform founded on Socrates' philosophy.

In his great dialogue, *The Republic*, Plato devised an ideal state based on standards that would rescue his native Athens from the evils that had befallen it. For Plato, the just state could not be founded on tradition (for inherited attitudes did not derive from rational standards), nor on the doctrine of might being right (a principle taught by radical Sophists and practiced by Athenian statesmen). A just state for Plato conformed to universally valid principles and aimed at the moral improvement of its citizens, not at increasing its power and material possessions. Such a state required leaders distinguished by their wisdom and virtue rather than by sophistic cleverness and eloquence.

Fundamental to Plato's political theory as formulated in *The Republic* was his criticism of Athenian democracy. An aristocrat by birth and temperament, Plato believed that it was foolish to expect the common man to think intelligently about foreign policy, economics, or other vital matters of state. Yet the common man was permitted to speak in the Assembly, to vote, and, by lot, to be selected for executive office. A second weakness of democracy was that leaders were chosen and followed for nonessential reasons like persuasive speech, good looks, wealth, and family background.

A third danger of democracy was that it could degenerate into anarchy, said Plato. Intoxicated by liberty, the citizens of a democracy could lose all sense of balance, self-discipline, and respect for law: "The citizens become so sensitive that they resent the slightest application of control as intolerable tyranny, and in their resolve to have no master they end up by disregarding even the law, written or unwritten."[5]

As the democratic city falls into disorder, a fourth weakness of democracy will become evident. A demagogue will be able to gain power by promising to plunder the rich to benefit the poor. To retain his hold over the state, the tyrant "begins by stirring up one war after another, in order that the people may feel their need of a leader."[6] Because of these inherent weaknesses of democracy, Plato insisted that Athens would be governed properly only when the wisest men, the philosophers, attained power.

Plato rejected the fundamental principle of Athenian democracy: that the average person is capable of participating sensibly in public affairs. People would not entrust the care of a sick person to just anyone, said Plato, nor would they allow a novice to guide a ship during a storm. Yet, in a democracy, amateurs were permitted to run the government and to supervise the education of the young—no wonder Athenian society was disintegrating. Plato felt that these duties should be performed only by the best people in the city, the philosophers who would approach human problems with reason and wisdom derived from knowledge of the world of unchanging and perfect Ideas. Only these possessors of truth would be competent to rule, said Plato.

Plato divided people into three groups: those who demonstrated philosophic ability should be rulers; those whose natural bent revealed exceptional courage should be soldiers; those driven by desire, the great masses, should be producers (tradesmen, artisans, or farmers). The philosophers were selected by a rigorous system of education open to all children. Those not demonstrating sufficient intelligence or strength of character were to be weeded out to become workers or warriors, depending on their natural aptitudes. After many years of education and practical military and administrative experience, the philosophers were to be entrusted with political power. If they had been properly educated, the philosopher-rulers would not seek personal wealth or personal power; they would be concerned with pursuing justice and serving the community. The philosophers were to be absolute rulers. Although the people would have lost their right to participate in political decisions, they would have gained a well-governed state whose leaders, distinguished by their wisdom, integrity, and sense of responsibility, sought only the common good. Only thus, said Plato, could the individual and the community achieve well-being.

Aristotle: Creative Synthesis

Aristotle (384–322 B.C.) stands at the apex of Greek thought because he achieved a creative synthesis of the knowledge and theories of earlier thinkers. The range of Aristotle's interests and intellect is extraordinary. He was the leading expert of his time in every field of knowledge, with the possible exception of mathematics.

Aristotle undertook the monumental task of organizing and systematizing the thought of the Pre-Socratics, Socrates, and Plato. He shared with the natural philosophers a desire to understand the physical universe; he shared with Socrates and Plato the belief that reason was a person's highest faculty and that the polis was the primary formative institution of Greek life.

To the practical and empirically minded Aristotle, the Platonic notion of an independent and separate world of Forms beyond space and time seemed contrary to common sense. To comprehend reality, said Aristotle, one should not escape into another world. For him, Plato's two-world philosophy suffered from too much mystery, mysticism, and poetic fancy; moroever, Plato undervalued the world of facts and objects revealed through sight, hearing, and touch, a world that Aristotle valued. Like Plato, Aristotle desired to comprehend the essence of things and held that understanding universal principles is the ultimate aim of knowledge. But unlike Plato, he did not turn away from the world of things to obtain such knowledge. Possessing a scientist's curiosity to understand nature, Aristotle respected knowledge obtained through the senses.

For Aristotle, the Forms were not located in a higher world outside and beyond phenomena, but existed in things themselves. He said that through human experience with such things as men, horses, and white objects, the essence of man, horse, and whiteness can be discovered through reason; the Form of Man, the Form of Horse, and the Form of Whiteness can be determined. These universals, which apply to all men, all horses, and all white things, were for both Aristotle and Plato the true objects of knowledge. For Plato, these Forms existed independently of particular objects, so the Forms for men or horses or whiteness or triangles or temples existed, whether or not representations of these Ideas in the form of material objects were made known to the senses. For Aristotle, however, without examination of particular things, universal Ideas could not be determined. Whereas Plato's use of reason tended to stress otherworldliness, Aristotle tried to bring philosophy back to earth.

By holding that certainty in knowledge comes from reason alone and not from the senses, Plato was predisposed toward mathematics and metaphysics—pure thought that transcends the world of change and material objects. By stressing the importance of knowledge acquired through the rational examination of sense experience, Aristotle favored the development of empirical sciences—physics, biology, zoology, botany, and other disciplines based on the observation and investigation of nature and the recording of data.

Ethical Thought   Like Socrates and Plato, Aristotle believed that a knowledge of ethics was possible and that it must be based on reason. For Aristotle, the good life was the examined life; it meant making intelligent decisions when confronted with specific problems. Persons could achieve happiness when they exercised the distinctively human trait of reasoning, when they applied their knowledge relevantly to life, and when their behavior was governed by intelligence and not by whim, tradition, or authority.

Aristotle recognized that people are not entirely rational, that there is a passionate element of the human personality that can never be eradicated or ignored. Aristotle held that surrendering completely to desire was to descend to the level of beasts, but that denying the passions and living as an ascetic was a foolish and unreasonable rejection of human nature. Aristotle maintained that by proper training, people could learn to regulate their desires. They could achieve moral well-being, or virtue, when they avoided extremes of behavior and rationally chose the way of moderation. "Nothing in excess" is the key to Aristotle's ethics.

Political Thought   Aristotle's *Politics* complements his *Ethics*. To live the good life, he said, a person must do it as a member of a political community. Only the polis would provide people with an opportunity to lead a rational and moral existence. With this assertion, Aristotle demonstrated a typically Greek attitude.

Like Plato, Aristotle presumed that political life could be rationally understood and intelligently directed. He emphasized the importance of the rule of law. He placed his trust in law rather than in individuals, for they are subject to passions. Aristotle recognized that at times laws should be altered but recommended great caution; otherwise, people would lose respect for law and legal procedure.

Tyranny and revolution, Aristotle said, can threaten the rule of law and the well-being of the citizen. To prevent revolution, the state must maintain "the spirit of obedience to law. . . . Men should not think it slavery to live according to the rule of the constitution, for it is their salvation."[7]

Aristotle held "that the best political community is formed by citizens of the middle class, and that those states are likely to be well-administered in which the middle class is large and stronger if possible than the other classes [the wealthy and the poor]." Both the rich, who excel in "beauty, strength, birth, [and] wealth," and the poor, who are "very weak or very much disgraced [find it] difficult to follow rational principle. Of these two the one sort grow into violence and great criminals, the others into rogues and petty rascals." The rich are unwilling "to submit to authority . . . for when they are boys, by reason of the luxury in which they are brought up, they never learn even at school, the habit of obedience." Consequently, the wealthy "can only rule despotically." On the other hand, the poor "are too degraded to command and must be ruled like slaves."[8] Middle-class citizens are less afflicted by envy than the poor and are more likely than the rich to view their fellow citizens as equals.

Art

The classical age of Greek art spans the years from the end of the Persian Wars (479 B.C.) to the death of Alexander the Great (323 B.C.). During this period standards were established that would dominate Western art until the emergence of modern art in the late nineteenth century. Greek art coincided with Greek achievement in all other areas. Like Greek philosophy and politics, it too applied reason to human experience and made the transition from a mythopoeic-religious world-view to a world perceived as orderly and rational. It gradually transformed the supernatural religious themes with which it was at first preoccupied into secular human themes. Classical art was representational—that is, it strove to imitate reality, to represent the objective world realistically, as it appeared to the human eye. Artists carefully observed nature and human beings and sought to achieve an exact knowledge of human anatomy; they tried to portray accurately the body at rest and in motion. They knew when muscles should be taut or relaxed, one hip lower than the other, the torso and neck slightly twisted—in other words, they succeeded in transforming marble or bronze into a human likeness that seemed alive. Yet although it was realistic and naturalistic, Greek art was also idealistic, aspiring to a finer, more perfect representation of what was seen, depicting the essence and form of a thing more truly than it actually appeared. Thus a Greek statue resembled no specific individual but revealed a flawless human form, without wrinkles, warts, scars, or other imperfections.

In achieving an accurate representation of objects and in holding that there were rules of beauty that the mind could discover, the Greek artist employed an approach consistent with the new scientific outlook. The Greek temple, for example, is an organized unity obeying nature's laws of equilibrium and harmony; classical sculpture captured the basic laws that govern life in motion. Such art based on reason, which draws the mind's attention to the clear outlines of the outer world, also draws attention to the mind itself, making the human being the master and center of an intelligible world and the master of his own person.

The Greek artist, just like the Greek philosopher, proclaimed the importance and creative capacity of the individual person. He exemplified the humanist spirit that characterized all aspects of Greek culture. Classical art placed people in their natural environment, made the human form the focal point of attention, and exalted the nobility, dignity, self-assurance, and beauty of the human being.

Drama

Greek poets and dramatists, like philosophers and artists, gave expression to the rise of the individual and the emerging humanist values. One of the earliest and best of the Greek poets was Sappho, who lived about 600 B.C. on the island of Lesbos. Sappho established a school to teach music and singing to well-to-do girls and to prepare them for marriage. With great tenderness, Sappho wrote poems of friendship and love.

Pindar (c. 518–438 B.C.) was another Greek lyric poet. In his poem of praise for a victorious athlete, Pindar expressed the aristocratic view of excellence. Life is essentially tragic—triumphs are short-lived, misfortunes are many, and ultimately death overtakes all; still, man must demonstrate his worth by striving for excellence.

Theater at Epidaurus.   Built c. 330 B.C., the acoustics of this theater are still perfect. Just as splendid are the plays of Aeschylus, Sophocles, Euripides, and Aristophanes, which were performed there. (*Bildarchiv Foto Marburg/Art Resource*)

The high point of Greek poetry is the drama, an art form that originated in Greece. The Greek dramatist portrayed the sufferings, weaknesses, and triumphs of individuals. Just as a Greek sculptor shaped a clear visual image of the human form, a Greek dramatist brought the inner life of a human being into sharp focus and tried to find the deeper meaning of human experience. Thus, in both art and drama, the growing self-awareness of the individual was evident.

Drama originated in the religious festivals honoring Dionysus, the god of wine and agricultural fertility. A profound innovation in these sacred performances, which included choral songs and dances, occurred in the last part of the sixth century B.C. Thespis, the first actor known to history, stepped out of the chorus and engaged it in dialogue. By separating himself from the choral group, Thespis demonstrated a new awareness of the individual.

With only one actor and a chorus, however, the possibilities for dramatic action and human conflicts were limited. Then Aeschylus introduced a second actor in his dramas, and Sophocles a third. Dialogue between individuals thus became possible. The Greek actors wore masks, and by changing them, each actor could play several roles in the same performance. This flexibility allowed the dramatists to depict the clash and interplay of human wills and passions on a greater scale.

A parallel development to Socratic dialectics—dialogue between thinking individuals—occurred in Greek drama. Greek tragedy evolved as a continuous striving toward humanization and individualization. By setting characters in conflict against each other, dramatists showed individuals as active subjects responsible for their behavior and decisions.

Like the natural philosophers, Greek dramatists saw an inner logic to the universe, which they called Fate or Destiny; both physical and social worlds obeyed laws. When people were stubborn, narrow-minded, arrogant, or immoderate, they were punished. The order in the universe required it. In being free to make decisions, the dramatists said, individuals have the potential for greatness, but in choosing wrongly, unintelligently, they bring disaster to themselves and others.

Also like philosophy, Greek tragedy entailed rational reflection. The tragic hero was not a passive victim of fate. He was a thinking human being who felt a need to comprehend his position, to explain the reasons for his actions, and to analyze his feelings.

The essence of Greek tragedy lies in the tragic hero's struggle against cosmic forces and insurmountable obstacles that eventually crush him. But what impressed the Greek spectators (and today's readers of Greek drama) was not the vulnerability nor weaknesses of human beings but their courage and determination in the face of these forces.

The three great Athenian tragedians were Aeschylus (525–456 B.C.). Sophocles (c. 496–406 B.C.), and Euripides (c. 485–405 B.C.). Aeschylus believed that the world was governed by divine justice, which could not be violated with impunity, and that when individuals evinced *hubris* (overweening pride or arrogance), which led them to overstep the bounds of moderation, they must be punished. Another principal theme was that through suffering, people acquired knowledge: the terrible consequences of sins against the divine order should remind all to think and act with moderation and caution.

Sophocles maintained that individuals should shape their character in the way a sculptor shapes a form—according to laws of proportion. Sophocles felt that when the principles of harmony were violated by immoderate behavior, a person's character would be thrown off balance and misfortune would strike.

The rationalist spirit of Greek philosophy permeated the tragedies of Euripides. Like the Sophists, Euripides subjected the problems of human life to critical analysis and challenged human conventions. Women's conflicts, the moral implications of adultery, the role of the gods, the rearing of children, and the meaning of war were carefully scrutinized in his plays. Euripides blended a poet's insight with the psychologist's probing to reveal the tangled world of human passions and souls in torment.

Greek dramatists also wrote comedies. Aristophanes (c. 448–c. 326 B.C.), the greatest of the Greek comic playwrights, lampooned Athenian statesmen and intellectuals and censured government policies. Behind Aristophanes' sharp wit was a deadly seriousness; he sought an end to the ruinous Peloponnesian War and to reaffirm traditional values that had been undermined by the Sophists.

History

The Mesopotamians and the Egyptians kept annals that purported to narrate the deeds of gods and their human agents, the priest-kings or god-kings. The Hebrews valued history, but believing that God acted in human affairs, they did not remove historical events from the realm of religious-mythical thought. The Greeks initiated a different approach to the study of history. As the gods were eliminated from the nature philosophers' explanations for the origins of things in the natural world, mythical elements also were removed from the writing of history. Greek historians asked themselves questions about the deeds of people, based their answers on available evidence, and wrote in prose, the language of rational thought. They not only narrated events but also examined causes.

Herodotus

Often called the "father of history," Herodotus (c. 484–c. 424 B.C.) wrote a history of the Persian Wars. The central theme of this book, *Histories*, is the contrast between Near Eastern despotism and Greek freedom and the subsequent clash of these two world-views in the wars. Though Herodotus found much to praise in the Persian Empire, he was struck by a lack of freedom and what he considered barbarity. Herodotus emphasized that the mentality of the free citizen was foreign to the East, where men were trained to obey the ruler's commands absolutely. Not the rule of law but the whim of despots prevailed in the East.

Another theme evident in Herodotus' work was punishment for hubris. In seeking to become king of both Asia and Europe, Xerxes had acted arrogantly; although he behaved as if he were superhuman, "he too was human, and was sure to be disappointed of his great expectations."[9] Like the Greek tragedians, Herodotus drew universal moral principles from human behavior.

In several ways Herodotus was a historian rather than a teller of tales. First, he asked questions about the past, instead of merely repeating ancient legends; he tried to discover what had happened and the motivations behind the actions. Second, Herodotus at times demonstrated a cautious and critical attitude toward his sources of information. Third, while the gods appeared in Herodotus' narrative, they played a far less important role than they did in Greek popular mythology. Nevertheless, by retaining a belief in the significance of dreams, omens, and oracles, and by allowing for divine intervention, Herodotus fell short of being a thoroughgoing rationalist. His writings contain the embryo of rational history. Thucydides brought it to maturity.

Thucydides

Thucydides (c. 460–c. 400 B.C.) also concentrated on a great political crisis confronting the Hellenic world—the Peloponnesian War. Living in Periclean Athens, whose life blood was politics, Thucydides regarded the motives of statesmen and the acts of government as the essence of history. He did not just catalogue facts, but sought those general concepts and principles that the facts illustrated. In Thucydides' history, there was no place for myths, for legends, for the fabulous—all hindrances to historical truth. He recognized that a work of history was a creation of the rational mind and not an expression of the poetic imagination. The historian seeks to learn and to enlighten, not to entertain.

Rejecting the notion that the gods interfere in history, Thucydides looked for the social forces and human decisions behind events. Undoubtedly, he was influenced by Hippocratic doctors who frowned on divine explanations for disease and distinguished between the symptoms of a disease and its causes. Where Herodotus occasionally lapsed into supernatural explanations, Thucydides wrote history in which the gods were absent, and he denied their intervention in human affairs.

In addition to being a historian, Thucydides was also a political philosopher with a specific view of governments and statesmen. He warned against the dangers of extremism unleashed by the strains of war, and he believed that when reason was forsaken, the state's plight would worsen. He had contempt for statesmen who waged war lightly, acting from impulse, reckless daring, and an insatiable appetite for territory.

The Hellenistic Age: The Second Stage
of Greek Civilization

Greek civilization, or Hellenism, passed through three disinct stages—the Hellenic Age, the Hellenistic Age, and the Greco-Roman Age. The Hellenic Age began around 800 B.C. with the early city-states, reached its height in the fifth century B.C., and endured until the death of Alexander the Great in 323 B.C. From that date the ancient world entered the Hellenistic Age, which ended in 30 B.C., when Egypt, the last major Hellenistic state, fell to Rome. The Greco-Roman Age lasted 500 years, encompassing the period of the Roman Empire up to the collapse of the empire's western half in the last part of the fifth century A.D.

Although the Hellenistic Age absorbed the heritage of classical (Hellenic) Greece, its style of civilization changed. During the first phase of Hellenism, the polis had been the center of political life. The polis had given the individual identity, and only within the polis could a Greek live a good and civilized life. With the coming of the Hellenistic Age, this situation changed. The city-state was eclipsed in power and importance by kingdoms and empires. Although cities retained a large measure of autonomy in domestic affairs, they had lost their freedom of action in foreign affairs. No longer were they the self-sufficient and independent communities of the Hellenic period. Unable to stand up to kingdoms, the city-state had become an outmoded institution. The bonds between the individual and the city loosened. People had to deal with the feelings of isolation and insecurity produced by the decline of the polis.

As a result of Alexander the Great's conquests of the lands between Greece and India, tens of thousands of Greek soldiers, merchants, and administrators settled in eastern lands. This mixing of Greek and Near Eastern peoples and cultures defines the Hellenistic Age.

In the Hellenic Age, Greek philosophers had a limited conception of humanity, dividing the world into Greek and barbarian. In the Hellenistic Age, the intermingling of Greeks and Near Easterners caused a shift in focus from the city to the *oikoumene* (the inhabited world); parochialism gave way to universalism and cosmopolitanism as people began to think of themselves as members of a world community. Philosophers came to regard the civilized world as one city, the city of humanity.

Alexander the Great

After the assassination of Philip of Macedon in 336 B.C., his twenty-year-old son, Alexander, succeeded to the throne. Alexander inherited a proud and fiery temperament from his mother. From his tutor Aristotle, Alexander acquired an appreciation for Greek culture, particularly the Homeric epics. Undoubtedly, the young Alexander was aroused by these stories of legendary heroes, particularly of Achilles, and their striving for personal glory. Alexander acquired military skills and qualities of leadership from his father.

Mosaic of a Lion Hunt.   This pebble mosaic floor may be an illustration of a rescue of Alexander by his friend Krateros; it was found at the Macedonian capital, Pella. The lion hunt as a theme in art appears in Egyptian, Assyrian, and Mycenaean cultures; the king is the guardian of his flock and must protect it from predators. Subduing lions may also be an allusion to one of the labors of Hercules. (*Pella Museum/ TAPService, Athens*)

Alexander also inherited from Philip an overriding policy of state—the invasion of Persia. With an army of 35,000 men, Macedonians and Greeks combined, he crossed into Asia Minor in 334 B.C. and eventually advanced all the way to India. In these campaigns, Alexander proved himself to be a superb strategist and leader of men. Winning every battle, his army carved an empire that stretched from Greece to India.

The world after Alexander differed sharply from that existing before he took up the sword. Alexander's conquests brought West and East closer together, marking a new epoch. Alexander himself helped implement this transformation. He took a Persian bride, arranged for 80 of his officers and 10,000 of his soldiers to marry oriental women, and planned to incorporate 30,000 Persian youths into his army. Alexander founded Greek-style cities in Asia, where Greek settlers mixed with orientals.

As Greeks acquired greater knowledge of the Near East, the parochial-mindedness of the polis gave way in many ways to a world outlook. As trade and travel between West and East expanded, as Greek merchants and soldiers settled in Asiatic lands, and as Greek culture spread to non-Greeks, the distinctions between barbarian and Greek lessened. Although Alexander never united all the peoples in a world-state, his career pushed the world in a new direction, toward a fusion of disparate peoples and the intermingling of cultural traditions.

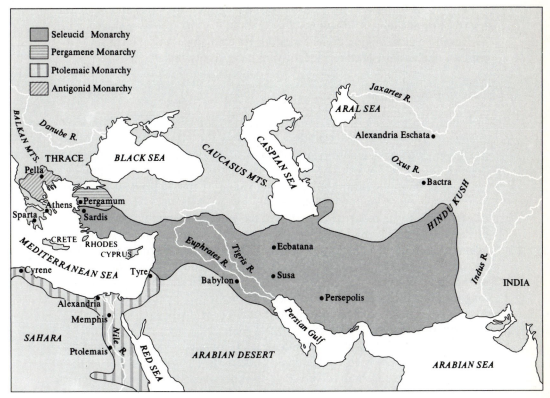

Map 3.2   The Division of Alexander's Empire and the Spread of Hellenism

The Competing Dynasties

In 323 B.C., Alexander, not yet thirty-three years of age, died, probably of a fever. After his premature death, his generals engaged in a long and bitter struggle to see who would succeed the conqueror. Since none of the generals or their heirs had enough power to hold together Alexander's vast empire, the wars of succession ended in a stalemate. By 275 B.C., the empire was fractured into three dynasties: the Ptolemies in Egypt, the Seleucids in Asia, and the Antigonids in Macedonia. Macedonia—Alexander's native country—continued to dominate the Greek cities, which periodically tried to break its hold. Later, the kingdom of Pergamum in western Asia Minor emerged as the fourth Hellenistic monarchy.

In the third century B.C., Ptolemaic Egypt was the foremost power in the Hellenistic world. The Seleucid Empire, which stretched from the Mediterranean to the frontiers of India and encompassed many different peoples, attempted to extend its power in the west but was resisted by the Ptolemies. Finally, the Seleucid ruler Antiochus III (223–187 B.C.) defeated the Ptolemaic forces and established Seleucid control over Phoenicia and Palestine. Taking advantage of Egypt's defeat, Macedonia seized several of Egypt's territories.

Rome, a new power, became increasingly drawn into the affairs of the quarrelsome Hellenistic kingdoms. By the middle of the second century B.C., it had imposed its will upon them. From this time on, the political fortunes of the western and eastern Mediterranean were inextricably linked.

Cosmopolitanism

Hellenistic society was characterized by a mingling of peoples and an interchange of cultures. Greek traditions spread to the Near East, while Mesopotamian, Egyptian, Hebrew, and Persian traditions—particularly religious beliefs—moved westward. The parochialism of the city-state was replaced by a growing cosmopolitanism. Although the rulers of the Hellenistic kingdoms were Macedonians and their high officials and generals were Greeks, the style of government was modeled after that of the ancient oriental kingdoms. In the Hellenic Age, the law had expressed the will of the community, but in this new age of monarchy, the kings were the law. The Macedonian rulers encouraged the oriental practice of worshiping the king as a god or as a representative of the gods. In Egypt, for example, the priests conferred on the Macedonian king the same divine powers and titles traditionally held by Egyptian pharaohs. Also, in accord with ancient tradition, statues of the divine king were installed in Egyptian temples.

The Seleucids, following Alexander's lead, founded cities in the east patterned after the city-states of Greece. Thousands of Greeks settled in these cities, which were Greek in architecture and contained Greek schools, temples, theaters, and gymnasia. Hellenistic kings brought books, paintings, and statues to their cities from Greece. Hellenistic cities, inhabited by tens of thousands of people from many lands and dominated by a Hellenized upper class, served as centers and agents of Hellenism, which non-Greeks adopted. The cities in Egypt and Syria saw the emergence of a native elite who spoke Greek, wore Greek-style clothing, and adopted Greek customs. *Koine,* a form of Greek, came to be spoken throughout much of the Mediterranean world.

The greatest city of the time and the one most representative of the Hellenistic Age was Alexandria, founded by Alexander the Great. Strategically located at one of the mouths of the Nile, Alexandria became a center of commerce and culture. The most populous city of the Mediterranean world, Alexandria at the beginning of the Christian era contained perhaps a million people—Egyptians, Persians, Macedonians, Greeks, Jews, Syrians, and Arabs. The city was an unrivaled commercial center; goods from the Mediterranean world, east Africa, Arabia, and India circulated in its marketplaces. This cosmopolitan center also attracted poets, philosophers, physicians, astronomers, and mathematicians.

All phases of cultural life were permeated by cultural exchange. Sculpture showed the influence of many lands. Historians wrote world histories, not just local histories. Greek astronomers worked with data collected over the centuries by the Babylonians. The Hebrew Scriptures were translated into Greek for use by Greek-speaking Jews, and Jewish thinkers began to take note of

Greek philosophy. Greeks increasingly demonstrated a fascination for oriental religious cults. Philosophers helped to break down the barriers between peoples by asserting that all inhabit a single fatherland.

The spread of Greek civilization from the Aegean to the Indus River gave the Hellenistic world a cultural common denominator, but Hellenization did not transform the East and make it one with the West. Hellenization was limited almost entirely to the cities, and in many urban centers it was often only a thin veneer. Many Egyptians in Alexandria learned Greek, and some assumed Greek names, but for most, Hellenization did not go much deeper. In the countryside, there was not even the veneer of Greek culture. Retaining traditional attitudes, the countryside in the East resisted Greek ways. In the villages, local and traditional law, local languages, and family customs remained unchanged; and religion, the most important ingredient of the civilizations of the Near East, also kept its traditional character.

Hellenistic Culture

History

The leading historian of the Hellenistic Age was Polybius (c. 200–118 B.C.), whose history of the rise of Rome is one of the great works of historical literature. Reflecting the universal tendencies of the Hellenistic Age, Polybius endeavored to explain how Rome had progressed from a city-state to a world conqueror. As a disciple of Thucydides, Polybius sought rational explanations for human events. Also like Thucydides, he relied on eyewitness accounts (including his own personal experiences), checked sources, and strove for objectivity.

Science

During the Hellenistic Age, Greek scientific achievement reached its height. When Alexander invaded Asia Minor, the former student of Aristotle brought along surveyors, engineers, scientists, and historians, who continued with him into Asia. The vast amount of data in botany, zoology, geography, and astronomy collected by Alexander's staff stimulated an outburst of activity. Hellenistic science, says historian Benjamin Farrington, stood "on the threshold of the modern world. When modern science began in the sixteenth century, it took up where the Greeks left off."[10]

Because of its state-supported museum, Alexandria attracted leading scholars and superseded Athens in scientific investigation. The museum contained a library of more than half a million volumes, as well as botanical gardens and an observatory. It was really a research institute in which some of the best minds of the day studied and worked.

Alexandrian doctors advanced medical skills. They improved surgical instruments and techniques, and through dissecting bodies, they added to anatomical knowledge. Through their research, they discovered organs of the body not known heretofore, made the distinction between arteries and veins, divided nerves into those comprising the motor and sensory systems, and identified the brain as the source of intelligence. Their investigations advanced knowledge of anatomy and physiology to a level that was not significantly improved until the sixteenth century A.D.

Knowledge in the fields of astronomy and mathematics also increased. Eighteen centuries before Copernicus, Alexandrian astronomer Aristarchus (310–230 B.C.) said that the sun was the center of the universe, that the planets revolved around it, and that the stars are situated at great distances from the earth. But these revolutionary ideas were not accepted, and the belief in an earth-centered universe persisted. In geometry, Euclid, an Alexandrian mathematician who lived around 300 B.C., creatively synthesized earlier developments. Euclid's hundreds of geometrical proofs, derived from reasoning alone, are a profound witness to the power of the rational mind.

Eratosthenes (c. 275–195 B.C.), an Alexandrian geographer, sought a scientific understanding of the enlarged world. He divided the planet into climatic zones, declared that the oceans are joined, and with extraordinary ingenuity and accuracy measured the earth's circumference. Archimedes of Syracuse (287–212 B.C.), who studied at Alexandria, was a mathematician, a physicist, and an ingenious inventor. His mechanical inventions, including war engines, dazzled his contemporaries. However, in typically Greek fashion, Archimedes dismissed his practical inventions, preferring to be remembered as a theoretician.

Philosophy

Hellenistic thinkers preserved the rational tradition of Greek philosophy, but they also transformed it, for they had to adapt thought to the requirements of a cosmopolitan society. In the Hellenic Age, the starting point of philosophy was the citizen's relationship to the city; in the Hellenistic Age, the point of departure was the solitary individual's relationship to humanity, his personal destiny in a complex world. Philosophy tried to deal with the feeling of alienation resulting from the weakening of the individual's attachment to the polis and to arrive at a conception of community that corresponded to the social realities of a world grown larger. It aspired to make persons ethically independent so that they could achieve happiness in a hostile and competitive world. In striving for tranquillity of mind and relief from conflict, Hellenistic thinkers reflected the general anxiety that pervaded their society.

Epicureanism   Two principal schools of philosophy arose in the Hellenistic world; Epicureanism and Stoicism. In the tradition of Plato and Aristotle, Epicurus (342–270 B.C.) founded a school at Athens at the end of the fourth century B.C. In significant ways Epicurus broke with the attitude of the Hellenic Age. Unlike classical Greek philosophers, Epicurus, reflecting the Greeks' changing relationship to the city, taught the value of passivity and withdrawal

Epicurus. The direct gaze of this marble head of Epicurus shows an inner calm, which was the goal of Epicurean philosophy. In the tradition of Greek philosophy, Epicurus maintained that happiness came from a rationally ordered life. But unlike fifth-century Greeks, Epicurus urged his followers not to engage in public affairs. (*The Metropolitan Museum of Art, Rogers Fund, 1911, 11.90*)

from civic life. To him, citizenship was not a prerequisite for individual happiness. Wise persons, said Epicurus, would refrain from engaging in public affairs, for politics could deprive them of their self-sufficiency, their freedom to choose and to act. Nor would wise individuals pursue wealth, power, or fame, for the pursuit would only provoke anxiety. For the same reason, wise persons would not surrender to hate or love, desires that distress the soul. Nor could there be happiness when they worried about dying or pleasing the gods.

To Epicurus, fear that the gods interfered in human life and could inflict suffering after death was the principal cause of anxiety. To remove this source of human anguish, he favored a theory of nature that had no place for the activity of gods. Therefore he adopted the physics of Democritus, which taught that all things consist of atoms in motion. In a universe of colliding atoms, there could be no higher intelligence ordering things; there was no room for divine activity. Epicurus taught that the gods probably did exist, but that they could not influence human affairs, so individuals could order their own lives. People could achieve happiness, said Epicurus, when their bodies were "free from pain" and minds "released from worry and fear." Although Epicurus wanted to increase pleasure for the individual, he rejected unbridled hedonism. Because happiness must be pursued rationally, he believed, those merely sensuous pleasures that have unpleasant aftereffects (such as overeating and overdrinking) are to be avoided. In general, Epicurus espoused the traditional Greek view of moderation and prudence. By opening his philosophy to men and women, slave and free, Greek and barbarian, and by separating ethics from politics, Epicurus fashioned a philosophy adapted to the post-Alexandrian world of kingdoms and universal culture.

Stoicism   About the same time as the founding of Epicurus' school, Zeno (335–263 B.C.) also opened a school in Athens. Zeno's teachings, called Stoicism (because his school was located in the *Stoa,* or colonnade), became the most important philosophy in the Hellenistic world. By teaching that the world constituted a single society, Stoicism gave theoretical expression to the world-mindedness of the age. By arriving at the concept of a world-state, the city of humanity, Stoicism offered an answer to the problem of community and alienation posed by the decline of the city-state. By stressing inner strength in dealing with life's misfortunes, Stoicism offered an avenue to individual happiness in a world fraught with uncertainty.

At the core of Stoicism was the belief that the universe contained a principle of order, variously called the Divine Fire, God, and Divine Reason (*Logos*). This ruling principle underlay reality and permeated all things; it accounted for the orderliness of nature. The Stoics reasoned that because people are part of the universe, they too shared in the logos that operated throughout the cosmos. The logos was implanted in every human soul; it enabled people to act intelligently, and to comprehend the principles of order that governed nature. Since reason was common to all, human beings were essentially brothers and fundamentally equal. Reason gave individuals dignity and enabled them to recognize and respect the dignity of others. To the Stoics, all people, Greek and barbarian, free and slave, rich and poor, were fellow human beings, and one law, the law of nature, applied to all human beings. Thus the Stoics, like the Hebrews, arrived at the idea of the oneness of humanity.

Like Socrates, the Stoics believed that a person's distinctive quality was the ability to reason and that happiness came from the disciplining of emotions by the rational part of the soul. Also like Socrates, the Stoics maintained that individuals should progress morally, should perfect themselves. In the Stoic view, wise persons ordered their lives according to the natural law—the law of reason—that underlay the cosmos. This harmony with the logos would give them the inner strength to resist the torments inflicted by others, by fate, and by their own passionate natures. Self-mastery and inner peace, or happiness, would follow. Such individuals remain undisturbed by life's misfortunes, for their souls are their own. Even slaves were not denied this inner freedom; although their bodies were subjected to the power of their masters, their minds still remained independent and free.

Stoicism had an enduring influence on the Western mind. To some Roman political theorists, the Empire fulfilled the Stoic ideal of a world community in

The Laocoön Group, Late Second Century B.C.   This marble statue, sculpted by Agesander, Polydorus, and Athenodorus, all of Rhodes, portrays a Greek legend included in Virgil's *Aeneid.* A priest of Apollo, Laocoön, and his twin sons, are depicted in the death embrace of sea serpents—punishment for breaking the priest's oath of celibacy. The twisting movement and the profusion of angles characterize Hellenistic art, which abandoned the simplicity, balance, and repose of classical Greek art. (*Bildarchiv Foto Marburg/Art Resource*)

which people of different nationalities held citizenship and were governed by a worldwide law that accorded with the law of reason, or natural law that operated throughout the universe. Stoic beliefs—by nature we are all members of one family, each person is significant, distinctions of rank and race are of no account, and human law should not conflict with natural law—were incorporated into Roman jurisprudence, Christian thought, and modern liberalism. There is continuity between Stoic thought and the principle of inalienable rights stated in the Declaration of Independence.

The Greek Achievement: Reason, Freedom, Humanism

Like other ancient peoples, the Greeks warred, massacred, and enslaved; they could be cruel, arrogant, contentious, and superstitious; and they often violated their ideals. But their achievement was unquestionably of profound historical significance. Western thought begins with the Greeks, who first defined the individual by his capacity to reason. It was the great achievement of the Greek spirit to rise above magic, miracles, mystery, authority, and custom and to discover the means of giving rational order to nature and society. Every aspect of Greek civilization—science, philosophy, art, literature, politics, historical writing—showed a growing reliance on human reason and a diminishing dependence on the gods.

In Mesopotamia and Egypt, people had no clear conception of their individual worth and no understanding of political liberty. They were not citizens, but subjects who marched to the command of a ruler whose power originated with the gods; such royal power was not imposed on an unwilling population, but was religiously accepted and obeyed.

In contrast, the Greeks created political freedom. They saw the state as a community of free citizens who made laws in their own interest. The Greeks held that men are capable of governing themselves and they valued active citizenship. For the Greeks, the state was a civilizing agent that permitted people to live the good life. Greek political thinkers arrived at a conception of the rational or legal state in which law was an expression of reason, not of whim or divine commands; of justice, not of might; of the general good of the community, not of self-interest.

The Greeks also gave to Western civilization a conception of inner, or ethical, freedom. People were free to choose between shame and honor, cowardice and duty, moderation and excess. The heroes of Greek tragedy suffered, not because they were puppets being manipulated by higher powers, but because they possessed the freedom of decision. The idea of ethical freedom reached its highest point with Socrates. To shape oneself according to ideals known to the mind, to become an autonomous and self-directed person, became for the Greeks the highest form of freedom.

During the Hellenistic Age, the Greeks, like the Hebrews earlier, arrived at the idea of universalism, the oneness of humanity. Stoic philosophers taught that all people, because of their ability to reason, are fundamentally alike and can be governed by the same laws. This idea is at the root of the modern principle of natural or human rights, which are the birthright of each individual.

Underlying everything accomplished by the Greeks was a humanist attitude toward life. The Greeks expressed a belief in the worth, significance, and dignity of the individual; they called for the maximum cultivation of human talent, the full development of human personality, and the deliberate pursuit of excellence. In valuing the human personality, the Greek humanists did not approve of living without restraints; they aimed at creating a higher type of man. Such a man would mold himself according to worthy standards; he would make his life as harmonious and flawless as a work of art. This aspiration required effort, discipline, and intelligence. Fundamental to the Greek humanist outlook was the belief that man could master himself. Although people could not alter the course of nature, for there was an order to the universe over which neither human beings nor gods had control, the humanist believed that people could control their own lives.

By discovering theoretical reason, by defining political freedom, and by

Chronology 3.1 ✪ The Greeks

1700–1450 B.C.*	Height of Minoan civilization
1400–1230	Height of Mycenaean civilization
1100–800	Dark Age
c. 700	Homer
750–550	Age of colonization
594	Solon is given power to institute reforms
507	Cleisthenes broadens democratic institutions
480	Xerxes of Persia invades Greece; Greek naval victory at Salamis
479	Spartans defeat Persians at Plataea, ending Persian Wars
431	Start of Peloponnesian War
404	Athens surrenders to Sparta, ending Peloponnesian War
387	Plato founds a school at Athens
359	Philip II becomes king of Macedonia
338	Battle of Chaeronea; Greek city-states fall under dominion of Macedonia
323 B.C.	Death of Alexander the Great

*Some dates are approximations.

affirming the worth and potential of human personality, the Greeks broke with the past and founded the rational and humanist tradition of the West. "Had Greek civilization never existed," says poet W. H. Auden, "we would never have become fully conscious, which is to say that we would never have become, for better or worse, fully human."[11]

Notes

1. H. D. F. Kitto, *The Greeks* (Baltimore: Penguin Books, 1957), p. 60
2. Werner Jaeger, *Paideia: The Ideals of Greek Culture,* vol. I (New York: Oxford University Press, 1945), p. 8.
3. Kitto, *The Greeks,* p. 78.
4. Thucydides, *The Peloponnesian War,* trans. by Rex Warner (Baltimore: Penguin Books, 1954), bk. 2, ch. 4.
5. Plato, *The Republic,* trans. by F. M. Cornford (New York: Oxford University Press, 1945), p. 289.
6. Ibid., p. 293.

7. *Politics*, in Richard McKeon, ed.,
   Basic Works of Aristotle (New
   York: Random House, 1941),
   pp. 1246, 1251.
8. Ibid., pp. 1220–1221.
9. Herodotus, *The Histories*, trans. by
   Aubrey de Sélincourt (Baltimore:
   Penguin Books, 1954), p. 485.

10. Benjamin Farrington, *Greek Science,*
    (Baltimore: Penguin Books, 1961),
    p. 301.
11. W. H. Auden, ed., *The Portable
    Greek Reader* (New York: Viking,
    1952), p. 38.

Suggested Reading

Boardman, John, et al., *The Oxford History of the Classical World* (1986). Essays on all facets of Greek culture.

Copleston, Frederick, *A History of Philosophy,* vol. I (1962). An excellent analysis of Greek philosophy.

Cornford, F. M., *Before and After Socrates* (1968). The essential meaning of Greek philosophy clearly presented.

Ferguson, John, *The Heritage of Hellenism* (1973). A good introduction to Hellenistic culture.

Fine, John V. A., *The Ancient Greeks* (1983). An up-to-date, reliable analysis of Greek history.

Finley, M. I., ed., *The Legacy of Greece* (1981). Essays on all phases of Greek culture.

Frost, Frank J., *Greek Society* (1987). Social and economic life in ancient Greece.

Grant, Michael, *From Alexander to Cleopatra* (1982). A fine survey of all phases of Hellenistic society and culture.

Hooper, Finley, *Greek Realities* (1978). A literate and sensitive presentation of Greek society and culture.

Jaeger, Werner, *Paideia: The Ideals of Greek Culture* (1939–1944). A three-volume work on Greek culture by a distinguished classicist. The treatment of Homer, the early Greek philosophers, and the Sophists in volume I is masterful.

Jones, W. T., *A History of Western Philosophy,* vol. I (1962). Clearly written; contains useful passages from original sources.

Kitto, H. D. F., *The Greeks* (1957). A stimulating survey of Greek life and thought.

Wallbank, F. W., *The Hellenistic World* (1982). A survey of the Hellenistic world that makes judicious use of quotations from original sources.

Webster, T. B. L., *Athenian Culture and Society* (1973). Discusses Athenian religion, crafts, art, drama, education, and so on.

Review Questions

1. Why is Homer called "the shaper of Greek civilization"?
2. How did the Greek polis break with the theocratic politics of the Near East?
3. Describe the basic features and the limitations of Athenian democracy.
4. What were the causes of the Peloponnesian War? What was the impact of the Peloponnesian War on the Greek world?
5. Explain how Greek political life demonstrated both the best and the worst features of freedom, both the capabilities and the limitations of reason.
6. What was the achievement of the Ionian natural philosophers?
7. How did the Sophists advance the tradition of reason initiated by the natural philosophers? How did they contribute to a spiritual crisis in Athens?
8. What was Socrates' answer to the problems posed by the Sophists?
9. Describe the essential features of Plato's *Republic* and the reasons that led him to write it.

10. How did Aristotle both criticize and accept Plato's theory of Ideas? What do Aristotle's political and ethical thought have in common?
11. Greek art was realistic, idealistic, and humanistic. Explain.
12. Why do the Greek plays have perennial appeal?
13. What were the basic differences between the Hellenic and Hellenistic ages?
14. How did Alexander the Great contribute to the shaping of the Hellenistic Age?
15. Hellenistic science stood on the threshold of the modern world. Explain.
16. What problems concerned Hellenistic philosophers?
17. What was the enduring significance of Stoicism?
18. The Greeks broke with the mythopoeic outlook of the ancient Near East and conceived a world-view that is the foundation of Western civilization. Discuss.

Chapter ⟁ 4

Rome: From City-State to World Empire

Rome's great achievement was to transcend the narrow political orientation of the city-state and to create a world-state that unified the different nations of the Mediterranean world. Regarding the polis as the only means to the good life, the Greeks had not desired a larger political unit and had almost totally excluded foreigners from citizenship. Although Hellenistic philosophers had conceived the possibility of a world community, Hellenistic politics could not shape one. But Rome overcame the limitations of the city-state mentality and developed an empirewide system of law and citizenship. The Hebrews were distinguished by their prophets, and the Greeks by their philosophers; Rome's genius found expression in law and government.

Historians divide Roman history into two broad periods: the period of the Republic began in 509 B.C. with the overthrow of the Etruscan monarchy, and that of the Empire started in 27 B.C. when Octavian (Augustus) became in effect the first Roman emperor, ending almost five hundred years of republican self-government. By conquering the Mediterranean world and extending its law and, in some instances, citizenship to different nationalities, the Roman Republic transcended the parochialism typical of the city-state. The Republic initiated the trend toward political and legal universalism, which reached fruition in the second phase of Roman history, the Empire. ⟁

Evolution of the Roman Constitution

By the eighth century B.C., peasant communities existed on some of Rome's seven hills near the Tiber River in central Italy. To the north and south stood

Etruscan Sarcophagus, c. 520 B.C.   Some archaic stylistic features of early Greek art are present in the Etruscan couple on this terra cotta sarcophagus lid, but none of the awkwardness. Also, unlike the still formality of Egyptian tomb statuary, the figures appear relaxed and much more lifelike. (*Deutsches Archäologisches Institut, Rome*)

Etruscan and Greek cities whose higher civilizations were gradually absorbed by the Romans. The origin of the Etruscans remains a mystery, although some scholars believe that they came from Asia Minor and settled in northern Italy. From them, Romans acquired architectural styles and skills in road construction, sanitation, hydraulic engineering including underground conduits, metallurgy, ceramics, and portrait sculpture. Etruscan words and names entered the Latin language, and Etruscan gods were assimilated by Roman religion.

The Etruscans had expanded their territory in Italy during the seventh and sixth centuries B.C., and they controlled the monarchy in Rome. Defeated by Celts, Greeks, and finally Romans, by the third century B.C. the Etruscans ceased to exercise any political power in Italy.

Rome became a republic at the end of the sixth century B.C., when the landowning aristocrats, or patricians, overthrew the Etruscan king. As in the Greek cities, the transition from theocratic monarchy to republic offered possibilities for political and legal growth. In the opening phase of republican history, religion governed the people, dictated the law, and legitimized the rule of the patricians, who regarded themselves as the preservers of sacred traditions. Gradually the Romans loosened the ties between religion and politics and hammered out a constitutional system that paralleled the Greek achievement of rationalizing and secularizing politics and law. In time the Romans, like the Greeks, came to view law as an expression of the public will and not as the creation of god-kings, priest-kings, or a priestly caste.

The impetus for the growth of the Roman constitution came from a conflict—known as the Struggle of the Orders—between the patricians and the commoners, or plebeians. At the beginning of the fifth century B.C., the patrician-dominated government was composed of two consuls together with the Centuriate Assembly and the Senate. Patricians owned most of the land and controlled the army. The executive heads of government were the two annually elected consuls, who came from the nobility; they commanded the army, served as judges, and initiated legislation.

The Centuriate Assembly was a popular assembly but, because of voting procedures, was controlled by the nobility. The assembly elected consuls and other magistrates and made the laws, which also needed Senate approval. The Senate advised the assembly but did not itself enact laws; it controlled public finances and foreign policy. Senators either were appointed for life terms by the consuls or were former magistrates. The Senate was the principal organ of patrician power.

The tension between patricians and commoners stemmed from plebeian grievances, which included enslavement for debt, discrimination in the courts, prevention of intermarriage with patricians, lack of political representation, and the absence of a written code of laws. Resentful of their inferior status, the plebeians organized and waged a struggle for political, legal, and social equality.

The plebeians had one decisive weapon: their threat to secede from Rome, that is, not to pay taxes, work, or serve in the army. Realizing that Rome, which was constantly involved in warfare on the Italian peninsula, could not endure without plebeian help, the pragmatic patricians grudgingly made concessions. Thus the plebeians slowly gained legal equality.

Early in the fifth century the plebeians won the right to form their own assembly (the Plebeian Assembly when later enlarged was called the Tribal Assembly). This Assembly could elect officials called tribunes, who were empowered to protect plebeian rights. As a result of plebeian pressure, in about 450 B.C. the first Roman code of laws was written; called the Twelve Tables, it gave plebeians some degree of protection against unfair and oppressive patrician officials, who could interpret customary law in an arbitrary way. Other concessions gained later by the plebeians included the right to intermarry with patricians, access to the highest political, judicial, and religious offices in the state, and the elimination of slavery as payment for debt. In 287 B.C., a date generally recognized as the termination of the plebeian-patrician struggle, the acts of the Tribal Assembly became binding on all and did not need Senate approval.

Although the plebeians had gained legal equality and the right to sit in the Senate and to hold high offices, power was still concentrated in a ruling oligarchy, now consisting of patricians and influential plebeians who had joined forces with the old nobility. Marriages between patricians and politically powerful plebeians strengthened this alliance. As wealthy plebeians generally became tribunes, they tended to side with the old nobility rather than to defend the interests of poor plebeians. By using bribes, the ruling oligarchy maintained control over the Assembly, and the Senate remained a bastion of aristocratic power. Regarding themselves as Rome's finest citizens, the ruling oligarchy led Rome during its period of expansion and demonstrated a sense of responsibility and a talent for statesmanship.

During the two-hundred-year Struggle of the Orders, the Romans forged a constitutional system based on civic needs rather than on religious mystery. The essential duty of government ceased to be the regular performance of religious rituals and became the maintenance of order at home and the preservation of Roman might and dignity in international relations. Although the Romans retained the ceremonies and practices of their ancestral religion, public interest, not religious tradition, determined the content of law and was the standard by which all the important acts of the city were judged. In the opening stage of republican history, law was priestly and sacred, spoken only by priests and known only to men of religious families. Gradually, as law was written, debated, and altered, it became disentangled from religion. Another step in this process of secularization and rationalization occurred when the study and interpretation of law passed from the hands of priests to a class of professional jurists, who analyzed, classified, systematized, and sought common-sense solutions to legal problems.

The Roman constitution was not a product of abstract thought, nor was it the gift of a great lawmaker like the Athenian Solon. Rather, like the English constitution, the Roman constitution evolved gradually and empirically in response to specific needs. The Romans, unlike the Greeks, were distinguished by practicality and common sense, not by a love of abstract thought. In their pragmatic and empirical fashion, they gradually developed the procedures of public politics and the legal state.

Roman Expansion to 146 B.C.

At the time of the Struggle of the Orders, Rome was also extending its power over the Italian peninsula. Without civic harmony and stability, it could not have achieved expansion. By 146 B.C., it had become the dominant power in the Mediterranean world.

Roman expansion occurred in three main stages: the uniting of the Italian peninsula, which gave Rome the manpower that transformed it from a city-state into a great power; the collision with Carthage, from which Rome emerged as ruler of the western Mediterranean; and the subjugation of the Hellenistic states, which brought Romans in close contact with Greek civilization. As Rome expanded territorially, its leaders enlarged their vision. Instead of restricting citizenship to people having ethnic kinship, Rome assimilated other peoples into its political community. As law had grown to cope with the earlier grievances of the plebeians, it adjusted to the new situations resulting from the creation of a multinational empire. The city of Rome was evolving into the city of humanity—the cosmopolis envisioned by the Stoics.

The Uniting of Italy

During the first stage of expansion, Rome extended its hegemony over Italy, subduing in the process neighboring Latin kinsmen, semicivilized Italian tribes, the once dominant Etruscans, and Greek city-states in southern Italy. Rome's conquest of Italy stemmed in part from superior military organization and discipline. Copying the Greeks, the Romans organized their soldiers into battle formations; in contrast, their opponents often fought as disorganized hordes that were prone to panic and flight. Romans also willingly made sacrifices so that Rome might endure. In conquering Italy, they were united by a moral and religious devotion to their city strong enough to overcome social conflict, factional disputes, and personal ambition.

Despite its army's strength, Rome could not have mastered Italy without the cooperation of other Italian peoples. Instead of reducing adversaries to slavery and taking all their land—a not uncommon method of warfare in the ancient world—Rome endeavored, through generous treatment, to gain the loyalty of conquered people. Some defeated communities retained a measure of self-government but turned the conduct of foreign affairs over to Rome and contributed contingents to the army when Rome went to war. Other conquered people received partial or full citizenship. In extending its dominion over Italy, Rome displayed a remarkable talent for converting former enemies into allies and eventually into Roman citizens. No Greek city had ever envisaged integrating nonnatives into its political community.

The Conquest of the Mediterranean World

When Rome finished unifying Italy, there were five great powers in the Mediterranean area: the Seleucid monarchy in the Near East, the Ptolemaic monarchy in Egypt, the kingdom of Macedonia, Carthage in the western Mediterranean, and the Roman-dominated Italian Confederation. One hundred and twenty years later—in 146 B.C.—Rome had subjected these states to its dominion.

Roman expansion beyond Italy did not proceed according to a set plan. Indeed, some Roman leaders considered involvement in foreign adventures a threat to both Rome's security and its traditional way of life. However, as its interests grew, Rome was drawn into conflicts, and without planning it acquired an overseas empire.

Shortly after asserting supremacy in Italy, Rome engaged Carthage, the other great power in the western Mediterranean, in a prolonged conflict, the

Map 4.1   The Growth of Rome: From Republic to Empire   ▶

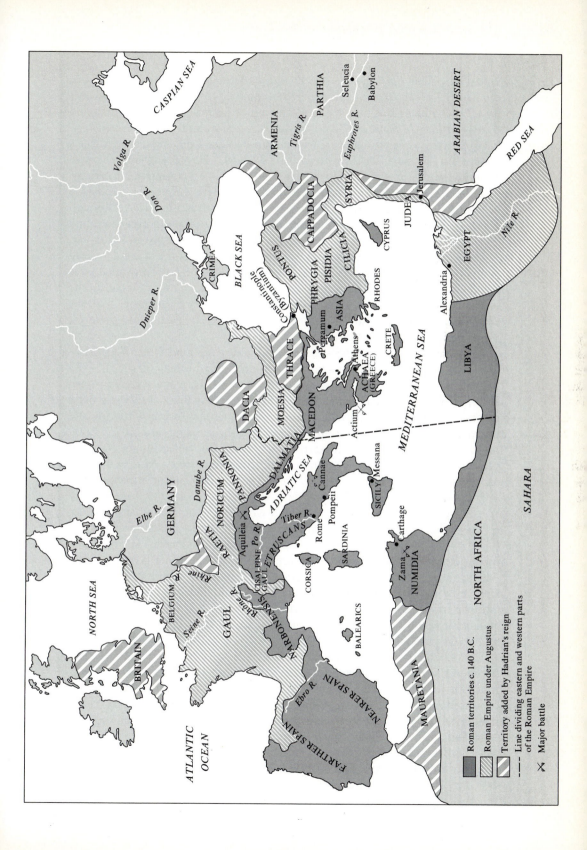

CASPIAN SEA

PARTHIA

Seleucia •
Babylon •

ARMENIA

Tigris R.

Volga R.

Euphrates R.

ARABIAN DESERT

RED SEA

Don R.

CAPPADOCIA

SYRIA

Nile R.

Jerusalem •

JUDEA

Dnieper R.

BLACK SEA

PONTUS

PHRYGIA

PISIDIA

CILICIA

CYPRUS

EGYPT

Alexandria •

CRIMEA

Constantinople
(Byzantium) •

Pergamum •

ASIA

RHODES

CRETE

Athens •

MEDITERRANEAN SEA

LIBYA

THRACE

MACEDON

ACHAEA
(GREECE)

Actium ✕

DACIA

MOESIA

DALMATIA

ADRIATIC SEA

Danube R.

NORICUM

PANNONIA

GERMANY

Elbe R.

Cannae •

Messana •

SICILY

RAETIA

Aquileia ✕

CISALPINE
GAUL

Po R.

ETRUSCANS

Rome •

Pompeii •

SARDINIA

Carthage •

Zama ✕

NUMIDIA

Tiber R.

NORTH AFRICA

SAHARA

Rhine R.

BELGIUM

GAUL

Seine R.

Rhône R.

NARBONENSIS

CORSICA

BALEARICS

MAURETANIA

NORTH SEA

BRITAIN

ATLANTIC
OCEAN

NEARER SPAIN

FARTHER SPAIN

Ebro R.

◼ Roman territories c. 140 B.C.

▨ Roman Empire under Augustus

▨ Territory added by Hadrian's reign

– – – Line dividing eastern and western parts
of the Roman Empire

✕ Major battle

First Punic War (264–241 B.C.). Founded about 800 B.C. by Phoenicians, the North African city of Carthage had become a prosperous commercial center. The Carthaginians had acquired an empire comprising North Africa and coastal regions of southern Spain, Sardinia, Corsica, and western Sicily.

War between the two great powers began because Rome feared Carthage's designs on the northern Sicilian city of Messana. Rome was apprehensive about the southern Italian city-states that were its allies, fearing that Carthage would use Messana either to attack them or to interfere with their trade. Rome decided that the security of its allies required intervention in Sicily. Although Rome suffered severe losses—including the annihilation of an army that had invaded North Africa and the destruction of hundreds of ships in battle and storms—the Romans never considered anything but a victor's peace. Drawing manpower from loyal allies throughout Italy, Rome finally prevailed over Carthage, which had to surrender Sicily to Rome. Three years later, Rome seized the islands of Corsica and Sardinia from a weakened Carthage. With the acquisition of these territories beyond Italy, which were made into provinces, Rome had the beginnings of an empire.

Carthaginian expansion in Spain precipitated the Second Punic War (218–201 B.C.). The Carthaginian army was commanded by Hannibal (247–183 B.C.), whose military genius astounded the ancients. Hannibal led a seasoned army, complete with war elephants for charging enemy lines, across mountain passes so steep and icy that men and animals sometimes lost their footing and fell to their deaths. Some 26,000 men survived the crossing into Italy; 15,000 more were recruited from Gallic tribesmen of the Po Valley. At the battle of Cannae (216 B.C.), Hannibal's army completely destroyed a Roman army of 60,000 soldiers, the largest single force Rome had ever put into the field.

These were the Republic's worst days. Nevertheless, says the Roman historian Livy, the Romans did not breathe a word of peace. Hannibal could not follow up his victory at Cannae with a finishing blow, for Rome wisely would not allow its army to be lured into another major engagement. Nor did Hannibal possess the manpower to capture the city itself. Rome invaded North Africa, threatening Carthage and forcing Hannibal to withdraw his troops from Italy in order to defend his homeland. Hannibal, who had won every battle in Italy, was defeated at the battle of Zama in North Africa in 202 B.C., ending the Second Punic War. Carthage was compelled to surrender Spain and to give up its elephants and its navy.

The Second Punic War left Rome the sole great power in the western Mediterranean; it also hastened Rome's entry into the politics of the Hellenistic world. In the year after Cannae, during Rome's darkest ordeal, Philip V of Macedonia entered into an alliance with Hannibal. Fearing that the Macedonian ruler might have intentions of invading Italy, Rome initiated the First Macedonian War, which ended in a Roman victory in 205 B.C. To end Macedonian influence in Greece, which Rome increasingly viewed as a Roman protectorate, the Romans fought two other wars with Macedonia. Finally, in 148 B.C., Rome created the province of Macedonia.

Intervention in Greece then led to Roman involvement in the Hellenistic kingdoms of the Near East and Asia Minor—Seleucia, Egypt, and Pergamum. The Hellenistic states became client kingdoms of Rome, and consequently lost their freedom of action in foreign affairs.

In 146 B.C., the same year that Rome's hegemony over the Hellenistic world was assured, Rome concluded the Third Punic War with Carthage. Although Carthage was a second-rate power and no longer a threat to Rome's security, Rome had launched this war of annihilation against Carthage in 149 B.C. The Romans were driven by old hatreds and the traumatic memory of Hannibal's near-conquest. Rome sold Carthaginian survivors into slavery, obliterated the city, and turned the land into the Roman province of Africa. Rome's savage and irrational behavior toward a helpless Carthage was an early sign of the deterioration of senatorial leadership; there would be others.

Rome had not yet reached the limits of its expansion, but there was no doubt that by 146 B.C. the Mediterranean world had been subjected to its will. No power could stand up to Rome.

Consequences of Expansion

Expansion had important consequences for Rome and the Mediterranean world. Thousands of Greeks, many of them educated persons who had been enslaved as a result of Rome's eastern conquests, came to Rome. This influx accelerated the process of Hellenization begun earlier with Rome's contact with the Greek cities of southern Italy.

A crucial consequence of expansion was Roman contact with the legal experience of other peoples, including the Greeks. Roman jurists, demonstrating the Roman virtues of pragmatism and common sense, selectively incorporated into Roman law elements of the legal codes and traditions of these nations. Thus Roman jurists gradually and empirically fashioned the *jus gentium,* the law of nations or peoples, which eventually was applied throughout the Empire.

Roman conquerors transported to Italy hundreds of thousands of war captives, including Greeks, from all over the empire. The more fortunate slaves worked as craftsmen and servants; the luckless and more numerous toiled on the growing number of plantations or died early, laboring in mines. Roman masters often treated their slaves brutally. Although slave uprisings were not common, their ferocity terrified the Romans. In 135 B.C., slaves in Sicily revolted and captured some key towns, defeating Roman forces before being subdued. In 73 B.C., gladiators led by Spartacus broke out of their barracks and were joined by tens of thousands of runaways. Spartacus aimed to escape into Gaul and Thrace, the homelands of many slaves. His slave army defeated Roman armies and devastated southern Italy before the superior might of Rome prevailed. Some 6,000 of the defeated slaves were crucified.

Roman governors, lesser officials, and businessmen found the provinces a source of quick wealth; they were generally unrestrained by the Senate, which was responsible for administering the overseas territories. Exploitation, corruption, and extortion soon ran rampant. The Roman nobility proved unfit to manage a world empire.

Despite numerous examples of misrule in the provinces, there were many positive features of Roman administration. Rome generally allowed its subjects a large measure of self-government and did not interfere with religion and local customs. Usually the Roman taxes worked out to be no higher, and in some instances were lower, than those under previous regimes. And most important, Rome reduced the endemic warfare that had plagued these regions.

Culture in the Republic

A chief consequence of expansion was increased contact with Greek culture. During the third century B.C., Greek civilization started to exercise an increasing and fruitful influence upon the Roman mind. Greek teachers, both slave and free, came to Rome and introduced Romans to Hellenic cultural achievements. As they conquered the eastern Mediterranean, Roman generals began to ship libraries and works of art from Greek cities to Rome. In time, Romans acquired from Greece knowledge of scientific thought, philosophy, medicine, and geography. Roman writers and orators used Greek history, poetry, and oratory as models. Adopting the humanist outlook of the Greeks, the Romans came to value human intelligence and eloquent and graceful prose and poetry. Wealthy Romans retained Greek tutors, poets, and philosophers in their households and sent their sons to Athens to study. Thus, Rome creatively assimilated the Greek achievement and transmitted it to others, thereby extending the orbit of Hellenism.

Plautus (c. 254–184 B.C.), Rome's greatest playwright, adopted features of fourth- and third-century Greek comedy. His plays had Greek characters and took place in Greek settings; the actors wore the Greek style of dress. But the plays also contained familiar elements that appealed to Roman audiences—scenes of gluttony, drunkenness, womanizing, and the pains of love.

Another playwright, Terence (c. 190–159 B.C.), was originally from North Africa, and was brought to Rome as a slave. His owner, a Roman senator, provided the talented youth with an education and freed him. Terence's humor, restrained and refined, lacked the boisterousness of Plautus' writing that appealed to the Roman audience, but his style was technically superior.

Catullus (87–54 B.C.) is generally regarded as one of the world's great lyric poets. He was a native of northern Italy whose father provided him with a gentleman's education. Tormented by an ill-fated love, Catullus wrote memorable poems dealing with passion and its torments.

Lucretius (c. 94–c. 55 B.C.), the leading Roman Epicurean philosopher, was influenced by the conflict fostered by two generals, Marius and Sulla, which is discussed later in this chapter. Distraught by the seemingly endless strife, Lucretius yearned for philosophic tranquillity. Like Epicurus, he believed that religion prompted people to perform evil deeds and caused them to experience terrible anxiety about death and eternal punishment. In his work *On the Nature of Things,* Lucretius expressed his appreciation of Epicurus. Like his mentor, Lucretius advanced a materialistic conception of nature and denounced superstition and religion for fostering psychological distress. He proposed that the simple life, devoid of political involvement and excessive passion, was the highest good and the path that would lead from emotional turmoil to peace of mind.

Cicero (106–43 B.C.), a leading Roman statesman, was also a distinguished orator, an unsurpassed Latin stylist, and a student of Greek philosophy. His letters, more than eight hundred of which have survived, provide modern historians with valuable insights into late republican politics. Dedicated to republicanism, Cicero sought to prevent one-man rule. He adopted the Stoic belief that natural law governs the universe and applies to all, that all belong to a common humanity, and that reason is the individual's noblest faculty. Stoicism was the most influential philosophoy in Rome. Its stress on virtuous conduct and performance of duty coincided with Roman ideals, and its doctrine of natural law that applies to all nations harmonized with the requirements of a world empire.

The Collapse of the Republic

In 146 B.C., Roman might spanned the Mediterranean world. After that year the principal concerns of the Republic no longer were foreign invasions, but adjusting city-state institutions to the demands of empire and overcoming critical social and political problems at home. In both instances the Republic was unequal to the challenge. Instead of developing a professional civil service to administer the conquered lands, Roman leaders attempted to govern an empire with city-state institutions that had evolved for a different purpose. In addition, the Republic showed little concern for the welfare of its subjects, and provincial rule worsened as governors, tax collectors, and soldiers shamelessly exploited the provincials.

During Rome's march to empire, all its classes had demonstrated a magnificent civic spirit in fighting foreign wars. With Carthage and Macedonia no longer threats to Rome, this cooperation deteriorated. Internal dissension tore Rome apart as the ferocity and drive for domination formerly directed against foreign enemies turned inward against fellow Romans. Civil war replaced foreign war.

The Gracchi Revolution

The downhill slide of the Republic was triggered by an agricultural crisis. In the long war with Hannibal in Italy, many farms were devastated. With many Roman soldier-farmers serving long periods in the army, fields lay neglected.

Returning veterans lacked the money to restore their land; they were forced to sell their farms to wealthy landowners at low prices.

Another factor that helped to squeeze out the small farmowners was the importation of hundreds of thousands of slaves to work on large plantations called *latifundia*. Farmers who had formerly increased meager incomes by working for wages on neighboring large estates no longer were needed. Sinking ever deeper into poverty and debt, farmers gave up their lands and went to Rome seeking work. The dispossessed peasantry found little to do in Rome, where there was not enough industry to provide them with employment and where much of the work was done by slaves. The once-sturdy and independent Roman farmer, who had done all that his country had asked of him, was becoming part of a vast urban underclass—poor, embittered, and alienated.

In 133 B.C., Tiberius Gracchus (163–133 B.C.), who came from one of Rome's most honored families, was elected tribune. Distressed by the injustice done to the peasantry and recognizing that the Roman army depended on the loyalty of small landowners, Tiberius made himself the spokesman for land reform. He proposed a simple and moderate solution for the problem of the landless peasants: he would re-enact an old law barring any Roman from using more than 312 acres of the state-owned land obtained in the process of uniting Italy. For many years the upper class had ignored this law, occupying vast tracts of public land as squatters and treating this land as their own. By enforcing the law, Tiberius hoped to free land for distribution to landless citizens.

Rome's leading families viewed Tiberius as a revolutionary who threatened their property and political authority. They also feared that he was seeking to stir up the poor in order to gain political power for himself. To preserve the status quo, with wealth and power concentrated in the hands of a few hundred families, senatorial extremists killed Tiberius and some three hundred of his followers, dumping their bodies into the Tiber.

The cause of land reform was next taken up by Gaius Gracchus (153–121 B.C.), a younger brother of Tiberius who was elected tribune in 123 B.C. Gaius aided the poor by reintroducing his brother's plan for land distribution and by enabling them to buy grain from the state at less than half the market price. But like his brother, Gaius aroused the anger of the senatorial class. A brief civil war raged in Rome during which Gaius Gracchus (who may have committed suicide) and 3,000 of his followers perished. By killing the Gracchi, the Senate had substituted violence for reason and made murder a means of coping with troublesome opposition.

Soon the club and the dagger became common weapons in Roman politics, thereby hurling Rome into an era of political violence that ended with the destruction of the Republic. Though the Senate considered itself the guardian of republican liberty, in reality it was expressing the determination of a few hundred families to retain their control over the state. It is a classic example of a once-creative minority clinging tenaciously to power long after it had ceased to govern effectively, or to inspire allegiance. Roman politics in the century after the Gracchi was bedeviled by intrigues, rivalries, personal ambition, and political violence. The Senate behaved like a decadent oligarchy, and the Tribal Assembly, which had become the voice of the urban mob, demonstrated a weakness for demagogues, an openness to bribery, and an abundance of deceit and incompetence. The Roman Republic had passed the peak of its greatness.

Rival Generals

Marius (157–86 B.C.), who became consul in 107 B.C., adopted a military policy that eventually contributed to the wrecking of the Republic. Short of troops for a campaign in Numidia in North Africa, Marius disposed of the traditional property requirement for entrance into the army and filled his legions with volunteers from the urban poor, a dangerous precedent. These new soldiers, disillusioned with Rome, served only because Marius held out the promise of pay, loot, and land grants after discharge. Their loyalty was given not to Rome but to Marius, and they remained loyal to their commander only as long as he fulfilled his promises.

Marius had set an example that other ambitious commanders followed. They saw that a general could use his army to advance his political career, that by retaining the confidence of his soldiers, he could cow the Senate and dictate Roman policy. The army, no longer an instrument of government, became a private possession of generals. Seeing its authority undermined by generals appointed by the Assembly, the Senate was forced to seek army commanders who would champion the cause of senatorial rule. In time, Rome would be engulfed in civil wars, as rival generals used their troops to further their own ambitions or political affiliations.

Meanwhile, the Senate continued to deal ineffectively with Rome's problems. When Rome's Italian allies pressed for citizenship, the Senate refused to make concessions. The Senate's shortsightedness plunged Italy into a terrible war, known as the Social War (91–88 B.C.). As war ravaged the peninsula, the Romans reversed their policy and conferred citizenship on the Italians. The unnecessary and ruinous rebellion petered out.

A conflict between Marius and Sulla (138–78 B.C.), who had distinguished himself in the Social War, over who would command an army in the east led to a prolonged civil war. Sulla won the first round. But then Marius and his troops retook the city and in a frenzy lashed out at Sulla's supporters. The killing lasted for five days and nights. Marius died shortly afterwards. Sulla quickly subdued Marius' supporters on his return and instituted a terror that far surpassed Marius' violence.

Sulla believed that only rule by an aristocratic oligarchy could protect Rome from future military adventurers and assure domestic peace. He therefore restored the Senate's right to veto acts of the Assembly, limited the power of the tribunes and the Assembly, and reduced the military authority of provincial governors to prevent any march on Rome. To make the Senate less oligarchical, he increased its membership to six hundred. Having put through these reforms, Sulla retired.

Bust of Caesar.   Julius Caesar tried to rescue a dying Roman world by imposing strong rule. He paved the way for the transition from Republic to imperial rule. (*Ewing Galloway*)

Julius Caesar

But the Senate failed to wield its restored authority effectively. The Republic was still menaced by military commanders who used their troops for their own political advantage, and underlying problems remained unsolved. In 60 B.C., a triumvirate (a ruling group of three) consisting of Julius Caesar (c. 100–44 B.C.), a politician, Pompey, a general, and Crassus, a wealthy banker, conspired to take over Rome. The ablest of the three was Caesar.

Recognizing the importance of a military command as a prerequisite for political prominence, Caesar gained command of the legions in Gaul in 59 B.C. The following year he began the conquest of that part of Gaul outside of Roman control. The successful Gallic campaigns and invasion of Britain revealed Caesar's exceptional talent for generalship. Indeed, his victories alarmed the Senate, which feared that Caesar would use his devoted troops and soaring reputation to seize control of the state.

Meanwhile, the trimvirate had fallen apart. In 53 B.C., Crassus had perished with his army in a disastrous campaign against the Parthians in the East.

Pompey, who was jealous of Caesar's success and eager to expand his own power, drew closer to the Senate. Supported by Pompey, the Senate ordered Caesar to relinquish his command. Without his troops, Caesar realized, he would be defenseless; he decided instead to march on Rome. After he crossed the Rubicon River into Italy in 49 B.C., civil war again ravaged the Republic. Pompey proved no match for so talented a general; the Senate acknowledged Caesar's victory and appointed him to be dictator for ten years.

Caesar realized that republican institutions no longer operated effectively and that only strong and enlightened leadership could permanently end the civil warfare destroying Rome. He fought exploitation in the provinces and generously extended citizenship to more provincials. To aid the poor in Rome, he began a public works program that provided employment and beautified the city. He also relocated over 100,000 veterans and members of Rome's lower class to the provinces, where he gave them land.

In February of 44 B.C., Rome's ruling class—jealous of Caesar's success and power and afraid of his ambition—became thoroughly alarmed when his temporary dictatorship was converted into a lifelong office. The aristocracy saw this event as the end of senatorial government and their rule, which they equated with liberty, and as the beginnings of a Hellenistic type of monarchy. A group of aristocrats, regarding themselves as defenders of republican traditions more than four and a half centuries old, assassinated Caesar on March 15 in the year 44 B.C.

The Republic's Last Years

The assassination of Julius Caesar did not restore republican liberty, but plunged Rome into renewed civil war. Two of Caesar's trusted lieutenants, Mark Antony and Lepidus, joined with Octavian, Caesar's adopted son, and defeated the armies of Brutus and Cassius, two instigators of Caesar's death. After Lepidus was forced into political obscurity, Antony and Octavian fought each other with the empire as the prize. In 31 B.C., at the naval battle of Actium in western Greece, Octavian crushed the forces of Antony and his wife, Egypt's Queen Cleopatra. Octavian emerged as master of Rome and four years later became, in effect, the first Roman emperor.

The Roman Republic, which had amassed power to a degree hitherto unknown in the ancient world, was wrecked not by foreign invasion but by internal weaknesses: the degeneration of senatorial leadership, and the willingness of politicians to use violence; the formation of private armies in which soldiers gave their loyalty to their commander rather than to Rome; the transformation of a self-reliant peasantry into an impoverished and demoralized city rabble; and the deterioration of those ancient virtues that had been the source of the state's vitality. Before 146 B.C., the threat posed by foreign enemies, particularly Carthage, forced Romans to work together for the benefit of the state. This social cohesion broke down when foreign danger was reduced.

Augustus and the Foundations of the Roman Empire

After Octavian's forces defeated those of Antony and Cleopatra at the battle of Actium, no opponents could stand up to him. The century of civil war, political murder, corruption, and mismanagement had exhausted the Mediterranean world, which longed for order. Like Caesar before him, Octavian recognized that only a strong monarchy could rescue Rome from civil war and anarchy. But learning from Caesar's assassination, he also knew that republican ideals were far from dead. To exercise autocratic power openly like a Hellenistic monarch would have aroused the hostility of the Roman ruling class, whose assistance and good will Octavian desired.

Octavian demonstrated his political genius by reconciling his military monarchy with republican institutions—he held absolute power without abruptly breaking with a republican past. Magistrates were still elected and assemblies still met; the Senate administered certain provinces, retained its treasury, and was invited to advise Octavian. With some truth, Octavian could claim that he ruled in partnership with the Senate. By maintaining the façade of the Republic, Octavian camouflaged his absolute power and contained senatorial opposition, which had already been weakened by the deaths of leading nobles in battle or in the purges that Octavian had instituted against his enemies.

In 27 B.C., Octavian shrewdly offered to surrender his power, knowing that the Senate, purged of opposition, would demand that he continue to lead the state. By this act, Octavian could claim to be a legitimate constitutional ruler leading a government of law, not one of a lawless despotism so hateful to the Roman mentality. In keeping with his policy of maintaining the appearance of traditional republican government, Octavian refused to be called king or even, like Caesar, dictator; instead, he cleverly disguised his autocratic rule by taking the inoffensive title *Princeps* (First Citizen). The Senate also conferred upon him the semireligious and revered name of *Augustus*.

Augustus' reign signified the end of the Roman Republic and the beginning of the Roman Empire, the termination of aristocratic politics and the emergence of one-man rule. Despite his introduction of autocratic rule, however, Augustus was by no means a self-seeking tyrant, but a creative statesman. Heir to the Roman tradition of civic duty, he regarded his power as a public trust delegated to him by the Roman people. He was faithful to the classical ideal that the state should promote the good life by protecting civilization from barbarism and ignorance, and he sought to rescue a dying Roman world.

Augustus instituted reforms and improvements throughout the Empire. He reformed the army to guard against the re-emergence of ambitious generals like those whose rivalries and private armies had wrecked the Republic. He maintained the loyalty of his soldiers by assuring that veterans, on discharge, would receive substantial bonuses and land in Italy or in the provinces. For the city of Rome, Augustus had aqueducts and water mains built that brought water to most Roman homes. He created a fire brigade that reduced the danger of great conflagrations in crowded tenement districts, and he organized a police force to contain violence. He improved the distribution of free grain to the impoverished proletariat, and financed out of his own funds the popular gladiatorial combats. In Italy, Augustus had roads repaired, fostered public works, and arranged for Italians to play a more important role in the administration of the Empire. He earned the gratitude of the provincials by correcting tax abuses, by fighting corruption and extortion, and by improving the quality of governors and enabling aggrieved provincials to bring charges against Roman officials.

The Pax Romana

The brilliant statesmanship of Augustus inaugurated Rome's greatest age. For the next two hundred years the Mediterranean world enjoyed the blessings of the *pax Romana,* the Roman Peace. The ancient world had never experienced such a long period of peace, order, efficient administration, and prosperity. Although both proficient and inept rulers succeeded Augustus, the essential features of the pax Romana persisted.

The Successors of Augustus

The first four emperors who succeeded Augustus were related either to him or to his third wife, Livia. They constituted the Julio-Claudian dynasty, which ruled from A.D. 14 to A.D. 68. Although their reigns were marked by conspiracies, summary executions, and assassinations, the great achievements of Augustus were preserved.

The Julio-Claudian dynasty came to an end in A.D. 68, when Emperor Nero committed suicide. Nero had grown increasingly tyrannical and had lost the confidence of the people, the senatorial class, and the generals, who rose in revolt. In the year following his death, anarchy reigned as military leaders competed for the throne. After a bloody civil war, the execution of two emperors, and the suicide of another, Vespasian gained the Principate. His reign (A.D. 69–79) marked the beginning of the Flavian dynasty. By having the great Colosseum of Rome constructed for gladiatorial contests, he earned the gratitude of the city's inhabitants. Vespasian also had nationalist uprisings put down in Gaul and Judea.

In Judea, Roman rule clashed with Jewish religious-national sentiments. Recognizing the tenaciousness with which Jews clung to their faith, the Roman leaders deliberately refrained from interfering with Hebraic religious beliefs and practices. Numerous privileges, such as exemption from emperor worship because it conflicted with the requirements of strict monotheism, were extended to Jews not only in Judea but throughout the Empire. But sometimes the Romans engaged in activities that outraged the Jews. For example, the Emperor Caligula (A.D. 37–41) ordered that a golden statue of himself be placed in Jerusalem's temple. To the Jews, this display of a pagan idol in their

The Colosseum, Rome, A.D. 70–80.   The amphitheatrum Flavianum, which is now called the Colosseum, was built during the reign of Vespasian. It could seat some 50,000 spectators who came to watch the gladiator contests and beast-hunts. (*A. F. Kersting*)

midst was an abomination; the order was rescinded when the Jews demonstrated their readiness to resist.

Relations between the Jews of Judea and the Roman authorities deteriorated progressively in succeeding decades. Militant Jews who rejected Roman rule as a threat to the purity of Jewish life urged their people to take up arms. Feeling a religious obligation to re-establish an independent kingdom in their ancient homeland and unable to reconcile themselves to Roman rule, the Jews launched a full-scale war of liberation in A.D. 66. In A.D. 70, after a five-month siege had inflicted terrible punishment on the Jews, Roman armies captured Jerusalem and destroyed the temple.

Vespasian was succeeded by his sons Titus (A.D. 79–81) and Domitian (A.D. 81–96). The reign of Titus was made memorable by the eruption of Vesuvius, which devastated the towns of Pompeii and Herculaneum. After Titus' brief time as emperor, his younger brother Domitian became ruler. After crushing a revolt led by the Roman commander in Upper Germany, a frightened Domitian executed many leading Romans. These actions led to his assassination in A.D. 96, ending the Flavian dynasty.

The Senate selected one of its own, Nerva, to succeed the murdered Domitian. Nerva's reign (A.D. 96–98) was brief and uneventful. But he introduced a

practice that would endure until A.D. 180: he adopted as his son and desig-
nated as his heir a man with proven ability, Trajan, the governor of Upper
Germany. This adoptive system assured a succession of competent rulers.

Trajan (ruled A.D. 98–117) eased the burden of taxation in the provinces,
provided for the needs of poor children, and had public works built. With his
enlarged army he conquered Dacia (parts of Rumania and Hungary), where he
seized vast quantities of gold and silver and made the territory into a Roman
province, adding to the large frontier Rome had to protect.

Trajan's successor, Hadrian (A.D. 117–138), strengthened border defenses
in Britain, and fought the second Hebrew revolt in Judea (A.D. 132–135).
After initial successes, including the capture of Jerusalem, the Jews were again
defeated by superior Roman might. The majority of Palestinian Jews were
killed, sold as slaves, or forced to seek refuge in other lands. The Romans
renamed the province Syria Palestina; they forbade Jews to enter Jerusalem,
except once a year, and encouraged non-Jews to settle the land. Although the
Jews continued to maintain a presence in Palestine, they had become a dispossessed and dispersed people.

After Hadrian came another ruler who had a long reign, Antoninus Pius
(A.D. 138–161). He introduced humane and just reforms, in particular, limits
on the right of masters to torture their slaves to obtain evidence, and the
establishment of the principle that an accused person be considered innocent
until proven guilty. During Antoninus' reign the Empire remained peaceful
and prosperous.

Marcus Aurelius (A.D. 161–180), the next emperor, was also a philosopher
whose *Meditations* was an eloquent expression of Stoic thought. His reign was
marked by renewed conflict in the East with the kingdom of Parthia. The
Roman legions were victorious in this campaign, but brought back from the
East an epidemic that decimated the population of the Empire.

From the accession of Nerva in A.D. 96 to the death of Marcus Aurelius in
A.D. 180, the Roman Empire was ruled by the "Five Good Emperors." During
this period the Empire was at the height of its power and prosperity, and nearly
all its peoples benefited. The four emperors preceding Marcus Aurelius had no
living sons, so they resorted to the adoptive system in selecting successors,
which served Rome effectively. But Marcus Aurelius chose his own son Commodus to succeed him. With the accession of Commodus, a misfit and a
megalomaniac, in A.D. 180, the pax Romana came to an end.

The Time of Happiness

The Romans called the pax Romana the "Time of Happiness." This period
was the fulfillment of Rome's mission—the creation of a world-state that
provided peace, security, ordered civilization, and the rule of law. Roman
legions defended the Rhine-Danube river frontiers from incursions by German
tribesmen, held the Parthians at bay in the East, and subdued the few uprisings
that occurred. Nerva's adoptive system of selecting emperors provided Rome
with internal stability and a succession of emperors with exceptional ability.

These Roman emperors did not use military force needlessly, but fought for sensible political goals; generals did not wage war recklessly, but tried to limit casualties, avoid risks, and deter conflicts by a show of force.

Constructive Rule   Roman rule was constructive. The Romans built roads, improved harbors, cleared forests, drained swamps, irrigated deserts, and cultivated undeveloped lands. They constructed aqueducts that brought fresh water for drinking and bathing to large numbers of people, and effective sewage systems that added to the quality of life. Goods were transported over roads made safe by Roman soldiers and across a Mediterranean Sea swept clear of pirates. A wide variety of goods circulated throughout the Empire. A stable currency, generally not subject to depreciation, contributed to the economic well-being of the Mediterranean world.

Scores of new cities sprang up, and old ones grew larger and wealthier. Although these municipalities had lost their power to wage war and had to bow to the will of the emperors, they retained considerable freedom of action in local matters. Imperial troops guarded against civil wars within the cities and prevented warfare between cities—two traditional weaknesses of city life in the ancient world. The municipalities served as centers of Greco-Roman civilization, which spread to the farthest reaches of the Mediterranean, continuing a process initiated during the Hellenistic Age. Citizenship, generously granted, was finally extended to virtually all free men by an edict of A.D. 212.

Improved Conditions for Slaves and Women   Conditions improved for those at the bottom of society, the slaves. At the time of Augustus, slaves may have accounted for a quarter of the population of Italy. But their numbers declined as Rome engaged in fewer wars of conquest. The freeing of slaves also became more common during the Empire. Freed slaves became citizens, with most of the rights and privileges of other citizens; their children suffered no legal disabilities whatsoever. During the Republic, slaves had been terribly abused; they were often mutilated, thrown to wild beasts, crucified, or burned alive. Several emperors issued decrees protecting slaves from cruel masters.

The status of women gradually improved during the Republic. In the early days of the Republic, a woman lived under the absolute authority first of her father, then of her husband. By the time of the Empire, a woman could own property and, if divorced, keep her dowry. A father no longer forced his daughter to marry against her will. Women could make business arrangements and draw up wills without the consent of their husbands. Roman women, unlike their Greek counterparts, were not secluded in their homes, but could come and go as they pleased. Upper-class women of Rome had far greater opportunities for education than those of Greece had. The history of the Empire, indeed Roman history in general, was filled with talented and influential women.

Law and Order   From Britain to the Arabian Desert, from the Danube River to the sands of the Sahara, some seventy million people with differing native languages, customs, and histories were united by Roman rule into a world community. Unlike those of the Republic, when corruption and exploitation in the provinces were notorious, officials of the Empire felt a high sense of responsibility to preserve the Roman peace, institute Roman justice, and spread Roman civilization.

In creating a stable and orderly political community with an expansive conception of citizenship, Rome resolved the problems posed by the limitations of the Greek city-state—civil war, intercity warfare, and a parochial attitude that divided men into Greek and non-Greek. Rome also brought to fruition an ideal of the Greek city-state—the protection and promotion of civilized life. By constructing a world community that broke down barriers between nations, by preserving and spreading Greco-Roman civilization, and by developing a rational system of law that applied to all humanity, Rome completed the trend toward universalism and cosmopolitanism that had emerged in the Hellenistic Age.

Roman Culture and Law During the Pax Romana

During the late Roman Republic, Rome had creatively assimilated the Greek achievement (see pages 88–89) and transmitted it to others, thereby extending the orbit of Hellenism. Rome had acquired Greek scientific thought, philosophy, medicine, and geography. Roman writers used Greek models; sharing in the humanist outlook of the Greeks, they valued human intelligence and achievement and expressed themselves in a graceful and eloquent style.

Literature and History   Roman cultural life reached its high point during the reign of Augustus, when Rome experienced the golden age of Latin literature. At the request of Augustus, who wanted a literary epic to glorify the Empire and his role in founding it, Virgil wrote the *Aeneid,* a masterpiece in world literature. Virgil ascribed to Rome a divine mission to bring peace and civilized life to the world, and he praised Augustus as a divinely appointed ruler who had fulfilled Rome's mission. The Greeks might be better sculptors, orators, and thinkers, said Virgil, but only the Romans knew how to govern an empire.

In his *History of Rome,* Livy (59 B.C.–A.D. 17) also glorified Roman character, customs, and deeds. He praised Augustus for attempting to revive traditional Roman morality, to which Livy felt a strong attachment. Although Livy was a lesser historian than Thucydides or Polybius, his work was still a major achievement, particularly in its depiction of the Roman character that helped make Rome great.

Roman writers who excelled in poetry include Horace (65–8 B.C.), the son of a freed slave. He broadened his education by studying literature and philosophy in Athens, and Greek ideals are reflected in his writings. Horace enjoyed the luxury of country estates, banquets, fine clothes, and courtesans along with the simple pleasures of mountain streams and clear skies. His poetry touched on many themes—the joy of good wine, the value of moderation, and the beauty of friendship. Unlike Horace, Virgil, or Livy, Ovid (43 B.C.–A.D. 17) did not experience the civil wars during his adult years. Consequently he was less inclined to praise the Augustan peace. His poetry showed a preference for romance and humor, and he is best remembered for his advice to lovers.

The writers who lived after the Augustan age mostly were of a lesser quality than the preceding men. The historian Tacitus (A.D. 55–c. 118) was an exception. Sympathetic to republican institutions, Tacitus denounced Roman emperors and the imperial system in his *Histories* and *Annals*. In *Germania,* he turned his sights on the habits of the Germanic peoples. He describes the Germans as undisciplined but heroic and brave, with a strong love of freedom. Another outstanding writer was the satirist Juvenal (A.D. c. 55–138). His works attacked evils of Roman society, such as the misconduct of emperors, the haughtiness of the wealthy, the barbaric tastes of commoners, the failures of parents, and the noise, congestion, and poverty of the capital.

Philosophy   Stoicism was the principal philosophy of the pax Romana, and its leading exponents were Seneca, Epictetus (A.D. c. 60–c. 117), and Marcus Aurelius. Perpetuating the rational tradition of Greek philosophy, Rome's early Stoics saw the universe as governed by reason and esteemed the human intellect. Like Socrates, they sought the highest good in this world, not in an afterlife, and envisioned no power above human reason. Moral values were obtained from reason alone. The individual was self-sufficient, and depended entirely on rational faculties for knowing and doing good. Stoics valued the self-sufficient person who attains virtue and wisdom by exercising rational control over his life. The Stoic doctrine that all people, because of their capacity to reason, belong to a common humanity coincided with the requirements of the multinational Roman Empire.

The Stoic conception of God underwent a gradual transformation that reflected the religious yearnings of the times. For the early Stoics, God was an intellectual necessity, an impersonal principle that gave order to the universe. For later Roman Stoics, God had become a moral necessity that comforted and reassured people. While maintaining the traditional Stoic belief that the individual can attain virtue through unaided reason, Epictetus and Marcus Aurelius came close to seeking God's help to live properly. The gap between Greek philosophy and Christianity was narrowing.

Science   The two most prominent scientists during the Greco-Roman age were Ptolemy, a mathematician, geographer, and astronomer who worked at Alexandria in the second century A.D., and Galen (A.D. c. 130–c. 201), who investigated medicine and anatomy. Ptolemy's thirteen-volume work, *Mathematical Composition*—more commonly known as the *Almagest,* a Greek-Arabic term meaning "the greatest"—summed up antiquity's knowledge of astronomy and became the authoritative text during the Middle Ages. In the Ptolemaic system, a motionless, round earth stood in the center of the universe; the moon, sun, and planets moved about the earth in circles, or in combinations of circles. The Ptolemaic system was built on a faulty premise, as modern astronomy eventually showed; however, it did work, that is, it did provide a model of the universe that adequately accounted for most observed phenomena. The Ptolemaic system was not challenged until the middle of the sixteenth century.

As Ptolemy's system dominated astronomy, so the theories of Galen dominated medicine down to modern times. By dissecting both dead and living animals, Galen attempted a rational investigation of the body's working parts. Although his work contains many errors, he made essential contributions to a knowledge of anatomy.

Art and Architecture   Romans borrowed art forms from other peoples, particularly the Greeks, but they borrowed creatively, transforming and enhancing their inheritance. Roman portraiture continued trends initiated during the Hellenistic Age. Hellenistic art, like Hellenistic philosophy, expressed a heightened awareness of the individual. Whereas Hellenic sculpture aimed to depict ideal beauty—the perfect body and face—Hellenistic sculpture captured individual character and expression, often of ordinary people. This movement from idealism to realism was carried further by Roman sculptors who realistically carved every detail of a subject's face—unruly hair, prominent nose, lines and wrinkles, a jaw that showed weakness or strength. Sculpture also gave expression to the imperial ideal. Statues of emperors conveyed nobility and authority; reliefs commemorating victories glorified Roman might and grandeur.

In architecture, the Romans most creatively transformed the Greek inheritance. The Greek temple was intended to be viewed from the outside; the focus was exclusively on the superbly balanced exterior. By using arches, vaults, and domes, the Romans built structures with large, magnificent interiors. The vast interior, massive walls, and overarching dome of the famous Pantheon, a temple built in the early second century during the reign of Hadrian, symbolizes the power and majesty of the Roman world-state.

Law   Expressing the Roman yearning for order and justice, law was Rome's great legacy to Western civilization. Roman law passed through two essential stages—the formation of civil law (*jus civile*) and the formation of the law of nations (*jus gentium*). The basic features of the civil law evolved during the two-hundred-year Struggle of the Orders, at the same time that Rome was extending its dominion over Italy. The Twelve Tables, drawn up in the early days of the patrician-plebeian struggle, established written rules of criminal and civil law for the Roman state that applied to all citizens. Over the centuries, the civil law was expanded by statutes passed by the assemblies, by the legal decisions of jurisdictional magistrates, by the rulings of emperors, and by the commentaries of professional jurists who, aided by familiarity with Greek logic, engaged in systematic legal analysis.

During the period of the Republic's expansion outside of Italy, contact with the Greeks and other peoples led to the development of the second branch of Roman law, the law of nations (*jus gentium*), which combined Roman civil law with principles selectively drawn from the legal tradition of Greeks and other peoples. Roman jurists identified the *jus gentium* with the natural law (*jus naturale*) of the Stoics. The jurists said that a law should accord with

Pont du Gard, Nîmes, France, 19 B.C.   The discovery and use of concrete by the Romans enabled the Empire to carry out a vast program of public works. Among the achievements of the Empire was a water transport system, the aqueduct; some aqueducts functioned for many centuries, and this one is now used as a viaduct. (*French Government Tourist Office*)

rational principles inherent in nature—uniform norms that are capable of being discerned by rational people. Serving to bind different peoples together, the law of nations harmonized with the requirements of a world empire and with Stoic ideals, as Cicero pointed out: "True law is right reason in agreement with nature; it is of universal application, unchanging and everlasting. And there will not be different laws at Rome and at Athens or different laws now and in the future, but one eternal and unchangeable law will be valid for all nations and all times."[1] The law of nations came to be applied throughout the Empire, although it never entirely supplanted local law. In the eyes of the law, a citizen was not a Syrian or a Briton or a Spaniard, but a Roman.

Following the fall of the Roman Empire, Roman law fell into disuse in western Europe. Gradually reintroduced in the twelfth century, it came to form the basis of the common law in all Western lands except Britain and its dependencies. Some provisions of Roman law are readily recognizable in modern legal systems, as the following excerpts illustrate:

> *Justice is a constant, unfailing disposition to give everyone his legal due.*

> No one is compelled to defend a cause against his will.
>
> No one suffers a penalty for what he thinks.
>
> In the case of major offenses it makes a difference whether something is committed purposefully or accidentally.
>
> In inflicting penalties, the age . . . of the guilty party must be taken into account.[2]

Entertainment   Despite its many achievements, Roman civilization presents a paradox. On the one hand, Roman culture and law evidence high standards of civilization; on the other hand, the Romans institutionalized barbaric practices. The major forms of entertainment both in the Republic and the Empire were chariot races, wild-animal shows, and gladiatorial combat. Chariot races were gala events in which the most skillful riders and the finest and best-trained stallions raced in an atmosphere of incredible excitement. The charioteers, many of them slaves hoping that victory would bring them freedom, became popular heroes.

The Romans craved brutal spectacles. One form of entertainment pitted wild beasts against each other or against men armed with spears. Another consisted of battles, sometimes to the death, between highly trained gladiators. The gladiators, mainly slaves and condemned criminals, learned their craft at schools run by professional trainers. Some gladiators entered the arena armed with a sword, others with a trident and a net. If the spectators were displeased with a losing gladiator's performance, they would call for his immediate execution. Over the centuries, these spectacles grew more bizarre. Hundreds of tigers were set against elephants and bulls; wild bulls tore apart men dressed in animal skins; women battled in the arena; dwarfs fought each other.

Signs of Trouble

The pax Romana was one of the finest periods in world history. But even during the Time of Happiness, signs of trouble appeared, which grew to crisis proportions in the third century. The Empire's internal stability was always precarious. Unrest in Egypt, Gaul, and Judea demonstrated that not all people at all times welcomed the grand majesty of the Roman peace, that localist and separatist tendencies persisted in a universal empire. In the centuries that followed, as Rome staggered under the weight of economic, political, and military difficulties, these native loyalties reasserted themselves. Increasingly the masses and even the Romanized elite of the cities withdrew their support from the Roman world-state.

Social and Economic Weaknesses

A healthy world-state required empirewide trade to serve as an economic base for political unity, expanding agricultural production to feed the cities, and growing internal mass markets to stimulate industrial production. But the economy of the Empire during the pax Romana had serious defects. The means of communication and transportation were slow, which hindered long-distance commerce. Many nobles, considering it unworthy for a gentleman to engage in business, chose to squander their wealth rather than invest it in commercial or industrial enterprises. Thus, deprived of the stimulus of capital investment, the economy could not expand.

Ultimately, only a small portion of the population—the middle and upper classes of the cities: landlords, merchants, and administrators—reaped the benefits of the Roman peace. They basked in luxury, leisure, and culture. The privileged class bought off the urban poor with bread and circuses, but occasionally mass discontent expressed itself in mob violence. Outside the cities, the peasantry, still the great bulk of the population, was exploited to provide cheap food for the city dwellers. Between town and countryside, an enormous cultural gap existed. In reality, the cities were small islands of high culture surrounded by a sea of peasant barbarism.

Such a parasitical, exploitative, and elitist social system might function in periods of peace and tranquillity, but could it survive crises? Would the impoverished people of town and country—the overwhelming majority of the population—remain loyal to a state whose benefits barely extended to them and whose sophisticated culture, which they hardly comprehended, virtually excluded them?

Cultural Stagnation and Transformation

Perhaps the most dangerous sign for the future was the spiritual paralysis that crept over the ordered world of pax Romana. A weary and sterile Hellenism underlay the Roman peace. The ancient world was undergoing a transformation of values that foreshadowed the end of Greco-Roman civilization.

During the second century A.D., Greco-Roman civilization lost its creative energies, and the values of classical humanism were challenged by mythic-religious movements. No longer regarding reason as a satisfying guide to life, the educated elite subordinated their intellect to feelings and an unregulated imagination. People no longer found the affairs of this world to have purpose; they placed their hope in life after death. The Roman world was undergoing a religious revolution and was seeking a new vision of the divine.

The application of reason to nature and society was the great achievement of the Greek mind. But, despite its many triumphs, Greek rationalism never entirely subdued the mythic-religious mentality, which draws its strength from human emotion. The masses of peasants and slaves remained attracted to religious forms. Ritual, mystery, magic, and ecstasy never lost their hold on the ancient world—nor, indeed, have they in our own scientific and technological society. During the Hellenistic Age the tide of rationalism gradually receded, and the nonrational, an ever-present undercurrent, showed renewed vigor. This resurgence of the mythical mentality could be seen in the popularity of the

Sacred Relief: Mithras Sacrifices a Bull. The spread and popularity of mystery religions during the Empire was one sign of spiritual malaise. Mithras, god of the soldiers, and his cult were widespread. Of all the mystery religions, Mithraism was Christianity's most serious rival. (*Cincinnati Art Museum, Gift of Mr. and Mrs. Fletcher E. Nyce, 1968*)

occult, magic, alchemy, and astrology; people turned for deliverance to magicians, astrologers, and exorcists.

They also became devotees of the many Eastern religious cults that promised personal salvation. The proliferation of oriental mystery religions was a clear expression of this transformation of classical values. During the Hellenistic era, slaves, merchants, and soldiers brought many religious cults westward from Persia, Babylon, Syria, Egypt, and Asia Minor. The various mystery cults possessed many common features. Their rites were secret, revealed only to members. Converts underwent initiation rites and were bound by oath to secrecy. The initiates, in a state of rapture, attempted to unite with the deity after first purifying themselves through baptism (sometimes with the blood of a bull), fasting, having their heads shaved, or drinking from a sacred vessel. Communion was achieved by donning the god's robe, eating a sacred meal, or visiting the god's sanctuary; cultists were certain that their particular savior-god would protect them from misfortune and ensure their soul's immortality. More and more people felt that the good life could not be achieved by individuals through their own efforts; they needed outside help.

Like the mystery religions, philosophy reached for something beyond this world in order to comfort the individual. Philosophers eventually sought escape from this world through union with a divine presence greater than human power. In Neo-Platonism, which replaced Stoicism as the dominant school of philosophy in the Late Roman Empire, religious yearnings were transformed into a religious system that transcended reason. Plotinus (A.D. c. 205–c. 270), the most influential spokesman of Neo-Platonism, subordinated philosophy to mysticism. Plato's philosophy, we have seen, contained both a major and a minor key. The major key stressed a rational interpretation of the human community and called for reforming the polis on the basis of knowledge, whereas the minor key urged the soul to rise to a higher world of reality. Although Plotinus retained Platonic rationalism (he viewed the individual as a reasoning being and used rational argument to explain his religious orientation), he was intrigued by Plato's otherworldliness.

What Plotinus desired was union with the One or the Good, sometimes called God—the source of all existence. Plotinus felt that the intellect could neither describe nor understand the One, which transcended all knowing, and that joining with the One required a mystical leap, a purification of the soul so that it could return to its true eternal home. For Plotinus, philosophy became a religious experience, a contemplation of the eternal through spiritual intoxication. In comparison to this union with the divine One, of what value was knowledge of the sensible world or a concern for human affairs? For Plotinus this world was a sea of tears and troubles from which the individual yearned to escape. Reality was not in this world, but beyond it, and the principal goal of life was not comprehension of the natural world nor the fulfillment of human potential nor the betterment of the human community, but knowledge of the One. Thus, his philosophy broke with the essential meaning of classical humanism.

By the Late Roman Empire, mystery religions intoxicated the masses, and mystical philosophy beguiled the educated elite. Classical civilization was undergoing a transformation. Philosophy had become subordinate to religious belief; secular values seemed inferior to religious experience. The earthly city had raised its eyes toward heaven. The culture of the Roman world was moving in a direction in which the quest for the divine was to predominate over all human enterprises.

The Decline of Rome

Third-Century Crisis

In the third century, the ordered civilization of the pax Romana ended. Several elements caused this disruption. The Roman Empire was plunged into military anarchy, was raided by Germanic tribes, and was burdened by economic dislocations.

The degeneration of the army was a prime reason for the crisis. During the great peace, the army had remained an excellent fighting force, renowned for its discipline, organization, and loyalty. In the third century A.D., however, there was a marked deterioration in the quality of Roman soldiers. Lacking

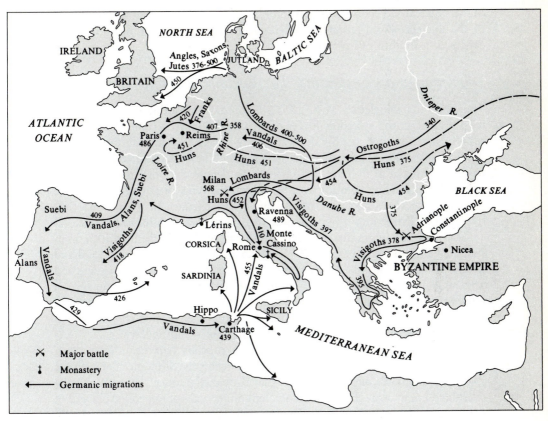

Map 4.2   Incursions and Migrations, c. A.D. 300–500

loyalty to Rome and greedy for spoils, soldiers used their weapons to prey on civilians and to make and unmake emperors. From A.D. 235 to 285, military mutiny and civil war raged, as legion fought legion, and many emperors were assassinated. The once stalwart army neglected its duty of defending the borders and disrupted the internal life of the Empire.

Taking advantage of the military anarchy, Germanic tribesmen crossed the Rhine-Danube frontier to loot and destroy. A reborn Persian Empire, led by the Sassanid Dynasty, attacked and for a while conquered Roman lands in the east. Some sections of the Empire, notably in Gaul, attempted to break away; these moves reflected an assertion of local patriotism over Roman universalism. The "city of mankind" was crumbling.

These eruptions had severe economic repercussions. Cities were pillaged and destroyed, farmlands ruined, and trade disrupted. To obtain funds and supplies for the military, emperors confiscated goods, exacted forced labor, and debased the coinage, causing inflation. These measures brought ruin to the middle class. Invasions, civil war, rising prices, a debased coinage, declining agricultural production, disrupted transportation, and the excessive demands of the state caused economic havoc and famine in the cities. The urban centers of the ancient world, creators and disseminators of high civilization, were caught in a rhythm of breakdown.

Diocletian and Constantine: The Regimented State

The emperors Diocletian (A.D. 285–305) and Constantine (A.D. 306–337) tried to contain the awesome forces of disintegration. At a time when agricultural production was steadily declining, they had to feed the city poor and an army of 400,000 strung out over the Empire. They also had to prevent renewed outbreaks of military anarchy and to defend the borders against barbarian attacks. Their solution was to tighten the reins of government and to squeeze more taxes and requisitions out of the citizens. In the process they transformed Rome into a bureaucratic, regimented, and militarized state.

Cities lost their traditional right of local self-government, which consolidated a trend started earlier. To ensure continuous production of food and goods, as well as the collection of taxes, the state forced unskilled workers and artisans to hold their jobs for life and to pass them on to their children. For the same reasons, peasants were turned into virtual serfs, bound to the land that they cultivated. An army of government agents was formed to hunt down peasants who fled the land to escape crushing taxes and poverty.

Also frozen into their positions were city officials (*curiales*). They often found it necessary to furnish from their own pockets the difference between the state's tax demands and the amount that they could collect from an already overtaxed population. This system of a hereditary class of tax collectors and of crippling taxes to pay for a vastly expanded bureaucracy and military establishment enfeebled urban trade and industry. These conditions killed the civic spirit of townsmen, who desperately sought escape. By overburdening urban dwellers with taxes and regulations, Diocletian and Constantine shattered the vitality of city life on which Roman prosperity and civilization depended.

Rome was now governed by an oriental despotism, a highly centralized monarchy regimenting the lives of its subjects. Whereas Augustus had upheld the classical ideal that the commonwealth was a means of fostering the good life for the individual, Diocletian adopted the oriental attitude that the individual lives for the state. To guard against military insurrection, he appointed a loyal general to govern the western provinces of the Empire while he ruled the East; although both emperors bore the title Augustus, Diocletian remained superior. By building an imperial capital, Constantinople, at the Bosporus, a strait where Asia meets Europe, Constantine furthered this trend of dividing the Empire into eastern and western halves.

Barbarian Invasions

By imposing some order on what had been approaching chaos, Diocletian and Constantine prevented the Empire from collapsing. Rome had been given a reprieve. But in the last part of the fourth century the problem of guarding the frontier grew more acute.

The Huns, a savage Mongol people from central Asia, swept across the plains of Russia and put pressure on the Visigoths, a Germanic tribe that had migrated into southeastern Europe. Terrified of the Huns, the Goths sought refuge within the Roman Empire. Hoping to increase his manpower and unable to stop the panic-stricken Germans, Emperor Valens permitted them to cross the Danube frontier. But two years later, in 378, the Goths and the Romans fought each other in a historic battle at Adrianople. This battle signified that Rome could no longer defend its borders. The Visigoths now plundered the Balkans at will. The Germanic tribes increased their pressure on the Empire's borders, which finally collapsed at the end of 406, as Vandals, Alans, Suebi, and other tribes joined the Goths in devastating and overrunning the Empire's western provinces. In 410, the Visigoths sacked Rome.

Economic conditions continued to deteriorate. Cities in Britain, Gaul, Germany, and Spain lay abandoned. Other metropolises saw their populations dwindle and production stagnate. The great network of Roman roads was not maintained, and trade in the West almost disappeared or passed into the hands of Greeks, Syrians, and Jews from the east.

In 451 Attila (c. 406–453), called "the Scourge of God," led his Huns into Gaul, where he was defeated by a coalition of Germans and the remnants of the Roman army. He died two years later, having come within a hairsbreadth of turning Europe into a province of a Mongolian empire. But Rome's misfortunes persisted. In 455, Rome was again sacked, this time by the Vandals. Additional regions fell under the control of Germanic chieftains. Germanic soldiers in the pay of Rome gained control of the government and dictated the choice of emperor. In 476, German officers overthrew the Roman Emperor Romulus and placed a fellow German, Odoacer, on the throne. This act is traditionally regarded as the end of the Roman Empire in the west.

The Underlying Reasons for Decline

What were the underlying causes for the decline and fall of the Roman Empire in the west? Surely no other question has intrigued the historical imagination more than this one. Implicit in the answers suggested by historians and philosophers is a concern for their own civilization. Will it suffer the same fate as Rome?

To analyze so monumental a development as the fall of Rome, some preliminary observations are necessary. First, the fall of Rome was a process lasting hundreds of years; it was not a single event that occurred in A.D. 476. Second, only the western half of the Empire fell. The eastern half—wealthier, more populous, less afflicted with civil wars, and less exposed to barbarian invasions—survived as the Byzantine Empire until the middle of the fifteenth century. Third, no single explanation suffices to account for Rome's decline; multiple forces operated concurrently to bring about the fall.

The Role of the Barbarians   The pressures exerted by the barbarians along an immense frontier aggravated Rome's internal problems. The barbarian attacks left border regions impoverished and depopulated. The Empire imposed high taxes and labor services on its citizens in order to strengthen the armed forces, causing the overburdened middle and lower classes to hate the imperial government that took so much from them.

Spiritual Considerations   The classical mentality, once brimming with confidence about the potentialities of the individual and the power of the intellect, suffered a failure of nerve. The urban upper class, upon whom the responsibility for preserving cosmopolitan Greco-Roman culture traditionally rested, became dissolute and apathetic, no longer taking an interest in public life. The aristocrats secluded themselves behind the walls of their fortified country estates; many did not lift a finger to help the Empire. The townsmen demonstrated their disenchantment by avoiding public service and by rarely organizing resistance forces against the barbarian invaders. The great bulk of the Roman citizenry, apathetic and indifferent, simply gave up, despite the fact that they overwhelmingly outnumbered the barbarian hordes.

Political and Military Considerations   The Roman government itself contributed to this spiritual malaise through its increasingly autocratic tendencies, which culminated in the regimented rule of Diocletian and Constantine. The insatiable demands and regulations of the state in the Late Roman Empire sapped the initiative and civic spirit of its citizens. The ruined middle and lower classes withdrew their loyalty. For many the state had become the enemy, and its administration was hated and feared more than the barbarians.

In the Late Roman Empire, the quality of Roman soldiers deteriorated, and the legions failed to defend the borders, even though they outnumbered the German invaders. During the third century the army consisted predominantly of the provincial peasantry. These nonurban, non-Italian, semicivilized soldiers, often the dregs of society, were not committed to Greco-Roman civilization. They had little comprehension of Rome's mission, and at times used their power to attack the cities and towns. The emperors also recruited large numbers of barbarians into the army to fill depleted ranks. Ultimately, the army consisted predominantly of barbarians, as both legionnaires and officers. Although these Germans made brave soldiers, they too had little loyalty to Greco-Roman civilization and to the Roman state. Moreover, barbarian units serving with the Roman army under their own commanders did not easily submit to traditional discipline or training. This deterioration of the Roman army occurred because many young citizens evaded conscription. No longer imbued with patriotism, they considered military service a servitude to be shunned.

Economic Considerations   Among the economic causes contributing to the decline of the Roman Empire in the west were population decline, the failure to achieve a breakthrough in technology, the heavy burden of taxation, and the economic decentralization that abetted political decentralization.

Largely because of war and epidemics, the population of the Empire may have shrunk from 70 million during the pax Romana to 50 million in the Late Roman Empire. This decline adversely affected the Empire in at least three important ways. First, at the same time that the population was declining, the costs of running the Empire were spiraling, which created a terrible burden for taxpayers. Second, fewer workers were available for agriculture, the most important industry of the Empire. Third, population decline reduced the manpower available for the army, forcing emperors to permit the establishment of Germanic colonies within the Empire's borders to serve as feeders for the army. This situation led to the barbarization of the army.

The failure to expand industry and commerce was another economic reason for the Empire's decline. Instead of expanding industry and trade, towns maintained their wealth by exploiting the countryside. The Roman cities were centers of civilized life and opulence, but they lacked industries. They spent, but they did not produce. The towns were dominated by landlords whose estates lay beyond the city and whose income derived from grain, oil, and wine. Manufacturing was rudimentary, confined essentially to textiles, pottery, furniture, and glassware. The methods of production were simple, the market limited, the cost of transportation high, and agricultural productivity low—the labor of perhaps nineteen peasants was required to support one townsman. Such a fundamentally unhealthy economy could not weather the dislocations caused by uninterrupted warfare and the demands of a mushrooming bureaucracy and military.

With the barbarians pressing on the borders, the increased military expenditures overstrained the Empire's resources. To pay for the food, uniforms, arms, and armor of the soldiers, taxes rose, growing too heavy for peasants and townsmen. The state also requisitioned wood and grain and demanded that citizens maintain roads and bridges. The government often resorted to force to collect taxes and exact services. Crushed by these demands, many peasants simply abandoned their farms and sought the protection of large landowners, or turned to banditry.

Contributing to the economic decentralization was the growth of industries on *latifundia,* the large fortified estates owned by wealthy aristocrats. Producing exclusively for the local market, these estates contributed to the impoverishment of urban centers by reducing the number of customers available to buy goods made in the cities. As life grew more desperate, urban craftsmen and small farmers sought the protection of these large landlords, whose estates grew in size and importance. The growth of latifundia was accompanied by the decline of cities and the transformation of independent peasants into virtual serfs.

These great estates were also new centers of political power that the imperial government could not curb. A new society was taking shape in the Late Roman Empire. The center of gravity had shifted from the city to the landed estate, from the imperial bureaucrats to the local aristocrats. These developments epitomized the decay of ancient civilization and presaged the Middle Ages.

Chronology 4.1 ❧ Rome

509 B.C.	Expulsion of the Etruscan monarch
287	The end of the Struggle of the Orders
264–241	First Punic War; Rome acquires provinces
218–201	Second Punic War; Hannibal is defeated
133–122	Land reforms by the Gracchi brothers; they are murdered by the Senate
88–83	Conflict between Sulla and the forces of Marius; Sulla emerges as dictator
49–44	Caesar is dictator of Rome
27 B.C.	Octavian assumes the title *Augustus* and becomes, in effect, the first Roman emperor; start of the pax Romana
A.D. 180	Marcus Aurelius dies; the end of the pax Romana
212	Roman citizenship is granted to virtually all free inhabitants of Roman provinces
235–285	Military anarchy; attacks by barbarians
285–305	Diocletian tries to deal with the crisis by creating a regimented state
378	Battle of Adrianople; the Goths defeat the Roman legions
406	Borders collapse, and barbarians pour into the Empire
476	The end of the Roman Empire in the West

The Roman Achievement

Rome left the West a rich heritage that endured for centuries. The idea of a world empire united by a common law and effective government never died. In the centuries following the collapse of Rome, people continued to be attracted to the idea of a unified and peaceful world-state. By preserving and adding to the philosophy, literature, science, and arts of ancient Greece, Rome strengthened the foundations of the Western cultural tradition. Latin, the language of Rome, lived on long after Rome perished. The Western church fathers wrote in Latin, and during the Middle Ages, Latin was the language of learning, literature, and law. From Latin came Italian, French, Spanish, Portuguese, and Romanian. Roman law, the quintessential expression of Roman genius, influenced church law and formed the basis of the legal codes of most

European states. Finally, Christianity, the core religion of the West, was born within the Roman Empire and was greatly influenced by Roman law and organization.

Notes

1. Cicero, *De Re Publica,* trans. by C. W. Keyes (Cambridge, Mass.: Harvard University Press, Loeb Classical Library, 1928), 3.22 (p. 211).

2. Naphtali Lewis and Meyer Reinhold, *Roman Civilization: Sourcebook II: The Empire* (New York: Harper & Row, 1966), pp. 535, 539, 540, 547.

Suggested Reading

Boardman, John, et al., eds., *The Oxford History of the Classical World* (1986). Essays on all facets of Roman culture.

Boren, H. C., *Roman Society* (1977). A social, economic, and cultural history of the Republic and the Empire; written with the student in mind.

Chambers, Mortimer, ed., *The Fall of Rome* (1963). A valuable collection of readings.

Christ, Karl, *The Romans* (1984). A recent survey.

Crawford, M., *The Roman Republic* (1982). A recent and reliable survey, with many quotations from original sources.

Grant, Michael, *History of Rome* (1978). A synthesis of Roman history by a leading classical scholar; valuable for both the Republic and the Empire.

Lewis, Naphtali, and Reinhold, Meyer, eds., *Roman Civilization* (1966). A two-volume collection of source readings.

Ogilvie, R. M., *Roman Literature and Society* (1980). An introductory survey of Latin literature.

Veyne, Paul, ed., *A History of Private Life* (1987). All phases of Roman social life.

Wardman, Alan, *Rome's Debt to Greece* (1976). Roman attitudes toward the Greek world.

White, Lynn, ed., *The Transformation of the Roman World* (1973). A useful collection of essays on the transformation of the ancient world and the emergence of the Middle Ages.

Review Questions

1. What were the causes, results, and significance of the plebeian-patrician controversy?
2. What factors enabled Rome to conquer Italy? What were the consequences of Roman expansion?
3. How was Roman cultural life influenced by Greek civilization?
4. Analyze the reasons for the collapse of the Roman Republic.
5. The Roman world-state completed the trend toward cosmopolitanism and universalism that had emerged during the Hellenistic Age. Discuss this statement.
6. How did Roman law incorporate Stoic principles? What does modern law owe to Roman law?
7. Describe the crisis that afflicted Rome in the third century.
8. How did Diocletian and Constantine try to deal with the Empire's crisis?
9. Analyze the spiritual, military, political, and economic reasons for the decline of the Roman Empire.

Chapter ✌ 5

Early Christianity:
A World Religion

As confidence in human reason and hope for happiness in this world waned in the last centuries of the Roman Empire, a new outlook began to take hold. Evident in philosophy and in the popularity of oriental religions, this viewpoint stressed escape from an oppressive world and communion with a higher reality. Christianity evolved and expanded within this setting of declining classicism and heightening other-worldliness. As one response to a declining Hellenism, Christianity offered a spiritually disillusioned Greco-Roman world a reason for living—the hope of personal immortality. The triumph of Christianity marked a break with classical antiquity and a new stage in the evolution of the West, for there was a fundamental difference between the classical and the Christian concepts of God, the individual, and the purpose of life. ✦

Origins of Christianity

Judaism in the First Century B.C.

A Palestinian Jew named Jesus was executed by the Roman authorities during the reign of Tiberius (A.D. 14–37), who was Augustus' successor. At the time, few people paid much attention to what proved to be one of the most pivotal events in world history. In the quest for the historical Jesus, scholars have stressed the importance of both his Jewishness and the religious ferment that prevailed in Palestine in the first century B.C. Jesus' ethical teachings are rooted in the moral outlook of Old Testament prophets and, says Andrew M. Greeley, a student of religion, must be viewed as

> *a logical extension of the Hebrew Scriptures . . . a product of the whole religious environment of which Jesus was a part. Jesus defined*

> *himself as a Jew, was highly conscious of the Jewishness of his message*
> *and would have found it impossible to conceive of himself as anything*
> *but Jewish. . . . The teachings of Jesus, then, must be placed squarely in*
> *the Jewish religious context of the time.*[1]

In the first century B.C., four principal social-religious parties or sects existed among the Palestinian Jews: Sadducees, Pharisees, Essenes, and Zealots. Composed of the upper stratum of Jewish society—influential landed gentry and hereditary priests who controlled the temple in Jerusalem—the Sadducees insisted on a strict interpretation of Mosaic Law and the perpetuation of temple ceremonies. Challenging the Sadducees, the Pharisees adopted a more flexible attitude toward Mosaic Law; they allowed for discussion and varying interpretations of the Law and granted authority to oral tradition as well as to written Scripture. The Pharisees had the support of the bulk of the Jewish nation. The third religious party, the Essenes, established a semimonastic community near the Dead Sea. Another sect, the Zealots, demanded that the Jews neither pay taxes to Rome nor acknowledge the authority of the Roman emperor. Devoted patriots, the Zealots engaged in acts of resistance to Rome, which culminated in the great revolt of A.D. 66–70 (see page 96).

The concept of personal immortality is barely mentioned in the Hebrew Scriptures. Unlike the Sadducees, the Pharisees believed in life after death. A later addition to Hebrew religious thought, probably acquired from Persia, the idea had gained wide acceptance by the time of Jesus. The Essenes, too, believed in the physical resurrection of the body, but gave this doctrine a more compelling meaning by tying it to the immediate coming of God's kingdom.

In addition to the afterlife, another widely recognized idea in the first century B.C. was the belief in a Messiah, a redeemer chosen by God to liberate Israel from foreign rule. In the days of the Messiah, it was predicted, Israel would be free, the exiles would return, and the Jews would be blessed with peace, unity, and prosperity. Jesus (c. 4 B.C.–c. A.D. 29) performed his ministry within this context of Jewish religious-national expectations and longings. The hopes of Jesus' early followers encompassed a lower-class dissatisfaction with the aristocratic Sadducees, a Pharisee emphasis on prophetic ideals and the afterlife, an Essene preoccupation with the end-of-days, a belief in the nearness of God and the need for repentance, and a conquered people's yearning for a Messiah who would liberate their land from Roman rule and establish God's reign.

Jesus: Moral Transformation of the Individual

Jesus himself wrote nothing, and nothing was written about him during his lifetime. In the generations following his death, both Roman and Jewish historians paid him scant attention. Consequently, virtually everything we know about Jesus derives from the Bible's New Testament, which was written decades after Jesus' death by devotees seeking to convey a religious truth and to propagate a faith. Modern historians have rigorously and critically analyzed the New Testament; their analyses have provided some insights into Jesus and his beliefs, though much about him remains obscure.

At about the age of thirty, no doubt influenced by John the Baptist, Jesus began to preach the imminent coming of the reign of God and the need for repentance—a moral transformation so that a person could gain entrance into God's kingdom. For Jesus, the coming of the kingdom was imminent; the process leading to the establishment of God's kingdom on earth had already begun. A new order would soon be established in which God would govern his people righteously and mercifully. Hence the present moment became critical for him—a time for spiritual preparedness and penitence—because an individual's thoughts, goals, and actions would determine whether he or she would gain entrance to the kingdom. People must change their attitudes, he said. They must eliminate base, lustful, hostile, and selfish feelings; they must stop pursuing wealth and power; they must purify their hearts and show their love for God and their fellow human beings.

Although Jesus did not intend to lead his fellow Jews away from their ancestral religion, he was distressed with the Judaism of his day. The rabbis taught the Golden Rule, as well as God's love and mercy for his children, but it seemed to Jesus that these ethical considerations were being undermined by an exaggerated rabbinical concern with ritual, restrictions, and the fine points of the Law, and that the center of Judaism had shifted from prophetic values to obedience to rules and prohibitions regulating the smallest details of daily life. Such legalism and ritualism, Jesus held, dealt only with an individual's visible behavior; they did not penetrate to the person's inner being and lead to a moral transformation. The inner person concerned Jesus, and it was an inner change that he sought. With the fervor of a prophet, he urged a moral transformation of human character through a direct encounter between the individual and God.

Jewish scribes and priests, guardians of the faith, regarded Jesus as a troublemaker who threatened ancient traditions and undermined respect for the Sabbath. To the Romans who ruled Palestine, Jesus was a political agitator who could ignite Jewish messianic expectations into a revolt against Rome. After Jewish leaders turned Jesus over to the Roman authorities, the Roman procurator, Pontius Pilate, sentenced him to death by crucifixion.

Some Jews, believing that Jesus was an inspired prophet or even the long-awaited Messiah, had become his followers—the chief of these were the Twelve Disciples. At the time of Jesus' death, Christianity was not a separate religion but a small Hebrew sect with dim prospects for survival. What established the Christian movement and gave it strength was the belief of Jesus' followers that he was raised from the dead on the third day after he was buried. The doctrine of the resurrection made possible the belief in Jesus as a divine savior-god, who had come to earth to show people the way to heaven.

In the years immediately following the crucifixion, the religion of Jesus was confined almost exclusively to Jews, who could more appropriately be called Jewish-Christians. The word *Christian* came from a name given Jesus: *Christ* (the Lord's Anointed, the Messiah). Before Christianity could realize the universal implications of Jesus' teachings and become a world religion, as distinct from a Jewish sect, it had to extricate itself from Jewish ritual, politics, and culture. This achievement was the work of a Hellenized Jew named Saul, known to the world as Saint Paul.

Saint Paul: From a Jewish Sect to a World Religion

Saint Paul (A.D. c. 5–c. 67) came from the Greek city of Tarsus in southeastern Asia Minor. He belonged to the Diaspora, or the "Dispersion"—the millions of Jews living outside Palestine. Non-Jews, or *Gentiles,* coming into contact with Jews of the Diaspora, were often favorably impressed with Hebrew monotheism, ethics, and family life. Some Gentiles embraced Hebrew monotheism, but refused to adhere to provisions of the Law requiring circumcision and dietary regulations. Among these Gentiles and non-Palestinian Jews who

Saint Paul. Early Christian art brought to an end the classical concern with the visible real world. Mosaics of translucent glass, such as this of Saint Paul, transformed the interiors of churches into heavenly abodes. Bodies assumed unnatural poses and became spiritualized. (*Scala/Art Resource*)

were greatly influenced by the Greco-Roman milieu, Jesus' Apostles would find receptive listeners.

At first Saul persecuted the followers of Jesus, but then he underwent a spiritual transformation and became a convert to Jesus. Serving as a zealous missionary of Jewish Christianity in the Diaspora, Saint Paul preached to his fellow Jews in synagogues. Recognizing that the Christian message applied to non-Jews as well, Paul urged spreading it to the Gentiles. In the process of his missionary activity—and he traveled extensively through the Roman Empire—Paul formulated doctrines that represented a fundamental break with Judaism and became the heart of this new religion. Paul taught that all people, both Jew and Gentile, were sinners, as a consequence of Adam's original defiance of God; that Jesus was a savior-god who had come to earth to save all people from sin and death; that by dying on the cross, he had atoned for the sins of all and made it possible for all to have eternal life in heaven; and that by believing in Jesus, people could gain this salvation. Alone, the individual was helpless, possessed by sin, unable to overcome his or her wicked nature. Jesus was the only hope, said Paul.

In attempting to reach the Gentiles, Saint Paul had to disentangle Christianity from a Jewish sociocultural context. Thus, he held that neither Gentile nor Jewish followers of Jesus were bound by the hundreds of rituals and rules that constitute Mosaic Law. As a consequence of Jesus' coming, Paul insisted, Mosaic regulations were obsolete and a hindrance to missionary activity among the Gentiles. To Paul, the new Christian community was the true fulfillment of Judaism; it was granted the promise that God had earlier bestowed on Israel. The Jews regarded their faith as a national religion, bound organically with the history of their people. For Paul, the new Christian community was not a nation but an *oikoumene,* a world community. To this extent, Christianity shared in the universalism of the Hellenistic Age. Paul held that Jesus not only fulfilled the messianic aspirations of the Jews, but fulfilled the spiritual needs and expectations of all peoples.

In preaching the doctrine of a risen Savior and insisting that Mosaic Law had been superseded, Paul, whatever his intentions, was breaking with his Jewish roots and transforming a Jewish sect into a new religion. Separating Christianity from Judaism enormously increased its appeal for non-Jews who were attracted to Hebrew ethical monotheism but repelled by circumcision, dietary regulations, and other strict requirements of Mosaic Law. Paul built on the personalism and universalism implicit in the teachings of Jesus (and the Hebrew prophets) to create a religion intended not for a people with its own particular history, culture, and land, but for all humanity.

Spread and Triumph of Christianity

By establishing Christianity's independence from Judaism, Saint Paul made the new religion fit for export to the Greco-Roman world. But its growth was

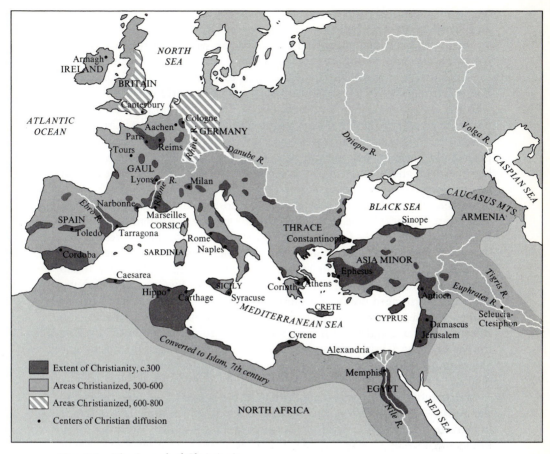

Map 5.1   The Spread of Christianity

slow. Originating in the first century, Christianity took firm root in the second, grew extensively in the third, and became the official religion of the Roman Empire at the end of the fourth century.

The Appeal of Christianity

The triumph of Christianity was related to a corresponding decline in the vitality of Hellenism and a shift in cultural emphasis—a movement from reason to emotion and revelation. Offering comforting solutions to the existential problems of life and death, religion demonstrated a greater capacity to stir human hearts than reason did. Hellenism had invented the tools of rational thought, but the power of mythical thought was never entirely subdued. By the Late Roman Empire, science and philosophy were unable to compete with mysticism and myth. Mystery cults, which promised personal salvation, were spreading and gaining followers. Neo-Platonists yearned for a mystical union with the One. Astrology and magic, which offered supernatural explanations for the operations of nature, were also popular. This drift away from rational and worldly values helped prepare the way for Christianity. In a culturally stagnating and spiritually troubled Greco-Roman world, Christianity gave to life a new meaning and offered to disillusioned men and women a new hope.

The Christian message of a divine Savior, a concerned Father, and brotherly love inspired people who were dissatisfied with the world of here-and-now, who felt no attachment to city or empire, who derived no inspiration from philosophy, and who suffered from a profound sense of loneliness. Christianity offered the individual what the city and the Roman world-state could not: a profoundly personal relationship with God, an intimate connection with a higher world, and membership in a community of the faithful who cared for one another.

Stressing the intellect and self-reliance, Greco-Roman thought did not provide for the emotional needs of the ordinary person. Christianity addressed itself to this defect in the Greco-Roman outlook. The poor, the oppressed, and the slaves were attracted to the personality, life, death, and resurrection of Jesus, his love for all, and his concern for suffering humanity. They found spiritual sustenance in a religion that offered a hand of love, that taught that a person of worth need not be well-born, rich, educated, or talented. To people burdened with misfortune and terrified by death, Christianity held the promise of eternal life, a kingdom of heaven where they would be comforted by God the Father. Thus, Christianity gave to the common person what the aristocratic values of Greco-Roman civilization generally did not—hope and a sense of dignity.

Christianity's success was due not only to the appeal of its message but to the power of an institution, the Christian church, which grew into a strong organization uniting the faithful. To city-dwellers—lonely, alienated, disillusioned with public affairs, stranded mortals groping for a sense of community—the church that called its members brother and sister filled an elemental need of human beings to belong. The church welcomed women converts, who were often the first to join and brought their menfolk after them. Among other reasons, the church attracted women because it commanded that husbands treat their wives kindly, remain faithful, and provide for the children. The church won new converts and retained the loyalty of the old ones by providing social services for the poor and infirm, welcoming slaves, criminals, sinners, and other outcasts, and offering a hand of brotherhood and comfort during difficult times.

The ability of an evolving Christianity to assimilate elements from Greek philosophy and even from the mystery religions also contributed in no small measure to its growth. By becoming infused with Greek philosophy, Christianity was able to present itself in terms intelligible to those versed in Greek learning, and was thus able to attract some educated people. Because some Christian doctrines (a risen savior-god, a virgin and her child, life after death), practices (baptism), and holy days (December 25) either paralleled or were adopted from the mystery religions, it became relatively easy to win converts from these rivals.

Christianity and Rome

Generally tolerant of religions, the Roman government at first did not significantly interfere with Christianity. Indeed, Christianity benefited in many ways from its association with the Roman Empire. Christian missionaries traveled throughout the Empire, over roads and across seas made safe by Roman arms. The common Greek dialect, the *koine,* spoken in most parts of the Empire, facilitated the task of missionaries. Had the Mediterranean world been fractured into separate and competing states, the spread of Christianity might well have faced an insurmountable obstacle. The universalism of the Roman Empire, which made citizenship available to peoples of many nationalities, prepared the way for the universalism of Christianity, which welcomed membership from all nations.

As the number of Christians increased, Roman officials began to fear the Christians as subversives, preaching allegiance to God and not to Rome. To many Romans, Christians were enemies of the social order—strange people who would not accept the state gods, would not engage in Roman festivals, scorned gladiator contests, stayed away from public baths, glorified nonviolence, refused to honor deceased emperors as gods, and worshiped a crucified criminal as Lord. Romans ultimately found in Christians a universal scapegoat for the ills burdening the Empire, such as famines, plagues, and military reverses. In an effort to stamp out Christianity, emperors resorted to persecution. Christians were imprisoned, beaten, starved, burned alive, torn apart by wild beasts in the arena for the amusement of the Romans, and crucified. However, the persecutions did not last long enough to extirpate the new religion. Actually, they strengthened the determination of most of the faithful and won new converts who were awed by the extraordinary courage of the martyrs, who willingly died for their faith.

Unable to crush Christianity by persecution, Roman emperors decided to gain the support of the growing number of Christians within the Empire. In A.D. 313, Constantine, genuinely attracted to Christianity, issued the Edict of Milan, granting toleration to Christians. By A.D. 392, Theodosius I had made Christianity the state religion of the Empire and declared the worship of pagan gods illegal.

Christianity and Greek Philosophy

Christianity synthesized both the Hebrew and the Greco-Roman traditions. Having emerged from Judaism, it assimilated Hebrew monotheism and prophetic morality and retained the Old Testament as the Word of God. As the new religion evolved, it also assimilated elements of Greek philosophy. But there was a struggle between conservatives who wanted no dealings with pagan philosophy and those believers who recognized the value of Greek thought to Christianity.

To conservative church fathers, classical philosophy was all in error because it did not derive from divine revelation. As the final statement of God's truth,

Christianity superseded both pagan philosophy and pagan religions. These conservatives feared that studying classical authors would contaminate Christian morality (did not Plato propose a community of wives, and did not the dramatists treat violent passions?) and promote heresy (was not classical literature replete with references to pagan gods?). For these church fathers there could be no compromise between Greek philosophy and Christian revelation.

Some early church fathers, however, defended the value of studying classical literature. They maintained that Greek philosophy contained a dim glimmer of God's truth, a pre-Christian insight into divine wisdom. Christ had corrected and fulfilled an insight reached by the philosophic mind. Knowledge of Greek philosophy, they argued, helped a Christian to explain his beliefs logically and to argue intelligently with pagan critics of Christian teachings.

Utilizing the language and categories of Greek philosophy, Christian intellectuals transformed Christianity from a simple ethical creed into a theoretical system, a theology. This effort to express Christian beliefs in terms of Greek rationalism is referred to as the Hellenization of Christianity. Greek philosophy enabled Christians to explain in rational terms God's existence and revelation.

Christ was depicted as the divine *logos* (reason) in human form. The Stoic teaching that all people are fundamentally equal because they share in universal reason could be formulated in Christian terms—that all are united in Christ. Stoic ethics, which stressed moderation, self-control, and brotherhood, could be assimilated by Christian revelation. Particularly in Platonism, which drew a distinction between a world perceived by the senses and a higher order open to the intellect, Christian thinkers found a congenial vehicle for expressing Christian beliefs. The perfect and universal Forms, or Ideas, which Plato maintained were the true goal of knowledge and the source of ethical standards, were held by Christians to exist in God's mind.

That Greek philosophy exercised a hold over church doctrine is of immense importance; it meant that rational thought, the priceless achievement of the Greek mind, was not lost. But this Hellenization of Christianity was not a triumph of classicism over Christianity. The reverse is the essential truth: Christianity triumphed over Hellenism; Greek philosophy had to sacrifice its essential autonomy to the requirements of Christian revelation, that is, reason had to fit into a Christian framework. Moreover, although Christianity made use of Greek philosophy, Christian truth ultimately rested on faith, not reason.

Growth of Christian Organization, Doctrine, and Attitudes

Early in its history the church developed along hierarchical lines. Those members of the Christian community who had the authority to preside over the celebration of the Mass—breaking bread and offering wine as Christ had done in the Last Supper—were called either priests or bishops. Gradually the designation *bishop* was reserved for the one clergyman in the community with the authority to resolve disputes over doctrines and practices. Regarded as the successors to Christ's Twelve Disciples, bishops supervised religious activities within their regions.

The Primacy of the Bishop of Rome

The bishop of Rome, later to be called the pope, claimed primacy over the other bishops. In developing the case for their supremacy over the church organization, bishops of Rome increasingly referred to the famous New Testament passage in which Jesus says to his Disciple Simon (also called Peter): " 'And I tell you, you are Peter, and on this rock I will build my church' " (Matthew 16:18). Because *Peter* in Greek means *rock* (*petra*), it was argued that Christ had chosen Peter to succeed him as ruler of the universal church. It was commonly accepted that Saint Peter had established a church in Rome and was martyred there, so it was argued further that the Roman bishop inherited the power that Christ had passed on to Peter.

The Rise of Monasticism

Inspired by Jesus' example of self-denial and seeking to escape from the agonies and corruptions of this world, some ardent Christians withdrew to deserts and mountains in search of spiritual renewal. In their zeal for holiness they sometimes practiced extreme forms of asceticism—self-flogging, wearing spiked corsets, eating only herbs, or living for years on a column many feet above the ground. Gradually, colonies of these hermits sprang up, particularly in Egypt; in time, the leaders of these monastic communities drew up written rules that required monks to refrain from bodily abuses and to engage in manual labor.

The monastic ideal spread from east to west. The principal figure in the shaping of monasticism in the West was Saint Benedict, who founded a monastery at Monte Cassino, Italy, in 529. The rule of Saint Benedict called for the monks to live in poverty and to study, labor, and obey the abbot, the head of the monastery. Monks were required to pray often, work hard, talk little, and surrender private property. In imposing discipline and regulations, Benedict eliminated the excessive and eccentric individualism of the early monks; he socialized and institutionalized the spiritual impulse that led monks to withdraw from the world. Benedict demonstrated the same genius for administration that Romans had shown in organizing and governing their Empire. His rule became the standard for monasteries in Western Europe.

Doctrinal Disputes

Christ's sayings and actions were preserved by word of mouth. Sometime around A.D. 66–70, Saint Mark formulated the Christian message from this oral tradition and perhaps from some material that had been put in writing

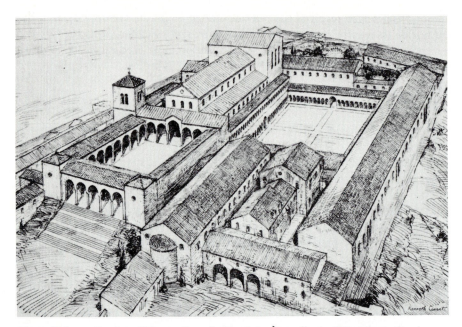

Plan of Monte Cassino Abbey.   Founded by Saint Benedict in 529, Monte Cassino Abbey still serves as a religious community today, although the buildings have had to be rebuilt several times after the ravages of war. Benedict's rule instructed monks to live in poverty, to labor, to study, and to aid the sick and the poor. (*From Kenneth John Conant,* The Pelican History of Art: Carolingian and Romanesque Architecture, 800–1200 [*Penguin Books, 1959*]. *Reprinted by permission of Penguin Books Ltd.*)

earlier. Later Saint Matthew and Saint Luke, relying heavily on Mark's account, wrote somewhat longer Gospels. The Gospels of Mark, Matthew, and Luke are called *synoptic* because their approach to Jesus is very similar. The remaining Gospel, written by Saint John, varies significantly from the Synoptic Gospels. The Synoptic Gospels, The Gospel According to Saint John, Acts of the Apostles, the twenty-one Epistles, including those written by Saint Paul, and Revelation constitute the twenty-seven Books of the Christian New Testament.

The early Christians had a Bible and a clergy to teach it. But Holy Writ could be interpreted differently by equally sincere believers, and controversies over doctrine threatened the unity of the early church. The most important controversy concerned how people viewed the relationship between God and Christ. Arius (A.D. 250–336), a Greek priest in Alexandria, led one faction; he denied the complete divinity of Christ—one of the basic tenets of the church. To Arius, Christ was more than man but less than God; there was no permanent union between God and Christ; the Father alone was eternal and truly God. The Council of Nicaea (A.D. 325), the first assembly of bishops from all parts of the Roman world, was called to settle the controversy. The Council condemned Arius and ruled that God and Christ were of the same substance, coequal and coeternal. The position adopted at Nicaea became the basis of the Nicene Creed, which remains the official doctrine of the church. Although Arianism, the name given Arius' heresy, won converts for a time, it eventually lost supporters.

Christianity and Society

Although salvation was their ultimate aim, Christians still had to dwell within the world and deal with its imperfections. In the process, Christian thinkers challenged some of the mores of Greco-Roman society and formulated attitudes that would endure for centuries. Influenced by passages in the New Testament that condemned acts of revenge and the shedding of blood, some early Christians refused military service. Others, however, held that in a sinful world defense of the state was necessary, and without concealment or apology they served in the army. After Roman emperors professed Christianity, Christians began to serve the government with greater frequency. With the barbarians menacing the borders, these officials could not advocate nonviolence. Christian theorists began to argue that under certain circumstances—to punish injustice or to restore peace—war was just. But even such wars must not entail unnecessary violence.

Sharing in the patriarchal tradition of Jewish society, Saint Paul subjected the wife to her husband's authority. "Wives, be subject to your husbands, as to the Lord. For the husband is the head of the wife as Christ is the head of the church" (Ephesians 5:22–23).[2] But Paul also held that all are baptized in Christ: "There is neither Jew nor Greek, there is neither slave nor free, there is neither male nor female; for you are all one in Christ Jesus" (Galatians 3:28). Consequently, both sexes were subject to divine law; both men and women possessed moral autonomy. The early church held to strict standards on sexual matters. It condemned adultery and held virginity for spiritual reasons in high esteem.

Christians waged no war against slavery, which was widely practiced and universally accepted in the ancient world. Saint Paul commanded slaves to obey their masters, and many Christians were themselves slave owners. However, Christians taught that slaves too were children of God, sought their conversion, and urged owners not to treat them harshly.

Saint Augustine: The Christian World-View

During the early history of Christianity, many learned men, "fathers of the church," explained and defended church teachings. Most of the leading early fathers wrote in Greek, but in the middle of the fourth century, three great Latin writers—Saint Jerome, Saint Ambrose, and Saint Augustine—profoundly influenced the course of Christianity in the West.

Saint Jerome (A.D. 340–320) wrote about the lives of the saints and pro-

The Antioch Chalice. From the fourth century A.D., this cup is the earliest surviving Christian chalice. The transformation of the wine of the mass into the very blood of Christ was central to Christian worship. In later medieval times, historical kings and knights in literature would search for the original chalice of the Last Supper, the Holy Grail. (*The Metropolitan Museum of Art, The Cloisters Collection, 1950*)

moted the spread of monasticism. But his greatest achievement was the translation of the Old and New Testaments from Hebrew and Greek into Latin. Jerome's text, the common or Vulgate version of the Bible, became the official edition of the Bible for the western church.

Saint Ambrose (A.D. 340–397), bishop of Milan, Italy, instructed the clergy to deal humanely with the poor, the old, the sick, and the orphaned. He urged clerics not to pursue wealth, but to exercise humility and to avoid favoring the rich over the poor. Ambrose sought to defend the autonomy of the church against the power of the state. His dictum that "the Emperor is within the church, not above it" became a cardinal principle of the medieval church.

The most important Christian theoretician in the Late Roman Empire was Saint Augustine (A.D. 354–430), bishop of Hippo in North Africa and author of *The City of God*. Augustine became the principal architect of the Christian outlook that succeeded a dying classicism.

In 410, when Augustine was in his fifties, Visigoths sacked Rome—a disaster for which the classical consciousness was unprepared. Throughout the Empire people panicked. Pagans blamed the tragedy on Christianity. Even Christians expressed anxiety. Why were the righteous also suffering? Where was the kingdom of God on earth that had been prophesied? In *The City of God*, Augustine maintained that the worldly city could never be the central concern of Christians. The misfortunes of Rome, therefore, should not distress Christians unduly, for the true Christian was a citizen of a heavenly city that could not possibly be pillaged by ungodly barbarians, but would endure forever. Compared to God's heavenly city, the decline of Rome was unimportant. What really mattered in history, said Augustine, was not the coming to be or the passing away of cities and empires, but the individual's entrance into heaven or hell.

But Augustine did not hold that by his death Christ had opened the door to heaven for all. The majority of humanity remained condemned to eternal punishment, said Augustine; only a handful had the gift of faith and the promise of heaven. People could not by their own efforts overcome a sinful nature; a moral and spiritual regeneration stemmed not from human will power but from God's grace. The small number endowed with God's grace constituted the City of God. These people lived on earth as visitors only, for they awaited deliverance to the Kingdom of Christ. Most inhabitants of the earthly city were destined for eternal punishment in hell. A perpetual conflict existed between the two cities and between their inhabitants; one city stood for sin and corruption, the other for God's truth and perfection.

For Augustine, the highest good was not of this world but consisted of eternal life with God. His distinction between this higher world of perfection and a lower world of corruption remained influential throughout the Middle Ages.

Augustine repudiated the distinguishing feature of classical humanism—the autonomy of reason. For him, ultimate wisdom could not be achieved through rational thought alone; reason had to be guided by faith. Without faith there could be no true knowledge, no understanding. Philosophy had no validity if it did not first accept as absolutely true the existence of God and the authority of his revelation. Thus, Augustine upheld the primacy of faith, but he did not necessarily regard reason as an enemy of faith, and he did not call for an end to rational speculation. What he denied of the classical view was that reason *alone* could attain wisdom. The wisdom that Augustine sought was Christian wisdom, God's revelation to humanity. The starting point for this wisdom, he said, was belief in God and the Scriptures. For Augustine, secular knowledge for its own sake was of little value; the true significance of knowledge lay in its role as a tool for comprehending God's will. Augustine adapted the classical intellectual tradition to the requirements of Christian revelation.

With Augustine, the human-centered outlook of classical humanism—which for centuries had been undergoing transformation—gave way to a God-centered world-view. The fulfillment of God's will, not the full development of human talent, became the central concern of life.

Christianity and Classical Humanism: Alternative World-Views

Christianity and classical humanism are the two principal components of the Western tradition. The value that modern Western civilization places on the individual derives ultimately from classical humanism and the Judeo-Christian tradition. Classical humanists believed that individual worth came from the individual's capacity to reason, to shape his character and his life according to rational standards. Christianity also places great stress on the individual. In the Christian view, God cares for each person; he wants people to behave righteously and to enter heaven; Christ died for all because he loves humanity. Christianity espouses active love and genuine concern for fellow human beings.

But Christianity and classical humanism also represent two essentially different world-views. The triumph of the Christian outlook signified a break with the essential meaning of classical humanism; it pointed to the end of the world of antiquity and the beginning of an age of faith, the Middle Ages. With the victory of Christianity, the ultimate goal of life shifted. Life's purpose was no longer to achieve excellence in this world through the full and creative development of human talent, but to attain salvation in a heavenly city. A person's worldly accomplishments amounted to very little if he or she did not accept God and his revelation.

In the classical view, history had no ultimate end, no ultimate meaning; periods of happiness and misery repeated themselves endlessly. In the Christian view, history is filled with spiritual meaning. It is the profound drama of individuals struggling to overcome their original sin in order to gain eternal happiness in heaven. History began with Adam and Eve's defiance of God and would end when Christ returns to earth, when evil is eradicated, when God's will prevails.

Classicism held that there was no authority above reason; early Christianity taught that without God as the starting point, knowledge was formless, purposeless, and prone to error. Classicism held that ethical standards were laws of nature that reason could discover. Through reason, individuals could arrive at those values by which they should regulate their lives. Reason would enable them to govern desires and will; it would show them where their behavior was wrong and teach them how to correct it. Early Christianity, on the other hand, maintained that ethical standards emanated from the personal will of God. Without obedience to God's commands, people would remain wicked forever; the human will, essentially sinful, could not be transformed by the promptings of reason. Only when individuals turned to God for forgiveness and guidance—only then would they find the inner strength to overcome their sinful nature. People could not perfect themselves through scientific knowledge; spiritual insight and belief in God must serve as the first principle of their lives.

For classicism, the ultimate good was sought through independent thought and action; for Christianity, ultimate good comes through knowing, obeying,

---

Chronology 5.1 ☙ Early Christianity

A.D. 29	The crucifixion of Jesus
c. 34–64	Missionary activity of Saint Paul
c. 66–70	The Gospel According to Mark is written
250–260	A decade of brutal persecution of Christians by the Romans
313	Constantine grants toleration of Christianity
320	The first convent is founded
325	The Council of Nicaea rules that God and Christ are of the same substance, coequal and coeternal
392	Theodosius I makes Christianity the state religion
430	Death of Saint Augustine
529	Monte Cassino is founded by Saint Benedict

---

and loving God. In early Christianity, the good life was identified not with worldly achievement but with eternal life. Each person must make entrance into God's kingdom the central aim of life. For the next thousand years, this distinction between heaven and earth, this otherworldly, theocentric outlook, would define the Western mentality.

Notes

1. Andrew M. Greeley, "Hippie Hero? Superpatriot? Superstar? A Christmas Biography," *New York Times Magazine* (December 23, 1973), p. 28.
2. The biblical quotations are from the *Revised Standard Version Bible*, copyright 1946, 1952, 1971 by the Division of Christian Education of the National Council of the Churches of Christ in the USA, and used by permission.

Suggested Reading

Benko, Stephen, *Pagan Rome and the Early Christians* (1984). How Romans and Greeks viewed early Christianity.

Chadwick, Henry, *The Early Church* (1967). A survey of early Christianity in its social and ideological context.

Davies, J. G., *The Early Christian Church* (1967). A splendid introduction to the first five centuries of Christianity.

Meeks, Wayne A., *The Moral World of the First Christians* (1986). Continuity and discontinuity between the moral outlook of early Christianity and that of Jewish and Greco-Roman thought.

Pelikan, Jaroslav, *The Christian Tradi-*

tion (1971), vol. 1, *The Emergence of the Catholic Tradition*. The first of a five-volume series on the history of Christian doctrine.

Perkins, Pheme, *Reading the New Testa-ment* (1978). Introduces the beginning student to the New Testament.

Wilkin, Robert L., *The Christians as the Romans Saw Them* (1984). Pagan reaction to the rise of Christianity.

Review Questions

1. Why does the life of Jesus present a problem to the historian?
2. What were Jesus' basic teachings?
3. What is the relationship of early Christianity to Judaism?
4. How did Saint Paul transform a Jewish sect into a world religion?
5. What factors contributed to the triumph of Christianity in the Roman Empire?
6. Why did some early Christian thinkers object to the study of classical literature? What arguments were advanced by the defenders of classical learning? What was the outcome of this debate? Why was it significant?
7. What were Saint Augustine's attitudes toward the fall of Rome, the worldly city, humanity, and Greek philosophy?
8. Compare and contrast the worldviews of early Christianity and classical humanism.

Good Government in the City by Ambrogio Lorenzetti—Mural in Siena's Palazzo Pubblico. (*Scala/Art Resource*)

II · The Middle Ages: The Christian Centuries

500–1400

Chapter ✾ 6

The Rise of Europe:
Fusion of Classical,
Christian, and German Traditions

The triumph of Christianity and the establishment of Germanic kingdoms on once-Roman lands constituted a new phase in Western history: the end of the ancient world and the beginning of the Middle
Ages, a period that spanned a thousand years. In the ancient world,
the locus of Greco-Roman civilization was the Mediterranean Sea; the
heartland of medieval civilization gradually shifted to the north, to
regions of Europe that Greco-Roman civilization had barely penetrated. During the Middle Ages, a common European civilization
evolved that integrated Christian, Greco-Roman, and Germanic traditions. Christianity was at the center of medieval civilization; Rome
was the spiritual capital, and Latin the language of intellectual life;
Germanic customs pervaded social and legal relationships. In the Early
Middle Ages (500–1050), the new civilization was struggling to take
form; in the High Middle Ages (1050–1300), medieval civilization
reached its height. ✾

The Medieval East

Byzantium

Three new civilizations based on religion emerged from the ruins of the Roman
Empire: Byzantium, Islam, and Latin Christendom (western and central
Europe). Although the Roman Empire in the west fell to the German tribes, the
eastern provinces survived. They did so because they were richer and more

populous and because the main Germanic and Hunnish invasions were directed at the west. In the eastern regions, Byzantine civilization took shape. Its religion was Christianity, its culture Greek, and its machinery of administration Roman. The capital, Constantinople, was a fortress city perfectly situated to resist attacks from land and sea.

During the Early Middle Ages, Byzantine civilization was economically and culturally far more advanced than the Latin West. At a time when few Westerners (Latin Christians) could read or write, Byzantine scholars studied the literature, philosophy, science, and law of ancient Greece and Rome. Whereas trade and urban life had greatly declined in the West, Constantinople was a magnificent Byzantine city of schools, libraries, open squares, and bustling markets.

Over the centuries, many differences developed between the Byzantine church and the Roman church. The pope resisted domination by the Byzantine emperor, and the Byzantines would not accept the pope as head of all Christians. The two churches quarreled over ceremonies, holy days, the display of images, and the rights of the clergy. The final break came in 1054; The Christian church split into the Roman Catholic in the West and the Eastern (Greek) Orthodox in the East, a division that still persists.

Political and cultural differences widened the rift between Latin Christendom and Byzantium. In the Byzantine Empire, Greek was the language of religion and intellectual life; in the West, Latin predominated. Latin Christians refused to recognize that the Byzantine emperors were, as they claimed, successors to the Roman emperors. Byzantine emperors were absolute rulers who held that God had chosen them to rule and to institute divine will on earth. As successors to the Roman emperors, they claimed to rule all the lands once part of the Roman Empire.

At its height, under Emperor Justinian, who reigned from 527 to 565, the Byzantine Empire included Greece, Asia Minor, Italy, southern Spain, and parts of the Near East, North Africa, and the Balkans. Over the centuries, the Byzantines faced attacks from the Germanic Lombards and Visigoths, Persians, Muslim Arabs, Seljuk Turks, and Latin Christians. The death blow to the empire was dealt by the Ottoman Turks. Originally from central Asia, they had accepted Islam and had begun to build an empire. They drove the Byzantines from Asia Minor and conquered much of the Balkans. By the beginning of the fifteenth century, the Byzantine Empire consisted of only two small territories in Greece and the city of Constantinople. In 1453 the Ottoman Turks broke through Constantinople's great walls and looted the city. After more than a thousand years, the Byzantine Empire had come to an end.

During its thousand-year history, Byzantium made a significant impact on world history. First, it prevented the Muslim Arabs from advancing into eastern Europe. Had the Arabs broken through Byzantine defenses, much of Europe might have been converted to the new faith of Islam. Another far-reaching effect arose under Justinian, when the laws of ancient Rome were codified. This monumental achievement preserved Roman law's principles of reason and justice. Today's legal codes in much of Europe and Latin America

Hagia Sophia, Constantinople. The extensive interior mosaics that once transformed the vaults of Hagia Sophia into the golden sky of heaven linked this Byzantine structure with early Christian architecture. But the heights and vast domed interior were new and became the hallmarks of the First Golden Age of Byzantine art. The emperors strongly identified themselves with Christ, and elaborate church ceremonies necessitated the presence of the emperor. Hagia Sophia provided the dramatic setting. (*Bildarchiv Foto Marburg/Art Resource*)

trace their roots to the Roman law recorded by Justinian's lawyers. The Byzantines also preserved the philosophy, science, mathematics, and literature of ancient Greece. Contacts with Byzantine civilization stimulated learning in both the Islamic world to the east and Latin Christendom to the west. Byzantium also carried a higher civilization and Orthodox Christianity to some Slavic peoples, including the Russians, of eastern and southeastern Europe. Byzantium gave the Slavs legal principles, art forms, and an alphabet—the Cyrillic, based on the Greek—that enabled them to write in their own languages.

Islam

A second civilization to arise after Rome's fall was based on the vital new religion of Islam, which emerged in the seventh century among the Arabs of Arabia. Its founder was Muhammad (c. 570–632), a prosperous merchant in the trading city of Mecca. When Muhammad was about forty, he believed that he was visited by the Angel Gabriel, who ordered him to "recite in the name of the Lord!" Transformed by this vision, Muhammad was convinced that he had been chosen to serve as a prophet. Although most desert Arabs worshiped tribal gods, in the towns and trading centers many Arabs were familiar with Judaism and Christianity, and some had accepted the idea of one God. Rejecting the many deities of the tribal religions, Muhammad offered the Arabs a new monotheistic faith, *Islam,* which means "surrender to Allah" (God).

Islamic standards of morality and rules governing daily life are set by the Koran, which Muslims believe contains the words of Allah as revealed to Muhammad. Muslims see their religion as the completion and perfection of Judaism and Christianity. They regard the ancient Hebrew prophets as messengers of God, and value their message of compassion and the oneness of humanity. Muslims also regard Jesus as a great prophet, but do not believe that he was divine. Muslims view Muhammad as the last and greatest of the prophets and see him as entirely human; they worship only Allah, the creator and ruler of heaven and earth, an all-powerful god who is merciful, compassionate, and just. According to the Koran, on the Day of Judgment, unbelievers and the wicked will be dragged into a fearful place of "scorching winds and seething water. . . . Sinners shall eat bitter fruit and drink boiling water. . . ." Faithful Muslims who have lived virtuously are promised paradise, a garden of bodily pleasures and spiritual delights.

In a little more than two decades, Muhammad united the often feuding Arabian tribes into a powerful force dedicated to Allah and the spreading of the Islamic faith. After Muhammad's death in 632, his friend and father-in-law, Abu Bakr, became his successor, or caliph. Regarded as the defender of the faith, whose power derived from Allah, the caliph governed in accordance with Muslim law as defined in the Koran. The Islamic state was a theocracy in which government and religion were inseparable. Muslims viewed God as the source of all law and political authority and the caliph as his earthly deputy. Divine law regulated all aspects of human relations. The ruler who did not enforce Koranic law failed in his duties. Thus Islam was more than a religion; it was also a system of government, society, law, and thought that bound its adherents into an all-encompassing community. The idea of a society governed by the Koran remained deeply embedded in the Muslim mind over the centuries, and is still a powerful force today.

Islam gave the many Arab tribes the unity, discipline, and organization to succeed in their wars of conquest. Under the first four caliphs, who ruled from 632 to 661, the Arabs with breathtaking speed overran the Persian Empire, stripped Byzantium of some of its provinces, and invaded Europe. Muslim warriors believed that they were engaged in a holy war (*jihad*) to spread Islam to nonbelievers and that those who died in the jihad were assured a place in paradise. A desire to escape from the barren Arabian desert and to exploit the rich Byzantine and Persian lands was another compelling reason for expansion. In the east, Islam's territory eventually extended into India and to the borders of China; in the west, it encompassed North Africa and most of Spain. But the Muslims' northward push lost momentum and was halted in 732 at the battle of Tours in central France.

In the eighth and ninth centuries under the Abbasid caliphs, Muslim civilization entered its golden age. Islamic civilization creatively integrated Arabic, Byzantine, Persian, and Indian cultural traditions. During the Early Middle Ages, when learning was at a low point in western Europe, the Muslims

Physician (right) and Attendant Preparing a Cataplasm, 1224. This illustration is from a manuscript of the *Materia Medica* by Dioscorides, who served in the Roman Army in the first century A.D. The work describes and illustrates plants used for medicinal purposes. Through the centuries following the Fall of Rome, Arabic writers had edited and amplified the work, adding drawings like this one. This illustration (with Arabic cursive script) is from a copy made by Abdallah ibn al-Fadl, an Arab living in the thirteenth century. (*Courtesy of the Freer Gallery of Art, Smithsonian Institution, Washington, D.C., accession number 32.20*)

had forged a high civilization. Muslim science, philosophy, and mathematics rested largely on the achievements of the ancient Greeks. The Muslims acquired Greek learning from the older Persian and Byzantine civilizations, which had kept alive the Greek inheritance. By translating Greek works into Arabic and commenting on them, Muslim scholars performed the great historical task of preserving the philosophic and scientific heritage of ancient Greece. Greek learning, supplemented by original contributions of Muslim scholars and scientists, was also passed on to Christian Europe.

The Arab Empire, stretching from Spain to India, was unified by a common language (Arabic), a common faith, and a common culture. By the eleventh century, however, the Arabs began losing their dominance in the Islamic world. The Seljuk Turks, who had taken Asia Minor from the Byzantines, also conquered the Arabic lands of Syria, Palestine, and much of Persia. Although the Abbasid caliphs remained the religious and cultural leaders of Islam, political power was exercised by Seljuk sultans. In the eleventh and twelfth centuries, the Muslims lost Sicily and most of Spain to Christian knights, and European Crusaders carved out kingdoms in the Near East.

In the thirteenth century, Mongols led by Ghenghis Khan devastated Muslim lands; in the late fourteenth century, this time led by Tamerlane, they again plundered and massacred their way through Arab lands. After Tamerlane's death in 1404, his empire disintegrated, and its collapse left the way open for the Ottoman Turks.

The Ottoman Empire reached its height in the sixteenth century with the conquest of Egypt, North Africa, Syria, and the Arabian coast. The Ottomans developed an effective system of administration, but they could not restore the cultural brilliance, the thriving trade, or the prosperity that the Muslim world had known under the Abbasid caliphs of Baghdad.

Latin Christendom in the Early Middle Ages

Although Byzantium and Islam experienced centuries of cultural greatness, neither made the breakthroughs in science, technology, philosophy, economics, and political thought that gave rise to the modern world. This process would be the singular achievement of Europe. During the Early Middle Ages (500–1050), Latin Christendom was culturally far behind the two Eastern civilizations, but by the twelfth century it had caught up. In succeeding centuries it produced the movements that ushered in the modern age: Renaissance, Reformation, Scientific Revolution, Age of Enlightenment, French Revolution, and Industrial Revolution.

Political, Economic, and Intellectual Transformation

From the sixth to the eighth centuries, Europe was struggling to overcome the disorders created by the breakup of the Roman Empire and the deterioration of Greco-Roman civilization. A new civilization with its own distinctive style was taking root. It was based on the intermingling of Greco-Roman civilization and Christian and Germanic traditions. But it would take centuries for this new civilization to bear fruit.

In the fifth century, German invaders founded kingdoms in North Africa, Italy, Spain, Gaul, and Britain—lands formerly belonging to Rome. Even before the invasions, the Germans had acquired some knowledge of and attraction to Roman culture. Therefore, the new Germanic rulers sought not to destroy Roman civilization but to share in its advantages. For example, Theodoric the Great, the Ostrogoth ruler of Italy, retained the Roman senate, government officials, civil service, and schools; the Burgundians in Gaul and the Visigoths in Spain maintained Roman law for their conquered subjects.

But the Germanic kingdoms, often torn by warfare, internal rebellion, and assassination, provided a poor political base on which to revive a decadent and dying classical civilization. Most of the kingdoms survived for only a short time and had no enduring impact. An exception to this trend occurred in Gaul and south Germany, where the most successful of the Germanic kingdoms was established by the Franks—the founders of the new Europe.

The Roman world was probably too far gone to be rescued, but even if this were not so, the Germans were culturally unprepared to play the role of rescuer. By the end of the seventh century the old Roman lands in the West showed a marked decline in central government, town life, commerce, and learning. The German invaders, while vigorous and brave, were essentially a rural and warrior people who were tribal in organization and outlook. Their native culture, without cities or written literature, was primitive in comparison to the literary, philosophic, scientific, and artistic achievements of the Greco-Roman world. The Germans were not equipped to reform the decaying Roman system of administration and taxation, to cope with the economic problems that had burdened the Empire, or to breathe new life into the dying humanist culture.

The distinguishing feature of classical civilization, the vitality of its urban institutions, had deteriorated in the Late Roman Empire. This shift from an urban to a rural economy accelerated under the kingdoms created by Germanic chieftains. Although towns did not vanish altogether, they continued to lose control over their surrounding countryside and to decline in wealth and importance. They were the headquarters of bishops, rather than centers of commerce and intellectual life. Italy remained an exception to this general trend. There Roman urban institutions persisted, even during the crudest period of the Early Middle Ages. Italian cities kept some metal currency in circulation and traded with each other and with Byzantium.

Greco-Roman humanism, which had been in retreat since the Late Roman Empire, continued its decline in the centuries immediately following Rome's demise. The old Roman upper classes abandoned their heritage and absorbed the ways of their Germanic conquerors; the Roman schools closed, and Roman law faded into disuse. Few people other than clerics could read and write Latin, and even learned clerics were rare. Knowledge of the Greek language in western Europe was almost totally lost, and the Latin rhetorical style deteriorated. Many literary works of classical antiquity were either lost or neglected. European culture was much poorer than the high civilizations of Byzantium, Islam, and ancient Rome.

During this period of cultural poverty, the few persons who were learned generally did not engage in original thought but salvaged and transmitted remnants of classical civilization. In a rudimentary way, they were struggling to create a Christian culture that combined the intellectual tradition of Greece and Rome with the religious teachings of the Christian church.

An important figure in the intellectual life of this transitional period was Boethius (480–c. 525), a descendant of a noble Italian family. Aspiring to rescue the intellectual heritage of antiquity, Boethius translated into Latin some of Aristotle's treatises on logic and wrote commentaries on Aristotle, Cicero, and Porphyry, a Neo-Platonist philosopher. Until the twelfth century, virtually all that Latin Christendom knew of Aristotle came from Boethius's translations and commentaries. Similarly, his work in mathematics, which contains fragments from Euclid, was the principal source for the study of that discipline in the Early Middle Ages. In his theological writings Boethius attempted to demonstrate that reason did not conflict with orthodoxy, an early attempt to attain a rational comprehension of belief—to join faith to reason, as he expressed it. Boethius's effort to examine Christian doctrines rationally, a principal feature of medieval philosophy, grew to maturity in the twelfth and thirteenth centuries.

Cassiodorus (c. 490–575), another Italian, collected Greek and Latin manuscripts and initiated the monastic practice of copying classical texts. Without this tradition, many key Christian and pagan works would undoubtedly have perished. In Spain, another "preserver" of ancient works, Isidore of Seville (c. 576–636) compiled an encyclopedia, *Etymologiae,* covering a diversity of topics from arithmetic to God to furniture. Isidore derived his information from many secular and religious sources. Quite understandably, his work contained many errors, particularly in its references to nature. For centuries, though, the *Etymologiae* served as a standard reference work and was found in every monastic library of note.

The translations and compilations made by Boethius, Cassiodorus, and Isidore, the books collected and copied by monks and nuns, and schools established in monasteries (particularly those in Ireland, England, and Italy) kept intellectual life from dying out completely in the Early Middle Ages.

The Church: The Shaper of Medieval Civilization

Christianity was the integrating principle, and the church was the dominant institution of the Middle Ages. During the Late Roman Empire, as the Roman state and its institutions decayed, the church gained in power and importance; its organization grew stronger and its membership increased. Unlike the Roman state, the church was a healthy and vital organism. The elite of the Roman Empire had severed their commitment to the values of classical civilization, whereas the church leaders were intensely devoted to their faith.

When the Empire collapsed, the church retained its administrative system and preserved elements of its civilization. The church served as a unifying and civilizing agent and provided people with an intelligible and purposeful conception of life and death. In a dying world, the church was the only institution capable of reconstructing civilized life. Thus, the Christian outlook, not the traditions of the German barbarians, was the foundation of medieval civilization. People saw themselves as participants in a great drama of salvation. There was only one truth—God's revelation to humanity. There was only one avenue to heaven, and it passed through the church. Membership in a universal church replaced citizenship in a universal empire. Across Europe, from Italy to Ireland, a new society centered on Christianity was forming.

Monks were instrumental in constructing the foundations of medieval civilization. During the seventh century, intellectual life on the Continent continued its steady decline. In the monasteries of England and Ireland, however, a tradition of learning persisted. In the early fifth century, Saint Patrick converted the Irish to Christianity. In Ireland, Latin became firmly entrenched as the language of both the church and scholars at a time when it was in danger of disappearing in many parts of the Continent. Irish clergymen preserved and cultivated Latin and even preserved some knowledge of Greek; they revived the use of Latin during their missionary activities on the Continent. In England, the Anglo-Saxons, who converted to Christianity mainly in the seventh century, also established monasteries that kept learning alive. In the sixth and seventh centuries, Irish and Anglo-Saxon monks became the chief agents for the conversion of the people in northern Europe. By converting pagans to Christianity, monks made possible a unitary European civilization based on a Christian foundation. By copying and preserving ancient texts, monks and nuns also kept alive elements of ancient civilization.

During the Early Middle Ages, when cities were in decay, monasteries were the principal cultural centers; they would remain so until the rebirth of towns in the High Middle Ages. Monasteries also offered succor to the sick and the destitute and served as places of refuge for travelers. To the medieval mind, the monk's and nun's selfless devotion to God, adoption of poverty, and dedication to prayer and contemplation represented the highest expression of the Christian way of life; it was the finest and most certain path to salvation.

The Early Middle Ages was a formative period for the papacy, as for society in general. A decisive figure in the strengthening of the papacy was Gregory I, known as the Great (590–604). One of the ablest of medieval popes, Gregory used Roman methods of administration to organize papal property in Italy, Sicily, Sardinia, Gaul, and other regions effectively. He strengthened his authority over bishops and monks, dispatched missionaries to England to win over the Anglo-Saxons, and set his sights on an alliance with the Franks; finally materializing 150 years later, this alliance was instrumental in the shaping of medieval history.

The Kingdom of the Franks

From their homeland in the Rhine River Valley, the Frankish tribes had expanded into Roman territory during the fourth and fifth centuries. The ruler Clovis united the various Frankish tribes and conquered most of Gaul. In 496, he converted to Roman Christianity. Clovis's conversion to Catholicism was an event of great significance. A number of other German kings had adopted the Arian form of Christianity, which the church had declared heretical. By embracing Roman Christianity, the Franks became a potential ally of the papacy.

Clovis's successors could not maintain control over their lands, and power passed to the mayor of the palace, the king's chief officer. Serving as mayor of the palace from 717 to 741, Charles Martel subjected all Frankish lands to his rule. In addition, at the battle of Tours in 732, he defeated the Muslims. Although the Muslims continued to occupy the Iberian Peninsula, they would advance no farther north into Europe.

Charles Martel was succeeded by his son Pepin the Short, who in 751 deposed the king. With the approval of the papacy and his nobles, Pepin was crowned king by Boniface, a prominent bishop. Two years later, Pope Stephen II anointed Pepin again as king of the Franks and appealed to him to protect the papacy from the Lombards, the last German tribe to invade formerly

Roman territory. Pepin crossed into Italy, defeated the Lombards, and turned over captured lands to the papacy. This famous Donation of Pepin made the pope ruler of the territory between Rome and Ravenna, which became known as the Papal States.

The Era of Charlemagne

The alliance between the Franks and the papacy was continued by Pepin's successor, Charlemagne (Charles the Great), who ruled from 768 to 814. Charlemagne continued the Carolingian policy of expanding the Frankish kingdom. He destroyed the Lombard kingdom and declared himself king of the Lombards. He added Bavaria to his kingdom, and after long, terrible wars, he forced the Saxons to submit to his rule and to convert to Christianity. He conquered a region in northern Spain, the Spanish March, that served as a buffer between the Christian Franks and the Muslims in Spain.

Immense difficulties arose in governing the expanded territories. Size seemed an insuperable obstacle to effective government, particularly since Charlemagne's administrative structure, lacking in trained personnel, was primitive by Islamic, Byzantine, or Roman standards. The empire was divided into about 250 counties administered by counts—nobles who were personally loyal to the ruler and who implemented the king's decisions.

On Christmas Day in Rome in the year 800, Pope Leo crowned Charlemagne Emperor of the Romans. The title signified that the tradition of a world empire still survived, despite the demise of the western Roman Empire three hundred years earlier. But because it was the pope who crowned Charlemagne, this meant that the emperor had a spiritual responsibility to spread and defend the faith. Thus Roman universalism was fused with Christian universalism.

The Frankish Empire, of course, was only a dim shadow of the Roman Empire. The Franks had no Roman law or Roman legions; there were no cities that were centers of economic and cultural activity; officials were not trained civil servants with a world outlook, but uneducated war chieftains with a tribal viewpoint. Yet Charlemagne's empire did embody the idea of a universal Christian empire, an ideal that would endure throughout the Middle Ages.

The crowning of a German ruler as emperor of the Romans by the head of the church represented the merging of German, Christian, and Roman traditions, which is the essential characteristic of medieval civilization. This blending of traditions was also evident on a cultural plane, for Charlemagne, a German warrior-king, showed respect for classical learning and Christianity, both non-Germanic traditions.

Charlemagne believed that it was his religious duty to raise the educational level of the clergy so that they understood and could properly teach the faith. He also fostered education to train administrators who would be capable of overseeing his kingdoms and royal estates; such men had to be literate. To achieve his purpose, Charlemagne gathered some of the finest scholars in Europe. Alcuin of Northumbria, England (735–804), was given charge of the

Map 6.1   The Carolingian World

palace school, attended by Charlemagne and his family, high lords, and youths training to serve the emperor.

The focus of the Carolingian Renaissance was predominantly Christian—an effort to train clergymen and improve their understanding of the Bible and the writings of the church fathers. This process raised the level of literacy and improved the Latin style. Most important, monastic copyists continued to preserve ancient texts, which otherwise might never have survived—the oldest surviving manuscripts of many ancient works are Carolingian copies.

The Coronation of Charlemagne as Emperor by Pope Leo III at St. Peter's.   Charlemagne felt it his duty to maintain the faith and defend the church and the pope.
(*Scala/Art Resource*)

Compared to the Greco-Roman past, to the cultural explosion of the twelfth
and thirteenth centuries, or to the great Italian Renaissance of the fifteenth
century, the Carolingian Renaissance seems slight indeed. But we must bear in
mind the cultural poverty that prevailed before the era of Charlemagne. The
Carolingian Renaissance reversed the process of cultural decay that characterized much of the Early Middle Ages. Learning would never again fall to the
low level it had reached in the centuries following the decline of Rome.

During the era of Charlemagne, a distinct European civilization took root. It
blended the Roman heritage of a world empire, the intellectual achievement of
the Greco-Roman mind, Christian otherworldliness, and the customs of the
Germanic peoples. This nascent western European civilization differed from
Byzantine and Islamic civilizations, and Europeans were growing conscious
of the difference. But the new civilization was still centuries away from fruition.

Charlemagne's empire also engendered the ideal of a unified Latin Christendom—a single Christian community under one government. The ideal of a
Christian world-state, Christendom, inspired many people, both clergy and
laity, and would reach its peak from the eleventh to the thirteenth centuries.

The Breakup of Charlemagne's Empire

After Charlemagne's death in 814, his son, Louis the Pious, inherited the throne. Louis aimed to preserve the empire, but the task was virtually impossible. The empire's strength rested more on the personal qualities of Charlemagne than on any firm economic or political foundation. Moreover, the empire was simply too large and consisted of too many diverse peoples to be governed effectively. Along with Frankish nobles who sought to increase their own power at the emperor's expense, Louis had to deal with his own rebellious sons. After Louis died in 840, the empire was divided among the three surviving sons.

The Treaty of Verdun in 843 gave Louis the German the eastern part of the empire, which marked the beginning of Germany; to Charles the Bald went the western part, which was the start of France; and Lothair received the Middle Kingdom, which extended from Rome to the North Sea. This Middle Kingdom would become a source of conflict between France and Germany into the twentieth century. As central authority waned, large landowners increasingly came to exercise authority in their own regions. Simultaneous invasions from all directions furthered this movement toward localism and decentralization.

In the ninth and tenth centuries, Latin Christendom was attacked on all sides. From bases in North Africa, Spain, and southern Gaul, Muslims ravaged coastal regions of southern Europe. The Magyars, originally from western Asia, had established themselves on the plains of the Danube; their horsemen launched lightning raids into northern Italy, western Germany, and parts of France. Defeated in Germany in 933 and again in 955, the Magyars withdrew to what is now Hungary; they ceased their raids and adopted Christianity.

Still another group of invaders, the Northmen, or Vikings, sailed south from Scandinavia on their long wooden ships to plunder the coasts and river valleys of western Europe. These ferocious warriors spread terror wherever they landed. Villages were devastated, ports were destroyed, and the population was decimated. Trade was at a standstill, coins were no longer circulated, and farms were turned into wastelands. The European economy collapsed, the political authority of kings disappeared, and cultural life and learning withered.

These terrible attacks heightened political insecurity and accelerated anew the process of decentralization that had begun with the decline of Rome. During these chaotic times, counts came to regard as their own the land that they administered and defended for their king. Similarly, the inhabitants of a district looked on the count or local lord as their ruler, for his men and fortresses protected them. In their regions, nobles exercised public power formerly held by kings. Europe had entered an age of feudalism, in which the essential unit of government was not a kingdom but a county or castellany, and political power was the private possession of local lords.

Feudal Society

Arising during a period of collapsing central authority, invasion, scanty public revenues, and declining commerce and town life, feudalism attempted to provide some order and security. Feudalism was not a planned system derived logically from general principles, but an improvised response to the challenge posed by ineffectual central authority. Feudal practices were not uniform but differed from locality to locality, and in some regions barely took root. Feudalism was a stopgap system of government that provided some order, justice, and law during an era of breakdown, localism, and transition. It remained the predominant political arrangement until kings reasserted their authority in the High and Late Middle Ages.

Vassalage

Feudal relationships enabled lords to increase their military strength. The need for military support was the principal reason for the practice of vassalage, in which a man, in a solemn ceremony, pledged loyalty to a lord. This feature of feudalism derived from an ancient German ceremony during which warriors swore personal allegiance to the head of the war-band. Among other things, the vassal gave military service to his lord and received in return a *fief*, which was usually land. This fief was inhabited by peasants, and the crops that they raised provided the vassal with his means of support.

In return for the fief and the lord's protection, the vassal owed several obligations to his lord. These duties included rendering military assistance and supplying knights for his lord; sitting in the lord's court and judging cases, such as the breach of feudal agreements between the lord and his other vassals; providing lodgings when the lord traveled through the vassal's territory; giving a gift when the lord's son was knighted or when his eldest daughter married; and raising a ransom if the lord were captured by an enemy.

Generally, both lord and vassal felt honor-bound to abide by the oath of loyalty. It became an accepted custom for a vassal to renounce his loyalty to his lord if the latter failed to protect him from enemies, mistreated him, or increased the vassal's obligations as fixed by the feudal contract. Similarly, if a vassal did not live up to his obligations, the lord would summon him to his court, where he would be tried for treachery. If found guilty, the vassal could lose his fief and perhaps his life. Sometimes disputes between vassals and lords erupted into warfare. Because a vassal often held land from more than one lord and sometimes was himself a lord to vassals, situations frequently became awkward, complex, and confusing. On occasion, a vassal had to decide to which lord he owed *liege homage* (prime loyalty).

As feudalism evolved, the king came to be regarded as the chief lord, who had granted fiefs to the great lords, who in turn had divided them into smaller units and regranted them to vassals. Thus all members of the ruling class, from the lowliest knights to the king, occupied a place in the feudal hierarchy. In theory the king was the highest political authority and the source of land tenure, but in actual fact he was often less powerful than other nobles of the realm. Feudalism would decline when kings converted their theoretical powers into actual powers.

Feudal Warriors

Feudal lords viewed manual labor and commerce as degrading for men of their rank. They considered only one vocation worthy—that of warrior. Through combat, the lord demonstrated his valor, earned his reputation, measured his individual worth, derived excitement, added to his wealth, and defended his rights. Warfare was his whole purpose in life. During the twelfth century, to relieve the boredom of peacetime, nobles staged gala tournaments in which knights, fighting singly or in teams, engaged each other in battle to prove their skill and courage and to win honor. The feudal glorification of combat became deeply ingrained in Western society, and has endured into the twentieth century. Over the centuries a code of behavior, called *chivalry*, evolved for the feudal nobility. A true knight was expected to fight bravely, to demonstrate loyalty to his lord, and to treat other knights with respect and courtesy.

The church, in time, interjected a religious element into the warrior culture of the feudal knight. It sought to use the fighting spirit of the feudal class for Christian ends—knights could assist the clergy in enforcing God's will. To the Germanic tradition of loyalty and courage was added a Christian component; as a Christian gentleman, a knight was expected to honor the laws of the church and to wield his sword in the service of God.

Regarding the private warfare of lords as a lawless violence that menaced social life, the church in the eleventh century imposed strictures called "the Peace of God" and "the Truce of God." These restrictions limited feudal warfare to certain days of the week and certain times of the year. Although only relatively effective, the Peace of God did offer Christian society some respite from plundering and incessant warfare.

Noblewomen

Feudal society was very much a man's world. In theory, women were held to be inferior to men; in practice, they were subjected to male authority. Fathers arranged the marriages of their daughters. Girls from aristocratic families were generally married at age sixteen or younger to men often twice their age; aristocratic girls who did not marry often had to enter a convent. The wife of the lord was at the mercy of her husband; if she annoyed him, she might expect a beating. But as the lady of the castle, she performed important duties. She assigned tasks to the servants, made medicines, preserved food, taught young girls how to sew, spin, and weave, and despite her subordinate position, took charge of the castle when her husband was away. Although the church taught that both men and women were precious to God and that marriage was a sacred rite, some clergymen viewed women as agents of the Devil—evil temptresses who, like the biblical Eve, lured men into sin.

Agrarian Society

Feudalism was built on an economic foundation known as *manorialism*. Although pockets of free peasantry remained, a village community (manor) consisting of serfs bound to the land became the essential agricultural arrangement in medieval society. The manorial village was the means of organizing an agricultural society with limited markets and money. Neither the lords who warred nor the clergymen who prayed performed economically productive work. Their ways of life were made possible by the toil of serfs.

The origins of manorialism can be traced in part to the Late Roman Empire, when peasants depended on the owners of large estates for protection and security. This practice developed further during the Early Middle Ages, especially during the invasions of Northmen, Magyars, and Muslims in the ninth and tenth centuries. Peasants continued to sacrifice their freedom in exchange for protection; in some cases, they were too weak to resist the encroachments of local magnates. Like feudalism, manorialism was not a neat system, but consisted of improvised relationships and practices that varied from region to region.

A lord controlled at least one manorial village; great lords might possess hundreds. A small manor had a dozen families; a large one had as many as fifty or sixty. The manorial village was never completely self-sufficient, because salt, millstones, and metalware were generally obtained from outside sources; it did, though, constitute a balanced economic setting. Peasants grew grain and raised cattle, sheep, goats, and hogs; blacksmiths, carpenters, and stonemasons did the building and repairing; the village priest cared for the souls of the inhabitants; and the lord defended the manor and administered the customary law.

When a manor was attacked by another lord, the peasants found protection inside the walls of their lord's house. By the twelfth century, this building had in many places become a well-fortified stone castle. Peasants generally lived, worked, and died on the lord's estate and were buried in the village churchyard. Few had any contact with the world beyond the village of their birth.

In return for protection and the right to cultivate fields and to pass these holdings on to his children, the serf owed obligations to his lord, and his personal freedom was restricted in a variety of ways. Bound to the land, he could not leave the manor without the lord's consent. Before a serf could marry, he had to obtain the lord's permission and pay a fee. The lord could select a wife for his serf and force him to marry her. Sometimes a serf, objecting to the lord's choice, preferred to pay a fine. These rules also applied to the serf's children, who inherited their parents' obligations. In addition to working his allotted land, the serf had to tend the fields reserved for the lord. Other services exacted by the lord included digging ditches, gathering firewood, building fences, repairing roads and bridges, and sewing clothes. Probably somewhat more than half the serf's workweek was devoted to fulfilling these labor obligations. Serfs also paid a variety of dues to the lord, including payments for using the lord's mill, bake-oven, and winepress.

Serfs derived some benefits from manorial relationships. They received protection during a chaotic era, and they possessed customary rights, which the lord often respected, to cottages and farmlands. If a lord demanded more services or dues than was customary, or if he interfered with their right to cottages or strips of farmland, the peasants might demonstrate their discontent by refusing to labor for the lord. Up to the fourteenth century, however, open rebellion was rare because lords possessed considerable military and legal power. The manorial system promoted attitudes of dependency and servility among the serfs; their hopes for a better life were directed toward heaven.

Economic Expansion During the High Middle Ages

Manorialism and feudalism presupposed an unchanging social order—clergy who prayed, lords who fought, and peasants who toiled. People believed that society functioned smoothly when each person accepted his or her status and performed his or her proper role. Consequently, a person's rights, duties, and relationship to law depended on one's ranking in the social order. To change position was to upset the organic unity of society. And no one, serfs included, should be deprived of the traditional rights associated with his or her rank. This arrangement was justified by the clergy, who maintained that "God himself has willed that among men, some must be lords and some serfs."[1]

The revival of urban economy and the re-emergence of central authority in the High Middle Ages (1050–1200) undermined feudal and manorial relationships. By the end of the eleventh century, Europe showed many signs of recovery. The invasions of Magyars and Vikings had ended, and powerful lords and kings imposed greater order in their territories. The High Middle Ages was a period of economic vitality. It witnessed an agricultural revolution, a commercial revolution, the rebirth of towns, and the rise of an enterprising and dynamic middle class.

An Agricultural Revolution

During the Middle Ages, important advances were made in agriculture. Many of these innovations occurred in the Early Middle Ages, but were only gradually adopted and were not used everywhere; however, in time, they markedly increased production. By the end of the thirteenth century, medieval agriculture had reached a technical level far superior to that of the ancient world.

One innovation was a heavy plow that cut deeply into the soil. This new plow enabled farmers to work more quickly and effectively. As a result, they could cultivate more land, including the heavy, moist soils of northern Europe, which had offered too much resistance to the light plow. Another important advance in agricultural technology was the invention of the collar harness. The old yoke harness worked well with oxen, but it tended to choke horses, which, because they move faster and have greater stamina than oxen, are more valuable for agricultural work. The widening use of the watermill by the tenth century and the introduction of windmills, which came into use in the twelfth century, replacing ancient hand-worked mills, saved labor in grinding grain.

The gradual emergence of the three-field system of managing agricultural land, particularly in northern Europe, increased production. In the old, widely used two-field system, half the land was planted in autumn with winter wheat, while the other half was left fallow to restore its fertility. In the new three-field system, one third of the land was planted in autumn with winter wheat, a second third was planted the following spring with oats and vegetables, and the last third remained fallow. The advantages of the three-field system were, first, that two-thirds of the land was farmed and only one-third was not in use, and second, that the diversification of crops made more vegetable protein available.

Increased agricultural production reduced the number of deaths from starvation and dietary disease and thus contributed to a population increase. Soon the farmlands of a manorial village could not support its growing population. Consequently, peasants had to look beyond their immediate surroundings and colonize trackless wastelands. Lords vigorously promoted this conversion of uncultivated soil into agricultural land because it increased their incomes. Monastic communities also actively engaged in this enterprise. Almost everywhere, peasants were draining swamps, clearing forests, and establishing new villages. Their endeavors during the eleventh and twelfth centuries brought vast areas of Europe under cultivation for the first time. New agricultural land was also acquired through expansion, the most notable example being the organized settlement of lands to the east by German colonists.

The colonizing and cultivation of virgin lands contributed to the decline of serfdom. Lords owned vast tracts of forests and swamps that would substantially increase their incomes if cleared, drained, and farmed. But serfs were often unwilling to move from their customary homes and fields to do the hard labor needed to cultivate these new lands. To lure serfs away from their villages, lords promised them freedom from most or all personal services. In many cases the settlers fulfilled their obligations to the lord by paying rent rather than by performing services or providing foodstuffs, thus making the transition from serfs to freemen. In time, they came to regard the land as their own.

The improvement in agricultural technology and the colonization of new lands altered the conditions of life in Europe. Surplus food and the increase in population freed people to work at nonfarming occupations, making possible the expansion of trade and the revival of town life.

The Revival of Trade

Expanding agricultural production, the termination of Viking attacks, greater political stability, and an increasing population produced a revival of commerce. During the Early Middle Ages, Italians and Jews kept alive a small amount of long-distance trade between Catholic Europe and the Byzantine and Islamic worlds. In the eleventh century, sea forces of Italian trading cities cleared the Mediterranean of Muslim fleets that preyed on Italian shipping. As in Roman times, goods could circulate once again from one end of the sea to the other. In the twelfth and thirteenth centuries, local, regional, and long-distance trade gained such a momentum that some historians describe the period as a commercial revolution that surpassed the commercial activity of the Roman Empire during the pax Romana.

Crucial to the growth of trade were international fairs, where merchants and craftsmen set up stalls and booths to display their wares. Because of ever-present robbers, lords provided protection for merchants carrying their wares to and from fairs. Each fair lasted about three to six weeks; then the merchants would move on to another site. The Champagne region in northeastern France was the great center for fairs.

The principal arteries of trade flowed between the eastern Mediterranean and the Italian cities, between Scandinavia and the Atlantic coast, between northern France, Flanders, and England, and from the Baltic Sea in the north to the Black Sea and Constantinople via Russian rivers.

Increased economic activity led to advances in business techniques. Since individual businessmen often lacked sufficient capital for large-scale enterprises, groups of merchants formed partnerships. By enabling merchants to pool their capital, reduce their risks, and expand their knowledge of profit-making opportunities, these arrangements furthered commerce. Underwriters insured cargoes; the development of banking and credit instruments made it unnecessary for merchants to carry large amounts of cash. The international fairs not only were centers of international trade, but also served as capital markets for international credit transactions. The arrangements made by fair-going merchants to settle their debts were the origin of the bill of exchange. The development of systematic bookkeeping was another improvement in business techniques. So too was the formation of a body of commercial law that defined the rules of conduct for debts and contracts.

The Rise of Towns

In the eleventh century, towns emerged anew throughout Europe, and in the next century they became active centers of commercial and intellectual life. Towns were a new and revolutionary force—socially, economically, and culturally. A new class of merchants and craftsmen came into being. This new class—the middle class—was made up of people who, unlike the lords and

Map 6.2   Medieval Trade Routes ▶

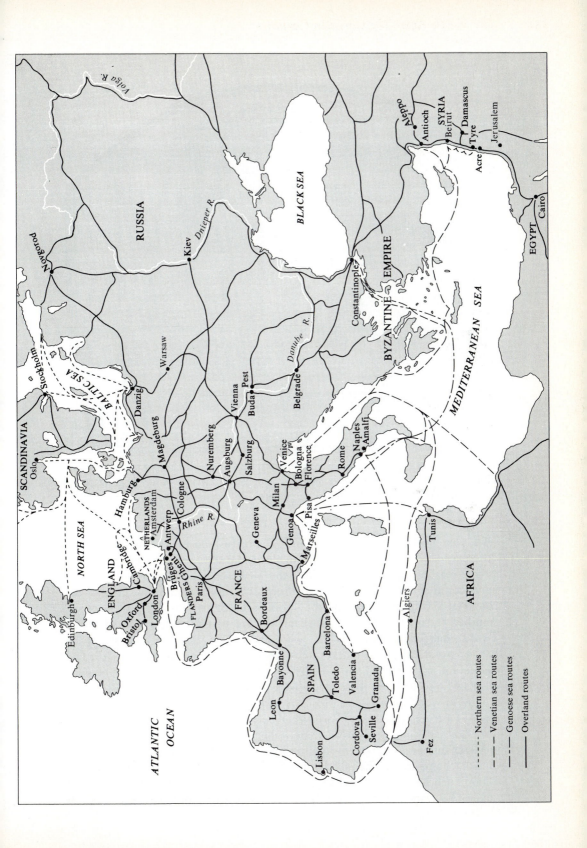

ATLANTIC OCEAN

NORTH SEA

BALTIC SEA

BLACK SEA

MEDITERRANEAN SEA

RUSSIA

Volga R.

Dnieper R.

Danube R.

Rhine R.

SCANDINAVIA

Novgorod

Stockholm

Oslo

Kiev

Warsaw

Danzig

Magdeburg

Hamburg

NETHERLANDS

Amsterdam

Antwerp

Cologne

Nuremberg

Augsburg

Salzburg

Vienna

Pest

Buda

Belgrade

Constantinople

BYZANTINE EMPIRE

ENGLAND

Edinburgh

Bristol

Oxford

Cambridge

London

Bruges

Ghent

FLANDERS

Paris

FRANCE

Bordeaux

Bayonne

Geneva

Milan

Genoa

Pisa

Marseilles

Venice

Bologna

Florence

Rome

Naples

Amalfi

Tunis

Algiers

AFRICA

Fez

SPAIN

Leon

Lisbon

Cordova

Seville

Granada

Valencia

Toledo

Barcelona

Aleppo

Antioch

SYRIA

Beirut

Damascus

Tyre

Acre

Jerusalem

Cairo

EGYPT

- - - - - Northern sea routes
― ― ― Venetian sea routes
― · ― · Genoese sea routes
―――― Overland routes

Local Market in Florence.   The expansion of trade sparked the rise of urban centers. Florence became one of the largest medieval merchant towns. A variety of goods were sold in open markets, like the one pictured here. (*Bibliothèque Municipale, Rouen*)

serfs, were not affiliated with the land. The townsman was a new man with a different value system from that of the lord, the serf, and the clergyman.

One reason for town growth was the increased food supply arising from advances in agricultural technology. Surplus farm production meant that the countryside could support an urban population of artisans and professionals. Another reason for the rise of urban centers was the expansion of trade. Towns emerged in locations that were natural for trade—sea coasts, riverbanks, crossroads, and market sites; they also sprang up outside fortified castles and monasteries and on surviving Roman sites. The colonies of merchants who gathered at these places were joined by peasants skilled in crafts or willing to work as laborers. Most towns had a small population; the largest ones—Florence, Ghent, and Paris—had between 50,000 and 100,000 inhabitants. Covering only small areas, these walled towns were crowded with people.

Merchants and craftsmen organized guilds to protect their members from outside competition. The merchant guild in a town prevented outsiders from doing much business. A craftsman new to a town had to be admitted to the guild of his trade before he could open a shop. Competition between members of the same guild was discouraged. To prevent any guild member from making significantly more money than another member, a guild required that its members work the same number of hours, pay employees the same wages, produce goods of equal quality, and charge customers a just price. These rules were strictly enforced.

Because many towns were situated on land belonging to lords or on the sites of old Roman towns ruled by bishops, these communities at first came under feudal authority. In some instances, lords encouraged the founding of towns, for urban industry and commerce brought wealth to the region. However, tensions soon developed between merchants who sought freedom from feudal restrictions and lords and bishops who wanted to preserve their authority over the towns. Townsmen, or burghers, refused to be treated as serfs bound to a lord and liable for personal services and customary dues. The burghers wanted to travel, trade, marry, and dispose of their property as they pleased; they wanted to make their own laws and levy their own taxes. Sometimes by fighting, but more often by payments of money, the townsmen obtained charters from the lords giving them the right to set up their own councils. These assemblies passed laws, collected taxes, and formed courts that enforced the laws. Towns became more or less self-governing city-states, the first since Greco-Roman days.

In a number of ways, towns loosened the hold of lords on serfs. Seeking freedom and fortune, serfs fled to the new towns where, according to custom, lords could no longer reclaim them after a year and a day. Enterprising serfs earned money by selling food to townsmen. When they acquired a sufficient sum, they bought their freedom from lords, who needed cash to pay for goods bought from merchants. Lords increasingly began to accept fixed cash payments from serfs in place of labor services or foodstuffs. As serfs met their obligations to lords with money, they gradually became rent-paying tenants, and in time were no longer bound to the lord's land. The manorial system of personal relations and mutual obligations was disintegrating.

The activities of townsmen made them a new breed; they engaged in business and had money and freedom. Their world was the market rather than the church, the castle, or the manor. Townsmen were freeing themselves from the prejudices both of feudal aristocrats, who considered trade and manual work degrading, and of the clergy, who cursed the pursuit of riches as an obstacle to salvation. The townsmen were critical, dynamic, and progressive—a force for change. Medieval towns nurtured the origins of the *bourgeoisie* (literally, "citizens of the burg," the walled town), the urban middle class, which would play a crucial role in modern European history.

The Rise of States

The revival of trade and the growth of towns were signs of a growing vitality in Latin Christendom. Another sign of strength was the greater order and security provided by the emergence of states. Aided by educated and trained officials who enforced royal law, tried people in royal courts, and collected royal taxes, kings expanded their territory and slowly fashioned strong central governments. These developments laid the foundations of European states. Not all areas followed the same pattern. Although England and France achieved a large measure of unity during the Middle Ages, Germany and Italy remained divided into numerous independent territories.

England

In 1066 the Normans—those Northmen who had first raided and then settled in France—conquered Anglo-Saxon England. Determined to establish effective control over his new kingdom, William the Conqueror, duke of Normandy, kept a sixth of conquered England for himself. In accordance with feudal practice, he distributed the rest among his Norman nobles, who swore an oath of loyalty to William and provided him with military assistance. But William made certain that no feudal baron had enough land or soldiers to threaten his power. The Norman conquest had led to the replacement of an Anglo-Saxon aristocracy with a Norman one.

To strengthen royal control, William retained some Anglo-Saxon administrative practices. The land remained divided into *shires* (counties) administered by *sheriffs* (royal agents). This structure gave the king control over local government. To determine how much money he could demand, William ordered a vast census taken of people and property in every village. This data, compiled in the *Domesday Book,* listed the quantities of tenants, cattle, sheep, pigs, and farm equipment throughout the realm. Thus, better than any other monarch of his day, William knew what the assets of his kingdom were. Because he had conquered England in one stroke, his successors did not have to travel the long, painful road to national unity followed by French monarchs.

A crucial development in shaping national unity was the emergence of *common law*. When Henry I became king in 1100, England had conflicting baronial claims and legal traditions that were a barrier to unity. There was the old Anglo-Saxon law, the feudal law introduced by the Normans from France, the church law, and the commercial law emerging among the town businessmen. During the reigns of Henry I (1100–1135) and Henry II (1154–1189), royal judges traveled to different parts of the kingdom. Throughout England, important cases began to be tried in the king's court rather than in local courts, thereby increasing royal power. The decisions of royal judges were recorded and used as guides for future cases. In this way, a law common to the whole land gradually came to prevail over the customary law of a specific locality. Because common law applied to all England, it served as a force for unity. It also provided a fairer system of justice. The common law remains the foundation of the English legal system.

Henry II made trial by jury a regular procedure for many cases heard in the king's court, laying the foundations of the modern judicial system. Henry II also ordered representatives of a given locality to report under oath to visiting royal judges any local persons who were suspected of murder or robbery. This indictment jury was the ancestor of the modern grand jury system.

King John (1199–1216) inadvertently precipitated a situation that led to another step in the political development of England. Fighting a costly and losing war with the king of France, John coerced his vassals into giving him more and more revenue; also he had punished some vassals without a proper trial. In 1215, the angry barons rebelled and compelled John to fix his seal to a document called the Great Charter, or *Magna Carta*. The Magna Carta is celebrated as the root of the unique English respect for basic rights and liberties. Although essentially a feudal document directed against a king who had violated feudal practices, the Magna Carta stated certain principles that could be interpreted more widely.

Over the centuries, these principles were expanded to protect the liberties of Englishmen against governmental oppression. The Magna Carta stated that no unusual feudal dues "shall be imposed in our kingdom except by the common consent of our kingdom." In time, this right came to mean that the king could not levy taxes without the consent of Parliament, the governmental body that represents the English people. The Magna Carta also provided that "no freeman shall be taken or imprisoned . . . save by the lawful judgment of his peers or by the law of the land." The barons who drew up the document had intended it to mean that they must be tried by fellow barons. As time passed, these words were regarded as a guarantee of trial by jury for all men, a prohibition against arbitrary arrest, and a command to dispense justice fully, freely, and equally. Implied in the Magna Carta is the idea that the king cannot rule as he pleases, but must govern according to the law—that not even the king can violate the law of the nation. Centuries afterward, when Englishmen sought to limit the king's power, they would interpret the Magna Carta in this way.

In Anglo-Saxon England the tradition had emerged that the king should consider the advice of the leading men in the land. Later, William the Conqueror continued this practice by seeking the opinions of leading nobles and bishops. In the thirteenth century it became accepted custom that the king should not decide major issues without consulting these advisers who assembled in the Great Council. Lesser landowners and townsmen also began to be summoned to meet with the king. These two groups were eventually called the House of Lords (bishops and nobles) and the House of Commons (knights and burghers). Thus the English Parliament evolved, and by the mid-fourteenth century it had become a permanent institution of government. Frequently in need of money but unable to levy new taxes without the approval of Parliament, the king had to turn to that body for help. Parliament used this control over money matters to increase its power. The tradition grew that the power to govern rested not with the king alone, but with the king and Parliament together.

During the Middle Ages, England became a centralized and unified state.

But the king did not have unlimited power; he was not above the law. The rights of the people were protected by certain principles implicit in the common law and the Magna Carta, and by the power of Parliament.

France

In the 150 years following Charlemagne's death, the western part of his empire, which was destined to become France, faced terrible ordeals. Charlemagne's heirs fought each other for the crown; the Vikings raided everywhere their ships would carry them; Muslims from Spain plundered the southern coast; and strong lords usurped power for themselves. With the Carolingian family unable to maintain the throne, the great lords elected the king. In 987, they chose Hugh Capet (987–996), the count of Paris. Because many great lords held territories far larger than those of Hugh, the French king did not seem a threat to noble power. But Hugh strengthened the French monarchy by having the lords also elect his son as his co-ruler. This practice endured until it became understood that the crown would remain with the Capetian family.

With the accession of Louis VI (1108–1137), a two-hundred-year period of steadily increasing royal power began. Louis started this trend by successfully subduing the barons in his own duchy. A decisive figure in the expansion of royal power was Philip Augustus (1180–1223). Philip struck successfully at King John of England (of Magna Carta fame), who held more territory in France than Philip did. When William, duke of Normandy in western France, conquered England in 1066, he became ruler of England and Normandy; William's great-grandson Henry II acquired much of southern France through marriage to Eleanor of Aquitaine in 1152. Thus, as a result of the Norman conquest and intermarriage, the destinies of France and England were closely intertwined until the end of the Middle Ages. By stripping King John of most of his French territory (Normandy, Anjou, and much of Aquitaine), Philip trebled the size of his kingdom and became stronger than any French lord.

In the thirteenth century the power of the French monarch continued to grow. Departing from feudal precedent, Louis IX (1226–1270) issued ordinances for the entire realm without seeking the consent of his vassals. Kings added to their lands by warfare and marriage; they devised new ways of raising money, including taxing the clergy. A particularly effective way of increasing the monarch's power was by extending royal justice. In the thirteenth century, the king's court, the Parlement, became the highest court in France. Quarrels between the king and his vassals were resolved in the Parlement, and many cases previously tried in lords' courts were transferred to the king's court.

In the beginning of the fourteenth century, Philip IV (the Fair) engaged in a struggle with the papacy. Seeking to demonstrate that he had the support of his subjects, Philip convened a national assembly called the *Estates General*, representing clergy, nobility, and townsmen. It would be called again to vote funds for the crown. But unlike the English Parliament, the Estates General never became an important body in French political life, and it never succeeded in controlling the monarch. While the basis for limited monarchy had been established in England, no comparable checks on the king's power developed in France. By the end of the Middle Ages, French kings had succeeded in creating a unified state. But regional and local loyalties remained strong and persisted for centuries.

Germany

After the destruction of Charlemagne's empire, its German territories were broken into large duchies. Following an ancient German practice, the ruling dukes elected one of their own as king. The German king, however, had little authority outside his own duchy. Some German kings tried not to antagonize the dukes, but Otto the Great (936–973) was determined to control them. He entered into an alliance with German bishops and archbishops who could provide him with fighting men and trained administrators—a policy continued by his successors. In 962, in emulation of the coronation of Charlemagne, the pope crowned Otto "Emperor of the Romans." (Later the title would be changed to Holy Roman emperor.)

Otto and his successors wanted to dominate Italy and the pope—an ambition that embroiled the Holy Roman emperor in a life-and-death struggle with the papacy. The papacy allied itself with the German dukes and the Italian cities, enemies of the emperor. The intervention in papal and Italian politics was the principal reason why German territories did not achieve unity in the Middle Ages.

The Growth of Papal Power

Accompanying economic recovery and increased political stability in the High Middle Ages was a growing spiritual vitality marked by several developments. Within the church, reform movements were attacking clerical abuses, and the papacy was growing more powerful. A holy war against the Muslims was drawing the Christian community closer together. During this period, the church tried with great determination to make society follow divine standards; that is, it tried to shape all institutions and expressions of the intellect according to a comprehensive Christian outlook.

As the sole interpreters of God's revelation and the sole ministers of his sacraments, the clergy imposed and supervised the moral outlook of Christendom. Divine grace was channeled through the sacraments, which could be administered only by the church, the indispensable intermediary between the individual and God. For those persons who resisted its authority, the church could impose the penalty of excommunication (expulsion from the church and denial of the sacraments, without which there could be no salvation).

The Gregorian Reform

By the tenth century, the church was Western Europe's leading landowner, owning much of Italy and vast properties in other lands. However, the papacy was in no position to exercise commanding leadership over Latin Christendom. The office of pope had fallen under the domination of aristocratic families; they conspired and on occasion murdered in order to place one of their own on the wealthy and powerful throne of Saint Peter. As the papacy became a prize for Rome's leading families, it was not at all unusual for popes themselves to be involved in conspiracies and assassinations. Also weakening the authority of the papacy were local lords, who dominated churches and monasteries by appointing bishops and abbots and by collecting the income from church taxes. These bishops and abbots, appointed by lords for political reasons, lacked the spiritual devotion to maintain high standards of discipline among the priests and monks.

What raised the power of the papacy to unprecedented heights was the emergence of a reform movement, particularly in French and German monasteries. High-minded monks called for a reawakening of spiritual fervor and the elimination of moral laxity among the clergy, especially a concern for worldly goods, the taking of mistresses, and a diminishing commitment to the Benedictine rule. Of the many monasteries that participated in this reform movement, the Benedictine monks of Cluny in Burgundy, France, were the most influential.

In the middle of the eleventh century, popes came under the influence of the monastic reformers. In 1059, a special synod convened by the reform-minded Pope Nicholas II moved to end the interference of Roman nobles and German Holy Roman emperors in the selection of the pope. Henceforth, a select group of clergymen called *cardinals* would essentially be responsible for choosing the pontiff.

The reform movement found its most zealous exponent in the person of Hildebrand, who became Pope Gregory VII in 1073. For Gregory, human society was part of a divinely ordered universe governed by God's universal law. As the supreme spiritual leader of Christendom, the pope was charged with the mission of establishing a Christian society on earth. As successor to Saint Peter, the pope had the final word on matters of faith and doctrine. All bishops came under his authority; so did kings, whose powers should be used for Christian ends. The pope was responsible for instructing rulers in the proper use of their God-given powers, and kings had the solemn duty to obey these instructions. If the king failed in his Christian duty, the pope could deny him his right to rule. Responsible for implementing God's law, the pope could never take a subordinate position to kings.

Like no other pope before him, Gregory VII made a determined effort to assert the pre-eminence of the papacy over both the church hierarchy and secular rulers. This determination led to a bitter struggle between the papacy and the German monarch and future Holy Roman emperor Henry IV. The dispute was a dramatic confrontation between two competing versions of the relationship between secular and spiritual authority.

Through his reforms, Gregory VII intended to improve the moral quality of the clergy and to liberate the church from all control by secular authorities. He forbade priests who had wives or concubines to celebrate mass, deposed clergy who had bought their offices, excommunicated bishops and abbots who received their estates from a lay lord, and expelled from the church lay lords who invested bishops with their office. The appointment of bishops, Pope Gregory insisted, should be controlled entirely by the church.

This last point touched off the conflict, called the *Investiture Controversy,* between Henry and Pope Gregory. Bishops served a dual function. On the one hand, they belonged to the spiritual community of the church; on the other, as members of the nobility and holders of estates, they were also integrated into the feudal order. Traditionally, emperors had both granted bishops their feudal authority and invested them with their spiritual authority. In maintaining that no lay rulers could confer ecclesiastial offices on their appointees, Pope Gregory threatened Henry's authority.

Seeking allies in the conflict with feudal nobility in earlier times, German kings had made vassals of the upper clergy. In return for a fief, bishops had agreed to provide troops for a monarch in his struggle against the lords. But if kings had no control over the appointment of bishops—in accordance with Pope Gregory's view—they would lose the allegiance, military support, and financial assistance of their most important allies. To German monarchs, bishops were officers of the state who served the throne. Moreover, by agreeing to Gregory's demands, German kings would lose their freedom of action and be dominated by the Roman pontiff. Henry IV regarded Gregory VII as a fanatic who trampled on custom, meddled in German state affairs, and threatened to subordinate kingship to the papacy.

With the approval of the German bishops, Henry called for Pope Gregory to descend from the throne of Saint Peter. Gregory in turn excommunicated Henry and deposed him as king. German lands were soon embroiled in a civil war, as German lords used the quarrel to strike at Henry's power. Finally Henry's troops crossed the Alps, successfully attacked Rome, and installed a new pope who in turn crowned Henry Emperor of the Romans. Gregory died in exile.

In 1122, the church and Emperor Henry V reached a compromise. Bishops were to be elected exclusively by the church and to be invested with the staff and the ring—symbols of spiritual power—by the archbishop, not the king. This change signified that the bishop owed his role as spiritual leader to the church only. But the king would grant the bishop the scepter, an act that would indicate that the bishop was also the recipient of a fief and the king's vassal, owing feudal obligations to the crown. This compromise, called the *Concordat of Worms,* recognized the dual function of the bishop as a spiritual leader in the church and a feudal landowner. Similar settlements were reached with the kings of France and England.

The conflict between the papacy and the German rulers continued after the Concordat of Worms—a contest for supremacy between the heir of Saint Peter and the heir of Charlemagne. German monarchs aimed at controlling the papacy and the prosperous north Italian cities. When Frederick I (1152–1190), known as Frederick Barbarossa ("Red Beard"), tried to assert authority over these cities, they resisted. In 1176, the armies of an alliance of Italian cities supported by the pope decisively defeated Frederick's forces at the battle of Legnano. The Italian infantry showed that it could defeat knights on horseback, and Frederick was compelled to recognize the independence of the Italian cities. His numerous expeditions to Italy weakened his authority; German princes strengthened themselves at the expense of the monarchy, thereby continuing to preclude German unity.

The Crusades

Like the movement for spiritual renewal associated with the Cluniac reformers, the Crusades—wars to regain the Holy Land from the Muslims—were an outpouring of Christian zeal and an attempt by the papacy to assert its preeminence. The Crusades were another sign—like the renewal of commerce and the growth of towns—of growing vitality and self-confidence. The victims of earlier Muslim attacks, Latin Christians now took the offensive.

The Crusades were also part of a general movement of expansion that took place in Europe during the High Middle Ages. By the middle of the eleventh century, Genoans and Pisans had driven the Muslims from Sardinia. By 1091, Normans from France had taken Sicily from the Muslims and southern Italy from Byzantium. With the support of the papacy, Christian knights engaged in the long struggle to drive the Muslims from Spain; by 1248, after more than two centuries of conflict, only the small southern kingdom of Granada remained in Muslim hands. Germans conquered and colonized lands south of the Baltic coast inhabited by non-Christian Slavs, Balts, and Prussians. German settlers brought with them Christianity and German language and culture. They cleared vast tracts of virgin land for farming and established towns in a region where urban life had virtually been unknown.

Seeking to regain lands taken from Byzantium by the Seljuk Turks, the Byzantine emperor Alexius appealed to the West for mercenaries. Pope Urban II, at the Council of Clermont (in France) in 1095, exaggerated the danger confronting Eastern Christianity. He called for a holy crusade against the heathen Turks, whom he accused of defiling and destroying Christian churches. A Christian army, mobilized by the papacy to defend the faith and to regain the Holy Land from nonbelievers, accorded with the papal concept of a just war; it would channel the energies of Europe's warrior class in a Christian direction.

What motivated the knights and others who responded to Urban's appeal?

Map 6.3   The Holy Roman Empire, c. 1200 ▶

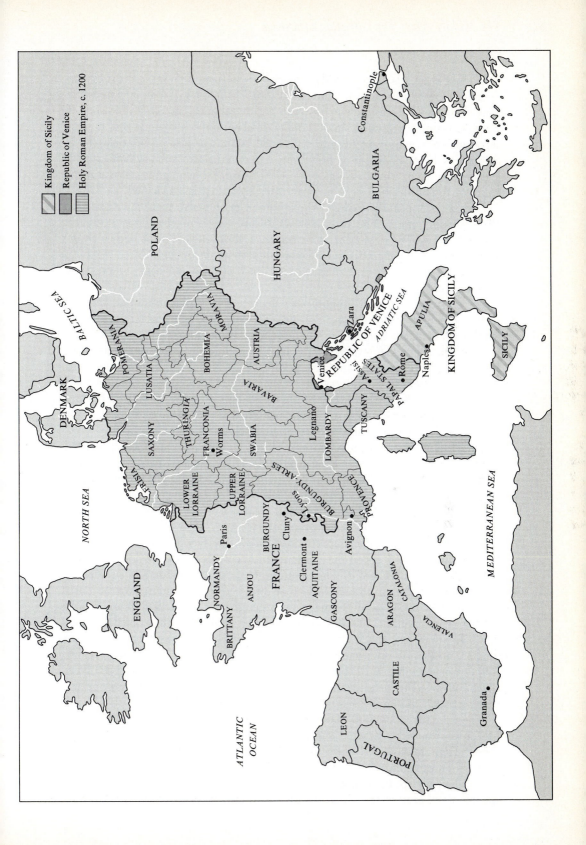

Kingdom of Sicily
Republic of Venice
Holy Roman Empire, c. 1200

CONSTANTINOPLE

BULGARIA

POLAND

HUNGARY

BALTIC SEA

DENMARK

POMERANIA

MORAVIA

BOHEMIA

AUSTRIA

LUSATIA

SAXONY

THURINGIA

FRANCONIA

Worms

BAVARIA

Zara

ADRIATIC SEA

REPUBLIC OF VENICE

Venice

Assisi

PAPAL STATES

Rome

APULIA

KINGDOM OF SICILY

Naples

SICILY

NORTH SEA

FRISIA

LOWER
LORRAINE

UPPER
LORRAINE

SWABIA

Legnano

LOMBARDY

TUSCANY

BURGUNDY-ARLES

Lyons

PROVENCE

Paris

BURGUNDY

Cluny

Avignon

ENGLAND

NORMANDY

ANJOU

FRANCE

Clermont

AQUITAINE

GASCONY

MEDITERRANEAN SEA

BRITTANY

CATALONIA

ARAGON

VALENCIA

ATLANTIC
OCEAN

CASTILE

LEON

PORTUGAL

Granada

No doubt the Crusaders regarded themselves as armed pilgrims dedicated to rescuing holy places from the hated Muslims. Moreover, Urban declared that participation in a crusade was itself an act of penance, an acceptable way of demonstrating sorrow for sin. To the warrior nobility, a crusade was a great adventure that promised glory and plunder, but it was also an opportunity to remit sins by engaging in a holy war. The enthusiasm with which knights became Christian warriors demonstrated the extent to which the warrior mentality of the nobles had become penetrated by Christian principles.

Stirred by popular preachers, the common people also became gripped by the crusading spirit. The most remarkable of the evangelists was Peter the Hermit. Swayed by this old man's eloquence, thousands of poor people abandoned their villages and joined Peter's march to Jerusalem. After reaching Constantinople, Peter's recruits crossed into Turkish territory, where they were massacred.

An army of Christian knights also departed for Constantinople. In June 1099, three years after leaving Europe, the army of knights stood outside the walls of Jerusalem. Using siege weapons, they broke into the city and slaughtered the Muslim and Jewish inhabitants. In addition to capturing Jerusalem, the Crusaders carved out four principalities in the Near East. Never resigned to the establishment of Christian states in their midst, Muslim leaders called for a *jihad*, or holy war. In 1144, one of the Crusader states, the County of Edessa, fell to the resurgent forces of Islam. Alarmed by the loss of Edessa, Pope Eugenius II called for a second Crusade, which was a complete failure.

After 1174, Saladin, a brilliant commander, became the most powerful leader in the Muslim Near East, and in 1187 he invaded Palestine. Saladin annihilated a Christian army near Nazareth and recaptured Jerusalem in 1187. This led to the Third Crusade, in which some of Europe's most prominent rulers participated—Richard I, the Lion-Hearted, of England; Philip Augustus of France; and Frederick Barbarossa of Germany. The Crusaders captured Acre and Jaffa, but Jerusalem remained in Muslim hands.

Pope Innocent III called the Fourth Crusade to demonstrate anew that the papacy was the shepherd of Christendom. However, the pope was enraged by the actions of the Crusaders, who first attacked the Christian port of Zara, controlled by the king of Hungary, and then looted and defiled churches and massacred inhabitants in Constantinople. This shameful behavior, along with the belief that the papacy was exploiting the crusading ideal to extend its own power, weakened both the papacy and the crusading zeal of Christendom. Other Crusades followed, but the position of the Christian states in the Near East continued to deteriorate. In 1291, almost two centuries after Pope Urban's appeal, the last Christian strongholds in the Near East fell.

The Crusades increased the wealth of the Italian cities that furnished transportation for the Crusaders and benefited from the increased trade with the East. They may have contributed to the decline of feudalism and the strengthening of monarchy, because many lords were killed in battle or squandered their wealth financing expeditions to the Holy Land. Over the centuries, people have praised the Crusades for inspiring idealism and heroism; others

Capture of Jerusalem.   "Mad with joy, we reached the city of Jerusalem on the Tuesday, eight days before the Ides of June, and laid siege to it," wrote one Crusader. Two months later, the Crusaders broke into the city and massacred its inhabitants. (*Bibliothèque Nationale, Paris*)

have castigated the movement for corrupting the Christian spirit, for unleashing religious intolerance and fanaticism that would lead to strife in future centuries.

Dissenters and Reformers

Freedom of religion is a modern concept; it was totally alien to the medieval outlook. Regarding itself as the possessor and guardian of divine truth, the church felt a profound obligation to purge Christendom of heresy—beliefs that challenged Christian orthodoxy. To the church, heretics had committed treason against God and were carriers of a deadly infection. Heresy was the work of Satan; lured by false ideas, people might abandon the true faith and deny themselves salvation. In the eyes of the church, heretics not only obstructed individual salvation, but also undermined the foundations of society.

To compel obedience, the church used its power of excommunication. An excommunicated person could not receive the sacraments or attend church services—fearful punishments in an age of faith. In dealing with a recalcitrant ruler, the church could declare an interdict on his territory, which in effect denied the ruler's subjects the sacraments (although exceptions could be made). The church hoped that the pressure exerted by an aroused populace would compel the offending ruler to mend his ways.

The church also conducted heresy trials. Before the thirteenth century, local bishops were responsible for locating heretics and putting them on trial. In 1233 the papacy established the Inquisition, a court specially designed to fight heresy. Accused heretics were presumed guilty until proven innocent, were not told the names of their accusers, and were not permitted lawyers. To wrest a confession from the accused, torture was permitted. Accused persons who persisted in their beliefs were turned over to the civil authorities to be burned at the stake.

The Waldensians   Dissent in the Middle Ages was often reformist in character. Inspired by the Gospels, reformers criticized the church for its wealth and involvement in worldly affairs; they called for a return to the simpler, purer life of Jesus and the Apostles.

In their zeal to emulate the moral purity and material poverty of the first followers of Jesus, these reform-minded dissenters attacked ecclesiastical authority. The Waldensians, followers of Peter Waldo, a rich merchant of Lyon, were a case in point. In the 1170s, Peter distributed his property to the poor and attracted both male and female supporters. Like their leader, they committed themselves to poverty and to preaching the Gospel in the *vernacular,* or native tongue, rather than in the church's Latin, which many Christians did not understand. The Waldensians considered themselves true Christians, faithful to the spirit of the apostolic church. Repelled by Waldensian attacks against the immorality of the clergy and by the fact that these laymen were preaching the Gospel without the permission of ecclesiastical authorities, the church condemned the movement as heretical. Despite persecution, however, the Waldensians continued to survive as a group in northern Italy.

The Cathari   Catharism was the most radical heresy to confront the medieval church. This belief represented a curious mixture of Eastern religious movements that had competed with Christianity in the days of the Roman Empire. Cathari tenets differed considerably from those of the church. The Cathari believed in an eternal conflict between the forces of the god of good and those of the god of evil. Because the evil god, whom they identified with the God of the Old Testament, created the world, this earthly home was evil. The soul, spiritual in nature, was good, but it was trapped in wicked flesh.

The Cathari taught that since the flesh is evil, Christ would not have taken a human form; hence he could not have suffered on the cross nor have been resurrected. Nor could God have issued forth from the evil flesh of the Virgin. According to Catharism, Jesus was not God but an angel. In order to enslave people, the evil god created the church, which demonstrated its wickedness by pursuing power and wealth. Repudiating the church, the Cathari organized their own ecclesiastical hierarchy.

The center for the Catharist heresy was southern France, where a strong tradition of protest existed against the moral laxity and materialism of the clergy. When the Cathari did not submit to peaceful persuasion, Innocent III called on kings and lords to exterminate Catharism with the sword. Lasting from 1208 to 1229, the war against the Cathari was marked by brutality and fanaticism.

The Franciscans and the Dominicans Driven by a zeal for reform, devout laymen condemned the clergy for moral abuses. Sometimes their piety and resentment exploded into heresy; other times it was channeled into movements that served the church. Such was the case with the two great orders of friars, Franciscans and Dominicans.

Like Peter Waldo, Saint Francis of Assisi (c. 1181–1226) came from a wealthy merchant family. After undergoing an intense religious experience, Francis abandoned his possessions and devoted his life to imitating Christ. Dressed as a beggar, he wandered into villages and towns preaching, healing, and befriending the poor, the helpless, the sick, and even lepers, whom everyone feared to approach. The saintly Francis soon attracted disciples called *Little Brothers*, who followed in the footsteps of their leader.

As the Franciscans grew in popularity, the papacy exercised greater control over their activities; in time the order was transformed from a spontaneous movement of inspired laymen into an organized agent of papal policy. The Franciscans served the church as teachers and missionaries in eastern Europe, North Africa, the Near East, and China. The papacy set aside Francis's prohibition against the Brothers owning churches, houses, and lands corporately. His desire to keep the movement a lay order was abandoned when the papacy granted the Brothers the right to hear confession. Francis's opposition to formal learning as irrelevant to preaching Gospel love was rejected when the movement began to urge university education for its members. Those who protested against these changes as a repudiation of Francis's spirit were persecuted, and a few were even burned at the stake as heretics.

The Dominican order was founded by Saint Dominic (c. 1170–1221), a Spanish nobleman who had preached against the Cathari in southern France. Believing that those well-versed in Christian teaching could best combat heresy, Dominic, unlike Francis, insisted that his followers engage in study. In time, the Dominicans became some of the leading theologians in the universities. Like the Franciscans, they went out into the world to preach the gospel and to proselytize. Dominican friars became the chief operators of the Inquisition. For their zeal in fighting heresy, they were known as the watchdogs of the Lord.

Innocent III: The Apex of Papal Power

During the pontificate of Innocent III (1198–1216), papal theocracy reached its zenith. More than any earlier pope, Innocent made the papacy the center of European political life; in the tradition of Gregory VII, he forcefully asserted the theory of papal monarchy. As head of the church, Vicar of Christ, and successor of Saint Peter, Innocent claimed the authority to intervene in the internal affairs of secular rulers when they threatened the good order of Christendom. According to Innocent, the pope, "lower than God but higher than man . . . judges all and is judged by no one."[2]

Innocent applied these principles of papal supremacy in his dealings with the princes of Europe. When King Philip Augustus of France repudiated Ingeborg of Denmark the day after their wedding and later divorced her to marry someone else, Innocent placed an interdict on France to compel Philip to take Ingeborg back. For two decades, Innocent III championed Ingeborg's cause, until she finally became the French queen. When King John of England rejected the papal candidate for archbishop of Canterbury, Stephen Langton, Innocent first laid an interdict on the country. Then he excommunicated John, who expressed his defiance by confiscating church property and by forcing many bishops into exile. However, when Innocent urged Philip Augustus of France to invade England, John backed down.

After the disastrous Fourth Crusade, Innocent's attention turned to the Cathari. Unable to eliminate the Catharist heresy in southern France through preaching, Innocent decided on force. An army of crusading knights broke the power of the nobles who protected the heretics. Innocent III sent legates to the region to arrest and try the Cathari. Under his successor, Dominican and Franciscan inquisitors completed the task of exterminating them.

The culminating expression of Innocent's supremacy was the Fourth Lateran Council, called in 1215. Composed of about twelve hundred clergy and representatives of secular rulers, the council issued several far-reaching orders. It maintained that the Eastern Orthodox church was subordinate to the Roman Catholic church; it prohibited the state from taxing the clergy, and declared laws detrimental to the church null and void. The council made bishops responsible for ferreting out heretics in their dioceses and ordered secular authorities to punish convicted heretics. It insisted on high standards of behavior for the clergy and required that each Catholic confess his or her sins to a priest at least once a year.

Christians and Jews

Latin Christendom's growing self-consciousness, which found expression in hostility to Muslims and condemnation of heresy, also sparked a hatred of Jews—a visibly alien group in a society dominated by the Christian world-view. In 1096, bands of Crusaders massacred Jews in French and German towns. In 1290, Jews were expelled from England, and in 1306 from France. Between 1290 and 1293, explusions, massacres, and forced conversions led to the virtual disappearance of a centuries-old Jewish community life in southern Italy. In Germany, savage riots periodically led to the torture and murder of Jews.

Several factors contributed to anti-Jewish feelings during the Middle Ages. To medieval Christians, the refusal of the Jews to embrace Christianity was an act of wickedness, particularly since the church taught that the coming of Christ had been prophesied by the Old Testament. Related to this prejudice was the depiction of the crucifixion in the Gospels. In the minds of medieval Christians, the crime of deicide—the killing of God—eternally stained the Jews as a people. The flames of hatred were fanned by the absurd allegation that Jews, made bloodthirsty by the spilling of Christ's blood, tortured and murdered Christians, particularly children, to obtain blood for ritual purposes. This blood libel was widely believed by the credulous masses and incited numerous riots that led to the murder, torture, and expulsion of countless Jews, despite the fact that popes condemned the charge as groundless.

The role of Jews as money lenders also contributed to animosity toward them. As Jews were increasingly excluded from international trade and were barred from the guilds, and in some areas from landholding, virtually the only means of livelihood open to them was money lending. This activity, which was forbidden to Christians, aroused the hatred of individual peasants, clergy, lords, and kings who did the borrowing.

The policy of the church toward the Jews was that they should not be harmed, but that they should live in humiliation. Hence the Fourth Lateran Council barred Jews from public office, required them to wear a distinguishing badge on their clothing, and ordered them to remain off the streets during Christian festivals. Christian art, literature, and religious instruction depicted the Jews in a derogatory manner. Deeply etched into the minds and hearts of Christians, the distorted image of the Jew as a contemptible creature persisted in the popular mentality into the twentieth century.

Despite their precarious position, medieval Jews maintained their faith, expanded their tradition of biblical and legal scholarship, and developed a flourishing Hebrew literature. The work of Jewish translators, doctors, and philosophers contributed substantially to the flowering of medieval culture in the High Middle Ages.

Europe in the High Middle Ages showed considerable vitality. The population increased, long-distance trade revived, new towns emerged, states started to take shape, and papal power increased. The culminating expression of this recovery and resurgence was the cultural awakening of the twelfth and thirteenth centuries, the high point of medieval civilization and a great creative period in Western history.

Chronology 6.1 ◊ The Early and High Middle Ages

496	Clovis adopts Roman Christianity
596	Pope Gregory I sends missionaries to convert the Anglo-Saxons
732	Charles Martel defeats the Muslims at Tours
768	Charlemagne becomes king of the Franks
800	Charlemagne is crowned emperor of the Romans by Pope Leo III
c. 840s	The height of Viking attacks
962	Otto I crowned emperor of the West, beginning the Holy Roman Empire
987	Hugh Capet becomes king of France
1054	The split between the Byzantine and Roman churches
1066	The Norman conquest of England
1075	Start of the Investiture Controversy
1096	Start of the First Crusade
1198–1216	Pontificate of Innocent III; the height of the church's power

Notes

1. Quoted in V. H. H. Green, *Medieval Civilization in Western Europe* (New York: St. Martin's Press, 1971), p. 35.

2. Excerpted in Brian Tierney, ed., *The Crisis of Church and State, 1050–1300* (Englewood Cliffs, N.J.: Prentice-Hall, 1964), p. 132.

Suggested Reading

Bark, W. C., *Origins of the Medieval World* (1960). The Early Middle Ages as a fresh beginning.

Dawson, Christopher, *The Making of Europe* (1957). Stresses the role of Christianity in shaping European civilization.

Gies, Frances, and Gies, Joseph, *Women in the Middle Ages* (1978). The narrative weaves in valuable quotations from medieval sources.

———, *Life in a Medieval Castle* (1974). The castle as the center of medieval life; passages from journals, songs, and account books permit medieval people to speak for themselves.

Laistner, M. L. W., *Thought and Letters in Western Europe A.D. 500 to 900* (1957). A comprehensive survey of European thought in the Early Middle Ages.

Lewis, A. R., *Emerging Medieval Europe* (1967). Good discussions of economic and social changes.

Lopez, R. S., *The Commercial Revolution of the Middle Ages, 950–1350* (1976). How an undeveloped society succeeded in developing itself.

Mayer, H. E., *The Crusades* (1972). A short, scholarly treatment.

Pounds, N. J. G., *An Economic History of Medieval Europe* (1974). A lucid survey.

Rorig, Fritz, *The Medieval Town* (1971). A study of medieval urban life.

Trachtenberg, Joshua, *The Devil and the Jews* (1961). The medieval conception of the Jew and its relationship to modern anti-Semitism.

White, Lynn, Jr., *Medieval Technology and Social Change* (1964). A study of medieval advances in technology.

Zacour, Norman, *An Introduction to Medieval Institutions* (1969). Comprehensive essays on all phases of medieval society.

Review Questions

1. What was the long-term influence of Byzantium on world history?
2. Characterize and discuss the significance of the Muslim intellectual achievement.
3. The civilization of Latin Christendom was a blending of Christian, Greco-Roman, and Germanic traditions. Explain this statement.
4. What was the significance of monks and nuns to medieval civilization?
5. What crucial developments occurred during the reign of Charlemagne? Why were they significant?
6. What conditions led to the rise of feudalism? How did feudal law differ from Roman law?
7. What advances in agriculture occurred during the Middle Ages? What was the effect of these advances?
8. What factors contributed to the rise of towns? What was the significance of the medieval town?
9. Identify and explain the importance of the following: William the Conqueror, common law, Magna Carta, and Parliament.
10. Why did Germany fail to achieve unity during the Middle Ages?
11. What prompted Urban II to call a crusade against the Turks? What prompted lords and commoners to go on a crusade? What was the final importance and outcome of the Crusades?
12. Why did the church regard Waldensians and Cathari as heretics?
13. What factors contributed to the rise of anti-Semitism during the Middle Ages? How does anti-Semitism demonstrate the power of mythical thinking?
14. The High Middle Ages showed many signs of recovery and vitality. Discuss this statement.

Chapter ⊗ 7

The Flowering of
Medieval Civilization:
The Christian Synthesis

The high point of papal power in the Middle Ages coincided with a cultural flowering in philosophy, the visual arts, and literature. Creative intellects achieved on a cultural level what the papacy accomplished on an institutional level—the integration of life around a Christian viewpoint. The High Middle Ages saw the restoration of some of the learning of the ancient world, the rise of universities, the emergence of an original form of architecture (the Gothic), and the erection of an imposing system of thought called *scholasticism*. Medieval theologian-philosophers fashioned Christian teachings into an all-embracing philosophy that represented the spiritual essence, the distinctive style of medieval civilization. They perfected what Christian thinkers in the Roman Empire had initiated and what the learned men of the Early Middle Ages has been groping for—a synthesis of Greek philosophy and Christian revelation. ⊗

Revival of Learning

In the late eleventh century, Latin Christendom began to experience a cultural revival; all areas of life showed vitality and creativeness. In the twelfth and thirteenth centuries, a rich civilization with a distinctive style united an educated elite in the lands from Britain to Sicily. Gothic cathedrals, an enduring testament to the creativity of the religious impulse, were erected throughout Europe. Universities sprang up in scores of cities. Roman authors were again read and their style imitated; the quality of written Latin—the language of the church, learning, and education—improved, and secular and religious poetry, both in Latin and in the vernacular, abounded. Roman law emerged anew in Italy, spread to northern Europe, and regained its importance (lost since Roman times) as worthy of study and scholarship. Some key works of ancient Greece were translated into Latin and studied in universities. Employing the rational tradition of Greece, men of genius harmonized Christian doctrines and Greek philosophy.

Several conditions contributed to this cultural explosion known as the Twelfth-Century Awakening. As attacks of Vikings, Muslims, and Magyars ended and kings and great lords imposed more order and stability, people found greater opportunities for travel and communication. The revival of trade and the growth of towns created a need for literacy and provided the wealth required to support learning. Growing contact with Islamic and Byzantine cultures led to the translation into Latin of ancient Greek works preserved by these Eastern civilizations. The Twelfth-Century Awakening was also kindled by the legacy of the Carolingian Renaissance, whose cultural lights had

Law Class at the University of Bologna.   The core of the medieval curriculum included the *trivium* and the *quadrivium*. Students mastered grammar, rhetoric, and dialectic—the "three ways" (trivium)—and then proceeded to mathematics, geometry, astronomy, and music (quadrivium). The technique of teaching was the *disputatio,* or oral disputation between master and student. (*Bildarchiv Preussischer Kulturbesitz*)

dimmed but never wholly vanished in the period of disorder following the dissolution of Charlemagne's empire.

In the Early Middle Ages the principal educational centers were the monastic schools. During the twelfth century, cathedral schools in towns grew in importance. Their teachers, paid a stipend by a local church, taught grammar, rhetoric, and logic. But the chief expression of expanding intellectual life was the university, a distinct creation of the Middle Ages. The first universities were not planned but grew up spontaneously. They arose as students eager for knowledge gathered around prominent teachers. The renewed importance of Roman law for business and politics, for example, drew students to Bologna to study with acknowledged masters.

University students attended lectures, studied for examinations, and earned degrees. They studied grammar, rhetoric, logic, arithmetic, geometry, astronomy, music, and when prepared, church law and theology, which was considered the queen of the sciences. The curriculum relied heavily on Latin translations of ancient texts, principally the works of Aristotle. In mathematics and astronomy, students read Latin translations of Euclid and Ptolemy, while students of medicine studied the works of two great medical men of the ancient world, Hippocrates and Galen.

Universities performed a vital function in the Middle Ages. Students learned the habit of reasoned argument. Universities trained professional secretaries and lawyers, who administered the affairs of church and state; these institutions of learning also produced theologians and philosophers, who shaped the climate of public opinion. The learning disseminated by universities tightened the cultural bonds that united Christian Europe, and established in the West a tradition of learning that has never died; there is direct continuity between the universities of our own day and medieval universities.

The Medieval World-View

A distinctive world-view based essentially on Christianity evolved during the Middle Ages. This outlook differed from both the Greco-Roman and the modern scientific and secular views of the world. In the Christian view, not the individual but the Creator determined what constituted the good life. Thus, reason that was not illuminated by revelation was either wrong or inadequate, for God had revealed the proper rules for the regulation of individual and social life. Ultimately, the good life was not of this world but came from a union with God in a higher world. This Christian belief as formulated by the church made life and death purposeful and intelligible. It was the outlook that dominated the thought of the Middle Ages.

The Universe: Higher and Lower Worlds

Medieval thinkers sharply differentiated between spirit and matter, between a realm of grace and an earthly realm, between a higher world of perfection and a lower world of imperfection. Moral values were derived from the higher world, which was also the final destination for the faithful. Two sets of laws operated in the medieval universe, one for the heavens and one for the earth. The cosmos was a giant ladder with God at the summit; earth, composed of base matter, stood at the bottom, just above hell.

From Aristotle and Ptolemy, medieval thinkers inherited the theory of an earth-centered universe—the geocentric theory—which they impregnated with Christian symbolism. The geocentric theory held that revolving around the motionless earth at uniform speeds were seven transparent spheres in which were embedded each of the seven "planets"—the moon, Mercury, Venus, the sun, Mars, Jupiter, and Saturn. A sphere of fixed stars enclosed this planetary system. Above the firmament of the stars were the three heavenly spheres: the outermost, the Empyrean Heaven, was the abode of God and the Elect; through the sphere below—the Prime Mover—God transmitted motion to the planetary spheres; beneath this was the lowermost sphere, the invisible Crystalline Heaven.

An earth-centered universe accorded with the Christian idea that God created the universe for men and women and that salvation was the essential aim of life. Because God had created people in his image, they deserved this central position in the universe. Although they might be living at the bottom rung of the cosmic ladder, only they, of all living things, had the capacity to ascend to heaven, the realm of perfection.

Also acceptable to the Christian mentality was the sharp distinction drawn by Aristotle between the world above the moon and the one below it. Aristotle held that terrestrial bodies on earth were made of four elements—earth, water, air, fire. Celestial bodies that occupied the region above the moon were composed of a fifth element, the ether, too clear, too pure, too perfect to be found on earth. The planets and stars existed in a world apart; they were made of the divine ether and followed celestial laws that did not apply to earthly objects. Whereas earthly bodies underwent change—ice converting to water, a burning log converting to ashes—heavenly objects were incorruptible, immune to all change. Unlike earthly objects, they were indestructible.

Heavenly bodies also followed different laws of motion from earthly objects. Aristotle said that it was natural for celestial bodies to move eternally in uniform circles, such motion being considered a sign of perfection. According to Aristotle, it was also natural for heavy bodies (stone) to fall downward and for light objects (fire, smoke) to move upward toward the celestial world; the falling stone and the rising smoke were finding their natural place in the universe.

The Individual: Sinful but Redeemable

At the center of medieval belief was the image of a perfect God and a wretched and sinful human being. God had given Adam and Eve freedom to choose; rebellious and presumptuous, they had used their freedom to disobey God. In doing so, they made evil an intrinsic part of the human personality. But God, who has not stopped loving human beings, had shown them the way out of sin. God became man and died so that human beings might be saved. Men and women were weak, egocentric, and sinful. With God's grace they could overcome their sinful nature and gain salvation; without grace, they were utterly helpless.

The medieval individual's understanding of himself or herself related to a comprehension of the universe as a hierarchy culminating in God. On earth, the basest objects were lifeless stones devoid of souls; higher than stones were plants, which possessed a primitive type of soul that allowed for reproduction and growth. Still higher were animals that had the capacity for motion and sensation. The highest of the animals were human beings, who, unlike other animals, could grasp some part of universal truth. Far superior to them were the angels, who apprehended God's truth without difficulty. At the summit of this graduated universe (the Great Chain of Being) was God, who was pure Being, without limitation, and the source of all existence. God's revelation reached down to humanity through the hierarchic order. From God, revelation passed to the angels, who were also arranged hierarchically. From the angels, the truth reached men and women, grasped first by prophets and apostles and then by the multitudes. Thus, all things in the universe, from angels to men and women to the lowest earthly objects, occupied a place peculiar to their nature and were linked by God in a great, unbroken chain.

Medieval individuals derived a sense of security from this hierarchical universe, in which the human position was clearly defined. True, they were sinners who dwelt on a corruptible earth at the bottom of the cosmic hierarchy. But they *could* ascend to the higher world of perfection above the moon. As children of God, they enjoyed the unique distinction that each human soul was precious and commanded respect.

Medieval thinkers also arranged knowledge in a hierarchic order: knowledge of spiritual things surpassed all worldly knowledge, all human sciences. To know what God wanted of the individual was the summit of self-knowledge and permitted entrance into heaven. Thus, God was both the source and the end of knowledge. The human capacity to think and to act freely constituted the image of God within each individual; it ennobled men and women and offered them the promise of associating with God in heaven. Human nobility might derive from intelligence and free will, but if individuals used these attributes to disobey God, they brought misery on themselves.

Philosophy, Science, and Law

Medieval philosophy, or *scholasticism,* attempted to apply reason to revelation. It tried to explain and clarify Christian teachings by means of concepts and principles of logic derived from Greek philosophy. Scholastics tried to show that the teachings of faith, although not derived from reason, were not contrary to reason. They tried to prove through reason what they already held to be true through faith. For example, the existence of God and the immortality of the soul, which every Christian accepted as articles of faith, could also, they thought, be demonstrated by reason. In struggling to harmonize faith with reason, medieval thinkers constructed an extraordinary synthesis of Christian revelation and Greek rationalism.

The scholastic masters used reason not to challenge faith but to serve faith—to elucidate, clarify, and buttress it. They did not break with the central concern of Christianity, that of earning God's grace and achieving salvation. Although this goal could be realized solely by faith, scholastic thinkers insisted that a science of nature did not obstruct the pursuit of grace and that philosophy could assist the devout in the contemplation of God. They did not reject Christian beliefs that were beyond the grasp of human reason and therefore could not be deduced by rational argument. Instead, they held that such truths rested entirely on revelation and were to be accepted on faith. To medieval thinkers, reason did not have an independent existence, but ultimately had to acknowledge a suprarational, superhuman standard of truth. They wanted rational thought to be directed by faith for Christian ends and guided by scriptural and ecclesiastical authority. Ultimately, faith had the final word.

Not all Christian thinkers welcomed the use of reason. Regarding Greek philosophy as an enemy of faith, a fabricator of heresies, and an obstacle to achieving communion of the soul with God, conservative theologians opposed the application of reason to Christian revelation. In a sense the conservatives were right. By giving renewed vitality to Greek thought, medieval philosophy nurtured a powerful force that would eventually shatter the medieval concepts of nature and society and weaken Christianity. Modern Western thought was created by philosophers' refusal to subordinate reason to Christian orthodoxy. Reason proved a double-edged sword: it both ennobled and undermined the medieval world-view.

Saint Anselm and Abelard

An early scholastic, Saint Anselm (1033–1109), was abbot of the Benedictine monastery of Le Bec in Normandy. He used rational argument to serve the interests of faith. Like Augustine before him and other thinkers who followed him, Anselm said that faith was a precondition for understanding. Without belief there could be no proper knowledge. He developed philosophical proof for the existence of God. Anselm argued as follows: We can conceive of no being greater than God. But if God were to exist only in thought and not in actuality, his greatness would be limited; he would be less than perfect. Hence he exists. Anselm's motive and method reveal something about the essence of medieval philosophy. He does not begin as a modern might: "If it can be proven that God exists, I will adopt the creed of Christianity; if not, I will either deny God's existence (atheism) or reserve judgment (agnosticism)." Rather, Anselm accepts God's existence as an established fact because he believes what Holy Scripture says and what the church teaches. He then proceeds to employ logical argument to demonstrate that God can be known not only through faith but also through reason. He would never use reason to subvert what he knows to be true by faith. In general, this attitude would characterize later medieval thinkers, who also applied reason to faith.

As a young teacher of theology at the Cathedral School of Notre Dame, Peter Abelard (1079–1142) acquired a reputation for brilliance and combativeness. His tragic affair with Héloïse, whom he tutored, has become one of the great romances in Western literature. Abelard's most determined opponent, Bernard of Clairvaux, accused Abelard of using the method of dialectical argument to attack faith. To Bernard, a monk and mystic, subjecting revealed truth to critical analysis was fraught with danger. Hearkening to Bernard's powerful voice, the church condemned Abelard and confined him to a monastery for the rest of his days.

Abelard believed that it was important to apply reason to faith and that careful and constant questioning led to wisdom. In *Sic et Non* (Yes and No), he took 150 theological issues, and by presenting passages from the Bible and the church fathers, showed that there were conflicting opinions. He suggested that the divergent opinions of authorities could be reconciled through proper use of dialectics. But like Anselm before him, Abelard did not intend to refute traditional church doctrines. Reason would buttress, not weaken, the authority of faith. He wrote after his condemnation in 1141: "I will never be a philosopher, if this is to speak against St. Paul; I would not be an Aristotle if this were to separate me from Christ. . . . I have set my building on the cornerstone on which Christ has built his Church. . . . I rest upon the rock that cannot be moved."[1]

Saint Thomas Aquinas: The Synthesis of Reason and Christianity

The introduction into Latin Christendom of the major works of Aristotle created a dilemma for religious authorities. Aristotle's comprehensive philosophy of nature and man, a product of human reason alone, conflicted in many instances with essential Christian doctrine. Whereas Christianity taught that God created the universe at a specific point in time, Aristotle held that the universe was eternal. Nor did Aristotle believe in the personal immortality of the soul, another cardinal principle of Christianity. Church officials feared that the dissemination of Aristotle's ideas and the use of Aristotelian logic would endanger faith. At various times in the first half of the thirteenth century they forbade teaching the scientific works of Aristotle at the University of Paris. But because the ban did not apply throughout Christendom and was not consistently enforced in Paris, Aristotle's philosophy continued to be studied.

Rejecting the position of conservatives who insisted that philosophy would contaminate faith, Saint Thomas Aquinas (c. 1225–1274) upheld the value of human reason and natural knowledge. He set about to reconcile Aristotelianism with Christianity. Aquinas taught at Paris and organized the Dominican school of theology in Naples. His greatest work, *Summa Theologica,* is a systematic exposition of Christian thought.

Can the teachings of faith conflict with the evidence of reason? For Aquinas, the answer was emphatically no. Since *both* faith and reason came from God, they were not in competition with each other but, properly understood, supported each other and formed an organic unity. Consequently, reason should not be feared, for it was another avenue to God. Because there was an inherent agreement between true faith and correct reason—they both ultimately stemmed from God—contradictions between the two were only a misleading appearance. Although philosophy had not yet been able to resolve the dilemma, for God no such contradictions existed. In heaven, human beings would attain complete knowledge as well as complete happiness. While on earth, however, they must allow faith to guide reason; they must not permit reason to oppose or undermine faith.

Because reason was no enemy of faith, its application to revelation should not be feared. As human reasoning became more proficient, said Aquinas, it also became more Christian, and apparent incompatibilities between faith and reason disappeared. Recognizing that both faith and reason point to the same truth, the wise person accepts the guidance of religion in all questions that relate directly to knowledge needed for salvation. There also existed a wide range of knowledge that God had not revealed and that was not required for salvation. Into this category fell much knowledge about the natural world of things and creatures, which human beings had perfect liberty to explore.

Thus, in exalting God, Aquinas also paid homage to human intelligence, proclaimed the value of rational activity, and asserted the importance of physical reality discovered through human senses. Therefore, he valued the natural philosophy of Aristotle. Correctly used, Aristotelian thought would provide faith with valuable assistance. To synthesize Aristotelianism with the divine revelation of Christianity was Aquinas's great effort. That the two could be harmonized he had no doubt. He made use of Aristotelian categories in his five proofs of God's existence. In his first proof, for example, Aquinas argued that a thing cannot move itself. Whatever is moved must be moved by something else, and that by something else again. "Therefore, it is necessary to arrive at a first mover, moved by no other; and this everyone understands to be God."[2]

Aquinas upheld the value of reason. To love the intellect was to honor God and not to diminish the truth of faith. He had confidence in the power of the rational mind to comprehend most of the truths of revelation, and he insisted that in nontheological questions about specific things in nature—those questions not affecting salvation—people should trust only to reason and experience. Thus, Aquinas gave new importance to the empirical world and to scientific speculation and human knowledge. The traditional medieval view based largely on Saint Augustine drew a sharp distinction between the higher world of grace and the lower world of nature, between the world of spirit and the world of sense experience. Knowledge derived from the natural world was often seen as an obstacle to true knowledge. Aquinas altered this tradition by affirming the importance of knowledge of the social order and the physical world. He gave to human reason and to worldly knowledge a new dignity. Thus, the City of Man was not merely a sinful place from which people tried to escape in order to enter God's city; it was worthy of investigation and understanding. But Aquinas remained a medieval and not a modern thinker, for he always subordinated reason to the needs of faith, and he never questioned the truth of the medieval Christian view of the world and the individual.

Science

During the Early Middle Ages, few scientific works from the ancient world were available to western Europeans. Scientific thought was at its lowest ebb since it had originated more than a thousand years earlier in Greece. In contrast, both Islamic and Byzantine civilizations preserved and in some instances added to the legacy of Greek science. In the High Middle Ages, however, many ancient texts were translated from Greek and Arabic into Latin, and entered Latin Christendom for the first time. The principal centers of translation were Spain, where Christian and Muslim civilizations met, and Sicily, which had been controlled by Byzantium up to the last part of the ninth century and then by Islam until Christian Normans completed conquest of the island by 1091.

In the thirteenth and fourteenth centuries, a genuine scientific movement did occur. Impressed with the naturalistic and empirical approach of Aristotle, some medieval schoolmen spent time examining physical nature. Among them was the Dominican Albert the Great (Albertus Magnus). Albert (c. 1206–1280) was born in Germany, studied at Padua, and taught at the University of Paris, where Thomas Aquinas was his student. To Albert, philosophy meant more than employing Greek reason to contemplate divine wisdom: it also meant making sense of nature. Albert devoted himself to editing and commenting on the vast body of Aristotle's works.

While retaining the Christian stress on God, revelation, the supernatural, and the afterlife, Albert (unlike many earlier Christian thinkers) considered nature a valid field for investigation. In his writings on geology, chemistry, botany, and zoology, Albert, like Aristotle, displayed a respect for the concrete details of nature, utilizing them as empirical evidence. Albert approved of inquiry into the material world, stressed the value of knowledge derived from experience with nature, sought rational explanations for natural occurrences, and held that theological debates should not stop scientific investigations.

Other scholars of the scientific movement included Robert Grosseteste (c. 1175–1253), chancellor of Oxford University. He declared that the roundness of the earth could be demonstrated by reason. In addition, he insisted that mathematics was necessary in order to understand the physical world, and he carried out experiments on the refraction of light. Another Englishman, the monk and philosopher Roger Bacon (c. 1214–1294), foreshadowed the modern attitude of using science to gain mastery over nature. Bacon valued the study of mathematics and read Arabic works on the reflection and refraction of light. Among his achievements were experiments in optics and the observation that light travels much faster than sound. His description of the anatomy of the vertebrate eye and optic nerves was the finest of that era, and he recommended dissecting the eyes of pigs and cows to obtain greater knowledge of the subject.

Medieval scholars did not make the breakthrough to modern science. They kept the belief that the earth was at the center of the universe and that different sets of laws operated on earth and in the heavens. They did not invent analytic geometry or calculus or arrive at the modern concept of inertia. Moreover, medieval science was never wholly removed from a theological setting. Modern science self-consciously seeks the advancement of specifically scientific knowledge, but in the Middle Ages, many questions involving nature were raised merely to clarify a religious problem.

Medieval scholars and philosophers did, however, advance knowledge about optics, the tides, and mechanics. They saw the importance of mathematics for interpreting nature, and they performed experiments. By translating and commenting on ancient Greek and Arabic works, medieval scholars provided future ages with ideas to reflect on and to surpass, a necessary precondition for the emergence of modern science. Medieval thinkers also developed an anti-Aristotelian physics that some historians of science believe influenced Galileo, the creator of modern mechanics, more than two centuries later.

Recovery of Roman Law

During the Early Middle Ages, western European law essentially consisted of Germanic customs, some of which had been put into writing. Some elements of Roman law endured as custom and practice, but the formal study of Roman law had disappeared. The late eleventh and twelfth centuries saw the revival of Roman law, particularly in Bologna, Italy. Irnerius lectured on the *Corpus Juris Civilis,* codified by Byzantine jurists in the sixth century, and he made Bologna the leading center for the study of Roman law. Irnerius and his students employed the methods of organization and logical analysis that scholastic theologians used in studying philosophical texts.

Unlike traditional Germanic law, Roman law assumed the existence of universal principles that could be grasped by the human intellect and expressed in the law of the state. Roman jurists had systematically and rationally structured the legal experience of the Roman people. The example of Roman law stimulated medieval jurists to organize their own legal tradition. Intellectuals increasingly came to insist upon both a rational analysis of evidence and judicial decisions based upon rational procedures. Law codes compiled in parts of France and Germany and in the kingdom of Castile were influenced by the recovery of Roman law.

Literature

Medieval literature was written both in Latin and in the vernacular. Much of medieval Latin literature consisted of religious hymns and dramas depicting

Millefleurs Tapestry: Two Musicians, School of the Loire, France, c. 1500. The courtly love tradition, in which women were worshiped and untouchable, inspired poetry. Troubadours sang this poetry, which expressed a changing attitude toward women. By inviting poets to their courts, and writing poetry themselves, noblewomen actively influenced the rituals and literature of courtly love. (*Collection of The Frick Art Museum, Pittsburgh, Pennsylvania*)

the life of Christ and saints. In their native tongues, medieval writers created different forms of poetry: *chansons de geste,* the *roman,* and *troubadour* songs, which emerged during the High Middle Ages.

The French chansons de geste—epic poems of heroic deeds that had first been told orally—were written in the vernacular of northern France. These poems dealt with Charlemagne's battles against the Muslims, with rebellious nobles, and with feudal warfare. The finest of these epic poems, *The Song of Roland,* expressed the vassal's loyalty to his lord and the Christian's devotion to his faith. Roland, Charlemagne's nephew, was killed in a battle with the Muslims. The *Nibelungenlied,* the best expression of the herioc epic in Germany, is often called "the *Iliad* of the Germans." Like its French counterpart, it dealt with heroic feats.

The roman—a blending of old legends, chivalric ideals, and Christian concepts—combined love with adventure, war, and the miraculous. Among the romans were the tales of King Arthur and his Round Table. Circulating by word of mouth for centuries, these tales spread from the British Isles to France and Germany. In the twelfth century, they were put into French verse.

Another form of medieval poetry, which flourished particularly in Provence in southern France, dealt with the romantic glorification of women. Sung by troubadours, many of them nobles, the courtly love poetry expressed a changing attitude toward women. Although medieval men generally regarded women as inferior and subordinate, courtly love poetry ascribed to noble ladies superior qualities of virtue. To the nobleman, the lady became a goddess worthy of all devotion, loyalty, and worship. He would honor her and serve her as he did his lord; for her love he would undergo any sacrifice.

Noblewomen actively influenced the rituals and literature of courtly love. They often invited poets to their courts and wrote poetry themselves. They demanded that knights treat them with gentleness and consideration, and that knights dress neatly, bathe often, play instruments, and compose (or at least recite) poetry. To prove worthy of his lady's love, a knight had to demonstrate patience, charm, bravery, and loyalty. By devoting himself to a lady, it was believed, a knight would ennoble his character.

Courtly love did not involve a husband-wife relationship, but a noble's admiration of and yearning for another woman of his class. Among nobles, marriages were arranged for political and economic reasons. The rituals of courtly love, it has been suggested, provided an expanded outlet for erotic feelings condemned by the church. They also expanded the skills and refined the tastes of the noble. The rough warrior acquired wit, manners, charm, and skill with words. He was becoming a courtier and a gentleman.

Written in the vernacular, *The Canterbury Tales* of Geoffrey Chaucer (c. 1340–1400) is a masterpiece of English literature. Chaucer chose as his theme twenty-nine pilgrims en route from London to the religious shrine at Canterbury. In describing the pilgrims, Chaucer displayed humor, charm, an understanding of human nature, and a superb grasp of the attitudes of the English. Few writers have pictured their times better.

The greatest literary figure of the Middle Ages was Dante Alighieri (1265–1321) of Florence. Dante appreciated the Roman classics and wrote not just in Latin, the traditional language of intellectual life, but in Italian, his native tongue. In this respect he anticipated the Renaissance. In the tradition of the troubadours, Dante wrote poems to his beloved Beatrice.

In the *Divine Comedy,* Dante synthesized the various elements of the medieval outlook and summed up, with immense feeling, the medieval understanding of the purpose of life. Written while Dante was in exile, the *Divine Comedy* describes the poet's journey through hell, purgatory, and paradise. Dante arranges hell into nine concentric circles; in each region, sinners are punished in proportion to their earthly sins. The poet experiences all of hell's torments—burning sand, violent storms, darkness, and fearful monsters who whip, claw, bite, and tear sinners apart. The ninth circle, the lowest, is reserved for Lucifer and traitors. Lucifer has three faces, each a different color, and two batlike wings. In each mouth he gnaws on the greatest traitors in history—Judas Iscariot, who betrayed Jesus, and Brutus and Cassius, who assassinated Caesar. Those condemned to hell are told: "All hope abandon, ye who enter in." In purgatory, Dante meets sinners who, although they undergo punishment, will eventually enter paradise. In paradise, an abode of light, music, and gentleness, the poet, guided by Beatrice, meets the great saints and the Virgin Mary. For an instant, he glimpses the Vision of God. In this indescribable mystical experience, the aim of life is realized.

Reims Façade. In Reims Cathedral, the High Gothic style makes a complete statement: the portals are deeply recessed with rich sculpture. The towers are symmetrical with an elaborate, heavily sculpted, connecting screen, and the rose window facing the front is so large that it serves as a translucent wall. (*Jean Roubier*)

Architecture

Two styles of architecture evolved during the Middle Ages: Romanesque and Gothic. The Romanesque style predominated in the eleventh and greater part of the twelfth centuries. Romanesque buildings—many of them monasteries as well as churches—contained massive walls supporting stone barrel vaults, rounded arches, and small windows. A construction of thick walls with few gaps for windows was necessary to hold up the great weight of the roofs. The interiors of Romanesque churches were dark, with an air of mystery, and the columns and walls were decorated with sculptured religious scenes. The development of the pointed arch allowed for supports that lessened the bearing pressure of the roof on the walls. This new style, the Gothic, allowed buildings to have lofty, vaulted ceilings, and huge windows, which made the interior lighter than Romanesque churches. The Romanesque church produced an impression of massive solidity; the Gothic cathedral, one of soaring grace.

The Gothic cathedral was a visual expression of the medieval view of a hierarchical universe. Historian Joan Kelly Gadol concludes: "Inside and out, the Gothic cathedral is one great movement upward through a mounting series of grades, one ascent through horizontal levels marked by arches, galleries, niches, and towers. . . . the material ascends to the spiritual, the natural is assumed into the supernatural—all in a gradated rise."[3] Magnificently de-

Tympanum of the South Portal of the Abbey Church of St. Pierre, Moissac, France, c. 1115–1135. This is a fine example of a Romanesque tympanum—the recessed, ornamented space within an arch above the church door. The relief sculptures of stylized figures fill the area. The Last Judgment was a popular theme for tympana; Christ's figure (center) dominates the area, and the Evangelists and their animal symbols appear beside him. (*Bulloz, Paris*)

signed stained-glass windows depicted scenes from the Bible and the lives of saints for the edification of the people, many of whom were illiterate. The subtle light of the stained glass windows evokes a religious experience. Light was a principal medieval metaphor for God. Although light itself is usually invisible, it enables human beings to see; similarly, God is invisible, but his existence makes possible the world of space and time. The Gothic style was to remain vigorous until the fifteenth century, spreading from France to England, Germany, Spain, and beyond. Revived from time to time thereafter, it has proved to be one of the most enduring styles in Western art and architecture.

The Fourteenth Century: An Age of Adversity

By the opening of the fourteenth century, Latin Christendom had experienced more than 250 years of growth. On an economic level, agricultural production had expanded, commerce and town life had revived, and the population had increased. On a political level, kings had become more powerful, bringing greater order and security over large areas. On a religious level, the papacy had demonstrated its strength as the spiritual leader of Christendom, and the clergy had been reformed. On a cultural level, a unified world-view blending faith and reason had been forged.

In the Late Middle Ages (roughly the fourteenth century), however, Latin Christendom was afflicted with severe problems. The earlier increases in agricultural production did not continue. Limited use of fertilizers and limited knowledge of conservation exhausted the topsoil. From 1301 to 1314 there was a general shortage of food, and from 1315 to 1317 famine struck Europe. Throughout the century, starvation and malnutrition were widespread.

Adding to the crisis was the Black Death, or bubonic plague. This disease was carried by fleas on black rats and probably first struck Mongolia in 1331–1332. From there it crossed into Russia. Carried back from Black Sea ports, the plague reached Sicily in 1347. Spreading swiftly throughout much of Europe, it attacked an already declining and undernourished population. The first crisis lasted until 1351, and other serious outbreaks occurred in later decades. The crowded cities and towns had the highest mortalities. Perhaps twenty million people—about one-quarter to one-third of the European population—perished in the worst natural disaster in recorded history.

The panic-stricken masses drifted into immorality and frenzied forms of religious life. Hysteria and popular superstition abounded. Flagellants marched from region to region, beating each other with sticks and whips in a desperate effort to appease God, who they believed had cursed them with the plague. Black magic, witchcraft, and sexual license found eager supporters. Dress became increasingly ostentatious and bizarre; art concentrated on morbid scenes of decaying flesh, dances of death, and the torments of Hell. Sometimes this hysteria was directed against Jews, who were accused of causing the plague by poisoning wells. Terrible massacres of Jews occurred despite the pleas of the papacy.

The millions of deaths caused production of food and goods to plummet and some prices to soar. Economic and social tensions, some of them antedating the Black Death, escalated into rebellions. Each rebellion had its own specific causes, but a general pattern characterized the uprisings in the countryside. When kings and lords, breaking with customary social relationships, imposed new and onerous regulations, the peasants rose in defense of their traditional rights. In 1323, the lords' attempt to reimpose old manorial obligations infuriated the free peasants of Flanders, whose condition had improved in earlier decades. The peasants' revolt lasted five bloody years. In 1358, French peasants took up arms in protest against the plundering of the countryside by

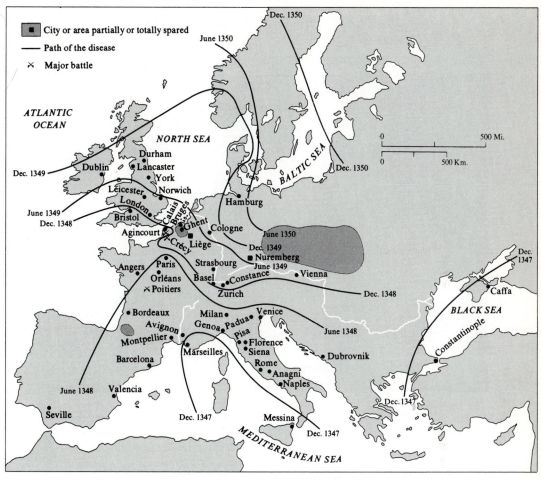

Map 7.1 Path of the Black Death, 1347–1350

soldiers. Perhaps 20,000 peasants died in the uprising known as the *Jacquerie*. In 1381, English peasants revolted, angered over legislation that tied them to the land and imposed new taxes. Like the revolts in Flanders and France, the uprising in England failed. To the landed aristocracy, the peasants were sinners attacking a social system ordained by God. Possessing superior might, the nobility suppressed the peasants, sometimes with savage cruelty.

Social unrest afflicted the towns as well as the countryside. The wage earners of Florence (1378), the weavers of Ghent (1382), and the poor of Paris (1382) rose up against the ruling oligarchies. These revolts were generally initiated not by the poorest and most downtrodden, but by those who had made some gains and were eager for more. The rebellions of the urban poor were crushed just as the peasant uprisings were.

The Jacquerie.   During the One Hundred Years' War, English mercenaries and French nobles pillaged the countryside in northeastern France. French peasants, enraged by the looting and further angered by the nobles' imposition of heavier dues, destroyed castles and killed their inhabitants. But the peasants' uprising was defeated and 20,000 were massacred. (*Bibliothèque Nationale, Paris*)

Compounding the adversity were the conflicts known as the Hundred Years' War (1337–1453). Because English kings had ruled parts of France, conflicts between the two monarchies were common. In the opening phase of the war, the English inflicted terrible defeats on French knights at the battles of Crécy (1346) and Poitiers (1356). Using longbows, which allowed them to shoot arrows rapidly, English archers cut down wave after wave of charging French cavalry. The war continued on and off throughout the fourteenth century. During periods of truce, gangs of unemployed soldiers roamed the French countryside killing and stealing, actions that precipitated the Jacquerie.

After the battle of Agincourt (1415), won by the English under Henry V, the English controlled most of northern France. It appeared that England would shortly conquer France and join the two lands under one crown. At this crucial moment in French history, a young and illiterate peasant girl, Joan of Arc (1412–1431), helped to rescue France. Believing that God commanded her to drive the English out of France, Joan rallied the demoralized French troops, leading them in battle. In 1429, she liberated the besieged city of Orléans. Imprisoned by the English, Joan was condemned as a heretic and a witch in 1431 by a hand-picked church court. She was burned at the stake. Inspired by Joan's death, the French drove the English from all French territory except for the port of Calais.

During the Hundred Years' War, French kings introduced new taxes that added substantially to their incomes. These monies furnished them with the means to organize a professional army of well-paid and loyal troops. By evoking a sense of pride and oneness in the French people, the war also contributed to a growing, but still incomplete, national unity. The English too emerged from the war with a greater sense of solidarity. However, the war had terrible consequences for the French peasants. Thousands of farmers were killed and valuable farmland was destroyed by English armies and marauding bands of mercenaries. In another portentous development, the later stages of the Hundred Years' War saw the use of gunpowder and heavy artillery.

The Decline of the Church

The principal sign of the decline of medieval civilization in the Late Middle Ages was the waning authority and prestige of the papacy. In the High Middle Ages the papacy had been the dominant institution in Christendom, but in the Late Middle Ages its power disintegrated. The medieval ideal of a unified Christian commonwealth guided by the papacy was shattered. Papal authority declined in the face of the growing power of kings who championed the parochial interests of states. Papal prestige and its capacity to command diminished as the pope became more embroiled in European politics. Many pious Christians felt that the pope behaved more like a secular ruler than like an Apostle of Christ. Political theorists and church reformers further undermined papal authority.

Conflict with France

Philip IV of France (1285–1314) taxed the church in his land to raise revenue for war. In doing so, he disregarded the church prohibition against taxing its property without papal permission. In the bull (papal decree) *Clericis laicos,* Pope Boniface VIII (1294–1303) decreed that kings and lords who imposed taxes on the clergy, and clergy who paid them, would incur the sentence of excommunication. Far from bowing to the pope's threat, Philip acted forcefully to assert his authority over the church in his kingdom. Boniface backed down from his position, declaring that the French king could tax the clergy in times of national emergency. Thus the matter was resolved to the advantage of the state.

The End of a Siege: English Soldiers Take a French Town, Late-Fifteenth-Century Illumination.   During the Hundred Years' War, scenes like this one were not uncommon. The conflicts that arose between the English and the French were partially caused by English rule in some areas of France. (*British Library*)

A second dispute had more disastrous consequences for Boniface. Philip tried and imprisoned a French bishop despite Boniface's warning that this was an illegal act and a violation of church law and tradition, which held that the church, not the state, must judge the clergy. Philip summoned the first meeting of the Estates General to gain the backing of the nation. Shortly afterward, Boniface threatened to excommunicate Philip. The outraged monarch attacked the papal summer palace at Anagni in September 1303 and captured the pope. Although Boniface was released, this terrible event proved too much for him, and a month later he died.

Boniface's successors, Benedict XI (1303–1304) and Clement V (1305–1314), tried to conciliate Philip. In particular, Clement decided to remain at Avignon, a town on the southeastern French frontier, where he had set up a temporary residence.

From 1309 to 1377, a period known as the *Babylonian Captivity,* the popes were all French. During this time, the papacy, removed from Rome and deprived of revenues from the Papal States in Italy, was often forced to pursue policies favorable to France. Worsening the papal image was growing anti-papalism among laymen, who were repelled by the luxurious style of living at Avignon and by the appointment of high churchmen to lands where they did not know the language and where they demonstrated little concern for the local population. Under these circumstances, more and more people questioned the value and necessity of the papacy. The conflict between Boniface and Philip provoked a battle of words between proponents of papal supremacy and defenders of royal rights.

The most important critique of clerical intrusion into worldly affairs was *The Defender of the Peace* (1324) by Marsiglio of Padua (c. 1290–c. 1343). Marsiglio held that the state ran according to its principles, which had nothing to do with religious commands originating in a higher realm. Religion dealt with a supranatural world and with principles of faith that could not be proved by reason, said Marsiglio. Politics, on the other hand, dealt with a natural world and with the affairs of the human community. And political thinkers should not try to make the earthly realm conform to articles of faith. For Marsiglio, the state was self-sufficient; it needed no instruction from a higher authority. Thus Marsiglio denied the essential premises of medieval papal political theory: that the pope, as God's vicar, was empowered to guide kings; that the state, as part of a divinely ordered world, must conform to and fulfill supranatural ends; and that the clergy were above the laws of the state. Marsiglio felt that the church should be a spiritual institution with no temporal power.

The Great Schism

Pope Gregory XI returned the papacy to Rome in 1377, ending the Babylonian Captivity. But the papacy was to endure an even greater humiliation—the Great Schism. Elected pope in 1378, Urban VI abused and imprisoned a number of cardinals. Fleeing from Rome, the cardinals declared that the election of Urban had been invalid and elected Clement VII as the new pope. Refusing to step down, Urban excommunicated Clement, who responded in kind. To the utter confusion and anguish of Christians throughout Europe, there were now two popes—Urban ruling from Rome and Clement from Avignon.

Prominent churchmen urged the convening of a general council—the Council of Pisa—to end the disgraceful schism. Held in 1409 and attended by hundreds of churchmen, the Council of Pisa deposed both Urban and Clement and elected a new pope. Neither deposed pope recognized the council's decision, so Christendom then had three popes! A new council was called at Constance in 1414. In the struggle that ensued, each of the three popes either abdicated or was deposed in favor of an appointment by the council. In 1417, the Great Schism ended.

During the first half of the fifteenth century, church councils met at Pisa (1409), Constance (1414–1418), and Basel (1431–1449) in order to end the schism, combat heresy, and reform the church. The Conciliar movement attempted to transform the papal monarchy into a constitutional system in which the pope's power would be regulated by a general council. Supporters of the movement held that the papacy could not reform the church as effectively as a general council representing the clergy. But the Conciliar movement ended in failure. As the Holy Roman emperor and then the French monarch withdrew support from the councils, the papacy regained its authority over the higher clergy. In 1460, Pope Pius II condemned the Conciliar movement as heretical.

The papacy was deeply embroiled in European power politics and often neglected its spiritual and moral responsibilities. Many devout Christians longed for a religious renewal, a return to simple piety; the papacy barely heard this cry for reform. The papacy's failure to provide creative leadership for reform made possible the Protestant Reformation of the sixteenth century. The Reformation, by splitting Christendom into Catholic and Protestant, destroyed forever the vision of a Christian world commonwealth guided by Christ's vicar, the pope.

Fourteenth-Century Heresies

Another threat to papal power and the medieval ideal of a universal Christian community guided by the church came from radical reformers who questioned the function and authority of the entire church hierarchy. These heretics in the Late Middle Ages were forerunners of the Protestant Reformation.

The two principal dissenters were the Englishman John Wycliffe (c. 1320–1384) and the Czech John Huss (c. 1369–1415). By stressing a personal relationship between the individual and God and by claiming the Bible itself, rather than church teachings, to be the ultimate Christian authority, they challenged the fundamental position of the medieval church: that the avenue to salvation passed through the church alone. They denounced the wealth of the higher clergy and sought a return to the spiritual purity and material poverty of the early church.

To Wycliffe, the wealthy, elaborately organized hierarchy of the church was unnecessary and wrong. The splendidly dressed and propertied bishops had no resemblance to the simple people who first followed Christ. Indeed, these worldly bishops headed by a princely and tyrannical pope were really anti-Christians, the "fiends of Hell." Wycliffe wanted the state to confiscate church property and the clergy to embrace poverty.

By denying that priests changed the bread and wine of communion into the substance of the body and blood of Christ, Wycliffe and Huss rejected the sacramental power of the clergy. Although both movements were declared heretical and Huss was burned at the stake, the church could not crush the dissenters' followers or eradicate their teachings. The doctrines of the Reformation would parallel the teachings of Wycliffe and Huss to some extent.

Breakup of the Thomistic Synthesis

In the Late Middle Ages, the papacy lost power as kings, political theorists, and religious dissenters effectively challenged papal claims to supreme leadership. Also breaking down was the great theological synthesis constructed by philosophers. The process of fragmentation seen in the history of the church also took place in philosophy, where Saint Thomas Aquinas's system had culminated the scholastic attempt to show the basic agreement of philosophy and religion. In the fourteenth century, a number of thinkers cast doubt on the possibility of synthesizing Aristotelianism and Christianity, that is, reason and faith. Denying that reason could demonstrate the truth of Christian doctrines with certainty, philosophers tried to separate reason from faith. Whereas Aquinas had said that reason proved or clarified much of revelation, fourteenth-century thinkers asserted that the basic propositions of Christianity were not open to rational proof. Whereas Aquinas had held that faith supplements and perfects reason, some philosophers were now proclaiming that reason often contradicts faith.

To be sure, this new outlook did not urge abandoning faith in favor of reason. Faith had to prevail in any conflict with reason because faith rested on God, the highest authority in the universe. But the relationship between reason and revelation was altered. Articles of faith, it was now held, had nothing to do with reason; they were to be believed, not proved. Reason was not an aid to theology, but a separate sphere of activity. This new attitude snapped the link between reason and faith that Aquinas had so skillfully forged. The scholastic synthesis was disintegrating.

A principal proponent of this new outlook was William of Ockham (c. 1280–1349). In contrast to Aquinas, Ockham insisted that natural reason could not prove God's existence, the soul's immortality, or any other essential Christian doctrine. Reason could only say that God probably exists and that he probably endowed man with an immortal soul. But it could not prove these propositions with *certainty*. The tenets of faith were beyond the reach of reason, said Ockham; there was no rational foundation to Christianity. For Ockham, reason and faith did not necessarily complement each other as they did for Aquinas; it was neither possible nor helpful to join reason to faith. He did not, however, seek to undermine faith—only to disengage it from reason.

In the process of proclaiming the authority of theology, Ockham also furthered using reason to comprehend nature. Ockham's approach, separating natural knowledge from religious dogma, made it easier to explore the natural world empirically without fitting it into a religious framework. With Ockham, then, we see a forerunner of the modern mentality: a separation of reason from religion and a growing interest in the empirical investigation of nature.

The Polos Embarking from Venice.   The journey of the Polos to the court of the Great Khan sees the medieval world almost at an end. The exploration of the East would soon be followed by voyages to Africa and the discovery of the New World. Commerce and trade would transform the Western economy. The role of the individual would change from that of a functioning member in an ordered political and spiritual realm to that of an explorer of new worlds: physical, intellectual, and artistic. (*Bodleian Library, Oxford, Ms. Bodley 264, fol. 218r*)

The Middle Ages and the Modern World: Continuity and Discontinuity

Medieval civilization began to decline in the fourteenth century, but no dark age comparable to the three centuries following Rome's fall descended on Europe; its economic and political institutions and technological skills had grown too strong. Instead, the waning of the Middle Ages opened up possibilities for another stage in Western civilization—the modern age. In innumerable ways, today's world is linked to the Middle Ages. European cities, the middle class, the state system, English common law, universities—all had their origins in the Middle Ages. During that period, important advances were made in business practices. By translating and commenting on the writings of Greek and Arabic thinkers, medieval scholars preserved a priceless intellectual heritage, without which the modern mind could never have evolved. And between the thought of the scholastics and that of early modern philosophers there are numerous connecting strands.

During the Middle Ages, Europeans began to take the lead over the Muslims, the Byzantines, the Chinese, and all the other peoples in the use of technology. Medieval technology and inventiveness stemmed in part from Christianity, which taught that God had created the world specifically for human beings to subdue and exploit. Consequently, medieval people tried to employ animal power and labor-saving machinery to relieve human drudgery. Moreover, Christianity taught that God was above nature, not within it, so for the Christian there was no spiritual obstacle to exploiting nature as there was, for example, for the Hindu. Unlike classical humanism, the Christian outlook did not consider manual work degrading—even monks combined it with their religious duties.

Believing that God's law was superior to state or national decrees, medieval philosophers provided a theoretical basis for opposing tyrannical kings who violated Christian principles. The idea that both the ruler and the ruled are bound by a higher law would, in a secularized form, become a principal element of modern liberal thought.

The Christian stress on the sacred worth of the individual and on the higher law of God has never ceased to influence Western civilization. Although in modern times the various Christian churches have not often taken the lead in political and social reform, the ideals identified with the Judeo-Christian tradition have become part of the common Western heritage. As such, they have inspired social reformers who may no longer identify with their ancestral religion.

Feudal traditions lasted long after the Middle Ages. Up to the French Revolution, for instance, French aristocrats enjoyed special privileges and exercised power over local government. In England, the aristocracy controlled local government until the Industrial Revolution transformed English society in the nineteenth century. Retaining the medieval ideal of the noble warrior, aristocrats continued to dominate the officer corps of European armies through the nineteenth century and even into the twentieth. Aristocratic notions of duty, honor, loyalty, and courtly love have also endured into the twentieth century.

Feudalism also contributed to the history of liberty. According to feudal theory the king, as a member of the feudal community, was duty-bound to honor agreements made by his vassals. Lords possessed personal rights that the king was obliged to respect. Resentful of a king who ran roughshod over customary feudal rights, lords also negotiated contracts with the crown, such as the famous Magna Carta, to define and guard their customary liberties. To protect themselves from the arbitrary behavior of a king, feudal lords initiated what came to be called *government by consent* and the *rule of law*.

Thus, in the Middle Ages there gradually emerged the ideas that law was not imposed on inferiors by an absolute monarch but required the collaboration of the king and his subjects; that the king, too, was bound by the law; and that lords had the right to resist a monarch who violated agreements. Related to these ideas, representative institutions also emerged with which the king was expected to consult on the realm's affairs. The most notable was the British Parliament, which, although it was subordinate to the king, became a permanent part of the state. Later, in the seventeenth century, Parliament would successfully challenge royal authority. Continuity therefore exists between the feudal tradition of a king bound by law and the modern practice of limiting the authority of the head of state.

Although the elements of continuity are clear, the characteristic outlook of the Middle Ages is as different from that of the modern age as it was from that of the ancient world. Religion was the integrating feature of the Middle Ages, whereas science and secularism determine the modern outlook. The period from the Italian Renaissance of the fifteenth century through the eighteenth-century Age of Enlightenment constituted a gradual breaking away from the medieval world-view—a rejection of the medieval conception of nature, society, the individual, and the purpose of life. This transition from medieval to modern was neither sudden nor complete, for there are no sharp demarcation lines separating historical periods. While many distinctively medieval ways endured in the sixteenth, seventeenth, and even eighteenth centuries, these centuries also saw the emergence of new patterns of thought and culture and of new political and economic forms that marked the emergence of modernity.

Medieval thought began with the existence of God and the truth of his revelation as interpreted by the church, which set the standards and defined the purposes for human endeavor. Medieval thinkers regarded reason without the guidance of revelation as deficient. Thus the medieval mind rejected the fundamental principle of Greek philosophy—the autonomy of reason.

Scholastics reasoned closely and carefully, drew fine distinctions, and at times demonstrated a critical attitude. They engaged in genuine philosophical speculation, but they did not allow philosophy to challenge the basic premises of their faith. Unlike either ancient or modern thinkers, medieval schoolmen believed ultimately that reason alone could not provide a unified view of nature or society. A rational soul had to be guided by a divine light. For all medieval philosophers, the natural order depended on a supernatural order for its origin and purpose. To understand the natural world properly, it was necessary to know its relationship to the higher world. The discoveries of reason had to conform to Scripture as interpreted by the church.

In the modern view, both nature and the human intellect are self-sufficient. Nature is a mathematical system that operates without miracles or any other form of divine intervention. To comprehend nature and society, the mind needs no divine assistance; it accepts no authority above reason. The modern mentality finds it unacceptable to reject the conclusions of science on the basis of clerical authority and revelation, or to base politics, law, or economics on religion; it refuses to accept dogma uncritically and insists on scientific proof.

The medieval philosopher arranged both nature and society into a hierarchic order. God was the source of moral values, and the church was responsible for teaching and upholding these ethical norms. Kings acquired their right to rule from God. The entire social structure constituted a hierarchy: the clergy guided society according to Christian standards; lords defended Christian society from its enemies; serfs, lowest in the social order, toiled for the good of all. In the hierarchy of knowledge, a lower form of knowledge derived from the senses, and the highest type of knowledge, theology, dealt with God's revelation. To the medieval mind this hierarchic ordering of nature, society, and knowledge had a divine sanction.

Rejecting the medieval division of the universe into higher and lower realms and superior and inferior substances, the modern view came to regard the universe as one and nature as uniform; the modern thinker studies mathematical law and chemical composition, not grades of perfection. Spiritual meaning is not sought in an examination of the material world. Roger Bacon, for example, described seven coverings of the eye and then concluded that God had fashioned the eye in this manner in order to express the seven gifts of the Spirit. This way of thinking is alien to the modern outlook.

The modern West also broke with the rigid division of medieval society into three orders: clergy, nobles, and commoners. Opposing the feudal principle that an individual's obligations and rights are a function of his or her rank in society, the modern West stressed equality of opportunity and equal treatment under the law. It rejected the idea that society should be guided by clergymen who possess a special wisdom, by nobles who were entitled to special privileges, and by a king who received his power from God.

The modern West also rejected the personal and customary character of feudal law. As the modern state developed, law assumed an impersonal and objective character. For example, if the lord demanded more than the customary forty days of military service, the vassal might refuse to comply, seeing the lord's request as an unpardonable violation of custom and agreement and an infringement on his liberties. In the modern state with a constitution and a representative government, if a new law increasing the length of military service is passed, it merely replaces the old law. People do not refuse to obey it because the government has broken faith or violated custom.

In the modern world, the individual's relationship to the universe has been radically transformed. Medieval people lived in a geocentric universe that was finite in space and time. The universe was small, enclosed by a sphere of stars beyond which were the heavens. The universe, it was believed, was some four thousand years old, and in the not too distant future, human history would come to an end. To medieval thinkers, human beings ranked below angels but were superior to inanimate objects, plants, and animals. People in the Middle Ages knew why they were on earth and what was expected of them; they never doubted that heaven would be their reward for living a Christian life. J. H. Randall, Jr., a historian of philosophy, eloquently sums up the medieval world-view:

Chronology 7.1 ⊕ The High and Late Middle Ages

c. 1100	Revival of the study of Roman law at Bologna
1163	Start of the construction of the Cathedral of Notre Dame
1267–1273	Saint Thomas Aquinas writes *Summa Theologica*
1309–1377	The Babylonian Captivity; the popes are French and influenced by the French monarchy
c. 1321	Dante completes the *Divine Comedy*
1337–1453	The Hundred Years' War between England and France
1347–1351	The Black Death reaches Italian ports and ravages Europe
1377	Pope Gregory XI returns the papacy to Rome
1378–1417	The Great Schism; Christendom has two and then three popes
1415	The battle of Agincourt—the French are defeated by Henry V of England; John Huss, a Bohemian religious reformer, is burned at the stake
1453	The English are driven from France, except Calais; the end of the Hundred Years' War
1460	Pope Pius II condemns the Conciliar Movement as heretical

The world was governed throughout by the omnipotent will and omniscient mind of God, whose sole interests were centered in man, his trial, his fall, his suffering and his glory. Worm of the dust as he was, man was yet the central object in the whole universe. . . . And when his destiny was completed, the heavens would be rolled up as a scroll and he would dwell with the Lord forever. Only those who rejected God's freely offered grace and with hardened hearts refused repentance would be cut off from this eternal life.[4]

This comforting medieval vision is alien to the modern outlook. Today, in a universe 15 billion years old in which the earth is a tiny speck floating in an endless cosmic ocean, where life evolved over tens of millions of years, many Westerners no longer are certain that human beings are special children of God; that heaven is their ultimate goal; that under their feet is hell; that God is an active agent in human history. To many intellectuals, life's purpose is sought solely within the limits of earthly existence. Science and secularism have driven Christianity and faith from their central position to the periphery of human concerns.

The modern outlook emerged gradually in the period from the Renaissance to the eighteenth-century Age of Enlightenment. Mathematics rendered the universe comprehensible. Economic and political thought broke free of the religious frame of reference. Science became the great hope of the future. The thinkers of the Enlightenment wanted to liberate humanity from superstition, ignorance, and traditions that could not pass the test of reason. Rejecting the Christian idea of a person's inherent sinfulness, they held that the individual was basically good and that evil resulted from faulty institutions, poor education, and bad leadership. Thus the concept of a rational and free society in which individuals could realize their potential slowly emerged.

Notes

1. Quoted in David Knowles, *The Evolution of Medieval Thought* (New York: Vintage Books, 1964), p. 123.
2. Thomas Aquinas, *Summa Theologica,* I.2.3.
3. Joan Gadol, *Leon Battista Alberti, Universal Man of the Early Renaissance* (Chicago: University of Chicago Press, 1969), pp. 149–150.
4. J. H. Randall, Jr., *The Making of the Modern Mind* (Boston: Houghton Mifflin, 1940), p. 34.

Suggested Reading

Brooke, Christopher, *The Twelfth-Century Renaissance* (1969). Surveys schools, learning, theology, literature, and leading figures.

Copleston, F. C., *A History of Medieval Philosophy* (1974). A lucid, comprehensive survey of medieval philosophy.

Gilson, Etienne, *Reason and Revelation in the Middle Ages* (1966). A superb brief exposition of the medieval philosophic tradition.

Haskins, C. H., *The Renaissance of the 12th Century* (1957). Reprint of a still-useful work.

Hay, Denys, *Europe in the Fourteenth and Fifteenth Centuries* (1966). A good survey of the Late Middle Ages.

Lerner, Robert E., *The Age of Adversity* (1968). A short, readable survey of the fourteenth century.

Ozment, Steven E., *The Age of Reform, 1250–1550* (1980). An intellectual and religious history of late medieval and Reformation Europe.

Pieper, Josef, *Scholasticism* (1964). Written with intelligence and grace.

Piltz, Anders, *The World of Medieval Learning* (1981). A clearly written, informative survey of medieval education and learning.

Wieruszowski, Helene, *The Medieval University* (1966). A good survey, followed by documents.

Review Questions

1. What factors contributed to the revival of learning in the late eleventh and twelfth centuries?
2. Describe the essential features of the medieval view of the universe. How does it differ from the modern view of the universe?
3. The medieval individual's understanding of himself or herself was related to a comprehension of the universe as a hierarchy culminating in God. Explain this statement.
4. What were scholastic philosophers trying to accomplish?

Art as History
500 B.C.–A.D. 1500

Historians rely on many different sources to arrive at a knowledge of the past. These sources include not only the written documents and literature of a people, but also their artistic creations—their architecture, sculpture, and painting. As you look at these works of art, what insights do they suggest about the historical times in which they were produced?

The Parthenon, Athens, 447–432 B.C. This Greek classical temple crowns the Acropolis above Athens. Dedicated to Athena, patron goddess of the city and of wisdom and the arts, the marble Parthenon once contained a huge ivory and gold statue of her. Its ruins reveal the perfect proportions and placement of the Parthenon, but they do not show that its façade was painted, as were the life-size sculptures that filled the triangular spaces above the rows of columns. What do the structure and style of the Parthenon suggest about Greek civilization? (*Scala/Art Resource*)

Metope from the Parthenon: Centaur and Lapith Fighting. Between the columns and the pediments of the Parthenon are relief sculptures called *metopes*. These squares contain simple compositions in high relief, that is, the figures stand out from the background, which was painted a strong color. The centaur (half man, half beast) and the Lapith (a Thessalonian Greek whose tribe defeated the centaurs) represents a mythological struggle. Why was this subject included in the temple decoration? (*Reproduced by courtesy of the Trustees of the British Museum*)

Earring with Nike Pendant, Second Half of Fourth Century, B.C. This Hellenistic gold earring (H. 2″) with its richly ornamented disc differs from the simple ornaments of the Periclean Age and reflects the complexities of the new era. What similarities in style exist among the Greek artifacts on these two pages, and how do they differ? (*Virginia Museum of Fine Arts, Richmond. Museum purchase, the Adolph D. and Wilkens C. Williams Fund*)

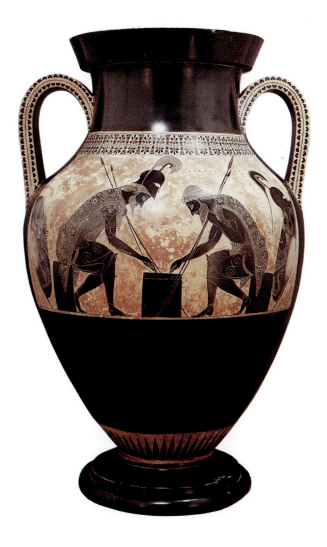

Black-figured Amphora: Achilles and Ajax Playing a Board Game, 540–530 B.C. Greeks not only built beautiful temples and skillfully sculpted ideal figures possessing grace, but they imparted beauty to everyday utensils like this amphora, a "vase" used to hold wine or oil. Here, figures from Homer's *Iliad* are shown enjoying a respite from the siege of Troy. What does this vessel and its ornamentation reveal about the Hellenic Greeks? (*Vatican Museum/Scala/Art Resource*)

Detail of Pompeian Wall Fresco: Lady Playing the Cithara. With the removal of lava and ash from Pompeii, a first-century Roman city appeared and has provided historians with much data on daily life almost twenty centuries ago. What does this fresco scene disclose about the state of Roman culture and the lives of Roman matrons? (*The Metropolitan Museum of Art, Rogers Fund, 1903*)

Stained Glass from Chartres Cathedral: Charlemagne Giving Orders for Building the Church of St. James. Dating from the early thirteenth century, Chartres is one of the outstanding Gothic cathedrals. Its stained-glass windows not only shed light in jeweled colors into the interior of the sanctuary, uplifting the spirit and raising the eyes of the worshiper but they also instruct and tell stories about heroes like Emperor Charlemagne, saints, and the Trinity. What might a medieval church-goer have learned from this window? (*Copyright Sonia Halliday and Laura Lushington*)

April (opposite) from **Les Très Riches Heures of Jean, Duke of Berry.** This page from a beautifully illustrated volume of prayers, which was made during 1413–1416, is one of the paintings of months appearing in this nobleman's book. What does this scene reveal about the lifestyle of nobles, both men and women? (*Chantilly, Musée Condé/Giraudon/Art Resource*)

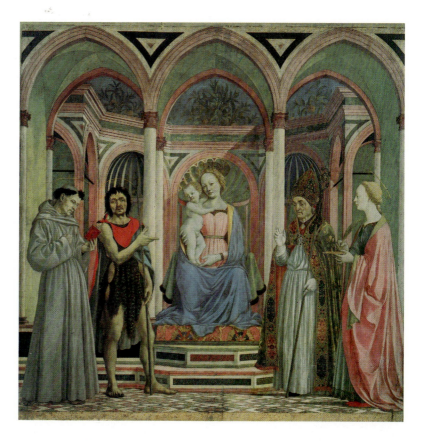

Domenico Veneziano (c. 1410–1461): Madonna and Child with Saints, c. 1445. This Florentine master painted the altar panel (6′ 7½″ × 6′ 11⅞″) in a new style, called *Sacra Conversazione* (sacred conversation). The enthroned Madonna and child are framed by architectural elements and are flanked by the formal, solemn figures of saints, who seem to converse with her or between themselves, or even with the onlooker. Saint John, to the left of the child and the Madonna, gazes out of the painting while he points to them, in effect directing the onlooker's eyes. Domenico's color scheme uses sunlight and spots of bright primary colors, together with pastels, to present a glowing scene. What elements in the painting indicate that it is an Early Renaissance work? (*Uffizi Gallery, Florence/Scala/Art Resource*)

**Raphael (1483–1520): Pope Leo X with His Nephews Giulio de'
Medici and Luigi de' Rossi, c. 1518.** A High Renaissance artist,
Raphael combined realism and the human ideal in his portraits. In
this panel, the pope's heavy features and his weak-looking nephews,
who are cardinals, do not present a flattering portrayal. But
Raphael's rendering of the dominant figure conveys power and dig-
nity. How does this treatment of human character differ from
Veneziano's Early Renaissance painting? (*Uffizi Gallery, Florence/
Scala/Art Resource*)

Foundation of the Academy of Sciences in 1666, by Testelin. The commemorative painting shows Louis XIV (seated) with Colbert at his side. (*Versailles/Cliché des Musées Nationaux*)

III ❧ The Rise of Modernity: From the Renaissance to the Enlightenment

1350–1789

Chapter ⚬ 8

Transition to the Modern Age:
Renaissance and Reformation

From the Italian Renaissance of the fifteenth century through the Age of Enlightenment of the eighteenth century, the outlook and institutions of the Middle Ages disintegrated and distinctly modern forms emerged. The radical change in European civilization could be seen on every level of society. On the economic level, commerce and industry expanded greatly, and capitalism largely replaced medieval forms of economic organization. On the political level, central government grew stronger at the expense of feudalism. On the religious level, the rise of Protestantism fragmented the unity of Christendom. On the social level, middle-class townspeople increasing in number and wealth, began to play a more important role in economic and cultural life. On the cultural level, the clergy lost its monopoly over learning, and the other-worldly orientation of the Middle Ages gave way to a secular outlook in literature and the arts. Theology, the queen of knowledge in the Middle Ages, surrendered its crown to science. Reason, which in the Middle Ages had been subordinate to revelation, asserted its independence.

Many of these tendencies manifested themselves dramatically during the Renaissance. The word *renaissance* means "rebirth," and it is used to refer to the attempt by artists and thinkers to recover and apply the ancient learning and standards of Greece and Rome. In historical terms, the Renaissance is both a cultural movement and a period. As a movement it was born in the city-states of northern Italy and spread to the rest of Europe. As a period it runs from about 1350 to 1600. Until the late fifteenth century the Renaissance was restricted to Italy. What happened there in the fourteenth and fifteenth centuries sharply contrasts with civilization in the rest of Europe, which until the end of the fifteenth century still belonged to the Late Middle Ages.

The nineteenth-century historian Jacob Burckhardt in his classic study, *The Civilization of the Renaissance in Italy* (1860), held that the Renaissance is the point of departure for the modern world. During the Renaissance, said Burckhardt, individuals showed an increasing concern for worldly life and self-consciously aspired to shape their destinies, an attitude that is the key to modernity.

Burckhardt's thesis has been challenged, particularly by medievalists who view the Renaissance as an extension of the Middle Ages, not as a sudden break with the past. These critics argue that Burckhardt neglected important links between medieval and Renaissance culture. A distinguishing feature of the Renaissance, the revival of classical learning, had already emerged in the High Middle Ages to such an extent that historians speak of "the renaissance of the twelfth century." The Renaissance owes much to the legal and scholastic studies that flourished in the Italian universities of Padua and Bologna before 1300. Town life and trade, hallmarks of Renaissance society, were also a heritage from the Middle Ages.

To be sure, the Renaissance was not a complete and sudden break with the Middle Ages. Many medieval ways and attitudes persisted. Nevertheless, Burckhardt's thesis that the Renaissance represents the birth of modernity has much to recommend it. Renaissance writers and artists themselves were aware of their age's novelty. They looked back on the medieval centuries as a "Dark Age" that followed the grandeur of ancient Greece and Rome, and they believed that they were experiencing a rebirth of cultural greatness. Renaissance artists and writers were fascinated with the cultural forms of Greece and Rome; they sought to imitate classical style and to capture the secular spirit of antiquity. In the process they broke with medieval artistic and literary forms. They valued the full development of human talent and expressed a new excitement about the possibilities of life in this world. This outlook represents a break from the Middle Ages and the emergence of modernity.

The Renaissance, then, was an age of transition that saw the rejection of certain elements of the medieval outlook, the revival of classical cultural forms, and the emergence of distinctly modern attitudes.

This rebirth began in Italy during the fourteenth century and gradually spread north and west to Germany, France, England, and Spain during the late fifteenth and the sixteenth centuries.

The Renaissance was one avenue to modernity; another was the Reformation. By dividing Europe into Catholic and Protestant, the Reformation ended medieval religious unity. It also accentuated the importance of the individual person, a distinctive feature of the modern outlook. It stressed individual conscience rather than clerical authority, called for a personal relationship between each man or woman and God, and called attention to the individual's inner religious capacities. ✤

Italy: Birthplace of the Renaissance

The city-states of northern Italy that spawned the Renaissance were developed urban centers where people had the wealth, freedom, and inclination to cultivate the arts and to enjoy the fruits of worldly life. In Italy, moreover, reminders of ancient Rome's grandeur were visible everywhere; Roman roads, monuments, and manuscripts intensified the Italians' links to their Roman past. Northern Italian city-states had developed as flourishing commercial and banking centers and had monopolized trade in the Mediterranean during the twelfth and thirteenth centuries. The predominance of business and commerce within these city-states meant that the feudal nobility, who held the land beyond the city walls, played a much less important part in government than they did elsewhere in Europe. By the end of the twelfth century, the city-states had adopted a fairly uniform pattern of republican self-government built around the office of a chief magistrate.

However, this republicanism proved precarious. During the fourteenth and early fifteenth centuries, republican institutions in one city after another toppled, giving way to rule by despots. The city-states had come to rely on mercenary troops, whose leaders, the notorious *condottieri*—unschooled in and owing no loyalty to the republican tradition—simply seized power during emergencies.

Florence, the leading city of the Renaissance, held out against the trend toward despotism for a long time. But by the mid-fifteenth century, even Florentine republicanism was giving way before the intrigues of a rich banking family, the Medici. They had installed themselves in power in the 1430s with the return of Cosimo de' Medici from exile. Cosimo's grandson, Lorenzo the Magnificent, completed the destruction of the republican constitution in 1480, when he managed to set up a government staffed by his supporters.

Lorenzo de' Medici. The Medici preferred to wield power behind the scenes through secret alliances and intrigue. Lorenzo, who became head of the family in his teens, fostered the notion of the good citizen; this portrait of him is by Agnolo Bronzino. (*Scala/Art Resource*)

LAVRENTIVS MEDICES   PETRI FILIVS.

Dramatically new ways of life emerged within the Italian city-states. Prosperous business people played a leading role in the political and cultural life of the city. With the expansion of commerce and industry, the feudal values of birth, military prowess, and a fixed hierarchy of lords and vassals decayed in favor of ambition and individual achievement, whether at court, in the counting house, or inside the artist's studio.

Art served as a focus of civic pride and patriotism. Members of the urban upper class became patrons of the arts, providing funds to support promising artists and writers. Just as rulers contended on the battlefield, they competed for art and artists to bolster their prestige. The popes, too, heaped wealth on artists to enhance their flagging prestige. They became the most lavish patrons of all, as the works of Michelangelo and Raphael testify.

The result of this new patronage by popes and patricians was an explosion of artistic creativity. The amount and especially the nature of this patronage also helped to shape both art and the artist. Portraiture became a separate genre for the first time since antiquity and was developed much further than ever before. Patrician rivalry and insecurity of status, fed by the Renaissance ethic of individual achievement and reward, produced a scramble for honor and reputation. This pursuit fostered the desire to be memorialized in a painting, if not in a sculpture. A painter like Titian was in great demand.

The great artists emerged as famous men by virtue of their exercise of brush and chisel. In the Middle Ages, artists had been regarded as craftsmen who did lowly (manual) labor and who, as a result, were to be accorded little, if any, status. Indeed, they remained anonymous for the most part. But the unparalleled Renaissance demand for art brought artists public recognition.

Renaissance society was also marked by a growing secular outlook. Intrigued by the active life of the city and eager to enjoy the worldly pleasures that their money could obtain, wealthy merchants and bankers moved away from the medieval preoccupation with salvation. To be sure, they were neither nonbelievers nor atheists, but increasingly religion had to compete with worldly concerns. Consequently, members of the urban upper class paid religion less heed, or at least did not allow it to interfere with their quest for the full life. The challenge and pleasure of living well in this world seemed more exciting than the promise of heaven. This outlook found concrete expression in Renaissance art and literature.

Individualism was another hallmark of Renaissance society. Urban life released people of wealth and talent from the old constraints of manor and church. The urban elite sought to assert their own personalities, to discover and to express their own particular feelings, to demonstrate their unique talents, to win fame and glory, and to fulfill their ambitions. This Renaissance ideal was explicitly elitist. It applied only to the few, entirely disregarding the masses; it valued what was distinctive and superior in an individual, not what was common to all; it was concerned with the distinctions of the few, not the needs or rights of the many. Individualism became deeply embedded in the Western soul and was expressed by artists who sought to capture individual character, by explorers who ventured into uncharted seas, by conquerors who carved out empires in the New World, and by merchant-capitalists who amassed fortunes.

The Renaissance Outlook: Humanism and Secular Politics

Humanism

The most characteristic intellectual movement of the Renaissance was *humanism,* an educational and cultural program based on the study of ancient Greek and Roman literature. The humanist attitude toward antiquity differed from that of medieval scholars. Medieval scholars sought to fit classical learning into a Christian world-view. Renaissance humanists, in contrast, did not subordinate the classics to the requirements of Christian doctrines; rather, they valued ancient literature for its own sake—for its clear and graceful style, for its insights into human nature. From the ancient classics, humanists expected to learn much that could not be provided by medieval writings—how to live well in this world and how to perform one's civic duties, for example. For the humanists the classics were a guide to the good life, the active life. To achieve self-cultivation, to write well, to speak well, and to live well, it was necessary to know the classics. In contrast to scholastic philosophers who used Greek philosophy to prove the truth of Christian doctrines, Italian humanists used classical learning to nourish their new interest in a worldly life. Whereas medieval scholars were familiar with only some ancient Latin writers, Renaissance humanists restored to circulation every Roman work that could be found. Similarly, whereas knowledge of Greek was very rare in Latin Christendom during the Middle Ages, Renaissance humanists increasingly cultivated the study of Greek in order to read Homer, Demosthenes, Plato, and other ancients in the original.

Although predominantly a secular movement, Italian humanism was not un-Christian. True, humanists often treated moral problems in a purely secular manner, but when they did deal with religious and theological questions, they did not challenge Christian belief or question the validity of the Bible. They did, however, attack scholasticism for its hairsplitting arguments and preoccupation with trivial questions. They stressed instead a purer form of Christianity based on the direct study of the Bible and writings by the church fathers.

An early humanist, sometimes called the father of humanism, was Petrarch (1304–1374). Petrarch and his followers carried the recovery of the classics further by making a systematic attempt to discover the classical roots of medieval Italian rhetoric. Petrarch's own efforts to learn Greek were largely unsuccessful, but by encouraging his students to master the ancient tongue, he advanced humanist learning. Petrarch was particularly drawn to Cicero, the ancient Roman orator. Following the example of Cicero, he insisted that education should consist not only of learning and knowing things, but also of learning how to communicate one's knowledge and how to use it for the public good. Therefore, the emphasis in education should be on rhetoric and moral philosophy, wisdom combined with eloquence. This was the key to virtue in the ruler, the citizen, and the republic. Petrarch helped to make Ciceronian values dominant among the humanists. His followers set up schools to inculcate the new Ciceronian educational ideal.

Implicit in the humanist educational ideal was a radical transformation of the Christian idea of human beings. According to the medieval (Augustinian) view, men and women, because of their sinful nature, were incapable of attaining excellence through their own efforts. They were completely subject to divine will. In contrast, the humanists, recalling the classical Greek concept of human beings, made the achievement of excellence through individual striving the end not only of education, but of life itself. Because individuals were capable of this goal, moreover, it was their duty to pursue it as the end of life. The pursuit was not effortless; indeed, it took extraordinary energy and skill.

People, then, were capable of excellence in every sphere and duty-bound to make the effort. This emphasis on human creative powers was one of the most characteristic and influential doctrines of the Renaissance. A classic expression of it is found in the *Oration on the Dignity of Man* (1486) by Giovanni Pico della Mirandola (1463–1494). Man, said Pico, has the freedom to shape his own life. Pico has God say to man: "We have made you a creature" such that "you may, as the free and proud shaper of your own being, fashion yourself in the form you may prefer."[1]

An attack on the medieval scholastics was implicit in the humanist educational ideal. From the humanist perspective, scholasticism failed not only because its terms and Latin usage were barbarous, but also because it did not provide useful knowledge. This humanist emphasis on the uses of knowledge also offered a stimulus to science and art.

So hostile were the humanists to all things scholastic and medieval that they reversed the prevailing view of history. The Christian view saw history as a simple unfolding of God's will and providence. The humanists stressed the importance of human actions and human wills in history—of people as active participants in the shaping of events. They characterized the epoch preceding their own as a period of declension from classical heights, and saw their own time as a period of rebirth, representing the recovery of classical wisdom and ideals. Thus, the humanists invented the notion of the Middle Ages as that period separating the ancient world from their own by a gulf of darkness. To the humanists, then, we owe the current periodization of history into ancient, medieval, and modern. There was also an element in the humanist view of today's idea of progress: they dared to think that they, "the moderns," might even surpass the ancient glories of Greece and Rome.

The humanist emphasis on historical scholarship yielded a method of critical inquiry that could help to undermine traditional loyalties and institutions. The work of Lorenzo Valla (c. 1407–1457) provides the clearest example of this trend. Educated as a classicist, Valla trained the guns of critical scholarship on the papacy in his most famous work, *Declamation Concerning the False Decretals of Constantine.* The papal claim to temporal authority rested on a document that purported to verify the so-called Donation of Constantine, whereby when the Emperor Constantine moved the capital to Constantinople in the fourth century, he had bestowed on the pope dominion over the entire western Empire. But Valla proved that the document was based on an eighth-century forgery because the language at certain points was unknown in Constantine's own time and did not come into use until much later.

Also embedded in the humanist re-evaluation of individual potential was a new appreciation of the moral significance of work. For the humanist the honor, fame, and even glory bestowed by one's city or patron for meritorious deeds was the ultimate reward for effort. The humanist pursuit of praise and reputation became something of a Renaissance cult.

A Revolution in Political Thought

Renaissance humanists turned away from the religious orientation of the Middle Ages and discussed the human condition in secular terms. In this way they opened up new possibilities for thinking about political and moral problems. Niccolò Machiavelli (1469–1527), a keen observer of Italian politics, regarded the Italian city-states, ruled by men whose authority rested solely on their cunning and effective use of force, as a new phenomenon that traditional political theory, concerned with ideal Christian ends, could not adequately explain. Italian princes made no effort to justify their policies on religious grounds; war was endemic, and powerful cities took over weaker ones; diplomacy was riddled with intrigue, betrayal, and bribery. In such a tooth-and-claw world, where political survival depended on alertness, cleverness, and strength, medieval theorists, who wanted the earthly realm to accord with standards revealed by God, seemed utterly irrelevant. Machiavelli simply wanted rulers to understand how to prepare and expand the state's power. In his book *The Prince,* he expounded a new political theory, one that had no place for Christian morality but that coincided with the emerging modern secular state. He himself was aware that his study of statecraft in the cold light of reason, free of religious and moral illusions, represented a new departure.

Machiavelli held that survival was the state's overriding aim; this consideration transcends any concern with moral or religious values and the interests of individual subjects. Removing questions of good and evil from the realm of political consideration, Machiavelli maintained that all means are permitted the prince when the state's survival is at stake. Successful princes, contended Machiavelli, have always been indifferent to moral and religious considerations—a lesson of history that rulers ignore at their peril. Thus, if the situation warrants it, the prince violates agreements with other rulers, goes back on his word with his subjects, and resorts to cruelty and terror.

Machiavelli broke with the distinguishing feature of medieval thought—the division of the universe into the higher world of the heavens and a lower earthly realm. To this extent, he did for politics what Galileo did a century

Giotto (c. 1276–1337): The Epiphany. Whether or not Giotto is classified as a Late Gothic or Early Renaissance painter, he was a revolutionary innovator. His choice of eye-level perspective and his habit of capturing dramatic gesture brought viewers directly into his pictorial space. (*The Metropolitan Museum of Art, John Stewart Kennedy Fund, 1911. 11.126.1*)

later for physics. Medieval thinkers held that rulers derived their power from God and had a religious obligation to govern in accord with God's commands. Rejecting completely this otherworldly, theocentric orientation, Machiavelli ascribed no divine origin or purpose to the state, but saw it as a natural entity; politics had nothing to do with God's intent or with moral precepts originating in a higher world. Machiavelli's significance as a political thinker consists in the fact that he removed political thought from a religious frame of reference and viewed the state and political behavior in the detached and dispassionate manner of a scientist. In secularizing and rationalizing political philosphy, he initiated a trend of thought that we recognize as distinctly modern.

Renaissance Art

The essential meaning of the Renaissance is conveyed through its art, particularly architecture, sculpture, and painting. Renaissance examples of all three art forms reflect a style that stressed proportion, balance, and harmony. These artistic values were achieved through a new, revolutionary conceptualization of space and spatial relations. Renaissance art also reflects to a considerable extent the values of Renaissance humanism, a return to classical models in architecture, to the rendering of the nude figure, and to a heroic vision of human beings.

Medieval art served a religious function and sought to represent spiritual aspiration; the world was a veil merely hinting at the other perfect and eternal world. Renaissance art did not stop expressing spiritual aspiration, but its setting and character differ altogether. This world is no longer a shroud, but becomes the *place* where people live, act, and worship. The reference is less to the other world and more to this world, and people are treated as creatures who find their spiritual destiny as they fulfill their human one. Renaissance art at its most distinctive represents a conscious revolt against the art of the Middle Ages. This revolt produced revolutionary discoveries that served as the foundation of Western art up to this century.

In art, as in philosophy, the Florentines played a leading role in this esthetic transformation. They, more than anyone else, were responsible for the way artists saw and drew for centuries and for the way most Western people still see or want to see. The first major contributor to Renaissance painting was the Florentine painter Giotto (c. 1276–1337). Borrowing from Byzantine painting, he created figures modeled by alterations in light and shade. He also developed several techniques of perspective, representing three-dimensional figures and objects on two-dimensional surfaces, so that they appear to stand in space. Giotto's figures also look remarkably alive. They are drawn and arranged in space to tell a story, and the expressions they wear and the illusion of movement they convey heighten the dramatic effect. Giotto's best works were *frescoes,* wall paintings painted while the plaster was still wet or *fresh*. Lionized in

Botticelli (1444–1510): The Birth of Venus.   Botticelli was a member of the Florentine group of Neo-Platonists. They tried to harmonize Greco-Roman ideals with those
of Christianity. The nude goddess is Venus, but the modest tilt of the head is the
traditional pose of the Virgin Mary. To Botticelli the beauty of Venus and the purity
of Mary were identical. (*Alinari/Art Resource*)

his own day, Giotto had no immediate successors, and his ideas were not taken
up and developed further for almost a century.

By the early fifteenth century the revival of classical learning had begun in
earnest. In Florence it had its artistic counterpart among a circle of architects,
painters, and sculptors who sought to revive classical art. The leader of this
group was an architect, Filippo Brunelleschi (1377–1446). He designed
churches (Florence Cathedral, for instance) reflecting classical models. To him,
we also owe a scientific discovery of the first importance in the history of art:
the rules of perspective. Giotto had revived the ancient technique of foreshort-
ening; Brunelleschi completed the discovery by rendering perspective in mathematical terms. Brunelleschi's devotion to ancient models and his new tool of
mathematical perspective set the stage for the further development of Renaissance painting. Brunelleschi's young Florentine friend Masaccio (1401–1428)
took up the challenge. Faithful to the new rules of perspective, Masaccio was
also concerned with painting statuesque figures and endowing his paintings
with a grandeur and simplicity whose inspiration is classical. Perspective came
with all the force of religious revelation.

In his work *On Painting*, Leon Battista Alberti (1404–1472), a humanist, scholar, and art theoretician, brought the Renaissance trend toward perspectival art to a summation by advancing the first mathematical theory of artistic perspective. By defining visual space and the relationship between the object and the observer in mathematical terms, Renaissance art and artistic theory paved the way for the development of the modern scientific approach to nature, which later found expression in the astronomy of Copernicus and the physics of Galileo.

Renaissance artists were dedicated to representing things as they are, or at least as they are seen to be. Part of the inspiration for this was also classical. The ancient ideal of beauty was the beautiful nude. Renaissance admiration for ancient art meant that artists for the first time since the fall of Rome studied anatomy; they learned to draw the human form by having models pose for them, a practice fundamental to artistic training to this day. Another member of Brunelleschi's circle, the Florentine sculptor Donatello (1386–1466), also showed renewed interest in the human form.

Among the great Renaissance artists were Leonardo da Vinci (1452–1519), Michelangelo Buonarroti (1475–1564), and Raphael Santi (1483–1520). All of them were closely associated with Florence, and all of them were contemporaries. Leonardo was a scientist and engineer as well as a great artist. He was an expert at fortifications and gunnery, an inventor, an anatomist, and a naturalist. He brought this close observation of nature to his paintings and combined it with powerful psychological insight to produce works that, although few in number, were of unsurpassed genius. Among the most important of these are *The Last Supper* and *La Gioconda* (the Mona Lisa). The Mona Lisa is an example of an artistic invention of Leonardo's—what the Italians call *sfumato*. Leonardo left the outlines of the face a little vague and shadowy; this freed it of any wooden quality, which more exact drawing would impart, and thus made it more lifelike and mysterious.

Michelangelo's creation of artistic harmony derived from a mastery of anatomy and drawing. His model in painting came from sculpture; his paintings are sculpted drawings. He was of course a sculptor of the highest genius, whose approach to his art was poetic and visionary. Instead of trying to impose form on marble, he thought of sculpting as releasing the form from the rock. Among his greatest sculptures are *David, Moses,* and *The Dying Slave.* Michelangelo was also an architect and, patronized by the pope, he designed the dome of the new St. Peter's basilica in Rome. But perhaps his most stupendous work was the ceiling of the Sistine Chapel in the Vatican, commissioned by Pope Julius II. In four years, working with little assistance, Michelangelo covered the empty space with the most monumental sculpted pictures ever painted, pictures that summarize the Old Testament story. The *Creation of Adam* is the most famous of these superlative frescoes.

Raphael, the last of these three artistic giants, is especially famous for the sweetness of his Madonnas. But he was capable of painting other subjects and conveying other moods, as he did in the portrait of his patron, *Pope Leo X with Two Cardinals.*

Michelangelo Buonarroti (1475–1564): Creation of Adam.   The art of Michelangelo relies on the human figure for expressive power, using virtually no background. In this painting, God propels himself effortlessly through the air, bringing the energy that will give life to the listless shell of Adam's recumbent body. The fresco is one of a series commissioned by Pope Julius II to decorate the ceiling of the Sistine Chapel in the Vatican in Rome. (*Scala/Art Resource*)

The Spread of the Renaissance

Aided by the invention of printing, the Renaissance spread to Germany, France, England, and Spain in the late fifteenth and the sixteenth centuries. In its migration northward, Renaissance culture adapted itself to conditions different from those in Italy, particularly the strength of lay piety. For example, the Brethren of the Common Life was a lay movement emphasizing education and practical piety. Intensely Christian and at the same time anticlerical, the people in such lay movements found in Renaissance culture tools for sharpening their wits against the clergy—not to undermine the faith, but rather to restore it to its Apostolic purity.

Thus, northern humanists were profoundly devoted to ancient learning, just as the humanists in Italy had been. But nothing in northern humanism compares to the paganizing trend associated with the Italian Renaissance. The northerners were chiefly interested in the question of what constituted original Christianity. They sought a model by which they might reform the corrupted church of their own time.

Humanism outside Italy was less concerned with the revival of classical values than with the reform of Christianity and society through a program of Christian humanism. The Christian humanists cultivated the new arts of rhetoric and history, as well as the classical languages—Latin, Greek, and

Hebrew. But the ultimate purpose of these pursuits was more religious than it had been in Italy, where secular interests predominated. Northern humanists used humanist scholarship and language to satirize and vilify medieval scholastic Christianity and to build a purer, more Scriptural Christianity. The discovery of accurate biblical texts, it was hoped, would lead to a great religious awakening. Protestant reformers, including Martin Luther, relied on humanist scholarship.

Erasmian Humanism

To Erasmus (c. 1466–1536) belongs the credit for making Renaissance humanism an international movement. He was educated in the Netherlands by the Brethren of the Common Life, which was one of the most advanced religious movements of the age, combining mystical piety with rigorous humanist pedagogy. Erasmus traveled throughout Europe as a humanist educator and biblical scholar. Like other Christian humanists, he trusted the power of words and used his pen to attack scholastic theology and clerical abuses and to promote his philosophy of Christ. His weapon was satire, and his *Praise of Folly* and *Colloquies* won him a reputation for acid wit vented at the expense of conventional religion.

True religion, Erasmus argued, does not depend on dogma, ritual, or clerical power. Rather it is revealed clearly and simply in the Bible and therefore is directly accessible to all people, from the wise and great to the poor and humble. Erasmian humanism stressed toleration, kindness, and respect for human rationality.

This clear but quiet voice was drowned out by the storms of the Reformation, and the Erasmian emphasis on the individual's natural capacities fell down before a renewed emphasis on human sinfulness and dogmatic theology. Erasmus was caught in the middle and condemned on all sides; for him, the Reformation was both a personal and historical tragedy. He had worked for peace and unity only to experience a spectacle of war and fragmentation. Erasmian humanism, however, survived these horrors as an ideal, and during the next two centuries, whenever thinkers sought toleration and rational religion, they looked back to Erasmus for inspiration.

French and English Humanism

Exemplifying the humanist spirit in France was François Rabelais (c. 1495–c. 1553), a former monk. In response to religious dogmatism, Rabelais asserted the essential goodness of the individual and the right to enjoy the world rather than be bound by the fear of a punishing God. In his folk epic, *Gargantua and Pantagruel,* he celebrated earthly life and earthly enjoyments, expressed an appreciation for secular learning and a confidence in human nature, and attacked monastic orders and clerical education for stifling the human spirit. Rabelais said that once freed from theology with its irrelevant concerns, and from narrow-minded clergy who deprived them of life's joys, people could by

Erasmus by Hans Holbein the Younger (c. 1497–1543).   The brilliance and honesty of Erasmus's philosophical treatises endeared him to both conservative Catholic and Protestant reformers. As a humanist and in his pursuit of truth, he travelled freely throughout Europe. (*Louvre/Cliché des Musées Nationaux*)

virtue of their native goodness, build a paradise on earth and disregard the one dreamed up by theologians. In *Gargantua and Pantagruel,* he imagined a monastery where men and women spend their lives "not in laws, statutes, or rules, but according to their own free will and pleasure." They slept and ate when they desired and learned to "read, write, sing, play upon several musical instruments, and speak five or six . . . languages and compose in them all very quaintly." Only one rule did they observe: "DO WHAT THOU WILT."[2]

The most influential humanist of the early English Renaissance was Sir Thomas More (1478–1535), who studied at Oxford. His impact arose from both his writing and his career. Trained as a lawyer, he became a successful civil servant and member of Parliament. His most famous book is *Utopia,* the major utopian treatise to be written in the West since Plato's *Republic* and one of the most original works of the entire Renaissance. Many humanists had attacked private wealth as the principal source of pride, greed, and human cruelty. But More was the only one to carry this insight to its logical conclusion: in *Utopia,* he called for the elimination of private property. He had too keen a sense of human weakness to think that people could become perfect, but he used *Utopia* to call attention to contemporary abuses and to suggest radical reforms. He exploited the satirical and ironical potential of recent overseas discoveries by setting *Utopia* among a non-Christian people, which made his criticism more caustic and pointed. More succeeded Cardinal Wolsey as Lord Chancellor under Henry VIII. But when the king broke with the Roman Catholic church, More resigned, unable to reconcile his conscience with the king's rejection of papal supremacy. Three years later, in July 1535, More was executed for treason for refusing to swear an oath acknowledging the king's ecclesiastical supremacy.

William Shakespeare (1564–1616), widely considered the greatest playwright the world has ever produced, gave expression to Renaissance values—honor, heroism, and the struggle against fate and fortune. But there is nothing conventional about Shakespeare's treatment of characters possessed of these virtues. His greatest plays, the tragedies (*King Lear, Julius Caesar,* and others), explore a common theme: men, even heroic men, despite virtue, are able only with the greatest difficulty, if at all, to overcome their human weaknesses. What fascinates Shakespeare is the contradiction between the Renaissance image of nobility, which is often the self-image of Shakespeare's heroes, and man's capacity for evil and self-destruction. The plays are thus intensely human, but so much so that humanism fades into the background. Thus, art transcends doctrine to represent life itself.

The Renaissance and the Modern Age

The Renaissance, then, marks the birth of modernity—in art, in the idea of the individual's role in history and in nature, and in society, politics, war, and diplomacy. Central to this birth is a bold new view of human nature: individuals in all endeavors are free of a given destiny imposed by God from the outside—free to make their own destiny, guided only by the example of the past, the force of present circumstances, and the drives of their own inner nature. Individuals, set free from theology, are seen to be the products, and in turn the shapers, of history. Their future is not wholly determined by providence, but is partly the work of their own free will.

Within the Italian city-states where the Renaissance was born, rich merchants were at least as important as the church hierarchy and the old nobility. Commercial wealth and a new politics produced a new culture that relied heavily on ancient Greece and Rome. This return to antiquity also entailed a rejection of the Middle Ages as dark, barbarous, and rude. The humanists clearly preferred the secular learning of ancient Greece and Rome to the clerical learning of the more recent past. The reason for this was obvious: the ancients had the same worldly concerns as the humanists; the scholastics did not.

The revival of antiquity by the humanists did not mean, however, that they identified completely with it. The revival itself was done too self-consciously for that. In the very act of looking back, the humanists differentiated themselves from the past and recognized that they were different. They were in this sense the first modern historians, because they could study and appreciate the past for its own sake and to some degree on its own terms.

In the works of Renaissance artists and thinkers, the world was to a large extent depicted and explained without reference to a higher supernatural realm of meaning and authority. This is clearly seen in Machiavelli's analysis of politics. Renaissance humanism exuded a deep confidence in the capacities of able people, instructed in the wisdom of the ancients, to understand and change the world. Renaissance realism, then, was mixed with idealism, and this potent combination departed sharply from the medieval outlook. In place of Christian resignation there grew a willingness to confront life directly and a belief that human beings can succeed even against great odds.

This new confidence is closely related to another distinctive feature of the Renaissance—the cult of the individual. Both prince and painter were motivated in part by the desire to display their talents and to satisfy their ambitions. This individual striving was rewarded and encouraged by the larger society of rich patrons and calculating princes who valued ability. Gone was the medieval Christian emphasis upon the virtue of self-denial and the sin of pride. Instead, the Renaissance placed the highest value on self-expression and self-fulfillment, on the realization of individual potential, especially of the gifted few. The Renaissance fostered an atmosphere in which talent, even genius, was allowed to flourish.

To be sure, the Renaissance image of the individual and the world, bold and novel, was the exclusive prerogative of a small, well-educated urban elite and did not reach down to include the masses. Nevertheless, the Renaissance set an example of what people might achieve in art and architecture, taste and refinement, education and urban culture. In many fields the Renaissance set the cultural standards of the modern age.

Background to the Reformation: The Medieval Church in Crisis

The Renaissance had revitalized European intellectual life and in the process discarded the medieval preoccupation with theology. Similarly, the Reformation marked the beginning of a new religious outlook. The Protestant Reformation, however, did not originate in the elite circles of humanistic scholars. Rather, it was sparked by Martin Luther (1483–1546), an obscure German monk and brilliant theologian. Luther instituted a rebellion against the church's authority that in less than one decade shattered irrevocably the religious unity of Christendom. The Reformation, begun in 1517, dominated European history throughout much of the sixteenth century.

The Roman Catholic church, centered in Rome, was the one European institution that transcended geographic, ethnic, linguistic, and national boundaries. For centuries it had extended its influence into every aspect of European society and culture. As a result, its massive wealth and power appeared to take predominance over its commitment to the search for holiness in this world and salvation in the next. Encumbered by wealth, addicted to international power, and protective of their own interests, the clergy, from the pope on down, became the center of a storm of criticism, starting in the Late Middle Ages.

In the fourteenth century, as kings increased their power and as urban centers with their sophisticated laity grew in size and numbers, people began to question the authority of the international church and its clergy. Political theorists rejected the pope's claim to supremacy over kings. The central idea of medieval Christendom—a Christian commonwealth led by the papacy—increasingly fell into disrepute. Theorists were arguing that the church was only a spiritual body, and therefore its power did not extend to the political realm. They said that the pope had no authority over kings, that the state needed no guidance from the papacy, and that the clergy were not above secular law. During the late fourteenth century Latin Christendom witnessed the first systematic attacks ever launched against the church. Church corruption—such as the selling of indulgences (see page 221), nepotism (the practice of appointing one's relatives to offices), the holding of many bishoprics, and the sexual indulgence of the clergy—was nothing new. What was new and startling was the willingness of educated and uneducated Christians to attack these practices publicly.

Thus, the Englishman John Wycliffe and the Bohemian John Huss (see page 192), both learned theologians, denounced the wealth of the clergy as a violation of Christ's precepts and attacked the church's authority at its root by arguing that the church did not control an individual's destiny. They maintained that salvation depends not on participating in the church's rituals nor on receiving its sacraments, but on accepting God's gift of faith.

Wycliffe's and Huss's efforts to initiate reform coincided with a powerful resurgence of religious feeling in the form of mysticism. Late medieval mystics sought an immediate and personal communication with God; such experiences inspired them to advocate concrete reforms for the purpose of renewing the church's spirituality. The church hierarchy inevitably regarded mysticism with some suspicion, for if individuals could experience God directly, they would seemingly have little need for the church and its rituals. In the fourteenth century, these mystical movements seldom became heretical. But in the sixteenth and seventeenth centuries, radical reformers often found in Christian mysticism a powerful alternative to institutional control and even to the necessity of a priesthood.

With the advent of Lutheranism, personal faith, rather than adherence to the practices of the church, became central to the religious life of European Protestants. Renaissance humanists had sought to reinstitute the wisdom of ancient times; Protestant reformers wanted to restore the spirit of early Christianity, in which faith seemed purer, believers more sincere, and clergy uncorrupted by luxury and power. By the 1540s, the Roman Catholic church had initiated its own internal reformation, but it came too late to stop the movement toward Protestantism in northern and western Europe.

The Lutheran Revolt

The Reformation was initiated by Martin Luther, who had experienced the personal agony of doubting the church's power to give salvation and who had the will and talent to convey that agony to all Christians and to win the support of powerful princes. As a young student, Luther fulfilled his father's wish and studied law, but at the age of twenty-one, he suddenly abandoned his legal studies to enter the Augustinian monastery at Erfurt. Luther began his search for spiritual and personal identity, and therefore for salvation, within the strict confinement and discipline of the monastery. He pursued his theological studies there and prepared for ordination into the priesthood.

The Break with Catholicism

As he studied and prayed, Luther grew increasingly terrified about the possibility of his damnation. As a monk he sought union with God, and he understood the church's teaching that salvation depended on faith, works (meaning acts of charity, prayer, fasting, and so on), and grace. He participated in the sacraments of the church, which according to its teaching were intended to give grace. Indeed, after his ordination, Luther administered the sacraments. Yet he still felt the weight of his sins, and nothing the church could offer seemed to relieve that burden. Seeking solace and salvation, Luther increasingly turned to reading the Bible. Two passages seemed to speak directly to him: "For in it the righteousness of God is revealed through faith for faith: as it is written, 'He who through faith is righteous shall live' " (Romans 1:17); and "They are justified by his grace as a gift, through the redemption which is in Christ Jesus" (Romans 3:24). In these two passages, Luther found, for the first time in his adult life, some hope for his own salvation. Faith, freely given by God through Christ, enables the recipient to receive salvation.

The concept of salvation by faith alone provided an answer to Luther's spiritual quest. Practicing such good works as prayer, fasting, pilgrimages, participation in the Mass and the other sacraments had never brought Luther peace of mind. He concluded that no amount of good works, however necessary for maintaining the Christian community, would bring salvation. Through reading the Bible and through faith alone, the Christian could find the meaning of earthly existence. For Luther, the true Christian was a courageous figure who faced the terrifying quest for salvation armed only with the hope that God had granted the gift of faith. The new Christian served others not to trade good works for salvation but solely to fulfill the demands of Christian love.

The starting point for the Reformation was Luther's attack in 1517 on the church's practice of selling indulgences. The church taught that some individuals go directly to heaven or hell, while others go to heaven only after spending time in purgatory; this waiting period is necessary for those who have sinned excessively in this life but who have had the good fortune to repent before death. To die in a state of mortal sin meant to suffer in hell eternally. Naturally people worried about how long they might have to spend in purgatory. Indulgences were intended to remit portions of that time and were granted to individuals by the church for their prayers, attendance at Mass, and almost any acts of charity—including monetary offerings to the church. This last good work was the most controversial, since it could easily appear that people were buying their way into heaven.

In the autumn of 1517 a monk named Tetzel was selling indulgences in the area near Wittenberg. Luther launched his attack on Tetzel and the selling of indulgences by tacking on the door of the Wittenberg castle church his ninety-five theses. Luther's theses (propositions) challenged the entire notion of selling indulgences, not only as a corrupt practice but also as a theologically unsound assumption—namely, that salvation can be earned by good works.

At the heart of Luther's argument in the ninety-five theses and in his later writings was the belief that the individual achieves salvation through inner religious feeling, a sense of contrition for sins, and trusting God's mercy. Luther also believed that church attendance, fasting, pilgrimages, charity, and other good works did not earn salvation. The church, in contrast, held that *both* faith and good works were necessary for salvation. Luther further insisted that every individual could discover the meaning of the Bible unaided by the clergy; the church, however, maintained that only the clergy could read and interpret the Bible properly. Luther argued that in matters of faith there was no difference between the clergy and the laity. Each person could receive faith directly and freely from God. But the church held that the clergy were intermediaries between individuals and God and that in effect Christians reached eternal salvation through the clergy. For Luther, no priest, no ceremony, no sacrament could bridge the gulf between the Creator and his creatures. Hope lay only in a personal relationship between the individual and God, as expressed through faith in God's mercy and grace. By holding that clergy and church rituals do not hold the key to salvation, Luther rejected the church's claim that it alone offered men and women the way to eternal life.

Recognizing that his life might be in danger if he continued to preach without a protector, Luther appealed for support to the prince of his district, Frederick, the elector of Saxony. The elector was a powerful man in international politics—one of seven lay and ecclesiastical princes who chose the Holy Roman emperor. Frederick's support convinced church officials, including the pope, that this monk would have to be dealt with cautiously. When in 1520 the pope finally acted against Luther, it was too late; Luther had been given the needed time to promote his views. He proclaimed that the pope was Antichrist and that the church was the "most lawless den of robbers, the most shameless of all brothels, the very kingdom of sin, death and Hell." When the papal bull excommunicating him was delivered, Luther burned it.

No longer members of the church, Luther and his followers established congregations for the purpose of Christian worship. Christians without the church needed protection, and in 1520 Luther published the *Address to the Christian Nobility of the German Nation*. In it, he appealed to the emperor and the German princes to reform the church and to cast off their allegiance to

Martin Luther (left) and the Wittenberg Reformers (Frederick of Saxony and Ulrich Zwingli in center) by Lucas Cranach the Younger. Luther benefited from his powerful protector, Frederick, who wielded influence in the church due to his office as elector of popes. Zwingli, a Swiss from Zurich, practiced a form of Christianity very close to that of Luther and claimed to have developed his ideas independently of Luther. (*The Toledo Museum of Art, Gift of Edward Drummond Libbey*)

the pope, who he argued had used taxes and political power to exploit them for centuries. His appeal produced some success; the Reformation flourished on the resentment against foreign papal intervention that had long festered in Germany. In this and other treatises, Luther made it clear that he wanted to present no threat to legitimate political authority, that is, to the power of the German princes.

In 1521, Charles V, the Holy Roman emperor, who was a devout Catholic, summoned Luther to Worms, giving him a pass of safe conduct. There Luther was to answer to the charge of heresy, both an ecclesiastical and a civil offense. When asked to recant, Luther replied: "Unless I am convinced of error by the testimony of Scripture or by clear reason . . . I cannot and will not recant anything, for it is neither safe nor honest to act against one's conscience. God help me. Amen." Shortly after this confrontation with the emperor, Luther went into hiding to escape arrest. During that one-year period he translated the New Testament into German. His followers, or Lutherans, were eventually called *Protestants,* those who protested against the established church, and the term became generic for all followers of the Reformation.

Print Shop, Sixteenth-Century Print.   Neither the Renaissance nor the Reformation would have been so widespread without printing, which was invented in Nuremberg in the 1450s. The printed word was the medium for the rapid transmission of Luther's and Calvin's revolutionary treatises, first in Germany and Switzerland and then elsewhere in Europe. (*The Bettmann Archive/BBC Hulton*)

The Appeal and Spread of Lutheranism

Spread rapidly by the new printing press, the tenets of Protestantism offered the hope of revitalization and renewal to its adherents. Lutheranism appealed to the devout, who resented the worldliness and lack of piety of many clergy. But the movement found its greatest following among German townspeople who objected to money flowing from their country to Rome in the form of church taxes and payment for church offices. In addition, the Reformation provided the nobility with the unprecedented opportunity to confiscate church lands, to eliminate church taxes, and to gain the support of their subjects by serving as leaders of a popular and dynamic religious movement. The Reformation also gave the nobles a way of resisting the Catholic Holy Roman emperor, Charles V, who wanted to extend his authority over the German princes. Resenting the Italian domination of the church, many other Germans who supported Martin Luther believed that they were freeing German Christians from foreign control.

Lutheranism also drew support from the peasants, who saw Luther as their champion against their oppressors—both lay and ecclesiastical lords and the townspeople. Indeed, in his writings and sermons, Luther often attacked the greed of the princes and bemoaned the plight of the poor. Undoubtedly,

Luther's successful confrontation with the authorities served to inspire the peasants. In 1524, these long-suffering people openly rebelled against their lords. The Peasants' Revolt spread to over one-third of Germany; some 300,000 people took up arms against their masters.

But Luther had no intention of associating his movement with a peasant uprising at the risk of alienating the nobility who supported him. Luther was a political conservative who hesitated to challenge secular authority. To him, the good Christian was an obedient subject. He virulently attacked the rebellious peasants, urging the nobility to become "both judge and executioner" and to "knock down, strangle, and stab" the insurgents. By 1525 the peasants had been put down by the sword. The failure of the Peasant's Revolt meant that the German peasantry remained among the most backward and oppressed until well into the nineteenth century.

Initially the Holy Roman emperor, who was at war with France over parts of Italy and whose eastern territories were threatened by the Ottoman Turks, hesitated to intervene militarily in the strife between Lutheran and Catholic princes, a delay that proved crucial. The religious conflict was settled by the Peace of Augsburg (1555), which decreed that each territorial prince should determine the religion of his subjects. Broadly speaking, northern Germany became largely Protestant while Bavaria and other southern territories remained in the Roman Catholic church. The Holy Roman emperor, who had been successfully challenged by the Lutheran princes, saw his power diminished. The decentralization of the empire and its division into Catholic and Protestant regions would block German unity until the last part of the nineteenth century.

The Spread of the Reformation

Nothing better illustrates people's dissatisfaction with the church in the early sixteenth century than the rapid spread of Protestantism. There was a pattern to this phenomenon. Protestantism grew strong in northern Europe—northern Germany, Scandinavia, the Netherlands, and England; it failed in the Latin countries, although not without a struggle in France. In general, Protestantism was an urban phenomenon, and it prospered where local magistrates supported it and where the distance from Rome was greatest.

Calvinism

The success of the Reformation outside Germany and Scandinavia derived largely from the work of John Calvin (1509–1564), a French scholar and theologian. Sometime in 1533 or 1534, Calvin met French followers of Luther and became convinced of the truth of the new theology. He began to spread its beliefs immediately after his conversion, and within a year he and his friends were in trouble with the civil and ecclesiastical authorities.

Calvin soon abandoned his humanistic and literary studies to become a preacher of the Reformation. From early in his religious experience, he emphasized the power of God over sinful and corrupt humanity. Calvin's God thundered and demanded obedience, and the terrible distance between God and the individual was mediated only by Christ. Calvin embraced a stern theology, holding that God's laws must be rigorously obeyed, that social and moral righteousness must be earnestly pursued, that political life must be carefully regulated, and that human emotions must be strictly controlled.

Even more than Luther, Calvin explained salvation in terms of uncertain predestination—that God, who grants grace for his own inscrutable reasons, knows in advance who will earn salvation and who will be condemned to hell. Calvin argued that although people are predestined to salvation or damnation, they can never know with certainty their fate in advance. This terrible decree could and did lead some people to despair. For others—in a paradox difficult for the modern mind to comprehend—Calvinism gave a sense of self-assurance and righteousness that made the saint, that is, the truly predestined man or woman, into a new kind of European. Most of Calvin's followers seemed to believe that in having comprehended the fact of predestination, they had received a bold insight into their unique relationship with God.

Calvinists were individuals who assumed that only unfailing dedication to God's law could be seen as a sign of salvation; thus, Calvinism made for stern men and women, active in their congregations and willing to suppress vice in themselves and others. Calvinism could also produce revolutionaries willing to defy any temporal authorities that were perceived to be in violation of God's laws. For Calvinists, obedience to Christian law became the dominating principle of life.

Forced to flee France, Calvin finally sought safety in Geneva, a small, prosperous Swiss city near the French border. There he eventually established a Protestant church that closely regulated the citizens' personal and social lives. Elders of the Calvinist church governed the city and imposed strict discipline in dress, sexual mores, church attendance, and business affairs; they severely punished irreligious and sinful behavior. Prosperous merchants as well as small shopkeepers saw in Calvinism a series of doctrines that justified the self-discipline they already exercised in their own lives and wished to impose on the unruly masses. They particularly approved of Calvin's economic views, for he saw nothing sinful about commercial activities, unlike many Catholic clergy.

Geneva became the center of international Protestantism. Calvin trained a new generation of Protestant reformers of many nationalities, who carried his message back to their homelands. Calvin's *Institutes of the Christian Religion* (1536), in its many editions, became (after the Bible) the leading textbook of the new theology. In the second half of the sixteenth century, Calvin's theology of predestination spread into France, England, the Netherlands, and parts of the Holy Roman Empire.

Map 8.1   The Protestant and the Catholic Reformations ▶

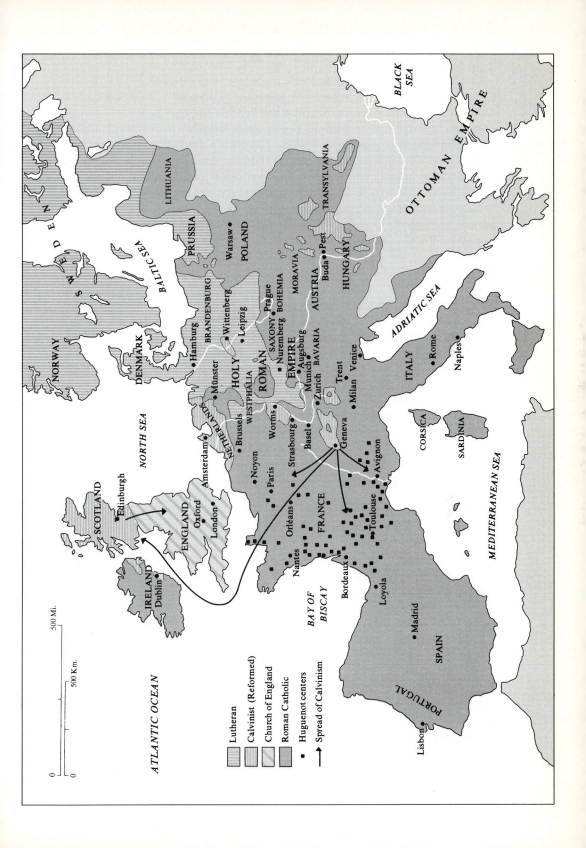

BLACK SEA

OTTOMAN EMPIRE

NORWAY

SWEDEN

LITHUANIA

PRUSSIA

BALTIC SEA

Warsaw

POLAND

BRANDENBURG

TRANSYLVANIA

DENMARK

Hamburg

Wittenberg

Leipzig

Prague

BOHEMIA

MORAVIA

Pest

Buda

HUNGARY

AUSTRIA

ADRIATIC SEA

Münster

HOLY

SAXONY

Nuremberg

Augsburg

BAVARIA

ROMAN

Rome

ITALY

Naples

WESTPHALIA

EMPIRE

Munich

Trent

Venice

Zurich

Milan

NETHERLANDS

Brussels

Worms

Basel

Strasbourg

Geneva

NORTH SEA

Amsterdam

SCOTLAND

Edinburgh

ENGLAND

Oxford

London

Noyon

Paris

Orléans

FRANCE

Avignon

CORSICA

SARDINIA

Toulouse

MEDITERRANEAN SEA

IRELAND

Dublin

Nantes

Bordeaux

BAY OF BISCAY

Loyola

Madrid

SPAIN

PORTUGAL

Lisbon

ATLANTIC OCEAN

500 Mi.

500 Km.

Lutheran

Calvinist (Reformed)

Church of England

Roman Catholic

■ Huguenot centers

→ Spread of Calvinism

Calvin always opposed any recourse to violence and supported the authority of magistrates. Yet when monarchy became their persecutor, his followers felt compelled to resist. Calvinist theologians became the first political theoreticians of modern times to publish cogent arguments for opposition to monarchy, and eventually for political revolution. In France and later in the Netherlands, Calvinism became a revolutionary ideology, complete with an underground organization composed of dedicated followers who challenged monarchical authority. In the seventeenth century, the English version of Calvinism—Puritanism—performed the same function. Thus, in certain circumstances, Calvinism possessed the moral force to undermine the claims of the monarchical state over the individual.

France

Although Protestantism was illegal in France after 1534, the Protestant minority, the Huguenots, grew, becoming a well-organized underground movement. Huguenot churches, often under the protection of powerful nobles, assumed an increasingly political character in response to monarchy-sponsored persecution. French Protestants became sufficiently organized and militant to challenge their persecutors, King Henry II and the Guise—one of the foremost Catholic families in Europe—and in 1562 civil war erupted between Catholics and Protestants. What followed was one of the most brutal religious wars in the history of Europe. In 1572, on Saint Bartholomew's Day, the gruesome slaughter of thousands of Protestant men, women, and children stained the streets with blood. So intense was the religious hatred at the time that the massacre inspired the pope to have a Mass said in thanksgiving for a Catholic "victory."

After nearly thirty years of brutal fighting throughout France, victory went to the Catholic side—but barely. Henry of Navarre, a Protestant leader, became King Henry IV, but only after he agreed to reconvert to Catholicism. Henry established a tentative peace by granting Protestants limited toleration. In 1598 he issued the Edict of Nantes, the first document in any national state that attempted to institutionalize a degree of religious toleration. In the seventeenth century the successors of Henry IV (who was assassinated in 1610) gradually weakened and then in 1685 revoked the edict. The theoretical foundations of toleration, as well as its practice, remained tenuous in early modern Europe.

England

The Reformation was initiated in England not by religious reformers but by the king himself. Henry VIII (1509–1547) removed the English church from the jurisdiction of the papacy because the pope refused to grant him an annulment of his marriage to his first wife. The English Reformation thus began as a political act on the part of a self-confident Renaissance king. But the Reformation's origins stretched back into the Middle Ages, for there was a long tradition of heresy as well as anticlericalism in England that had its roots in Wycliffe's actions in the fourteenth century.

When Henry VIII decided that he wanted a divorce from the Spanish princess Catherine of Aragon, in 1527–28, the pope in effect ignored his request. As the pope stalled, Henry grew more desperate—he needed a male heir and presumed that the failure to produce one lay with his wife. At the same time, he desired the shrewd and tempting Anne Boleyn. Henry VIII arranged to grant himself a divorce by severing England from the church. In 1534, with Parliament's approval he had himself declared supreme head of the Church of England. In 1536 he dissolved the monasteries and seized their property, which was distributed or sold to his loyal supporters. In most cases, it went to the lesser nobility and landed gentry. By involving Parliament and the gentry, Henry VIII turned the Reformation into a national movement.

In the eleven years following Henry's death in 1547, there were three monarchs. Henry VIII was succeeded by his son, Edward VI, a Protestant, who reigned from 1547 to 1553. On his death, he was succeeded by Mary (1553–1558), the daughter of Henry VIII and Catherine of Aragon. Mary, a devout Catholic, severely persecuted Protestants. By the 1558 succession of Elizabeth I, Henry's second daughter (by Anne Boleyn), England was a Protestant country again. Elizabeth's reign was characterized by a heightened sense of national identity and the persecution of Catholics, who were seen as a threat to national security. Fear of invasion by Spain, which was intent on returning England to the papacy, contributed to English anti-Catholicism.

The English, or Anglican, church as it developed in the sixteenth century differed to only a limited degree in its customs and ceremonies from the Roman Catholicism it replaced. The exact nature of England's Protestantism became a subject of growing dispute. Was the Anglican church to be truly Protestant? Were its services and churches to be simple, lacking in "popish" rites and rituals and centered on Scripture and sermon? Obviously, the powerful Anglican bishops would accept no form of Protestantism that might limit their privileges, ceremonial functions, and power. These issues contributed to the English Revolution of the seventeenth century (see pages 249–251).

The Radical Reformation

The leading Protestant reformers generally supported established political authorities, whether they were territorial princes or urban magistrates. For the reformers, human freedom was a spiritual, not a social, concept. Yet the Reformation did help trigger revolts among the artisan and peasant classes of central and then western Europe. By the 1520s, several radical reformers arose, often from the lower classes of European society, and attempted to channel popular religion and folk beliefs into a new version of reformed Christianity that spoke directly to the temporal and spiritual needs of the oppressed.

Radical reformers proclaimed that God's will was known by his saints—those predestined for salvation. They said that the poor would inherit the earth, which at present was ruled by the Antichrist; the saint's task was to purge this earth of evil to make it ready for Christ's Second Coming. For the radicals, the Scriptures, which spoke of God's love for the wretched and lowly, became an inspiration for social revolution. Luther, Calvin, and other reformers vigorously condemned the social doctrines that were preached by the radical reformers.

The largest group in the Radical Reformation prior to 1550 has the general name of *Anabaptists*. Having received the inner light—the message of salvation—Anabaptists felt born anew and yearned to be rebaptized. Anabaptists were new Christians, new persons led by the light of conscience to seek reform and renewal of all institutions in preparation for Christ's Second Coming.

In 1534, Anabaptists captured the city of Münster in Westphalia, near the western border of Germany. They seized the property of nonbelievers, burned all books except the Bible, and in a mood of jubilation and sexual excess, openly practiced polygamy. All the while the Anabaptists proclaimed that the Day of Judgment was close at hand. Provoked by their actions, Lutheran Prince Philip of Hesse and his army crushed the Anabaptists.

Because of this Anabaptist revolt, *Münster* became a byword for dangerous revolution in early modern Europe. Determined to prevent these wild enthusiasts from gaining strength in their own territories, princes attacked them with ferocity. In Münster today, the cages still hang from the church steeple where the Anabaptist leaders were tortured and left to die as a warning to all would-be imitators.

By the late sixteenth century, many radical movements had either gone underground or grown quiet. But a century later, during the English Revolution (1640–1660), the beliefs and political goals of the Radical Reformation again surfaced, threatening to push the revolution in a direction that its gentry leaders desperately feared. Although the radicals failed in England too, they left a tradition of democratic and antihierarchical thought. The radical assertion that saints, who have received the inner light, are the equal of anyone, regardless of social status, helped shape modern democratic thought.

The Catholic Response

The Protestant threat impelled the Roman Catholic church to institute reforms. In the first instance, the energy for reform came from ordinary clergy as well as lay people such as Ignatius Loyola (1491–1556). Trained as a soldier, this pious Spanish reformer sought to create a new religious order fusing the intellectual excellence of humanism with a reformed Catholicism that would appeal to powerful economic and political groups. Founded in 1534, the Society of Jesus, more commonly known as the Jesuits, became the backbone of the Catholic Reformation in southern and western Europe. The Jesuits combined traditional monastic discipline with a dedication to teaching and an emphasis on the power of preaching, and they sought to use both to win converts back to the church.

El Greco (1541–1614): Portrait of a Cardinal (probably Don Fernando Niño de Guevara).   The Spanish church fiercely opposed the Reformation. The Inquisition persecuted Protestants relentlessly. The tenseness of the sitter captures the wary militancy of Spanish Catholicism. The cardinal's cool glance is belied by his claw-like hand. (*The Metropolitan Museum of Art, Bequest of Mrs. H. O. Havemeyer, 1929. The H. O. Havemeyer Collection. 29.100.5*)

The Jesuits offered hope—a religious revival based on ceremony, tradition, and the power of the priest to offer forgiveness. In addition, they opened some of the finest schools in Europe. Just as the Lutherans in Germany sought to bring literacy to the masses so that they might read the Bible, the Jesuits sought to bring intellectual enhancement to the laity, especially to the rich and powerful. The Jesuits pursued positions as confessors to princes and urged them to press their efforts to strengthen the church in their territories.

By the 1540s the Counter Reformation was well under way. The leaders of this Catholic movement attacked many of the same abuses that had impelled Luther to speak out, but they avoided a break with the doctrinal and spiritual authority of the clergy.

The Counter Reformation also took aggressive and hostile measures against Protestantism. The church tried to counter the popular appeal of Protestantism by offering dramatic, emotional, even sentimental piety to the faithful. For individuals who were unmoved by this appeal to sentiment or by the church's more traditional spirituality and who allied with Protestant heresy, the church resorted to sterner measures. The Inquisition—the church court dealing with heretics—expanded its activities, and wherever Catholic jurisdiction prevailed, unrepentant heretics were subject to death or imprisonment. Catholics did not hold a monopoly on persecution: wherever Protestantism obtained official status—in England, Scotland, and Geneva, for instance—Catholics or religious radicals also sometimes faced persecution.

One of the Catholic church's main tools was censorship. By the 1520s the impulse to censor and burn dangerous books intensified dramatically as the church tried to prevent the spread of Protestant ideas. In the rush to eliminate heretical literature, the church condemned the works of reforming Catholic humanists as well as those by Protestants. The Index of Prohibited Books became an institutional part of the church's life. Over the centuries the works of many leading thinkers were placed on the Index, which was not abolished until 1966.

The Counter Reformation policies of enlightened education, vigorous preaching, church building, persecution, and censorship did succeed in bringing thousands of people, Germans and Bohemians in particular, back into the church. In addition, the church implemented some concrete changes in policy and doctrine. In 1545, the Council of Trent met to reform the church and to strengthen it to face the Protestant challenge. Over the many years that it was convened (until 1563), the council modified and unified church doctrine; abolished many corrupt practices, such as the selling of indulgences; and vested final authority in the papacy, thereby ending the long and bitter struggle within the church over papal authority. The Council of Trent purged the church and gave it doctrinal clarity on such matters as the roles of faith and good works in attaining salvation. It passed a decree that the church shall be the final arbiter of the Bible. All compromise with Protestantism was rejected (not that Protestants were anxious for it). The Reformation had split western Christendom irrevocably.

The Reformation and the Modern Age

At first glance, the Reformation would seem to have renewed the medieval stress on otherworldliness and reversed the direction toward a secularism that had been taken by the Renaissance. Yet the Reformation contributed substantially to the shaping of the modern world. It shattered the religious unity of Europe, the chief characteristic of the Middle Ages, and further weakened the church, the principal institution of medieval society, whose moral authority and political power waned considerably. To this day Europe remains a continent of Catholics and Protestants.

By strengthening the power of monarchs and magistrates at the expense of religious bodies, the Reformation furthered the growth of the modern state. Protestant rulers totally repudiated the pope's claim to temporal power and extended their authority over Protestant churches in their lands. In Catholic lands, the church reacted to the onslaught of Protestantism by supporting rather than challenging monarchs. Protestantism did not create the modern secular state; it did, however, help to free the state from subordination to religious authority. Such autonomy is an essential feature of modern political life.

Very indirectly, Protestantism contributed to the growth of political liberty—another ideal in the modern West. To be sure, neither Luther nor Calvin championed political freedom. Luther said that subjects should obey the commands of their rulers, and Calvinists created a theocracy in Geneva that closely regulated its citizens. Nevertheless, the Reformation provided a basis for challenging monarchical authority. During the religious wars, some Protestant theorists supported resistance to monarchs whose edicts, they believed, defied God's law as expressed in the Bible. This religious justification for rebelling against tyrannical authority helped fuel the English Revolution of the seventeenth century and the American Revolution a century later. Both revolutions were instrumental in creating the modern constitutional state. Moreover, the Protestant view that all believers—laity, clergy, lords, kings—were masters of their own spiritual destiny eroded hierarchical authority and accorded with emerging constitutional government.

The Reformation also contributed to the creation of an individualistic ethic that is characteristic of the modern world. Protestants sought a direct and personal relationship with God and interpreted the Bible for themselves. Facing the prospect of salvation or damnation entirely on their own, without the church to provide aid and security, and believing that God had chosen them to be saved, Protestants developed an inner confidence and assertiveness. This religious individualism was the counterpart of the intellectual individualism of the Renaissance humanists.

In 1904, the German sociologist Max Weber argued that Protestantism encouraged the growth of capitalism. Weber acknowledged that capitalism existed in Europe before the Reformation; merchant bankers in medieval Italian and German towns, for example, engaged in capitalist practices. But, he argued, Protestantism (particularly Calvinism) gave to capitalism a particular dynamism. Protestant businessmen believed that they had a religious obligation to make money, and their religion gave them the self-discipline to do it. According to Calvin's doctrine of predestination, salvation could not be attained through any worldly actions, but Calvin's followers came to believe that certain activities were signs that God was working through them, that they had indeed been elected. Thus Calvinists held that hard work, diligence, dutifulness, efficiency, frugality, and a disdain for hedonism—all virtues that contribute to rational and orderly business procedures and to business success—were signs of election. In effect, argued Weber, Protestantism gave religious approval, which Catholicism did not, to money-making and the businessman's way of life.

The tradition of individual striving for material gain, so much a part of Western culture today, developed out of what had once been a religious quest

Chronology 8.1 ◈ The Renaissance and the Reformation

1304–1374	Petrarch, "father of humanism"
c. 1445	Johann Gutenberg invents movable metal type
1513	Machiavelli writes *The Prince*
1517	Martin Luther writes his ninety-five theses and the Reformation begins
1520	Pope Leo X excommunicates Luther
1524–1526	The German peasants revolt
1529	The English Parliament accepts Henry VIII's Reformation
1534	Henry VIII is declared head of the Church of England; King Francis I of France declares Protestants heretics; Ignatius Loyola founds the Society of Jesus; Anabaptists, radical reformers, capture Münster in Westphalia
1535	Sir Thomas More, English humanist and author of *Utopia*, is executed for treason
1536–1564	Calvin leads the Reformation in Geneva with Guillaume (William) Farel
1545–1563	The Council of Trent
1555	The Peace of Augsburg

for salvation, made urgent in this world by the theology of the Protestant Reformation. Sixteenth-century Protestantism created a new, highly individual, spirituality. Survival in this world and salvation in the next came to depend on inner faith and self-discipline; for the prosperous, both eventually became useful in a highly competitive world where individuals rule their own lives and the labor of others and represent themselves and others in government.

Notes

1. Giovanni Pico della Mirandola, *Oration on the Dignity of Man,* trans. by A. Robert Caponigri (Chicago: Henry Regnery, 1956), p. 7.

2. François Rabelais, *Gargantua and Pantagruel,* trans. by Sir Thomas Urquhart (1883), I. 57.

Suggested Reading

Brucker, Gene A., *Renaissance Florence* (rev. ed., 1983). An excellent analysis of the city's physical character, its economic and social structure, its political and religious life, and its cultural achievements.

Burckhardt, Jacob, *The Civilization of the Renaissance in Italy* (1860). 2 vols. (1958). The first major interpretative synthesis of the Renaissance; still an essential resource.

Burke, Peter, *Popular Culture in Early Modern Europe* (1978). A fascinating account of the social underside from the Renaissance to the French Revolution.

Grimm, Harold J., *The Reformation Era,* 1500–1650, 2nd ed. (1973). The best and most complete narrative available.

Koenigsberger, H. G., and George L. Mosse, *Europe in the Sixteenth Century* (1968). Some very good chapters on the Reformation.

Ozment, Steven E., *The Reformation in the Cities* (1975). A good survey of the Reformation in Germany.

Pullan, Brian S., *A History of Early Renaissance Italy* (1973). A solid, brief account.

Skinner, Quentin, *The Foundations of Modern Political Thought,* 2 vols. (1978). The first volume covers the Renaissance; highly informed.

Review Questions

1. What is the connection between the Renaissance and the Middle Ages? What special conditions gave rise to the Italian Renaissance?
2. What is humanism and how did it begin? What did the humanists contribute to education and the writing of history?
3. How can it be said that Machiavelli invented a new politics?
4. What are the general features of Renaissance art?
5. What factors encouraged the spread of the Renaissance into the western European monarchies and the Rhineland?
6. Why is the Renaissance considered the departure from the Middle Ages and the beginning of modernity?
7. What were the medieval roots of the Reformation?
8. How did Luther's theology mark a break with the church? Why did many Germans become followers of Luther?
9. In what ways did the radical reformers differ from the other Protestants?
10. What role did the Jesuits and the Inquisition play in the Counter Reformation? What did the Counter Reformation accomplish?
11. How did the Reformation weaken medieval institutions and traditions?

Chapter ✪ 9

Political and Economic Transformation: National States, Overseas Expansion, Commercial Revolution

From the thirteenth to the seventeenth century a new and unique form of political organization emerged in the West: the dynastic or national state, which harnessed the material resources of its territory, directed the energies of the nobility into national service, and increasingly centralized political authority. The national state is the essential political institution of the modern West.

During the Middle Ages, some kings began to forge national states. However, medieval political forms differed considerably from those that developed later, in the early modern period. In the Middle Ages, feudal lords gave homage to their kings but retained power in their local territories, resisting the centralizing efforts of monarchs. Local and even national representative assemblies, which met frequently to give advice to kings, at times acted as a brake on the king's power. The clergy supported the monarch, but governed their congregations or monasteries as separate spiritual realms. The papacy challenged the authority of monarchs when it believed they did not fulfill their duty to rule in accordance with Christian teachings as interpreted by the church.

In early modern times, powerful monarchs subdued these competing systems of political authority and created a bureaucracy that coordinated and administered the activities of the central government.

Thus kings were the central figures in the creation of the national state. Strong dynastic states were formed wherever monarchs succeeded in subduing local aristocratic and ecclesiastical power systems. Where the monarchs failed, as they did in Germany and Italy, no viable states evolved until well into the nineteenth century.

By the early seventeenth century, Europeans had developed the concept of the state—an autonomous political entity to which its subjects owed duties and obligations. The essential prerequisite of the western concept of the state, as it emerged in the early modern period, was the idea of *sovereignty:* within its borders the state was supreme; all other institutions, both secular and religious, had to recognize the state's authority. The art of governing entailed molding the ambitions and strength of the powerful and wealthy into the state's service. The state, its power growing through war and taxation, had become the basic unit of political authority in the West.

In the sixteenth and seventeenth centuries, the idea of liberty, now so basic to western political life and thought, was only rarely discussed and generally only by Calvinist opponents of absolutism. Not until the mid-seventeenth century in England was there a body of political thought contending that human liberty was compatible with the new modern state. In general, despite the English (and Dutch) developments, absolutism dominated the political development of early modern Europe. It was not until the late eighteenth and nineteenth centuries that absolutism was widely challenged by advocates of liberty.

The principle of balance of power, an integral part of modern international relations, also emerged during early modern times. When one state threatened to dominate Europe, as did Spain under Philip II and France under Louis XIV, other states joined forces and resisted. The fear that one state would upset the balance of power and achieve European domination pervaded international relations in future centuries.

Seeking to enrich their treasuries and to extend their power, states promoted commercial growth and overseas expansion. The extension of European hegemony over much of the world was well under way by the eighteenth century. *&*

Hapsburg Spain

The Spanish political experience of the sixteenth century stands as one of the most extraordinary in the history of modern Europe. Spanish kings built a dynastic state that burst through its frontiers and encompassed Portugal, part of Italy, the Netherlands, and enormous areas in the New World. Spain became an intercontinental empire—the first in the West since Roman times.

In the eighth and ninth centuries, the Muslims controlled all of Spain except for some tiny Christian kingdoms in the far north. In the ninth century, these Christian states began a 500-year struggle—the Reconquest—to drive the Muslims from the Iberian Peninsula. By the middle of the thirteenth century, Granada in the south was all that remained of Muslim lands in Spain.

The 500-year struggle for Christian hegemony in the Iberian Peninsula left the Spanish fiercely religious and strongly suspicious of foreigners. Despite centuries of intermarriage with non-Christians, by the early sixteenth century, purity of blood and orthodoxy of faith became necessary for and synonymous with Spanish identity. In 1492 the Jews and the Muslims were physically expelled from Spain or forced to convert. This process of detection and conversion was supervised by the church, or more precisely, by the Inquisition. Run by clerics but responsive to state policies, the Inquisition existed to enforce religious uniformity and to ferret out the increasing numbers of Muslims and Jews who ostensibly converted to Catholicism but who remained secretly loyal to their own religions. Using its legal right to torture as well as burn heretics, the Inquisition represented the dark side of Spanish genius at conquest and administration, and its shadow stretched down through the centuries well into the twentieth.

Ferdinand and Isabella

In 1469, Ferdinand, heir to the throne of Aragon, married Isabella, heir to the throne of Castile. Although Ferdinand and Isabella did not give Spain a single legal and tax system or a common currency, their policies did contribute decisively to Spanish unity and power. They broke the power of aristocrats who had operated from their fortified castles in effect like kings, waging their private wars at will; they brought the Spanish church into alliance with the state; and in 1492 they drove the Muslims from Granada, their last territory in Spain. The crusade against the Muslim infidels accorded with the aims of the militant Spanish church. With a superior army, with the great aristocrats pacified, and with the church and the Inquisition under monarchical control, the Catholic kings expanded their interests and embarked on an imperialist foreign policy that made Spain dominant in the New World.

Isabella and Ferdinand.   With the marriage of Ferdinand of Aragon to Isabella of Castile, Spain came into being as a nation. At the battle of Granada, they defeated the last of the Islamic forces on the Spanish mainland. Columbus courted and won the patronage of Isabella. Monies that had previously been used to fight Islam were diverted to exploration. The wealth of the New World would repay her patronage beyond all expectation. (*Copyright reserved to H.M. The Queen*)

The Reign of Charles V: King of Spain and Holy Roman Emperor

Dynastic marriage constituted another crucial part of Ferdinand and Isabella's foreign policy. They strengthened their ties with the Austrian Hapsburg kings by marrying one of their children, Juana (called "the Mad" for her insanity), to Philip the Fair, son of Maximilian of Austria, the head of the ruling Hapsburg family. Philip and Juana's son Charles (1516–1556) inherited the kingdom of Ferdinand and Isabella; through his other grandparents, he also inherited the Netherlands, Austria, Sardinia, Sicily, the kingdom of Naples, and Franche Comté. In 1519, he was also elected Charles V, Holy Roman emperor. Charles became the most powerful ruler in Europe, but his reign also saw the emergence of political, economic, and social problems that eventually led to Spain's decline.

Charles's inheritance was simply too vast to be governed effectively, but that was only dimly perceived at the time. The Lutheran Reformation proved to be the first successful challenge to Hapsburg power. It was the first phase of a religious and political struggle between Catholic Spain and Protestant Europe that would dominate the last half of the sixteenth century.

The achievements of Charles V's reign rested on the twin instruments of army and bureaucracy. The Hapsburg empire in the New World was vastly extended and, on the whole, effectively administered and policed. Out of this sprawling empire with its exploited native populations came the greatest flow of gold and silver ever witnessed by Europeans. Constant warfare in Europe, coupled with the immensity of the Spanish administrative network, required a steady intake of capital. However, this easy access to capital appears to have been detrimental in the long run to the Spanish economy. There was no incentive for the development of domestic industry, bourgeois entrepreneurship, or international commerce. Moreover, constant war engendered and perpetuated a social order geared to the aggrandizement of a military class, rather than to the development of a commercial class. And although war expanded Spain's power in the sixteenth century, it sowed the seeds for the financial crises of the 1590s and beyond, and for the eventual decline of Spain as a world power.

Philip II

Philip II inherited the throne from his father, Charles V, who abdicated in 1556. Charles left his son with a vast empire in both the Old and New Worlds that had been administered competently enough, yet was also burdened by the specters of bankruptcy and heresy. A zeal for Catholicism ruled Philip's private conduct and infused his foreign policy. In the 1560s Philip sent the largest land army ever assembled in Europe into the Netherlands, with the intention of crushing Protestant-inspired opposition to Spanish authority. The ensuing revolt of the Netherlands lasted until 1609, and the Spanish lost their industrial heartland as a result of it.

The Dutch established a republic governed by the prosperous and progressive bourgeoisie. Rich from the fruits of manufacture and trade in everything from tulip bulbs to ships and slaves, the Dutch merchants ruled their cities and provinces with fierce pride. By the early seventeenth century, this new nation of only 1.5 million practiced the most innovative commercial and financial techniques in Europe.

Philip's disastrous attempt to invade England was also born of religious zeal. Philip regarded an assault on England, the main Protestant power, as a holy crusade against the "heretic and bastard," Queen Elizabeth; he particularly resented English assistance to the Protestant Dutch rebels. Sailing from Lisbon in May 1588, the Spanish Armada, carrying 22,000 seamen and soldiers, met with defeat. Its ships were too large and cumbersome to negotiate the treacherous English Channel, where the English ships easily outmaneuvered them and broke their formation with fire ships. Moreover, strong winds, typical for this time of year, drove the Armada out of striking position. The defeat had an enormous psychological effect on the Spanish, who saw it as divine punishment and openly pondered what they had done to incur God's displeasure.

The End of the Spanish Hapsburgs

After the defeat of the Armada, Spain gradually and reluctantly abandoned its imperial ambitions in northern Europe. The administrative structure built by Charles V and Philip II did remain strong throughout the seventeenth century; nevertheless, by the first quarter of the century, enormous weaknesses had surfaced in Spanish economic and social life. In 1596, Philip II was bankrupt, his vast wealth overextended by the cost of foreign wars. Bankruptcy reappeared at various times in the seventeenth century, while the agricultural economy, at the heart of any early modern nation, stagnated. The Spanish in their golden age had never devoted enough attention to increasing domestic production.

Despite setbacks, Spain was still capable of taking a very aggressive posture during the Thirty Years' War (1618–1648). The Austrian branch of the Hapsburg family joined forces with their Spanish cousins, and neither the Swedes and Germans nor the Dutch could stop them. Only French participation in the Thirty Years' War on the Protestant side tipped the balance decisively against the Hapsburgs. Spanish aggression brought no victories, and with the Peace of Westphalia (1648), Spain officially recognized the independence of the Netherlands and severed its diplomatic ties with the Austrian branch of the family.

By 1660, the imperial age of the Spanish Hapsburgs had come to an end. The rule of the Protestant princes had been secured in the Holy Roman Empire; the Protestant and Dutch Republic flourished; Portugal and its colony of Brazil were independent of Spain; and dominance over European affairs had passed to France. The quality of material life in Spain deteriorated rapidly, and the ever-present gap between rich and poor widened even more drastically. The traditional aristocracy and the church retained their land and power but failed conspicuously to produce effective leadership.

The Spanish experience illustrates two observations in the history of the European state. First, the state as empire could only survive and prosper if the domestic economic base remained sound. The Spanish reliance on bullion from its colonies and its failure to cultivate industry and to reform the taxation system spelled disaster. Second, states with a vital and aggressive bourgeoisie flourished at the expense of regions where aristocracy and church dominated and controlled society and its mores—Spain's situation. The latter social groups tended to despise manual labor, profit taking, and technological progress. Although kings and dynastic families originally created them, after 1700 the major dynastic states were increasingly nurtured by the economic activities of merchants and traders—by the bourgeoisie. Yet the bureaucracy of the dynastic states continued to be dominated by men drawn from the lesser aristocracy. This was nowhere truer than in France, where once again monarchs created the national state.

The Growth of French Power

Although both England and France effectively consolidated the power of their central governments, each became a model of a different form of statehood. The English model was a constitutional monarchy in which the king's power was limited by Parliament and the rights of the English people were protected by law and tradition. The French model emphasized at every turn the glory of the king and, by implication, the sovereignty of the state and its right to stand above the interests of its subjects. France's monarchy became absolute, and French kings emphasized that they had been selected by God to rule, a theory known as the divine right of kings. This theory gave monarchy a sanctity that various French kings used to enforce their commands over the population, including rebellious feudal lords.

The evolution of the French state was a very gradual process, one not completed until the late seventeenth century. In the Middle Ages the French monarchs recognized the rights of, and consulted with, representative assemblies called *Estates*. These assemblies (whether regional or national) were composed of deputies drawn from the various elites: the clergy, the nobility, and, significantly, the leaders of cities and towns in a given region. Early modern French kings increasingly wrested power from the nobility, reduced the significance of the Estates, and eliminated interference from the church.

Religion and the French State

In every emergent state, tension existed between the monarch and the papacy. At issue was control over the church within that territory—over its personnel, wealth, and, of course, its pulpits, from which an illiterate majority learned what their leaders believed they should know, not only in matters of religion but also about submission to civil authority. The monarch's power to make church appointments could ensure a complacent church, one that would preach obedience to royal authority and was compliant on matters of taxes.

For the French monarchs, centuries of tough bargaining with the papacy paid off in 1516, when Francis I (1515–1547) concluded the Concordat of Bologna. Under this agreement Pope Leo X permitted the French king to nominate, and therefore effectively to appoint, men of his choice to all the highest offices in the French church. The Concordat of Bologna laid the foundation for what became known as the *Gallican church*, a term signifying that

Map 9.1   Europe, 1648 ▶

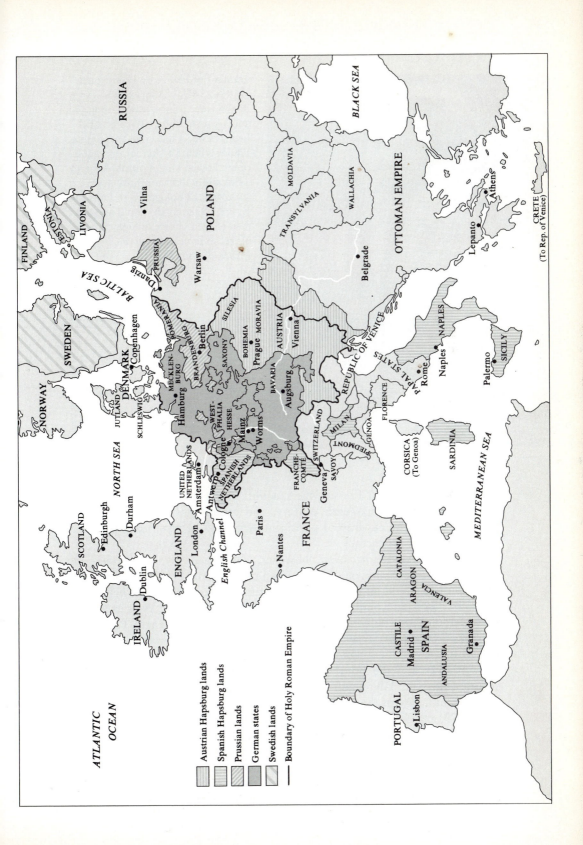

Francis I of France by Jean Clouet (1486–1541).   Francis I was a true Renaissance prince, power hungry and a patron of the arts. The aged Leonardo da Vinci ended his days at Francis's court at Amboise as guest of the French king. Francis was also a brilliant politician; through his concordat of Bologna with Pope Leo X, French monarchs could appoint men of their choice to high church offices in France. (*Louvre/Cliché des Musées Nationaux*)

the Catholic church in France was sanctioned and overseen by the French kings. By the early sixteenth century, the central government had been strengthened at the expense of papal authority and of traditional privileges enjoyed by local aristocracy.

The Protestant Reformation, however, challenged royal authority and threatened the very survival of France as a unified state. Francis I, fearful that Protestantism would undermine his authority, declared Protestant beliefs and practices illegal and punishable by fine, imprisonment, and even execution. However, the Protestant minority (the Huguenots) grew in strength. From 1562 to 1598, France experienced waves of religious wars that cost the king control over vast areas of the kingdom. The great aristocratic families, the Guise for the Catholics and the Bourbons for the Protestants, drew up armies that scourged the land, killing and maiming their religious opponents and dismantling the authority of the central government.

In 1579, extreme Huguenot theorists published the *Vindiciae contra Tyrannos*. This theoretical statement, combined with a call to action, was the first of its kind in early modern times. It justified rebellion against, and even the execution of, an unjust king. European monarchs might claim power and divinely sanctioned authority, but by the late sixteenth century, their subjects had available the moral justification to oppose by force, if necessary, their monarch's will, and this justification rested on Scripture and religious conviction. Significantly, this same treatise was translated into English in 1648, a year before Parliament publicly executed Charles I, king of England.

The Valois kings floundered in the face of this kind of political and religious opposition. The era of royal supremacy instituted by Francis I came to an abrupt end during the reign of his successor, Henry II (1547–1559). Wed to Catherine de' Medici, a member of the powerful Italian banking family, Henry occupied himself not with the concerns of government but with the pleasures of the hunt. The sons who succeeded Henry—Francis II (1559–1560), Charles IX (1560–1574), and Henry III (1574–1589)—were uniformly weak. Their mother, Catherine, who was the virtual ruler, ordered the execution of thousands of Protestants by royal troops in Paris—the infamous St. Bartholomew's Day Massacre (1572) which, with the bloodbath that followed, became a symbol of the excesses of religious zeal.

The civil wars begun in 1562 were renewed in the massacre's aftermath. They dragged on until the death of the last Valois king in 1589. The Valois failure to produce a male heir to the throne placed Henry, duke of Bourbon and a Protestant, in line to succeed to the French throne. Realizing that the overwhelmingly Catholic population would not accept a Protestant king, Henry (apparently without much regret) renounced his adopted religion and embraced the church. Henry IV (1589–1610) granted to his Protestant subjects and former followers a degree of religious toleration through the Edict of Nantes (1598), but they were never welcomed in significant numbers into the royal bureaucracy. Throughout the seventeenth century, every French king attempted to undermine the Protestants' regional power bases and ultimately to destroy their religious liberties.

The Consolidation of French Monarchical Power

The defeat of Protestantism as a national force set the stage for the final consolidation of the French state in the seventeenth century under the great Bourbon kings, Louis XIII and Louis XIV. Louis XIII (1610–1643) realized that his rule depended on an efficient and trustworthy bureaucracy, an ever-replenishable treasury, and constant vigilance against the localized claims to power made by the great aristocracy and by the Protestant cities and towns. Cardinal Richelieu, who served as Louis XIII's chief minister from 1624 to 1642, became the great architect of French absolutism.

Richelieu's morality rested on one sacred principle embodied in a phrase he invented: *raison d'état*, reason of state. Richelieu sought to serve the state by bringing under the king's control the disruptive and antimonarchical elements within French society. He increased the power of the central bureaucracy, attacked the power of independent, and often Protestant, towns and cities, and persecuted the Huguenots. Above all, he humbled the great nobles by limiting their effectiveness as councilors to the king and by prohibiting their traditional privileges, such as using a duel rather than court action to settle grievances. Reason of state also guided Richelieu's foreign policy. It necessitated France's

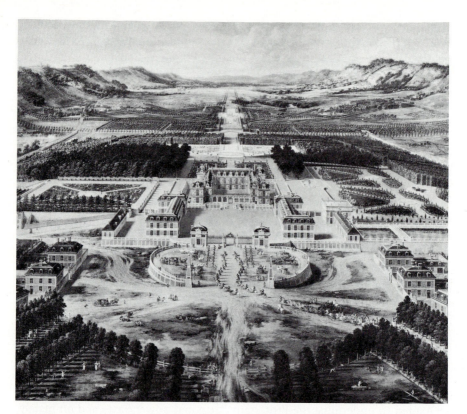

Versailles, Painted by Pierre Patel in 1668.   The splendor of Versailles, both the buildings and the extensive grounds, were widely imitated by European monarchs, and epitomized the power and wealth of the king. (*Versailles/Cliché des Musées Nationaux*)

turning against Catholic Spain and entering on the Protestant and hence anti-Spanish side in the war that was raging at the time in the Holy Roman Empire. The outcome of France's entry into the Thirty Years' War (1618–1648) produced a decided victory for French power on the Continent.

Richelieu died in 1642 and Louis XIII the following year. Cardinal Mazarin, who took charge during the minority of Louis XIV (who was five years old when Louis XIII died), continued Richelieu's policies. Mazarin's heavy-handed actions produced a rebellious reaction, the *Fronde*—a series of street riots that eventually cost the government control over Paris and lasted from 1648 to 1653. Centered in Paris and supported by the great aristocracy, the courts, and Paris's poorer classes, the Fronde threatened to develop into a full-scale uprising. It might have done so, but for one crucial factor: its leadership was fundamentally divided. Court judges (lesser nobles who had often just risen from the ranks of the bourgeoisie) deeply distrusted the great aristocrats and refused in the end to make common cause with them. And both groups feared disorders among the urban masses.

When Louis XIV finally assumed responsibility for governing in 1661, he vowed that the events he had witnessed as a child during the Fronde would never be repeated. In the course of his reign, he achieved the greatest degree of monarchical power held during the early modern period. No absolute monarch in Western Europe, before or at that time, had so much personal authority or commanded such a vast and effective military and administrative machine. Louis XIV's reign represents the culmination of a process of increasing monarchical authority that had been under way for centuries. Intelligent, cunning, and possessing a unique understanding of the requirements of his office, Louis XIV worked long hours at being king, and he never undertook a venture without an eye to his personal grandeur. The sumptuous royal palace at Versailles was built for that reason; similarly, etiquette and style were cultivated there on a scale never before seen in any European court.

When Mazarin died, Louis XIV did away with the office of first minister; he would rule France alone. The great nobles, "princes of the blood," enjoyed great social prestige but exercised decreasing political influence. Louis XIV treated the aristocrats to elaborate rituals, feasts, processions, displays, and banquets; but amid all the clamor, their political power dwindled.

Louis XIV's domestic policies centered around his incessant search for new revenues. Not only the building of Versailles but also wars cost money, and Louis XIV waged them to excess. To raise capital, he used the services of Jean Baptiste Colbert, a brilliant administrator who improved methods of tax collecting, promoted new industries, and encouraged international trade. Operating with a total bureaucracy of about a thousand officials and no longer bothering even to consult the parlements or Estates, Louis XIV ruled absolutely in accordance with the principle of divine right—that the monarch is selected to rule by God.

Yet Louis XIV's system was fatally flawed. Without any effective check on his power and dreams of international conquest, there was no limit imposed on the state's capacity to make war or on the ensuing national debt. Louis XIV coveted vast sections of the Holy Roman Empire; he also sought to check Dutch commercial prosperity and had designs on the Spanish Netherlands. By the 1680s, his domestic and foreign policies took on a violently aggressive posture. In 1685, he revoked the Edict of Nantes, forcing many of the country's remaining Protestants to flee. In 1689, he embarked on a military campaign to secure territory from the Holy Roman Empire. And in 1701, he tried to bring Spain under the control of the Bourbon dynasty. Louis XIV, however, underestimated the power of his northern rivals, England and the Netherlands. The combined power of England and the Netherlands in alliance with the Holy Roman Empire and the Austrians brought defeat to Louis XIV's ambitions.

Louis XIV's participation in these long wars emptied the royal treasury. By the late seventeenth century taxes had risen intolerably, and they were essentially levied on those least able to pay—the peasants. Thus, for the great majority of French people, absolutism meant a decline in living standards and a significant increase in mortality rates. Absolutism also meant increased surveillance over the population: royal authorities censored books; spied on heretics, Protestants, and freethinkers; and even tortured and executed opponents of state policy.

In the France of Louis XIV, the dynastic state had reached maturity and had begun to display some of its classic characteristics: centralized bureaucracy; royal patronage to enforce allegiance; a system of taxation universally but inequitably applied; and suppression of political opposition either through the use of patronage or, if necessary, through force. Another important feature was the state's cultivation of the arts and sciences as a means of increasing national power and prestige. Together, these policies enabled the French monarchy to achieve political stability, to enforce a uniform system of law, and to channel the country's wealth and resources into the service of the state as a whole.

Yet at his death in 1715, Louis XIV left his successors a system of bureaucracy and taxation that was vastly in need of overhaul but was still locked into the traditional social privileges of the church and nobility to an extent that made reform virtually impossible. The pattern of war, excessive taxation of the lower classes, and expenditure in excess of revenues had severely damaged French finances. Failure to reform the system led to the French Revolution of 1789.

The Growth of Limited Monarchy and Constitutionalism in England

In 1066, William, duke of Normandy and vassal to the French king, had invaded and conquered England, acquiring at a stroke the entire kingdom. In succeeding centuries, English monarchs continued to strengthen central authority and to tighten the bonds of national unity. At the same time, however, certain institutions and traditions evolved—common law, Magna Carta, and Parliament—that checked royal power and protected the rights of the English people.

Central government in England was threatened after the Hundred Years' War (1337–1453) when English aristocrats brought back from France a taste for warfare. In the ensuing civil war—the War of the Roses (1455–1485)—gangs of noblemen with retainers roamed the English countryside, and lawlessness prevailed for a generation. Only in 1485 did the Tudor family emerge triumphant.

The Tudor Achievement

Victory in the civil wars allowed Henry VII (1485–1509) to begin the Tudor dynasty. Henry VII's goal was to bring an unruly nobility into check. Toward this end, he brought commoners into the government; these commoners, unlike the great magnates, could be channeled into royal service because they craved what the king offered—financial rewards and elevated social status.

Although they did not fully displace the aristocracy, commoners were brought into Henry VII's inner circle, into the Privy Council, into the courts. The strength and efficiency of Tudor government were shown during the Reformation, when Henry VIII (1509–1547) made himself head of the English church.

The Protestant Reformation in England was a revolution in royal as well as ecclesiastical government. It attacked and defeated a main obstacle to monarchical authority—the power of the papacy. No change in religious practice could be instituted by the monarchy alone. Parliament's participation in the Reformation gave it a greater role and sense of importance than it had ever possessed in the past.

At Henry VIII's death, the Tudor bureaucracy and centralized government was strained to its utmost, yet it survived. The government weathered the reign of Henry's sickly son Edward VI (1547–1553) and the extreme Protestantism of some of his advisers, and it survived the brief and deeply troubled reign of Henry's first daughter, Mary (1553–1558), who attempted to return England to Catholicism. At Mary's death, England had come dangerously close to the religious instability and sectarian tension that undermined the French kings during the final decades of the sixteenth century.

Henry's second daughter, Elizabeth I, became queen in 1558. The Elizabethan period was characterized by a heightened sense of national identity. The English Reformation enhanced that sense, as did the increasing fear of foreign invasion by Spain. The fear was abated only by the defeat of the Spanish Armada in 1588. In the seventeenth century, the English would look back on Elizabeth's reign as a golden age. It was the calm before the storm, a time when a new commercial class was formed that, in the seventeenth century, would demand a greater say in government operations.

Religion played a vital role in this realignment of political interests and forces. Many of the old aristocracy clung to the Anglicanism of the Henrican Reformation, and in some cases to Catholicism. The newly risen gentry found in the Protestant Reformation of Switzerland and Germany a form of religious worship more suited to their independent and entrepreneurial spirit. Many of them embraced Puritanism, the English version of Calvinism.

The English Revolution, 1640–1689

The forces threatening established authority were dealt with ineffectively by the first two Stuart kings—James I (1603–1625) and Charles I (1625–1649). Both believed, as did their Continental counterparts, in royal absolutism, and both preached, through the established church, the doctrine of the divine right of kings. James I, an effective and shrewd administrator, conducted foreign policy without consulting Parliament, and Charles disbanded Parliament and attempted to collect taxes without its consent. These policies ended in disaster.

The English Revolution broke out in 1640 because Charles I needed new taxes to defend the realm against a Scottish invasion. Parliament, finally called after an eleven-year absence, refused his request unless he granted certain basic rights: Parliament to be consulted in matters of taxation, trial by jury, *habeas corpus,* and a truly Protestant church responsive to the beliefs and interests of its laity. Charles refused, for he saw these demands as an assault on royal authority. The ensuing civil war was directed by Parliament, financed by taxes and the merchants, and fought by the New Model Army led by Oliver Cromwell (1599–1658), a Puritan squire who gradually realized his potential for leadership.

The New Model Army was unmatched by any ever seen before in Europe. Parliament's rich supporters financed it, gentleman farmers led it, and religious zealots filled its ranks, along with the usual cross-section of poor artisans and day laborers. This army brought defeat to the king, his aristocratic followers, and the Anglican church's hierarchy.

In January 1649, Charles I was publicly executed by order of Parliament. During the interregnum (time between kings) of the next eleven years, one Parliament after another joined with the army to govern the country as a republic. In the distribution of power between the army and the Parliament, Cromwell proved to be a key element. He had the support of the army's officers and some of its rank and file, and he had been a member of Parliament for many years. His control over the army was secured, however, only after its rank and file was purged of radicals drawn largely from the poor. Some of these radicals wanted to level society, that is, to redistribute property and to give the vote to all male citizens.

After Cromwell died in 1658, the country was without effective leadership. Parliament, having secured the economic interests of its constituency (gentry, merchants, and some small landowners), chose to restore court and crown and invited the exiled son of the executed king to return to the kingship. Having learned the lesson his father had spurned, Charles II (1660–1685) never instituted royal absolutism.

But Charles's brother, James II (1685–1688), was a foolishly fearless Catholic and admirer of French absolutism. James gathered at his court a coterie of Catholic advisers and supporters of royal prerogative and attempted to bend Parliament and local government to the royal will. James's Catholicism was the crucial element in his failure. The Anglican church would not back him, and political forces similar to those that had gathered against his father, Charles I, in 1640 descended on him. The ruling elites, however, had learned their lesson back in the 1650s: civil war would produce social discontent among the masses. The upper classes wanted to avoid open warfare and preserve the monarchy as a constitutional authority, but not as an absolute one. Puritanism, with its sectarian fervor and its dangerous association with republicanism, was allowed to play no part in this second and last phase of the English Revolution.

In early 1688, Anglicans, some aristocrats, and opponents of royal prerogative formed a conspiracy against James II. Their purpose was to invite his son-in-law, William of Orange, *stadholder* (head) of the Netherlands and husband of James's Protestant daughter Mary, to invade England and rescue its government from James's control. James, who had lost the loyalty of key men in the army, powerful gentlemen in the counties, and the Anglican church, fled the country, and William and Mary were declared king and queen by act of Parliament.

This bloodless revolution—sometimes called the Glorious Revolution—created a new political and constitutional reality. Parliament secured its rights to assemble regularly and to vote on all matters of taxation; the rights of *habeas corpus* and trial by jury (for men of property and social status) were also secured. These rights were in turn legitimated in a constitutionally binding document, the Bill of Rights (1689). All Protestants, regardless of their sectarian bias, were granted toleration.

The English Revolution, in both its 1640 and its 1688 phases, secured English parliamentary government and the rule of law. Gradually the monarchical element in that system would yield to the power and authority of parliamentary ministers and state officials. The Revolution of 1688–89 was England's last revolution. In the nineteenth and twentieth centuries, parliamentary institutions would be gradually and peacefully reformed to express a more democratic social reality. The events of 1688–89 have rightly been described as "the year one," in that they fashioned a system of government that operated effectively in Britain and was also capable of being adopted with modification elsewhere. The British system became a model for other forms of bourgeois representative government adopted in France and former British colonies, beginning with the United States.

The Holy Roman Empire: The Failure to Unify Germany

In contrast to the French, English, Spanish, and Dutch experiences in the early modern period, the Germans failed to achieve national unity. This failure is tied to the history of the Holy Roman Empire. That union of various distinct central European territories was created in the tenth century when Otto I, in a deliberate attempt to revive Charlemagne's empire, was crowned emperor of the Romans. Later the title was changed to Holy Roman emperor, with the kingdom consisting of mostly German-speaking principalities.

Most medieval emperors busied themselves not with administering their territories but with attempting to secure control of the rich Italian peninsula and with challenging the rival authority of various popes. In the meantime, the German nobility extended and consolidated their rule over their peasants and over various towns and cities. Their aristocratic power remained a constant obstacle to German unity.

In the medieval and early modern periods the Holy Roman emperors were dependent on their most powerful noble lords—including an archbishop or two—because the office of emperor was an elected one, not the result of hereditary succession. German princes, some of whom were electors—such as the archbishops of Cologne and Mainz, the Hohenzollern elector of Brandenburg, the landgrave of Hesse, and the duke of Saxony—were fiercely independent. All belonged to the empire, yet all regarded themselves as autonomous powers. These decentralizing tendencies were highly developed by the fifteenth century. The Hapsburgs maneuvered themselves into a position from which they could monopolize the imperial elections. The empire became increasingly German and Hapsburg, with Worms as the seat of imperial power.

The centralizing efforts of the Hapsburg Holy Roman Emperors Maximillian I (1493–1519) and Charles V (1519–1556) were impeded by the Reformation, which bolstered the Germans' already well-developed tendencies toward local independence. The German nobility were all too ready to use the Reformation as a vindication of their local power, and indeed Luther made just such an appeal to their interests. War raged in Germany between the Hapsburgs and the Protestant princes, united for mutual protection in the Schmalkadic League. The Treaty of Augsburg (1555) conferred on every German prince the right to determine the religion of his subjects. The princes retained their power; a unified German state was never constructed by the Hapsburgs.

When an exhausted Emperor Charles V abdicated in 1556, he gave his kingdom to his son Philip and his brother Ferdinand. Philip inherited Spain and its colonies as well as the Netherlands, and Ferdinand acquired the Austrian territories. Two branches of the Hapsburg family were thus created. Throughout the sixteenth century the Austrian Hapsburgs barely managed to control these sprawling and deeply divided German territories. Religious disunity and the particularism and provinciality of the German nobility continued to prevent the creation of a German state.

The Austrian Hapsburg emperors, however, never missed an opportunity to further the cause of Catholicism and to strike at the power of the German nobility. No Hapsburg was ever more fervid in that regard than the Jesuit-trained Archduke Ferdinand II, who ascended to the throne in Vienna in 1619. His policies provoked a war within the empire that engulfed the whole of Europe. The Thirty Years' War (1618–1648) began when the Bohemians, whose anti-Catholic tendencies went back to fourteenth-century heretic John Huss, attempted to put a Protestant king on their throne. Austrian and Spanish Hapsburgs reacted by sending an army into the kingdom of Bohemia, and suddenly the whole empire was forced to take sides along religious lines. Bohemia suffered an almost unimaginable devastation; the ravaging Catholic army sacked and burned three-fourths of the kingdom's towns and practically exterminated its aristocracy.

Until the 1630s, it looked as if the Hapsburgs would be able to use the war to enhance their power and to promote centralization. But the intervention of Protestant Sweden, led by Gustavus Adolphus and encouraged by France, wrecked Hapsburg ambitions. The ensuing military conflict devastated vast areas of northern and central Europe. The civilian population suffered untold hardships. Partly because the French finally intervened directly, the Spanish Hapsburgs emerged from the Thirty Years' War with no benefits. At the Treaty of Westphalia (1648), the Austrian Hapsburgs gained firm control of the eastern states of the kingdom, with Vienna as their capital. Austria took shape as a dynastic state, while the German territories in the empire remained fragmented by the independent interests of the feudal nobility.

European Expansion

During the period from 1450 to 1750, western Europe entered an era of overseas exploration and economic expansion that transformed society. European adventurers discovered a new way to reach the rich trading centers of India by sailing around Africa. They also conquered, colonized, and exploited a new world across the Atlantic. These discoveries and conquests brought about an extraordinary increase in business activity and the supply of money, which stimulated the growth of capitalism. People's values changed in ways that were alien and hostile to the medieval outlook. By 1750, the model Christian in northwestern Europe was no longer the selfless saint but the enterprising businessman. The era of secluded manors and walled towns was drawing to a close. A world economy was emerging in which European economic life depended on the market in Eastern spices, African slaves, and American silver. During this age of exploration and commercial expansion, Europe generated a peculiar dynamism unmatched by any other civilization. A process was initiated that by 1900 would give Europe mastery over most of the globe and wide-ranging influence over other civilizations.

Forces Behind Expansion

Combined forces propelled Europeans outward and enabled them to dominate Asians, Africans, and American Indians. European monarchs, merchants, and aristocrats fostered expansion for power and profit; religion and technology played their part. As the numbers of the landed classes exceeded the supply of available land, the sons of the aristocracy looked beyond Europe for the lands and fortunes denied them at home. Nor was it unnatural for them to do so by plunder and conquest—their ancestors had done the same thing for centuries.

Merchants and shippers also had reason to look abroad. Trade between Europe, Africa, and the Orient had gone on for centuries, but always through intermediaries who increased the costs and decreased the profits on the European end. Gold had been transported by Arab nomads across the Sahara from the riverbeds of West Africa. Spices had been shipped from India and the East Indies by way of Muslim and Venetian merchants. Western European merchants now sought to break those monopolies by going directly to the source—to West Africa for gold, slaves, and pepper, and to India for pepper, spices, and silks.

The centralizing monarchical state also played its part in expansion. Monarchs who had successfully established royal hegemony at home, like Ferdinand and Isabella of Spain, looked for opportunities to extend their control overseas. From overseas empires came gold, silver, and commerce that paid for ever-more expensive royal government at home and for war against rival dynasties abroad.

Religion, too, helped in expansion. The crusading tradition was well established, especially on the Iberian Peninsula, where a 500-year struggle known as the Reconquest had taken place to drive out the Muslims. Cortés, the Spanish conqueror of Mexico, for example, saw himself as following in the footsteps of Paladin Roland, the great medieval military hero who had fought to drive back Muslims and pagans. Prince Henry the Navigator hoped that the Portuguese expansion into Africa would serve two purposes: the discovery of gold and the extension of Christianity at the expense of Islam.

Not only did the West have the will to expand, it also possessed the technology needed for successful expansion—in the form of armed sailing vessels. This factor distinguished the West from China and the lands of Islam and helps explain why the West, not the oriental civilizations, launched an age of conquest resulting in global mastery. Not only were sailing ships more maneuverable and faster in the open seas than galleys (ships propelled by oars), but the addition of guns below deck that could fire and cripple or sink distant enemy ships gave them another tactical advantage. The galleys of the Arabs in the Indian Ocean and the junks of the Chinese were not armed with such guns. In battle they relied instead on the ancient tactic of coming up alongside the enemy vessel, shearing off its oars, and boarding to fight on deck.

The gunned ship gave the West naval superiority from the beginning. The Portuguese, for example, made short work of the Muslim fleet sent to drive them out of the Indian Ocean in 1509. That victory at Diu, off the western coast of India, indicated that the West not only had found an all-water route to the Orient but was there to stay.

The Portuguese Empire

In the first half of the fifteenth century, a younger son of the king of Portugal, named Prince Henry the Navigator (1394–1460) by English writers, sponsored voyages of exploration and the nautical studies needed to undertake them. The Portuguese first expanded into islands in the Atlantic Ocean. In 1420 they began to settle Madeira and raise corn there, and in the 1430s they pushed into the Canaries and the Azores in search of new farmlands and slaves for their colonies. In the middle decades of the century they moved down the west African coast to the mouth of the Congo River and beyond, establishing trading posts as they went.

By the end of the fifteenth century, the Portuguese had developed a viable imperial economy among the ports of West Africa, their Atlantic islands, and western Europe—an economy based on sugar, black slaves, and gold. Africans panned gold in the riverbeds of central and western Africa, and the Portuguese purchased it at its source.

Map 9.2   Overseas Exploration and Conquest, c. 1400–1600 ▶

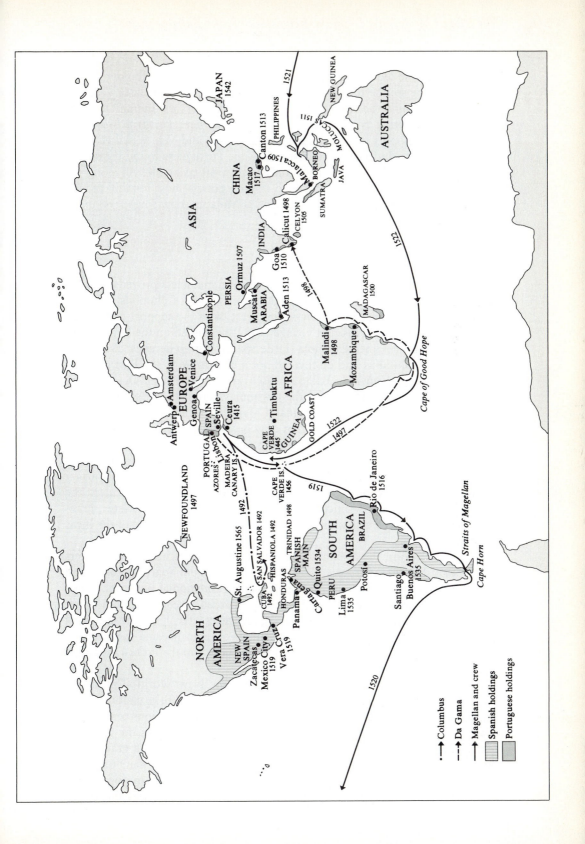

The Portuguese did not stop in western Africa. By 1488, Bartholomeu Dias had reached the southern tip of the African continent; a decade later Vasco da Gama sailed around the Cape of Good Hope and across the Indian Ocean to India. By discovering an all-water route to the Orient, Portugal broke the commercial monopoly of Eastern goods that Genoa and Venice had enjoyed. With this route to India and the East Indies, the Portuguese found the source of the spices needed to make dried and tough meat palatable. As along the African coast, they established fortified trading posts—most notably at Goa on the western coast of India (Malabar) and at Malacca (now Singapore) in the Malay Peninsula.

The Spanish Empire

Spain stumbled onto its overseas empire, which nonetheless proved to be the biggest and richest of any until the eighteenth century. Columbus, who believed that he could reach India by sailing west, won the support of Isabella, queen of Castile. But on his first voyage (1492) he landed on the large Caribbean island that he named Española (Little Spain). Within decades, two events revealed that Columbus had discovered not a new route to the East but new continents: Vasco Nuñez de Balboa's discovery of the Pacific Ocean at the Isthmus of Panama in 1513, and the circumnavigation of the globe (1519–1522) by the expedition led by Ferdinand Magellan, which sailed through the strait at the tip of South America that now bears his name.

Stories of the existence of large quantities of gold and silver to the west lured the Spaniards from their initial settlements in the Caribbean to Mexico. In 1519, Hernando Cortés landed on the Mexican coast with a small army; during two years of campaigning he managed to defeat the native rulers, the Aztecs, and to conquer Mexico for the Spanish crown. A decade later, Francisco Pizarro achieved a similar victory over the mountain empire of the Incas in Peru.

For good reasons, the Mexican and Peruvian conquests became the centers of the Spanish overseas empire. First, there were the gold hoards accumulated over the centuries by the rulers for religious and ceremonial purposes. When these supplies were exhausted, the Spanish discovered silver at Potosí in Upper Peru in 1545 and at Zacatecas in Mexico a few years later. From the middle of the century, the annual treasure fleets sailing to Spain became the financial bedrock of Philip II's war against the Muslim Turks and the Protestant Dutch and English.

Not only gold and silver lured Spaniards to the New World. The will to conquer and convert the pagan peoples of the New World continued the crusading spirit used against the Muslims during the five previous centuries of Spanish history. The rewards were what they had always been: the propagation of the true faith, service to the Crown, and handsome land grants. The land was especially attractive in the sixteenth century because the number of hidalgos (lesser nobility) was increasing with the general rise in population, and as a result the amount of land available to them at home was shrinking.

Indian Workers Mining for Gold, Overseen by Their Spanish Conquerors. The Spanish conquest of the Indians in Latin America filled the coffers of Spain with gold and silver. The native population was decimated, largely by disease, and most native artifacts were destroyed, regarded by the Europeans as heathen work and beneath their consideration. (*Historical Pictures Service, Chicago*)

In the New World, power and land gradually concentrated in fewer and fewer hands; especially royal officials, their associates, and the church gained substantially in wealth and privilege. As recurrent depressions ruined smaller landowners, they were forced to sell out to their bigger neighbors. On their conversion to Christianity, the Indians were persuaded to give more and more land to the church. Thus, Spanish America became permanently divided between the privileged elite and the impoverished masses.

The effects of conquest were severe in other ways. Between 1500 and 1600, the number of Indians shrank from about 20 million to little more than 2 million. The major cause of this catastrophe, however, was not forced labor but the diseases introduced from Europe—dysentery, malaria, hookworm, smallpox—against which the Indians had little or no natural resistance. Beginning in the 1540s, the position of the natives gradually improved as the Crown withdrew grants that gave authority over the natives and took increasing responsibility for controlling the Indians.

One group suffered even more than the Indians: the blacks. The natives at least escaped the degradation of slavery. But blacks were imported from Africa in increasing numbers, especially as the Indian population declined, to work as slaves in the fields and the mines. The Portuguese and, in the eighteenth century, the British were the most important slave traders. Africans were captured by rival black tribes in western Africa, then enslaved and sold to Europeans in ports along the west African coast. The Africans were then herded onto ships for passage to the New World under such brutal conditions that only about half survived. Those who did were sold at auction in the ports of the Caribbean and North America; sellers and buyers considered the age and physical condition of the slaves, with little or no regard for any other aspects of their well-being, such as family ties.

The Price Revolution

Linked to overseas expansion was another phenomenon—an unprecedented inflation during the sixteenth century known as the *price revolution*. For example, cereal prices multiplied by as much as eight times or more in certain regions in the course of the sixteenth century, and they continued to rise, although more slowly, during the first half of the next century. Economic historians have generally assumed that the prices of goods other than cereals increased by half as much as grain prices.

The main cause of the price revolution was the population growth during the late fifteenth and sixteenth centuries. The population of Europe almost doubled between 1460 and 1620. Until the middle of the seventeenth century, the number of mouths to feed outran the capacity of agriculture to supply basic foodstuffs, causing the vast majority of people to live close to subsistence. Until food production could catch up with the increasing population, prices, especially those of the staple food, bread, continued to rise.

The other principal cause of the price revolution was *probably* the silver that flowed into Europe from the New World via Spain, beginning in 1552. At some point the influx of silver may have exceeded the necessary expansion of the money supply and itself begun contributing to the inflation. The most that can now be said is that the price revolution was caused by *too many people with too much money chasing too few goods*. The effects of the price revolution were momentous.

The Expansion of Agriculture

The greatest effects of the price revolution were on farming. Food prices, rising roughly twice as much as the prices of other goods, spurred ambitious farmers to take advantage of the situation and to produce for the expanding market.

The opportunity for profit drove some farmers to work harder and manage their land better.

All over Europe, landlords held their properties in the form of manors. A particular type of rural society and economy had evolved on these manors in the Late Middle Ages. By the fifteenth century, much manor land was held by peasant-tenants according to the terms of a tenure known in England as *copy-hold*. The tenants had certain hereditary rights to the land in return for the performance of certain services and the payment of certain fees to the landlord. Principal among these rights was the use of the commons—the pasture, woods, and pond. For the copyholder, access to the commons often made the difference between subsistence and real want, because the land tilled on the manor might not produce enough to keep a family. Arable land was worked according to ancient custom. The land was divided into strips, and each peasant of the manor was assigned a certain number of strips. This whole pattern of peasant tillage and rights in the commons was known as the *open-field system*. After changing little for centuries, it was met head-on by the incentives generated by the price revolution.

In England, landlords aggressively pursued the possibilities for profit resulting from the inflation of farm prices. This pursuit required far-reaching changes in ancient manorial agriculture, changes that are called *enclosure*. The open-field system was geared to providing subsistence for the local village and, as such, prevented large-scale farming for a distant market. In the open-field system, the commons could not be diverted to the production of crops for sale. Moreover, the division of the arable land into strips reserved for each peasant made it difficult to engage in profitable commercial agriculture.

English landlords in the sixteenth century fought a two-pronged attack against the open-field system in their attempt to transform their holdings into market-oriented, commercial ventures. First they deprived their tenant peasantry of the use of the commons; then they changed the conditions of tenure from copyhold to leasehold. Whereas copyhold was heritable and fixed, leasehold was not. When a lease came up for renewal, the landlord could raise the rent beyond the tenant's capacity to pay. Restriction of rights to the commons deprived the poor tenant of critically needed produce. Both acts of the landlord forced peasants off the manor or into the landlord's employ as farm laborers. With tenants gone, fields could be incorporated into larger, more productive units. Landlords could hire labor at bargain prices because of the swelling population and the large supply of peasants forced off the land by enclosure. Subsistence farming gave way to commercial agriculture—the growing of a surplus for the marketplace. But rural poverty increased because of the mass evictions of tenant farmers.

In the fifteenth and sixteenth centuries, the Dutch developed a new kind of farming, known as *convertible husbandry*. This farming system employed a series of innovations that replaced the old three-field system of crop rotation, which had left one-third of the land unused at any given time. The new techniques used all the land every year and provided a more diversified agriculture.

The Expansion of Trade and Industry

The conditions of the price revolution also caused trade and industry to expand. Population growth exceeding the capacity of local food supplies stimulated commerce in basic foodstuffs—for example, the Baltic trade with western Europe. Equally important as a stimulus to trade and industry was the growing income of landlords, merchants, and in some instances, peasants. This income created a rising demand for consumer goods. Another factor in commercial and industrial expansion was the growth of the state. With increasing amounts of tax revenue to spend, the expanding monarchies of the sixteenth and seventeenth centuries bought more and more supplies—ships, weapons, uniforms, paper—and so spurred economic expansion.

Innovations in Business

Markets tended to shift from local to regional or even to international, a condition that gave rise to the merchant-capitalist. Unlike local producers, the merchant-capitalists' operations extended across local and national boundaries. An essential feature of merchant capitalism was the *putting-out system* of production. The manufacture of woolen textiles is a good example of how the system worked. The merchant-capitalist would buy the raw wool from English landlords who had enclosed their manors to take advantage of the rising price of wool. The merchant's agents collected the wool and took it (put it out) to nearby villages for spinning, dyeing, and weaving. The work was done in the cottages of peasants, many of whom had been evicted from the surrounding manors as a result of enclosure and therefore had to take what work they could get at the lowest possible wages. When the wool was processed into cloth, it was picked up and shipped to market.

Accompanying the emergence of the merchant-capitalist and the putting-out system was a cluster of other innovations in business life. Some of them had roots in the Middle Ages and were important in the evolution of the modern capitalist economy. Banking operations grew more sophisticated, making it possible for depositors to pay their debts by issuing written orders to their banks to make transfers to their creditors' accounts—the origins of the modern check. Accounting methods also improved. The widespread use of double-entry bookkeeping made errors immediately evident and gave a clear picture of the financial position of a commercial enterprise. Very important to overseas expansion was the form of business enterprise known as the joint-stock company, which allowed small investors to buy shares in a venture. These companies made possible the accumulation of the large amounts of capital needed for large-scale operations, like the building and deployment of merchant fleets, which were quite beyond the resources of one person.

Different Patterns of Commercial Development

England and the Netherlands   In both England and the United Provinces the favorable conditions led to large-scale commercial expansion. In the 1590s the

Inside the Amsterdam Stock Exchange by J. Berckheyde.   Seventeenth-century Holland saw the rise of a solid bourgeosie and produced an economic system that looked toward twentieth-century capitalism. Every available commodity was sold, from spices and slaves to tulips. (*Amsterdams Historisch Museum*)

Dutch devised a new ship, the *fluit,* or flyboat, to handle bulky grain shipments at the lowest possible cost. This innovation allowed them to capture the Baltic trade, which became a principal source of their phenomenal commercial expansion between 1560 and 1660. Equally dramatic was their commercial penetration of the Orient. Profits from the European carrying trade built ships that allowed the Dutch first to challenge and then to displace the Portuguese in the spice trade with the East Indies during the early seventeenth century. The Dutch chartered the United East India Company in 1602 and established trading posts in the islands, which were the beginnings of a Dutch empire that lasted until World War II.

The English traded throughout Europe in the sixteenth and seventeenth centuries, especially with Spain and the Netherlands. The seventeenth century saw the foundation of a British colonial empire along the Atlantic seaboard in North America from Maine to the Carolinas and in the West Indies, where the English managed to dislodge the Spanish in some places.

In both England and the United Provinces, government promoted the interests of business. In the late sixteenth and early seventeenth centuries the northern provinces of the Spanish Netherlands, centered on Holland, won their independence from Spain in a protracted struggle. Political power in these so-called United Provinces passed increasingly into the hands of an urban patriciate of merchants and manufacturers based in cities like Delft, Haarlem, and especially Amsterdam. There urban interests pursued public policies that served their pocketbooks. In England, because of the revolutionary transfer of power from the king to Parliament, economic policies more closely reflected the interests of big business, whether agricultural or commercial. Enclosure, for example, was abetted by parliamentary enactment. The Bank of England, founded in 1694, expanded credit and increased business confidence. The Navigation Acts, which proved troublesome to American colonists, required that all goods traded between England and its colonies be carried in English ships.

France and Spain   France benefited from commercial and industrial expansion, but not to the same degree as England. A principal reason for this was the aristocratic structure of French society. Family ties and social intercourse between aristocracy and merchants, such as existed in England, were largely absent in France. Consequently, the French aristocracy remained contemptuous of commerce. Also inhibiting economic expansion were the guilds—remnants of the Middle Ages that restricted competition and production. In France there was relatively less room than in England for the merchant-capitalist operating outside the guild structures.

Spain presents an even clearer example of failure to grasp the opportunities afforded by the price revolution. By the third quarter of the sixteenth century, Spain possessed the makings of economic expansion: unrivaled amounts of capital in the form of silver, a large and growing population, rising consumer demand, and a vast overseas empire. These factors did not bear fruit because the Spanish value system regarded business as a form of social heresy. The Spanish held in high esteem those gentlemen who possessed land gained through military service and crusading ardor, which enabled them to live on rents and privileges. So commerce and industry remained contemptible pursuits.

Numerous wars in the sixteenth century (with France, the Lutheran princes, the Ottoman Turks, the Dutch, and the English) put an increasing strain on the Spanish treasury, even with the annual shipments of silver from the New World. Spain spent its resources on maintaining and extending its imperial power and Catholicism, rather than on investing in economic expansion. In the end, the wars cost even more than Spain could handle. The Dutch for a time, and the English and the French more permanently, displaced Spain as the great power. The English and the Dutch had taken advantage of the opportunities presented by the price revolution; the Spanish had not.

The Fostering of Mercantile Capitalism

The changes described—especially in England and the Netherlands—represent a crucial stage in the development of the modern economic system known as *capitalism.* This is a system of *private enterprise:* the main economic decisions (what, how much, where, and at what price to produce, buy, and sell) are made by private individuals in their capacity as owners, workers, or consumers.

From 1450 to 1600, several conditions fostered a sustained incentive to invest and reinvest—a basic factor in the emergence of modern capitalism. One was the price revolution stemming from a supply of basic commodities that could not keep pace with rising demand. Prices continued to climb, creating the most powerful incentive of all to invest rather than to consume. Why spend now, those with surplus wealth must have asked, when investment in commercial farming, mining, shipping, and publishing (to name a few important outlets) is almost certain to yield greater wealth in the future?

Another stimulus for investment came from government—and this occurred in two ways. First, governments acted as giant consumers whose appetites throughout the early modern period were expanding. Merchants who supplied governments with everything from guns to frescoes not only prospered but were led to reinvest because of the constancy and growth of government demand. Governments also sponsored new forms of investment, whether to supply the debauched taste for new luxuries at the king's court or to meet the requirements of the military. Private investors also reaped incalculable advantages from overseas empires. Colonies supplied cheap raw materials and cheap (slave) labor and served as markets for exports. They greatly stimulated the construction of both ships and harbor facilities and the sale of insurance.

The second government stimulus was state policies, known as mercantilism, meant to augment national wealth and power. According to mercantilist theory, wealth from trade was measured in gold and silver, of which there was believed to be a more or less fixed quantity. The state's goal in international trade became to sell more abroad than it bought, that is, to establish a favorable balance of payments. When the amount received for sales abroad was greater than that spent for purchases, the difference would be an influx of precious metal into the state. By this logic, mercantilists were led to argue for the goal of national sufficiency: a country should try to supply most of its own needs to keep imports to a minimum.

To stimulate the national economy, governments subsidized new industries, chartered companies to engage in overseas trade, and broke down local trade barriers, such as guild regulations and internal tariffs. The price revolution, the concentration of wealth in private hands, and government activity combined to provide the foundation for sustained investment and for the emergence of mercantile capitalism. This new force in the world should not be confused with industrial capitalism. The latter evolved with the Industrial Revolution in eighteenth-century England, but mercantile capitalism paved the way for it.

Toward a Global Economy

The transformations considered in this chapter were among the most momentous in the world's history. In an unprecedented development, one small part of

Chronology 9.1 ⚜ Economic and Political Transformations

1394–1460	Henry the Navigator, prince of Portugal, encourages expansion into Africa for gold and his anti-Muslim crusade
1469	Ferdinand and Isabella begin their rule of Castile and Aragon
1485	Henry VII begins the reign of the Tudor dynasty in England
1488	Bartholomeu Dias reaches the tip of Africa
1492	Christopher Columbus reaches the Caribbean island of Española on his first voyage; the Jews are expelled from Spain; Granada, the last Muslim kingdom in Spain, is conquered, ending the Reconquest
1497	Vasco da Gama sails around Cape of Good Hope (Africa) to India
1519	Charles V of Spain becomes Hapsburg emperor of the Holy Roman Empire
1519–1521	Hernando Cortés conquers the Aztecs in Mexico
1531–1533	Francisco Pizarro conquers the Incas in Peru
1552	Silver from the New World flows into Europe via Spain, contributing to a price revolution
1556–1598	Philip II of Spain persecutes Jews and Muslims
1562–1598	Religious wars in France

the world, western Europe, had become the lord of the sea lanes, the master of many lands throughout the globe, and the banker and profit-taker in an emerging world economy. Western Europe's global hegemony was to last well into this century. In conquering and settling new lands, Europeans exported Western culture around the globe, a process that accelerated in the twentieth century.

The effects of overseas expansion were profound. The native populations of the New World were decimated. As a result of the labor shortage, millions of blacks were imported from Africa to work as slaves on plantations and in mines. Black slavery would produce large-scale effects on culture, politics, and society that have lasted to the present day.

The widespread circulation of plant and animal life also had great consequences. Horses and cattle were introduced to the New World. (So amazed were the Aztecs to see man on horseback that at first they thought horse and

Chronology 9.1 continued

1572	The St. Bartholomew's Day Massacre—Queen Catherine of France orders thousands of Protestants executed
1588	The Spanish Armada is defeated by the English fleet
1598	French Protestants are granted religious toleration by the Edict of Nantes
1624–1642	Cardinal Richelieu, Louis XIII's chief minister, determines royal policies
1640–1660	The English Revolution
1648	The Treaty of Westphalia ends the Thirty Years' War
1649	Charles I, Stuart king of England, is executed by an act of Parliament
1649–1660	England is co-ruled by Parliament and the army under Oliver Cromwell
1660	Charles II returns from exile and becomes king of England
1685	Louis XIV of France revokes the Edict of Nantes
1688–1689	Revolution in England; end of absolutism
1694	The Bank of England is founded
1701	Louis XIV tries to bring Spain under French control

rider were one demonic creature.) In return the Old World was introduced to corn, the tomato, and most important, the potato, which was to become a staple of the northern European diet. Manioc, from which tapioca is made, was transplanted from the New World to Africa, where it helped sustain the population.

Western Europe was wrenched out of the subsistence economy of the Middle Ages and launched on a course of sustained economic growth. This transformation resulted from the grafting of traditional forms, like primogeniture and holy war, onto new forces, like global exploration, price revolution, and convertible husbandry. Out of this change emerged the beginnings of a new economic system, mercantile capitalism, which in large measure provided the economic thrust for European world predominance and paved the way for the Industrial Revolution of the eighteenth and nineteenth centuries.

Suggested Reading

Anderson, Perry, *Lineages of the Absolutist State* (1974). An excellent survey, written from a Marxist perspective.

Cipolla, Carlo M., *Guns, Sails and Empires* (1965). Connections between technological innovation and overseas expansion, 1400 to 1700.

Davis, David Brion, *The Problem of Slavery in Western Culture* (1966). Authoritative and highly suggestive.

Davis, Ralph, *The Rise of the Atlantic Economies* (1973). A reliable recent survey of early modern economic history.

Elliott, J. H., *Imperial Spain, 1469–1716* (1963). An excellent survey of the major European power of the early modern period.

Koenigsberger, H. G., *Early Modern Europe, 1500–1789* (1987). The best survey of the period, by a master historian.

Parry, J. H., *The Age of Reconnaissance* (1963). A short survey of exploration.

Plumb, J. H., *The Growth of Political Stability in England, 1675–1725* (1967). A basic book, clear and readable.

Shennan, J. H., *The Origins of the Modern European State* (1974). An excellent brief introduction.

Review Questions

1. In what ways did early modern kings increase their power, and what relationship did they have to the commercial bourgeoisie in their countries?
2. What were the strengths and weaknesses of the Spanish state?
3. Why did England move in the direction of parliamentary government, while most countries on the Continent embraced absolutism? Describe the main factors.
4. What were the new forces for expansion operating in early modern Europe?
5. What is the connection between the price revolution and overseas expansion? What was the principal cause of the price revolution? Why?
6. What was enclosure? How did the price revolution encourage it?
7. What is mercantile capitalism? What three patterns of the distribution of wealth fostered its development?

Chapter ⚬ 10

Intellectual Transformation:
The Scientific Revolution and the
Age of Enlightenment

Starting in the late fourteenth century, the cohesive medieval world began to disintegrate, a process that lasted to the late seventeenth century. Not only did basic medieval institutions like feudalism and the church weaken, but the medieval view of the universe, or world-view, faded and was gradually replaced by the modern, scientific understanding of nature. This transformation occurred within the particular historical context created by the Renaissance and the Reformation, as well as by the growth in commercial prosperity and state power.

The unique contribution of the seventeenth-century Scientific Revolution to the making of the modern world-view lay in its new mechanical conception of nature, which enabled Westerners to discover and explain the laws of nature mathematically. They came to see nature as composed solely of matter whose motion, occurring in space and measurable by time, was governed by laws of force. This philosophically elegant construction renders the physical world knowable, and even possibly manageable.

The Scientific Revolution also entailed the discovery of a new scientific methodology of observation and experimentation. By the late seventeenth century, no one could entertain a serious interest in any aspect of the physical order without actually doing experiments or without observing, in a rigorous and systematic way, the behavior of physical phenomena. A new scientific culture had been born. During the eighteenth century, this method of inquiry became of vital importance as a model for progress in the human sciences as well as the natural sciences.

The eighteenth century is called the Age of Enlightenment, or Age of Reason, for during this period an educated elite, expressing supreme confidence in the power of reason, attempted a rational analysis of European institutions and beliefs. The Enlightenment was heavily indebted to the experimental method and the mechanical picture of the universe that were formed during the Scientific Revolution. Scientific research seemed to show that order and mathematically demonstrable laws were at work in the physical universe. The thinkers of the Enlightenment, called *philosophes,* argued that it should be possible to examine *human* institutions with the intention of imposing a comparable order and rationality. ✪

Medieval Cosmology

The unique character of the modern scientific outlook is most understandable in contrast with what went before it—the medieval understanding of the natural world and its physical properties. That understanding rested on a blend of Christian thought with theories derived from ancient Greek writers like Aristotle and Ptolemy.

The explanations given by Aristotle (384–322 B.C.) for the motion of heavy bodies permeated medieval scientific literature. In trying to understand motion, Aristotle had argued simply that it was in the nature of things to move in certain ways. A stone falls because it is absolutely heavy; fire rises because it is absolutely light. Weight is an absolute property of a physical thing; therefore, motion results from the properties of bodies, and not from the forces or laws of motion at work in nature.

Aristotle's physics fitted neatly into his *cosmology,* or world picture. The earth, being the heaviest object, lay stationary and suspended at the center of the universe. The sun, the planets, and the moon revolved in circles around the earth. Aristotle presumed that the planets were made of a kind of fine, luminous ether and were held in their circular orbits by luminous spheres, or "tracks." These spheres possessed a certain reality, although invisible to human beings, and hence they came to be known as the crystalline spheres.

Ptolemy of Alexandria produced the *Almagest* (A.D. 150), a handbook of Greek astronomy based on the theories of Aristotle. Central to that work was the assumption that a motionless earth stood at the center of the universe (although some Greeks had disputed the notion) and that the planets move about it in a series of circular orbits interrupted by smaller circular orbits called epicycles.* By the Late Middle Ages, Ptolemy's handbook, because of the support it lent to Aristotelian cosmology, had come to embody standard astronomical wisdom.

Medieval thinkers integrated the cosmology of Aristotle and Ptolemy into a Christian framework that drew a sharp distinction between the world beyond the moon and an earthly realm. Celestial bodies were composed of the divine ether, a substance too pure, too spiritual to be found on earth; heavenly bodies, unlike those on earth, were immune to all change and obeyed different laws of motion than earthly bodies did. The universe was not homogeneous but divided into a higher world of the heavens and a lower world of earth. Earth could not compare with the heavens in spiritual dignity, but God had nevertheless situated it in the center of the universe. Earth deserved this position of importance, for only here was the drama of salvation performed. This vision of the universe was to be shattered by the Scientific Revolution.

A New View of Nature

Renaissance Background

With the advent of the Renaissance, which began in Italy in the late fourteenth century, a new breed of intellectuals began to challenge medieval assumptions about human beings and nature, armed with a collection of newly discovered ancient Greek and Roman texts. The philosophy of Plato was seized on as an alternative to medieval scholasticism. The great strength of Plato's philosophy lay in his belief that one must look beyond the appearance of things to an invisible reality that is simple, rational, and mathematically explainable. Plato's search for this fundamental reality thus influenced thinkers of the Scientific Revolution, who found inspiration in the Platonic tradition that nature's truths apply universally and possess the elegance and simplicity of mathematics. With this impulse to mathematicize nature came the desire to describe it accurately. Thus, in addition to the humanists, Renaissance art, which aspired to depict the human body and the natural world as exactly as possible, is an antecedent of the Scientific Revolution.

The Copernican Revolution

The geocentric view of the universe postulated by Aristotle and Ptolemy was challenged by Nicolaus Copernicus (1473–1543), a Polish churchman, astronomer, and mathematician. As a young man, Copernicus enrolled in the

---

* Since, in reality, the path of a planet is not a circle, but an ellipse, Ptolemy used epicycles to save the appearance of circular motion. A planet revolved uniformly around a small circle, an epicycle, which in turn revolved around the earth on a large circle. By ascribing a sufficient number of epicycles to a given planet, thus creating a system of "wheels on wheels," astronomers could retain their commitment to the perfect circular motion of planets.

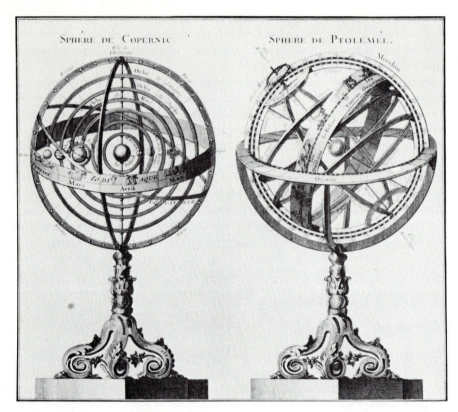

Armillary Spheres According to Copernicus and Ptolemy.   Copernicus overturned thirteen hundred years of cosmology with the appearance of his treatise on heavenly motion. The idea of a heliocentric universe supported by mathematical evidence brought the medieval mind-set to an irrefutable end. (*Smithsonian Institution Photo No. 65,420*)

University of Krakow, where he may have come under the influence of Renaissance Platonism, which was spreading outward from the Italian city-states. He also journeyed to Italy, and in Bologna and Padua he may have become aware of ancient Greek texts containing arguments for the sun being the center of the universe. The mathematical complexity of the Ptolemaic system troubled Copernicus, who believed that truth was the product of elegance and simplicity. Toward the end of his stay in Italy, he became convinced that the sun lay at the center of the universe, so he set out on a lifelong task to work out mathematical explanations of how a heliocentric universe operated. Because he did not want to engage in controversy with the followers of Aristotle, Copernicus did not publish his findings until 1543, in a work entitled *On the Revolutions of the Heavenly Spheres*. Legend says his book, which in effect began the Scientific Revolution, was brought to him on his deathbed.

His treatise on the universe retained some elements of the Aristotelian-Ptolemaic system. Copernicus never doubted Aristotle's basic notion of the perfect circular motion of the planets or the existence of crystalline spheres within which the stars revolved, and he retained many of Ptolemy's epicycles. But Copernicus proposed a heliocentric model of the universe that was mathematically simpler than Ptolemy's earth-centered universe. Thus, he eliminated some of Ptolemy's epicycles and cleared up various problems that had troubled astronomers who had based their work on an earth-centered universe. By removing the earth from its central position and by giving it motion—that is, by making the earth just another planet—Copernicus undermined the system of medieval cosmology and made the birth of modern astronomy possible. Because they were committed to the Aristotelian-Ptolemaic system and to biblical statements that supported it, most thinkers rejected Copernicus's conclusions.

Tycho and Kepler: The Laws of Planetary Motion

The most gifted astronomer in the generation after Copernicus, Tycho Brahe (1546–1601), never accepted the Copernican system. He did, however, realize more fully than any contemporaries the necessity for new observations. Aided by the king of Denmark, Tycho built the finest observatory in Europe to use in his work. Tycho's fame ultimately rests on his skill as a practicing astronomer.

Tycho Brahe and His Observatory's Interior.   Although Tycho Brahe remained a staunch Aristotelian, his observation of a new star in 1572 and a comet in 1577 challenged these traditional views. His precise scientific approach to astronomy and careful mathematical calculations were to be his greatest legacy. (*The British Library*)

He bequeathed to future generations precise calculations about the movements of heavenly bodies, which proved invaluable.

These calculations were put to greatest use by Johannes Kepler (1571–1630), a German who collaborated with Tycho during the latter's final years. Tycho bequeathed his astronomical papers to Kepler, who brought to this data a scientific vision that was both experimental and mystical. Kepler searched persistently for harmonious laws of planetary motion. He did so because he believed profoundly in the Platonic ideal: a spiritual force infuses the physical order; beneath appearances are harmony and unity; and the human mind can begin to comprehend that unity only through *gnosis*—a direct and mystical realization of unity—and through mathematics. Kepler believed that both approaches were compatible, and he managed to combine them. He believed in and practiced astrology (as did Tycho), and throughout his lifetime he tried to contact an ancient but lost and secret wisdom.

In the course of his studies and observations of the heavens, Kepler discovered the three basic laws of planetary motion. First, the orbits of the planets are elliptical, not circular as Aristotle and Ptolemy had assumed, and the sun is one focus of the ellipse. Unlike Tycho, Kepler accepted Copernicus's theory and provided proof for it. Kepler's second law demonstrated that the velocity of a planet is not uniform, as had been believed, but increases as its distance from the sun decreases. Kepler's third law—that the squares of the times taken by any two planets in their revolutions around the sun are in the same ratio as the cubes of their average distances from the sun—brought the planets together into a unified mathematical system.

The significance of Kepler's work was immense. He gave sound mathematical proof to Copernicus's theory, eliminated forever the use of epicycles that had saved the appearance of circular motion, and demonstrated that mathematical relationships can describe the planetary system. But Kepler left an important question unresolved: what kept the planets in their orbits? Why did they not fly out into space or crash into the sun? The answer would be supplied by Isaac Newton, who synthesized the astronomy of Copernicus and Kepler with the new physics developed by Galileo.

Galileo: Experimental Physics

At the same time that Kepler was developing a new astronomy, his contemporary, Galileo Galilei (1564–1642), was breaking with the older physics of Aristotle. A Pisan by birth, Galileo lived for many years in Padua, where he conducted some of his first experiments on the motion of bodies. Guided by the dominant philosophy of the Italian Renaissance—the revived doctrines of Plato—Galileo believed that beyond the visible world lay universal truths, subject to mathematical verification. Galileo insisted that the study of motion be based on mathematics. For this Late Renaissance natural philosopher, mathematics became the language of nature. Galileo also believed that only after experimenting can one discern the harmonious laws of the universe and give them mathematical expression.

Galileo established a fundamental principle of modern science—the order and uniformity of nature. There are no distinctions in rank or quality between the heavens and earth; heavenly bodies are not perfect and changeless as Aristotle had believed. In 1609, Galileo built a telescope through which he viewed the surface of the moon. The next year, in a treatise called *The Starry Messenger,* he proclaimed to the world that the moon "is not smooth, uniform, and precisely spherical as a great number of philosophers believe it and the other heavenly bodies to be, but is uneven, rough, and full of cavities . . . being not unlike the face of the earth, relieved by chains of mountains and deep valleys."[1] In addition, Galileo observed spots on the sun, providing further evidence that heavenly objects, like earthly objects, undergo change. There are no higher and lower worlds; nature is the same throughout.

Through his telescope Galileo also saw moons around Jupiter, a discovery that served to support the Copernican hypothesis. If Jupiter had moons, then all heavenly bodies did not orbit the earth. The moons of Jupiter removed a fundamental criticism leveled against Copernicus and opened up the possibility that indeed the earth, with its own moon, might be just like the planet Jupiter, and both might in turn revolve around a central point—the sun.

With Galileo, the science of Copernicus and the assault on Aristotle entered a new phase. Backed by teachers within the academic community who routinely taught the old astronomy, priests in Florence preached against Galileo, using Aristotle's writings and the Bible to back their attacks. In 1633, Galileo's teachings were condemned and he was placed under house arrest. Science as preached by Galileo was not, as he knew perfectly well, inherently dangerous to Catholicism. But the clergy and their academic allies saw it as a challenge to their power, and they could enlist the papacy and the Inquisition in their support. As a result, students of the new science in Catholic countries looked to Protestant countries as places to live or publish their books. Censorship worked to stifle intellectual inquiry, and by the middle of the seventeenth century science had become, because of historical circumstance, an increasingly Protestant and northern European phenomenon.

The Newtonian Synthesis

By the middle of the seventeenth century, largely because of the work of Copernicus, Kepler, and Galileo, Aristotle and Ptolemy had been dethroned. A new philosophy of nature and a new science had come into being whose essence lay in the mathematical expression of physical laws that describe matter in motion. Yet what was missing was an overriding law that could explain the motion observed in the heavens and on earth. This law was supplied by Isaac Newton (1642–1727).

In the *Principia Mathematica* of 1687, Newton not only formulated universal mathematical laws but offered a philosophy of nature that sought to explain the essential structure of the universe: matter is atomic in structure and is acted upon by immaterial forces that are placed in the universe by God. New-ton said that the motion of matter could be explained by three laws: inertia, that a body remains in a state of rest or continues its motion in a straight line unless impelled to change by forces impressed on it; acceleration, that the change in the motion of a body is proportional to the force acting on it; and that for every action there is an equal and opposite reaction.

Newton argued that these laws apply not only to observable matter on earth but also to the motion of planets in their orbits. He showed that planets did not remain in their orbits because circular motion was "natural" or because crys-talline spheres kept them in place. Rather, said Newton, planets keep to their orbits because every body in the universe exercises a force on every other body, a force that he called *universal gravitation.* Gravity is operative throughout the universe, whether on earth or in the heavens, and it is capable of mathematical expression. Newton built his theory on the work of other scientific giants, notably Kepler and Galileo; yet no one before him had possessed the breadth of vision, mathematical skill, and dedication to rigorous observation to com-bine this knowledge into one grand synthesis.

With Newton's discovery of universal gravitation, the Scientific Revolution reached its culmination. The universe could now be described as matter in motion; it was governed by invisible forces that operated everywhere, both on earth and in the heavens, and these forces could be expressed mathematically. The medieval picture of the universe as closed, earthbound, and earth-centered was replaced by a universe seen to be infinite and governed by universal laws. The earth was now regarded as simply another planet.

But what was God's role in this new universe? Newton and his circle labored to create a mechanical world picture that retained a central place for a provi-dential deity who operates constantly in the universe; at one time he believed that gravity was simply the will of God operating on the universe. As Newton said in the *Optiks,* the physical order "can be the effect of nothing else than the wisdom and skill of a powerful ever-living agent." Newton, a scientific genius, was also a deeply religious thinker who was committed to the maintenance of Protestantism in England.

Biology, Medicine, and Chemistry

The spectacular advances made in physics and astronomy in the sixteenth and seventeenth centuries were not matched in the biological sciences. Indeed, the day-to-day practice of medicine throughout western Europe changed little in the period from 1600 to 1700, for much of medical practice relied frequently on astrology. Doctors clung to the teachings of the ancient practitioners Galen and Hippocrates.

In general, Galenic medicine paid little attention to the discovery of specific cures for particular diseases. As a follower of Aristotle, Galen emphasized the elements that make up the body—he called their manifestations *humors.* A person with an excess of blood was sanguine; a person with too much bile was choleric. Health consisted of a restoration of balances among these various elements, so Galenic doctors often prescribed purges of one sort or another. The most famous of these was bloodletting, but sweating was also a favorite remedy. These methods were often as dangerous as the diseases they sought to cure, but they were taught religiously in the medical schools of Europe.

In 1543, the same year that Copernicus published his heliocentric theory, Andreas Vesalius (1514–1564), a Belgian surgeon, published *The Structure of the Human Body*. Opposing Galenic practice, Vesalius argued that observation and anatomical dissection were the keys to knowing how the human body works. By the late seventeenth century, doctors had learned a great deal about the body's structure and chemistry.

In *The Motion of the Heart and Blood in Animals* (1628), William Harvey (1578–1657), a British physician, showed that blood circulates in the body because of the pumping action of the heart muscle, breaking with Galen's view that the liver was the source of the blood in the veins and the heart was the source of arterial blood. In describing the heart as a mechanical pump, Harvey demonstrated the same tendency to mechanize nature that marked the revolution in astronomy and physics. Drawing conclusions after carefully observing and experimenting with living animals, Harvey employed the inductive method championed by Sir Francis Bacon.

Robert Boyle (1627–1691) was an English scientist who adopted the atomic explanation that matter is made up of small, hard, indestructible particles that behave with regularity and explain changes in gases, fluids, and solids. Boyle pioneered in the experimental method with such exciting and accurate results that by the time of his death, no serious scientist could attempt chemical experiments without following his guidelines. Thus the science of chemistry acquired its characteristic experimentalism; it was also based on an atomic theory of matter. But not until late in the eighteenth century was this new discipline applied to medical research.

Prophets and Proponents of the New Science

The accomplishments of the Scientific Revolution extend beyond the creation of a new model of the universe and new knowledge of the human body. They also include the formulation of a new method of inquiring into nature and the recognition that science can serve humanity. Two thinkers instrumental in articulating these implications of scientific advances were Sir Francis Bacon and René Descartes.

Bacon

Sir Francis Bacon (1561–1626), an English statesman and philosopher, vigorously supported the advancement of science and the scientific method. Although he had no laboratory and made no discoveries, he is deservedly regarded as a prophet of modern science because of his advocacy of the scientific method. Bacon recognized that medieval scholasticism was not suited for an emerging age of science, and he attributed science's limited progress over the ages to the interference of scholastic theologians who bent theories of nature to the requirements of Scripture. The scholastics, said Bacon, engaged in arid verbalism; they constructed elaborate systems that had little to do with the empirical world and did not increase understanding of nature. Bacon also attacked practitioners of astrology, magic, and alchemy for their errors, secretiveness, and enigmatic writings; he advocated instead cooperative, methodical, and publicly criticizable scientific research.

The method that Bacon championed as the best way to truth and new knowledge was the inductive approach: careful observation of nature, systematic accumulation of data, and experimentation. Because he gave supreme value to the direct observation of nature, Bacon is one of the founders of the empirical tradition in modern philosophy. The Baconian vision of progress in science leading to an improvement of the human condition inspired much scientific activity in the seventeenth century, particularly in England.

Descartes

The scientific method encompasses two approaches to knowledge, which usually complement each other: the empirical (inductive) and the rational (deductive). In the inductive approach, which is employed in descriptive sciences, such as biology, anatomy, and geology, general principles are derived from the analysis of data collected through observation and experiment. The essential features of the inductive method were championed by Bacon. In the deductive approach, which is employed in mathematics and theoretical physics, truths are derived in successive steps from first principles, or indubitable axioms. In the seventeenth century, the deductive method was formulated by René Descartes (1596–1650), a French mathematician and philosopher.

In his *Discourse on Method,* Descartes expressed his disenchantment with the learning of his day and "resolved to seek no other knowledge than that which I might find within myself, or perhaps in the great book of nature." Rejecting as "absolutely false anything of which I could have the least doubt," Descartes, who longed for certainty, searched for an incontrovertible truth that could serve as the first principle of knowledge, the basis of an all-encompassing philosophic system.

Descartes found there was one thing of which he was certain, one truth that was unshakable: that it was he who was doing the doubting and thinking. In his dictum "I think, therefore I am," he had his starting point of knowledge. Descartes is viewed as the founder of modern philosophy because he called for the individual to question and, if necessary, to overthrow all traditional beliefs, and he proclaimed the mind's inviolable autonomy and importance—its ability and right to comprehend truth.

Descartes held that it is the method of mathematics that produces certain knowledge. By applying mathematical reasoning to philosphic problems, we can achieve the same certainty and clarity evidenced in geometry. The mathe-

**René Descartes by Frans Hals
(c. 1580–1666).** Descartes is both
the father of modern philosophy and
the prophet of modern science. He
placed his faith above all in the human intellect and its ability to
achieve scientific knowledge, and
made significant practical contributions in algebra. (*Royal Museum of
Fine Arts, Copenhagen*)

matical or deductive approach he favored consists of finding a self-evident
principle, such as a geometric axiom, and then deducing other truths from it
through logical reasoning. Descartes was convinced that through *a priori* reasoning from general mathematical principles, one could deduce a complete and
comprehensive system of nature. His deductive method, with its mathematical
emphasis, perfectly complements Bacon's inductive approach, which stresses
observation and experimentation. The scientific achievements of modern times
have arisen from the skillful synchronization of induction and deduction.

Like Bacon, Descartes held that science served "the general good of mankind." It produced useful knowledge that enables us "to enjoy without any
trouble the fruits of the earth and all its comforts . . . especially . . . the
preservation of health." Bacon's and Descartes's confidence in science as a
boon for humanity was bequeathed to the Age of Enlightenment.

The Meaning of the Scientific Revolution

The Scientific Revolution was decisive in shaping the modern mentality; it
shattered the medieval view of the universe and replaced it with a wholly

different world-view. Gone was the belief that a motionless earth lay at the center of a universe that was finite and enclosed by a ring of stars. Gone too was the belief that the universe was divided into higher and lower worlds and that different laws of motion operated in the heavens and on earth. The universe was now viewed as a giant machine functioning according to universal laws that could be expressed mathematically; nature could be mastered.

The methodology that produced this new view of nature—the new science—played a crucial historical role in reorienting Western thought away from medieval theology and metaphysics and toward the study of physical and human problems. In the later Middle Ages, most men of learning were Aristotelians and theologians. But by the mid-eighteenth century, knowledge of Newtonian science and the dissemination of useful learning had become the goal of the educated classes. All knowledge, it was believed, could emulate scientific knowledge; it could be based on observation, experimentation, and rational deduction; it could be systematic, verifiable, progressive, and useful. At every turn the advocates of this new approach to learning hailed the scientists of the sixteenth and seventeenth centuries as proof that no institution or dogma had a monopoly on truth—the scientific approach would yield knowledge that might, if properly applied for the good of all people, produce a new and better age. Such an outlook gave thinkers new confidence in the power of the human mind to master nature and led them to examine European institutions and traditions with an inquiring, critical, and skeptical spirit. Thus inspired, the reformers of the eighteenth century would seek to create an age of enlightenment.

The Scientific Revolution ultimately weakened traditional Christianity. Applied to religious doctrines, Descartes' reliance on methodical doubt and clarity of thought and Bacon's insistence on careful observation eventually led thinkers to question miracles, prophecies, and other Christian beliefs. Theology came to be regarded as a separate and somewhat irrelevant area of intellectual inquiry that was not fit for the interests of practical, well-informed people. Not only Christian doctrines but also various widespread and popular beliefs in magic, witchcraft, and astrology came under attack.

Gradually the science of Newton became the science of western Europe: nature mechanized, analyzed, regulated, and mathematicized. As a result of the Scientific Revolution, Western thinkers came to believe more strongly than ever that nature could be mastered. Mechanical science, applied to canals, engines, pumps, and levers, became the science of industry. Thus the Scientific Revolution, operating on both intellectual and commercial levels, laid the groundwork for two major developments of the modern West—the Industrial Revolution and the Age of Enlightenment.

The Age of Enlightenment

The German philosopher Immanuel Kant (1724–1804) defined the Enlightenment as the bringing of "light into the dark corners of the mind," the dispelling of ignorance and superstition. Kant went to the heart of one aspect of the Enlightenment, that is, its insistence that each individual should reason independently, without recourse to the authority of the schools, churches, and universities.

Philosophes—the thinkers who aspired to examine and order human institutions—were found most commonly in the major European cities; Paris became the center of the Enlightenment during the 1770s. In essays, monthly journals, works of fiction, and even mildly pornographic and anonymous tales, they attacked many of the abuses of eighteenth-century society—religious fanaticism and intolerance, the idleness and corruption of the aristocracy, the use of torture, terrible prison conditions, slavery, and violations of natural rights. In essence, the philosophes condemned all vestiges of medieval culture. Inevitably, modern liberal thought, initiated by the Enlightenment, emerged as hostile to scholastic learning, priests, and eventually, in some quarters, to Christianity itself. The philosophes expressed confidence in science and reason, espoused humanitarianism, and struggled for religious liberty and freedom of thought and person. Combining these values with a secular orientation and a belief in future progress, the philosophes helped shape, if not define, the modern outlook.

The Science of Religion

Christianity Under Attack

No single thread had united Western culture more powerfully than Christianity. Until the eighteenth century, educated people, especially rulers and servants of the state, had to give allegiance to one or another of the Christian churches, however un-Christian their actions. The Enlightenment, however, produced the first widely read and systematic assault on Christianity launched from within the ranks of the educated. The philosophes argued that many Christian dogmas defied logic—for example, the conversion of the substance of bread and wine into the body and blood of Christ during the Eucharist—and they ridiculed theologians for arguing over obscure issues that seemed irrelevant to the human condition and a hindrance to clear thinking. "Theology amuses me," wrote Voltaire. "That's where we find the madness of the human spirit in all its plenitude." In the same spirit, the philosophes denounced the churches for inciting the fanaticism and intolerance that led to the horrors of the Crusades, the Inquisition, and the wars of the Reformation. They viewed Christianity's preoccupation with salvation and its belief in the depravity of human nature, a consequence of Adam and Eve's defiance of God, as barriers to social improvement and earthly happiness.

The leaders of the Enlightenment sought to repudiate traditional Christianity and to put in its place a rational system of ethics and philosophy based on scientific truths. Although some philosophes were atheists, most were *deists* who tried to make religion compatible with a scientific understanding of nature. Deists believed only those Christian doctrines that could meet the test of reason. For example, they considered it reasonable to believe in God, for only with a creator, they said, could such a superbly organized universe have come into being. But after God set the universe in motion, according to the deists, he took no further part in its operations. Thus, although deists retained a belief in God the Creator, they rejected clerical authority, revelation, original sin, and miracles. They held that biblical accounts of the resurrection and of Jesus walking on water or waking the dead could not be reconciled with natural law. Deists viewed Jesus as a great moral teacher, not as the son of God, and they regarded ethics, not faith, as the essence of religion; rational people, they said, served God best by treating their fellow human beings justly.

David Hume (1711–1776), a Scottish skeptic, attacked both revealed religion and the deists' natural religion. He maintained that all religious ideas, including Christian teachings and even the idea of God, stemmed ultimately from human fears and superstitions. Hume rejected the deist argument that this seemingly orderly universe required a designing mind to create it. The universe, said Hume, might very well be eternal, and the seeming universal order simply a natural condition that requires no explanation. Hume's attack made it impossible to establish a necessary link between a mechanical universe and a creator. As a consequence of Hume's critique, Christian belief rested more than ever before on faith, not reason.

Voltaire, the Philosophe

As a poet and writer struggling for recognition in Paris, the young François Marie Arouet, known to the world as Voltaire (1694–1778), encountered some of the new ideas that were being discussed in private gatherings (called *salons*) in Paris. Care had to be taken in the French capital by those educated people who wanted to read books and discuss ideas hostile to the church or to the Sorbonne, the clerically controlled university. The French printing presses were among the most tightly controlled and censored in Europe. Individuals had been imprisoned for writing, publishing, or owning books hostile to Catholic doctrine. Although Voltaire learned something of the new enlightened culture in Paris, it was in 1726, when he journeyed to London, that Voltaire the poet became Voltaire the philosophe.

In England, Voltaire became acquainted with the ideas of John Locke (1632–1704) and Isaac Newton. From Newton, Voltaire learned the mathematical laws that govern the universe; he witnessed the power of human reason to establish general rules that seemed to explain the behavior of physical objects. From Locke, Voltaire learned that people should believe only those ideas received from the senses. Locke's theory of learning, his *epistemology*, impressed many of the proponents of the Enlightenment. Again, the implications for religion were most serious: if people believe only those things that they experience, they will be unable to accept mysteries and doctrines simply because they are taught by churches and the clergy. Voltaire experienced considerable freedom of thought in England and saw a religious toleration that

Mme. Geoffrin's Salon.   The High Enlightenment in the 1750s had Paris as its capital. The new thinking concentrated on social inequalities, especially those that stifled talented human beings. The salons of exclusive Parisian society, such as that of Mme. Geoffrin, became the forum for the next generation of philosophers after Voltaire and Diderot. (*Giraudon/Art Resource*)

stood in stark contrast to the absolutism of the French kings and the power of the French clergy. He also witnessed a freer mixing of bourgeois and aristocratic social groups than was permitted in France at this time.

Throughout his life, Voltaire was a fierce supporter of the Enlightenment and a bitter critic of churches and the Inquisition. Although his books were banned in France, he probably did more there than any other philosophe to popularize the Enlightenment and to mock the authority of the clergy. In *Letters Concerning the English Nation* (1733), Voltaire praised English society and offered constitutional monarchy, new science, and religious toleration as models to be followed by all of Europe.

Voltaire was a practical reformer who campaigned for the rule of law, a freer press, religious toleration, humane treatment of criminals, and a more effective system of government administration. His writings constituted a radical attack on aspects of eighteenth-century French society. Yet, like so many philosophes, Voltaire feared the power of the people, especially if goaded by the clergy. He supported rule by reform-minded kings—enlightened despots.

Political Thought

The Enlightenment built on the secular and rational tradition in political thought developed by Machiavelli during the Renaissance and Thomas Hobbes during the English Revolution of the seventeenth century. Three major European thinkers and a host of minor ones wrote treatises on politics that remain relevant to this day: John Locke, *Two Treatises of Government* (1690); Baron de la Brède et de Montesquieu, *The Spirit of the Laws* (1748); and Jean Jacques Rousseau, *The Social Contract* (1762). All repudiated the divine right of kings and were concerned with checking the power of monarchy; each offered different formulas for achieving that goal.

Hobbes

A prerequisite for all Enlightenment political theorists was the work of Thomas Hobbes (1588–1679). All accepted Hobbes's belief that self-interest is a valid reason for engaging in political activity and his refusal to bring God into his system to justify the power of kings. Hobbes said that power did not rest on divine right but arose out of a contract made among men (women are not included in his system) who agreed to elevate the state, and hence the monarch, to a position of power over them. That contract, once made, could not be broken. As a consequence, the power of the government, whether embodied in a king or a parliament, was absolute.

Hobbes published his major work, *Leviathan,* in 1651, soon after England had been torn by civil war; thus, he was obsessed with the issue of political stability. He feared that, left to their own devices, men would kill one another; the "war of all against all"[2] would prevail without the firm hand of a sovereign to stop it. Hobbes's vision of human nature was dark and forbidding. In the state of nature, the original men had lived lives that could only have been "nasty, brutish, and short." Their only recourse was to set up a power over themselves that would restrain them. For Hobbes the state was, as he put it, a "mortal god," the only guarantee of peace and stability. He was the first political thinker to realize the extraordinary power that had come into existence with the creation of strong centralized governments.

Most Enlightenment theorists, however, beginning with John Locke, denied that governments possessed absolute power over their subjects, and to that extent they repudiated Hobbes. Many European thinkers of the eighteenth century, including Rousseau, also rejected Hobbes's gloomy view that human nature is greedy and warlike. Yet Hobbes was essential to the Enlightenment. He was a secular political theorist, and he sounded the death knell for the theory of the divine right of kings. Enlightenment political theorists started where he left off.

Locke

Probably the most widely read political philosopher during the first half of the eighteenth century was John Locke. His *Two Treatises of Government* was seen as a justification for the Revolution of 1688–89 and the notion of government by consent of the people. (Although they were published in 1690, Locke wrote the treatises before the English Revolution; that fact, however, was not known during the Enlightenment.)

Locke's theory, in its broad outlines, stated that the right to govern derived from the consent of the governed and was a form of contract. When people gave their consent to a government, they expected it to govern justly, to protect their property, and to ensure certain liberties for the propertied. If a government attempted to rule absolutely and arbitrarily—if it violated the natural rights of the individual—it reneged on its contract and forfeited the loyalty of its subjects. Such a government could legitimately be overthrown. Locke believed that a constitutional government that limited the power of rulers was the best defense of property and individual rights.

Late in the eighteenth century, Locke's ideas were used to justify liberal revolutions in both Europe and America. Indeed, the importance of Locke's political philosophy was not simply his recourse to contract theory as a justification of constitutional government; it was also his assertion that the community could take up arms against its sovereign in the name of the natural rights of liberty and property. Locke's ideas about the foundation of government had greater impact on the Continent and in America during the eighteenth century than they did in England.

Montesquieu

Baron de la Brède et de Montesquieu (1689–1755) was a French aristocrat who, like Voltaire, visited England late in the 1720s and knew the writings of Locke. Montesquieu had little sympathy for revolutions, but he did approve of constitutional monarchy. His primary concern was to check the unbridled authority of the French kings. In opposition to the Old Regime (French society before the Revolution of 1789), Montesquieu proposed a balanced system of government, with an executive branch offset by a legislature whose members were drawn from the landed and educated elements in society. Montesquieu genuinely believed that the aristocracy possessed a natural and sacred obligation to rule and that their honor called them to serve the community.

In stressing the rule of law and the importance of nonmonarchical authority, Montesquieu became a source for legitimating the authority of representative institutions. Hardly an advocate of democracy, he was nonetheless seen as a powerful critic of royal absolutism. His writings, particularly *The Spirit of the Laws,* established Montesquieu both as a major philosophe who possessed republican tendencies and as a critic of absolute monarchy and the Old Regime in France.

Rousseau

Not until the 1760s did democracy find its champion, in Jean Jacques Rousseau (1712–1778). Rousseau based his politics on contract theory—the people choose their government, and in so doing effectively give birth to civil society. But Rousseau further demanded that the contract be constantly renewed and that government be made immediately and directly responsible to the will of the people. *The Social Contract* opened with this stirring cry for reform: "Man is born free; and everywhere he is in chains," and went on to ask how that restriction could be changed. Freedom is in the very nature of man: "to renounce liberty is to renounce being a man, to surrender the rights of humanity and even its duties."

In *The Social Contract,* Rousseau tried to resolve the conflict between individual freedom and the demands of the state. His solution was a small state, modeled after the ancient Greek city-state, where people participated actively and directly in politics and were willing to sacrifice self-interest to the community's needs. To the ancient Greek, said Rousseau, the state was a moral association that made him a better person, and good citizenship was the highest form of excellence. The state, said Rousseau, should be based on the *general will*—that which is best for the community, which expresses its common interests. Rousseau wanted laws of the state to coincide with the general will; he felt that people have the wisdom to arrive at laws that serve the common good, but to do so they have to set aside selfish interests for the good of the community. For Rousseau, freedom consisted of obeying laws prescribed by citizens inspired by the general will. Citizens themselves must constitute the law-making body; law making cannot be entrusted to a single person or a small group.

For Rousseau, those who disobey laws—who act according to their private will rather than in accordance with the general will as expressed in law—degrade themselves and undermine the community. Therefore, government has the right to force citizens to be obedient—to compel them to exercise their individual wills in the proper way. Because of this view, several contemporary thinkers see Rousseau not only as a spokesman of modern democracy but also as a forerunner of modern dictatorships.

No philosopher of the Enlightenment was more dangerous to the Old Regime than Rousseau. His ideas were perceived as truly revolutionary, a direct challenge to the power of kings, churches, and aristocrats. During the French Revolution, his name would be invoked to justify democracy.

Social Thought

Psychology and Education

Just as Locke's *Two Treatises of Government* was instrumental in shaping the political thought of the Enlightenment, his *Essay Concerning Human Understanding* (1689) provided the theoretical foundations for an unprecedented interest in education. Locke's view that at birth the mind is blank, a clean slate, or *tabula rasa,* held two important implications. First, if human beings were not born with innate ideas, then they were not, as Christianity taught, inherently sinful. Second, a person's environment was the decisive force in shaping that person's character and intelligence. Nine of every ten men, wrote Locke, "are good or evil, useful or not, [because of] their education." Such a theory was eagerly received by the reform-minded philosophes, who preferred attributing wickedness to faulty institutions, improper rearing, and poor education—which could be remedied—rather than to a defective human nature.

Locke's doctrine that knowledge comes primarily through experience found its most extreme expression in the writings of Rousseau on education. In *Émile* (1762), Rousseau argued that individuals learn from nature, from people, or from things. Indeed, Rousseau wanted the early years of a child's education to be centered on developing the senses, not spent chained to a schoolroom desk. Later, attention would be paid to intellectual pursuits, then finally to morality. Rousseau grasped a fundamental principle of modern psychology, that the child is not a small adult, and childhood is not merely preparation for adulthood but a particular stage, with its own distinguishing characteristics, in human development. Children, said Rousseau astutely, should be permitted to behave like children.

Humanitarianism

Crime and Punishment   No society founded on the principles of the Enlightenment could condone the torture of prisoners and the inhumanity of a corrupt legal system. On that view, all the philosophes were clear, and they had plenty of evidence from their own societies on which to base their condemnation of torture and the inhumanity of the criminal justice system. Prisoners were often starved or exposed to disease, or both. In many Continental countries, where torture was still legal, prisoners could be subjected to brutal interrogation or to random punishment.

Fittingly, the most powerful critique of the European system of punishment came from Italy, where the Inquisition and its torture chambers had reigned for centuries with little opposition. In *On Crimes and Punishments* (1764), Cesare Beccaria (1738–1794), an Italian economist and criminologist inspired in part by Montesquieu, condemned torture as inhuman. He called it "a criterion fit for a cannibal," and an irrational way of determining guilt or innocence, for there are "innumerable examples of innocent persons who have confessed themselves criminals because of the agonies of torture." Influenced by Beccaria's work, reform-minded jurists, legislators, and ministers called for the elimination of torture from codes of criminal justice, and several European lands abolished torture in the eighteenth century.

Slavery   On both sides of the Atlantic during the eighteenth century, criticism of slavery was growing. At first it came from religious thinkers like the Quakers, who held that the light of God's truth works in every man and woman. Many philosophes in both America and Europe were familiar with Quaker

Slaves Processing Sugar in a Colonial Plantation.   This diagram shows slaves running machinery to grind sugar cane into pulp. In the colonies of European countries in the New World and other lands, subjected peoples were used to perform hard labor in the plantations and mines. The immorality of slavery was raised initially by religious thinkers, especially the Quakers, and then taken up by Diderot in his *Encyclopedia*. (*Courtesy of the University of Minnesota Libraries*)

attacks on slavery. The Enlightenment must be credited with bringing the problem of slavery into the forefront of public discussion in Europe and the American colonies. Throughout the eighteenth century, the emphasis placed by the Enlightenment on moral sensibility produced a literature that used shock to emphasize over and over again, and with genuine revulsion, the inhumanity of slavery.

By the second half of the century, strongly worded attacks on slavery were issued by a new generation of philosophes. With Rousseau in the vanguard, they condemned slavery as a violation of the natural rights of man. In a volume issued in 1755, the great *Encyclopedia* of the Enlightenment, edited by Denis Diderot, condemned slavery in no uncertain terms: "There is not a single one of these hapless souls . . . who does not have the right to be declared free . . . since neither his ruler nor his father nor anyone else had the right to dispose of his freedom."

Women

Not entirely unlike slaves, women had few property rights within marriage, and their physical abuse by husbands was widely regarded as beyond the purview of the law. Women's education was slighted, and social theorists had for centuries regarded them as inferiors. By the 1750s in Paris, however, rich women had become the organizers of fashionable salons where writers and enlightened reformers gathered for free and open conversation. Diderot attended such a salon, but Baron d'Holbach, who led the most famous gathering of the 1770s, specifically excluded women because he believed that they lowered the tone and seriousness of the discussion.

Mary Wollstonecraft (1759–1797), an English writer familiar with Enlightenment ideas, extended the principles of the Enlightenment to the position and status of women. In *Vindication of the Rights of Woman* (1792), she argued that "from the tyranny of man the greater part of female follies proceed." Calling for the extension of the principle of liberty to women and urging that equal public education be made available for both men and women, Wollstonecraft's *Vindication* became a text on which nineteenth-century reformers could and did build.

Economic Thought

The Enlightenment's emphasis on property as the foundation for individual rights and its search for uniform laws inspired by Newton's scientific achievement led to the development of the science of economics. Appropriately, that intellectual achievement occurred in the most advanced capitalistic nation in Europe, Great Britain. Not only were the British in the vanguard of capitalist expansion; by the third quarter of the eighteenth century, that expansion had brought on the start of the Industrial Revolution. Britain's new factories and markets for the manufacture and distribution of goods provided a natural laboratory where theorists schooled in the Enlightenment's insistence on observation and experimentation could observe the ebb and flow of capitalist production and distribution. In contrast to the harsh criticisms it leveled against existing institutions and old elites, the Enlightenment on the whole approved of the independent businessman—the entrepreneur.

And there was no one more approving than Adam Smith (1732–1790), whose *Wealth of Nations* (1776) became a kind of bible for those who regarded capitalist activity as uniformly worthwhile, never to be inhibited by government regulation. A professor in Glasgow, Scotland, Smith actually went out and observed factories at work; he was one of the first theorists to see the importance of the division of labor in making possible the manufacture of more and cheaper consumer goods.

By the middle of the eighteenth century, enlightened theorists all over

Europe, especially in England, Scotland, and France, had decided that self-interest was the foundation of all human actions and that at every turn government should assist people in expressing their interests and thus in finding true happiness. Of course, in the area of economic life, government had for centuries regulated most aspects of the market. The classic economic theory behind such regulation was mercantilism. Mercantilists believed that a constant shortage of riches—bullion, goods, whatever—existed, and that governments must direct economic activity in their states so as to compete successfully with other nations for a share of the world's scarce resources. It required enormous faith in the inherent usefulness of self-interest to assert that government should cease regulating economic activity, that the market should be allowed to be free. This doctrine of *laissez faire*—to leave the market to its own devices—was the centerpiece of Adam Smith's massive economic study on the origins of the wealth of nations.

Smith was not distressed by the apparent randomness of market forces. Beneath this superficial chaos he saw order—the same order he saw in physical nature through his understanding of the new science. He used the metaphor of "the invisible hand" to explain the source of this order; by that he probably meant Newton's regulatory God, made very distant by Smith, who was a deist. That hand would invisibly reconcile self-interest to the common or public interest. With the image of the invisible hand, Smith expressed his faith in the rationality of commercial society and laid the first principle for the modern science of capitalist economics.

The High Enlightenment

More than any other political system in western Europe, the Old Regime in France was directly threatened by the doctrines and reforming impulse of the Enlightenment. The Roman Catholic church was deeply entrenched in every aspect of life—landownership, control over universities and presses, and access to both the court and, through the pulpit, the people. For decades the church had brought its influence to bear against the philosophes, yet by 1750 the Enlightenment had penetrated learned circles and academies in Paris and the provinces. Censorship had produced the opposite of the desired effect: the more irreligious and atheistic the book or manuscript was, the more attractive and sought-after it became.

The most important work of the French Enlightenment was the multivolume *Encyclopedia* edited by Denis Diderot (1713–1784), who had spent six months in jail for his writings. Published in 1751 and in succeeding years and editions, the *Encyclopedia* initiated a new stage in the history of Enlightenment publishing. The new era thus ushered in, called the High Enlightenment, was characterized by a violent attack on the church's privileges and the very foundations of Christian belief. From the 1750s to the 1780s, Paris became the capital of the Enlightenment. The philosophes were no longer a persecuted minority. Instead, they became cultural heroes. The *Encyclopedia* had to be read by anyone claiming to be educated.

In his preface to the *Encyclopedia,* Diderot's collaborator, Jean d'Alembert (c. 1717–1783), wrote a powerful summation of the Enlightenment's highest ideals. He extolled Newton's science. The progress of geometry and mechanics in combination, d'Alembert wrote, "may be considered the most incontestable monument of the success to which the human mind can rise by its efforts." In turn, he urged that revealed religion should be reduced to a few precepts to be practiced; religion should, he implied, be made scientific and rational. The *Encyclopedia* itself was self-consciously modeled on Bacon's admonition that the scientist should first of all be a collector of facts; in addition, it gave dozens of examples of useful new mechanical devices.

D'Alembert's preface also praised the psychology of Locke: all that is known, is known through the senses. He added that all learning should be catalogued and made easily and readily available, that the printing press should serve the needs of enlightenment, and that literary societies should be set up that would encourage men of talent. D'Alembert added that "they should banish all inequalities that might exclude or discourage men who are endowed with talents that will enlighten others."[3]

The High Enlightenment's systematic, sustained, and occasionally violent attacks on the abuses of French society link it with the French Revolution. Although the philosophes themselves were political moderates who aimed at a gradual evolutionary transformation of society, their criticism of the existing order had revolutionary implications.

War, Revolution, and Politics

Warfare and Revolution

The dreams of the philosophes, articulated in almost every area of human experience, seemed unable to forestall troublesome developments in power politics, war, and diplomacy. The eighteenth century was dominated by two areas of extreme conflict: Anglo-French rivalry over control of territory in the New World and intense rivalry between Austria and Prussia over control of central Europe.

In 1740 Prussia, ruled by the aggressive Frederick the Great, launched a successful war against Austria and was rewarded with Silesia, which augmented the Prussian population by 50 percent. Maria Theresa, the Austrian queen, never forgave Frederick, and in 1756 formed an alliance with France against Prussia. The ensuing Seven Years' War (1756–1763), which involved every major European power, did not significantly change Europe, but it did reveal Prussia's growing might.

At the same time, the French and English fought over their claims in the New World. England's victory in the conflict (known in American history as the French and Indian War) deprived France of virtually all of its North

American possessions and set in motion a train of events that culminated in the American Revolution. The war drained the British treasury, and now Britain had the additional expense of paying for troops to guard the new North American territories that it had gained in the war. As strapped British taxpayers could not shoulder the whole burden, the members of Parliament thought it quite reasonable that American colonists help pay the bill; they reasoned that Britain had protected the colonists from the French and was still protecting them in their conflicts with Indians. New colonial taxes and import duties imposed by Parliament produced vigorous protests from the Americans.

The quarrel turned to bloodshed in April and June 1775, and on July 4, 1776, delegates from the various colonies adopted the Declaration of Independence, written mainly by Thomas Jefferson. Applying Locke's theory of natural rights, this document declared that government derives its power from the consent of the governed, that it is the duty of a government to protect the rights of its citizens, and that people have the right to "alter or abolish" a government that deprives them of their "unalienable rights."

Why were the American colonists so ready to revolt? For one thing, they had brought with them a highly idealized understanding of English liberties; long before 1776, they had extended representative institutions to include small property owners who probably could not have voted in England. The colonists had come to expect representative government, trial by jury, and protection from unlawful imprisonment. Each of the thirteen colonies had an elected assembly that acted like a miniature parliament; in these assemblies, Americans gained political experience and quickly learned to be self-governing.

Familiarity with the thought of the Enlightenment and the republican writers of the English Revolution also contributed to the Americans' awareness of liberty. The ideas of the philosophes traversed the Atlantic and influenced educated Americans, particularly Thomas Jefferson and Benjamin Franklin. Like the philosophes, American thinkers expressed a growing confidence in reason, valued freedom of religion and of thought, and championed the principle of natural rights.

Another source of hostility toward established authority among the American colonists was their religious traditions, particularly that of the Puritans, who believed that the Bible was infallible and its teachings a higher law than the law of the state. Like their counterparts in England, American Puritans challenged political and religious authorities who, in their view, contravened God's law. Thus, Puritans acquired two habits that were crucial to the development of political liberty—dissent and resistance. When transferred to the realm of politics, these Puritan tendencies led Americans to resist authority that they considered unjust.

American victory came in 1783 as a result of several factors. George Washington proved a superior leader, able to organize and retain the loyalty of his troops. France, seeking to avenge its defeat in the Seven Years' War, helped the

Map 10.1   Europe, 1789   ▶

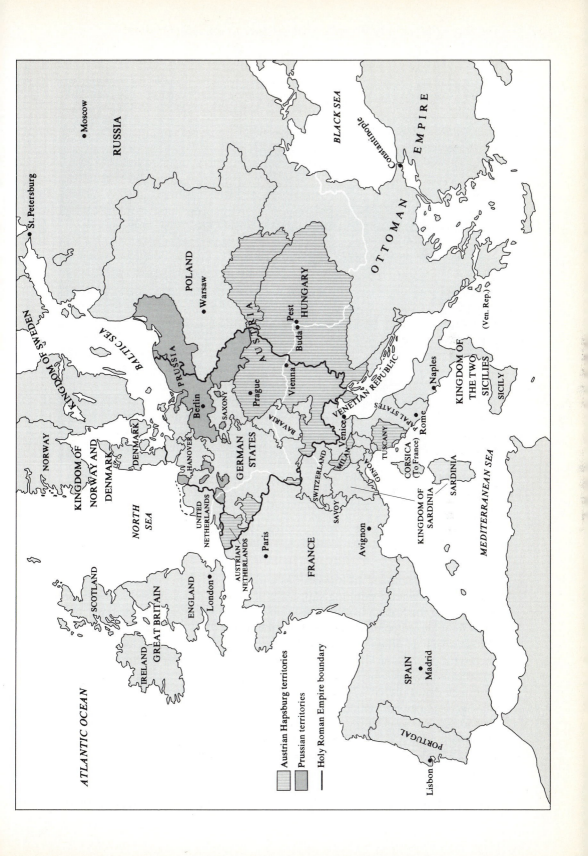

ATLANTIC OCEAN

RUSSIA

Moscow

St. Petersburg

KINGDOM OF SWEDEN

NORWAY

BALTIC SEA

POLAND

Warsaw

BLACK SEA

OTTOMAN EMPIRE

Constantinople

KINGDOM OF NORWAY AND DENMARK

DENMARK

PRUSSIA

Berlin

SAXONY

Prague

AUSTRIA

Vienna

Buda

Pest

HUNGARY

NORTH SEA

HANOVER

GERMAN STATES

BAVARIA

SWITZERLAND

VENETIAN REPUBLIC

(Ven. Rep.)

KINGDOM OF THE TWO SICILIES

Naples

SICILY

SCOTLAND

IRELAND

GREAT BRITAIN

ENGLAND

London

UNITED NETHERLANDS

AUSTRIAN NETHERLANDS

Paris

FRANCE

Avignon

SAVOY

GENOA

MILAN

Venice

TUSCANY

PAPAL STATES

Rome

CORSICA (To France)

SARDINIA

KINGDOM OF SARDINIA

MEDITERRANEAN SEA

SPAIN

Madrid

PORTUGAL

Lisbon

Austrian Hapsburg territories

Prussian territories

Holy Roman Empire boundary

The Signing of the Declaration of Independence, July 4, 1776 (detail) by John Trumbull. The success of the American Revolution was hailed as a victory of liberty over tyranny. Jefferson and Franklin were intimately familiar with the thinking of the Enlightenment and stressed a confidence in reason, freedom of religion and thought, and the existence of natural rights. (*Copyright Yale University Art Gallery*)

Americans with money and provisions and then in 1778 entered the conflict. Britain had difficulty shipping supplies across three thousand miles of ocean, was fighting the French in the West Indies and elsewhere at the same time, and ultimately lacked commitment to the struggle.

Reformers in other lands quickly interpreted the American victory as a successful struggle of liberty against tyranny. During the Revolution the various states drew up constitutions based on the principle of popular sovereignty and included bills of rights that protected individual liberty. They also managed, somewhat reluctantly, to forge a nation. Rejecting both monarchy and hereditary aristocracy, the Constitution of the United States created a republic in which power derived from the people. A system of separation of powers and checks and balances set safeguards against the abuse of power, and the Bill of Rights provided for protection of individual rights. To be sure, the ideals of liberty and equality were not extended to all people—slaves knew nothing of the freedom that white Americans cherished, and women were denied the vote and equal opportunity. But to reform-minded Europeans, it seemed that Americans were fulfilling the promise of the Enlightenment; they were creating a freer and better society.

Enlightened Despotism

The philosophes used the term *enlightened despotism* to refer to an ideal shared by many of them: the strong monarch who would implement rational reforms and remove obstacles to freedom. When historians use the term *enlightened despotism,* they generally are describing the reigns of specific European monarchs and their ministers—Frederick the Great in Prussia; Catherine the Great in Russia; Charles III of Spain; Maria Theresa and, to a greater extent, her son Joseph II in Austria; and Louis XV of France. These eighteenth-century monarchs instituted specific reforms in education, trade, and commerce, and against the clergy.

Behind the reforms of enlightened despots lay the realization that the struggle for power in Europe called for efficient government administration and ample funds. Enlightened despots appointed capable officials to oversee the administration of their kingdoms, eliminate costly corruption, and collect taxes properly. Rulers strengthened the economy by encouraging the expansion of commerce through reduced taxes on goods and through agricultural reforms. In Central and Eastern Europe some rulers moved toward abolishing serfdom or at least improving conditions for serfs. (In Western Europe, serfdom had virtually died out.) Provisions were made to care for widows, orphans, and invalids. Censorship was eased, greater religious freedom was granted to minorities, criminal codes were made less harsh, and there were some attempts at prison reform. By these measures enlightened despots hoped to inspire greater popular support for the nation, an important factor in the European power struggle.

However, if the Enlightenment meant the endorsement of reason over force and of peace and cosmopolitan unity over ruthless competition, then the foreign policies of these enlightened monarchs can only be regarded as despotic. The evidence for this view lies in a long series of aggressions. There were no major philosophes who did not grow disillusioned with "enlightened" monarchs.

The Enlightenment and the Modern World

Enlightenment thought was the culmination of a trend instituted by Renaissance artists and humanists who attacked medieval otherworldliness and gave value to individual achievement and the worldly life. It was a direct outgrowth of the Scientific Revolution, which provided a new method of inquiry and verification and demonstrated the power and self-sufficiency of the human intellect. If nature were autonomous—that is, if it operated according to natu-

---

Chronology 10.1 ❧ The Scientific Revolution and the Enlightenment

1543	Publication of Copernicus' *On the Revolutions of the Heavenly Spheres* marks the beginning of modern astronomy
1605	Publication of Bacon's *Advancement of Learning*
1610	Publication of Galileo's *The Starry Messenger,* which asserts the uniformity of nature
1632	Galileo's teachings are condemned by the church and he is placed under house arrest
1687	Publication of Newton's *Principia Mathematica*
1690	Publication of Locke's *Two Treatises of Government*
1733	Publication of Voltaire's *Letters Concerning the English Nation*
1751–1765	Publication of Diderot's *Encyclopedia*
1776	The Declaration of Independence
1789	The French Revolution

---

ral laws that did not require divine intervention—then the human intellect could also be autonomous. Through its own powers, it could uncover those general principles that operate in the social world as well as in nature.

The philosophes sought to analyze nature, government, religion, law, economics, and education through reason alone, without any reference to Christian teachings, and they rejected completely the claims of clerics to a special wisdom. The philosophes broke decisively with the medieval view that the individual is naturally depraved, that heaven is the true end of life, and that human values and norms derive from a higher reality and are made known through revelation. Instead, they upheld the potential goodness of the individual, regarded the good life on earth as the true end of life, and insisted that individuals could improve themselves and their society solely by the light of reason.

In addition, the political philosophies of Locke, Montesquieu, and Rousseau were based on an entirely new and modern concept of the relationship between the state and the individual: states should exist not simply to accumulate power unto themselves but also to enhance human happiness. From that perspective, monarchy and even oligarchy not based on merit began to seem increasingly less useful. And if happiness is a goal, then it must be assumed that some sort of progress is possible in history.

The French leaders of the late Enlightenment, in fact, possessed a wholehearted belief in the infinite possibility of human progress. If human knowledge is ever-increasing and dependent only on the ability to sense and experience the world, then surely, they believed, the human condition can constantly improve. Western thought has never entirely relinquished this brave dream.

The philosophes wanted a freer, more humane, and more rational society, but they feared the people and their potential for revolutionary action. As an alternative to revolution, most philosophes offered science as the universal improver of the human condition. Faith in reform without the necessity of revolution proved to be a doctrine for the elite of the salons. In that sense the French Revolution can be said to have repudiated the essential moderation of philosophes such as Voltaire, d'Alembert, and Kant. Yet the Enlightenment established a vision of humanity so independent of Christianity and so focused on the needs and abuses of present society that no established institution, once grown corrupt and ineffectual, could long withstand its penetrating critique. To that extent the writings of the philosophes point toward the democratic revolutions of the late eighteenth century. The writers of the Enlightenment also point toward ideals that remain strong in most democratic Western societies: religious toleration, a disdain for prejudice and superstition, a fear of unchecked political authority, and, of course, a belief in the power of the human mind to rectify defective institutions and social injustice.

Notes

1. Excerpted in Stillman Drake, ed., *Discoveries and Opinions of Galileo* (New York: Doubleday, 1957), p. 28.
2. Thomas Hobbes, *Leviathan*, ed. by C. B. Macpherson (Harmondsworth, England: Penguin, 1977), p. 189.
3. Jean Le Rond d'Alembert, *Preliminary Discourse to the Encyclopedia of Diderot*, trans. by Richard N. Schwab (New York: Bobbs-Merrill, 1963), pp. 101–102.

Suggested Reading

Anchor, Robert, *The Enlightenment Tradition* (1967). Good survey for the student.

Anderson, M. S., *Europe in the Eighteenth Century, 1713–1783* (1961). A good general survey of the century with excellent chapters on cultural and intellectual life.

Becker, Carl, *The Heavenly City of the Eighteenth-Century Philosophers* (1932). Still a provocative assessment of the Enlightenment's relation to Christianity.

Bernal, J. D., *Science in History* (1969). A learned classic that discusses the meaning of science in history.

Briggs, Robin, *The Scientific Revolution of the Seventeenth Century* (1969). A clearly written survey with documents.

Brumfitt, J. H., *The French Enlightenment* (1972). A useful survey.

Butterfield, Herbert, *The Origins of Modern Science* (1957). An analysis of the emergence of modern science.

Cassirer, Ernst, *The Philosophy of the Enlightenment* (1951). A classic and basic account of Enlightenment philosophy; difficult reading.

Cohen, I. B., *The Birth of a New Physics* (1960). Authoritative, but difficult for the novice.

Drake, Stillman, ed., *Discoveries and*

Opinions of Galileo (1957). A good place to start to learn Galileo's most important ideas.

Gay, Peter, *The Enlightenment, An Interpretation* (1967). A good survey.

Jacob, Margaret C., *The Cultural Meaning of the Scientific Revolution* (1988). Offers a general interpretation of the social context of the Scientific Revolution.

Kearney, Hugh, *Science and Social Change, 1500–1700* (1971). Includes a discussion of the social setting of the Scientific Revolution.

Woloch, Isser, *Eighteenth-Century Europe: Tradition and Progress, 1715–1789* (1982). An interesting general survey.

Review Questions

1. What was the difference between the scientific understanding of the universe and the medieval understanding of it?

2. Describe the major achievements of Copernicus, Kepler, Galileo, and Newton.

3. What role did the Scientific Revolution play in shaping the modern mentality?

4. What is meant by the Age of Enlightenment? Where did the Enlightenment begin, and what contributed to its spread?

5. How did Christianity come under attack by deists and skeptics?

6. In what ways does Voltaire exemplify the philosophes?

7. What were the essential characteristics of the political thought of each of the following: Hobbes, Locke, Montesquieu, and Rousseau? Make relevant comparisons and contrasts.

8. Describe Locke's theory of learning. What was its significance for the Enlightenment?

9. In what ways was the American Revolution based on Enlightenment principles?

10. The Enlightenment was a pivotal period in the shaping of the modern mentality. Discuss this statement.

Index

Student Evaluation of

Western Civilization: A Brief Survey

While a textbook is being written, the publisher works closely with the author(s) and with course instructors to be sure that the book is useful and interesting. Since the main reader of this textbook is you, the student, we at Houghton Mifflin Company would also like to know what you think about the quality of this text.

Please answer the questions below, and mail this response sheet to

College Marketing Services
Houghton Mifflin Company, One Beacon Street
Boston, MA 02108

We will appreciate reading your comments on the textbook.

1. Does the textbook cover the information necessary to master your course? Circle the appropriate number.

1	2	3	4
No, none of the information is there	Yes, some of the information is there	Yes, most of the information is there	Yes, almost all of the information is there

2. Was the textbook excessively difficult to read?

1	2	3	4
Yes, I often had to consult a dictionary	No, although there were some unfamiliar words	No, the book was not too difficult to read and understand	No, the textbook was almost too easy to read

3. Did the textbook hold your interest?

1	2	3	4
No, I often had trouble concentrating	Yes, but a few parts are dull	Yes, the text held my attention	Yes, I enjoyed many parts of the book

4. Which three chapters are the best?   Why?

5. Which three chapters are least effective?   Why?

6. Do any parts of the book stand out in your mind? Please identify them by page number or topic, and please explain why you remember these sections.

7. Do you have any general suggestions for improving the text?

Thank you for giving your reactions to this textbook.

(Optional)

Course Title _____

Name _____

College _____

City _____ *State* _____